# Strategies for Shaping Territorial Competitiveness



This book focuses on the main challenges that cities, regions and other territories at sub-national level face when it comes to designing and implementing a territorial strategy for economic development and competitiveness. There is a widespread recognition that territories need to construct strategies that focus on shaping sustainable competitive advantages. To do this they draw upon their own unique resources and capabilities alongside intelligence on existing technological and market trends. However, there is still a notorious lack of both theoretical and empirical research on this issue.

The first part of this book develops a theoretical framework for understanding and analysing territorial strategy. This framework asks three questions of territorial strategy – what for, what, and how – looking closely at the key relationship between strategy and policy. The second part is dedicated to exploring this framework in practice through application to a series of unique cases from around the world at different territorial levels, from regions such as the Basque Country, Navarre and Murcia in Spain, Okanagan (British Columbia) in Canada, Wales in the United Kingdom, and the cross-border region of the Øresund in Denmark–Sweden, as well as the city of Rafaela in Argentina. Each case offers something different and enables the framework to be thoroughly tested, generating concluding reflections that add real value for scholars and policy-makers interested in and working in the field of territorial strategy.

This volume is intended for the academic community, the policy community (government leaders, policy-makers, policy researchers and consultants) and university students and teachers at different levels interested in the areas of territorial competitiveness, regional development, competitiveness policies and processes of territorial strategy.

**Jesús M. Valdaliso** is Professor of Economic History and Institutions in the School of Economics and Business Administration at the University of the Basque Country in Bilbao, Spain.

**James R. Wilson** is a Senior Researcher at Orkestra-Basque Institute of Competitiveness, Spain, and faculty at Deusto Business School, University of Deusto, San Sebastián, Spain.

**Routledge Studies in Global Competition**
Edited by John Cantwell, *Rutgers, the State University of New Jersey, USA and David Mowery, University of California, Berkeley, USA*

*For a complete list of titles in this series, please visit www.routledge.com*

**37. Dynamic Capabilities Between Firm Organisation and Local Systems of Production**
*Edited by Riccardo Leoncini and Sandro Montresor*

**38. Localised Technological Change**
Towards the economics of complexity
*Cristiano Antonelli*

**39. Knowledge Economies**
Innovation, organization and location
*Wilfred Dolfsma*

**40. Governance and Innovation**
*Maria Brouwer*

**41. Public Policy for Regional Development**
*Edited by Jorge Martinez-Vazquez and François Vaillancourt*

**42. Evolutionary Economic Geography**
Location of production and the European Union
*Miroslav Jovanovic*

**43. Broadband Economics**
Lessons from Japan
*Takanori Ida*

**44. Targeting Regional Economic Development**
*Edited by Stephan J. Goetz, Steven C. Deller and Thomas R. Harris*

**45. Innovation, Knowledge and Power**
*Theodora Asimakou*

**46. Creativity, Innovation and the Cultural Economy**
*Edited by Andy C. Pratt and Paul Jeffcutt*

**47. Coopetition Strategy**
*Giovanni Battista Dagnino and Elena Rocco*

**48. Knowledge Intensive Entrepreneurship and Innovation Systems**
Evidence from Europe
*Edited by Franco Malerba*

**49. Innovation in Complex Social Systems**
*Edited by Petra Ahrweiler*

**50. Internationalization, Technological Change and the Theory of the Firm**
*Edited by Nicola De Liso and Riccardo Leoncini*

**51. Territory, Specialization and Globalization in European Manufacturing**
*By Helena Marques and Francisco Puig*

**52. Institutional Diversity and Innovation**
Continuing and emerging patterns in Japan and China
*Cornelia Storz and Sebastian Schäfer*

**53. Innovation and Economic Crisis**
*Daniele Archibugi and Andrea Filippetti*

**54. The Communications Industries in the Era of Convergence**
*Catherine Mulligan*

**55. Innovation, Technology and Knowledge**
*Charlie Karlsson, Borje Johansson and Roger R. Stough*

**56. Evolution of Competition Laws and their Enforcement**
*Pradeep S. Mehta*

**57. The Economics of Structural Change in Knowledge**
*Francesco Quatraro*

**58. Economic Geography and the Unequal Development of Regions**
*Jean-Claude Prager and Jacques-François Thisse*

**59. Social Networks, Innovation and the Knowledge Economy**
*Edited by Isabel Salavisa and Margarida Fontes*

**60. The Economics of Creativity**
Ideas, firms and markets
*Edited by Thierry Burger-Helmchen*

**61. Epistemic Economics and Organization**
Forms of rationality and governance for a discovery oriented economy
*Anna Grandori*

**62. Universities, Cities and Regions**
Loci for knowledge and innovation creation
*Edited by Roberta Capello, Agnieszka Olechnicka and Grzegorz Gorzelak*

**63. Strategies for Shaping Territorial Competitiveness**
*Edited by Jesús M. Valdaliso and James R. Wilson*

# Strategies for Shaping Territorial Competitiveness

**Edited by**
**Jesús M. Valdaliso and James R. Wilson**

Routledge
Taylor & Francis Group
LONDON AND NEW YORK

First published 2015 by Routledge

2 Park Square, Milton Park, Abingdon, Oxfordshire OX14 4RN
52 Vanderbilt Avenue, New York, NY 10017

*Routledge is an imprint of the Taylor & Francis Group, an informa business*

First issued in paperback 2020



*British Library Cataloguing in Publication Data*
A catalogue record for this book is available from the British Library

*Library of Congress Cataloging in Publication Data*
Strategies for shaping territorial competitiveness / edited by
Jesús M. Valdaliso and James R. Wilson.
pages cm
1. City planning. 2. Regional planning. 3. Sustainable development.
4. Competition. I. Valdaliso, Jesús Ma. (Jesús María)
HT165.5.S773 2015
307.1′216—dc23
2014041924

ISBN: 978-1-138-77771-2 (hbk)
ISBN: 978-0-367-66887-7 (pbk)

Typeset in Times New Roman
by Book Now Ltd, London

# Contents

# Figures

# Tables

# Contributors

**Mari José Aranguren** is General Director at Orkestra-Basque Institute of Competitiveness and faculty at Deusto Business School, University of Deusto, San Sebastián, Spain

**Pablo Costamagna** is Director of the Master on Territorial Development and faculty at the National Technological University of Argentina, Regional Faculty of Rafaela, Rafaela, Argentina

**Keith Culver** is a Professor in the Faculty of Management and Director of the Okanagan Sustainability Institute, University of British Columbia Okanagan campus, Kelowna, Canada.

**Nicky Dhaliwal** is an Interdisciplinary Graduate Studies PhD student, University of British Columbia Okanagan campus, Kelowna, Canada.

**Robert Huggins** is a Professor at the School of Planning and Geography at Cardiff University, Cardiff, UK

**Ola Jonsson** is an Associate Professor at the Department of Human Geography, Lund University, Lund, Sweden

**Christian Ketels** is Principal Associate at Harvard Business School's Institute for Strategy and Competitiveness, Cambridge, MA, USA

**Miren Larrea** is a Senior Researcher at Orkestra-Basque Institute of Competitiveness and faculty at Deusto Business School, University of Deusto, San Sebastián, Spain

**Edurne Magro** is a researcher at Orkestra-Basque Institute of Competitiveness and faculty at Deusto Business School, University of Deusto, Donostia-San Sebastian, Spain

**Malida Mooken** is a PhD student at Stirling Management School, University of Stirling, UK

**Claire Nauwelaers** is an independent policy expert, Louvain-la-Neuve, Belgium

**Mikel Navarro** is a Senior Researcher at Orkestra-Basque Institute of Competitiveness and a Professor at Deusto Business School, University of Deusto, San Sebastián, Spain

**Rhiannon Pugh** is a Researcher in the Institute for Entrepreneurship and Enterprise Development at Lancaster University, UK

**Roger Sugden** is a Professor and Dean of the Faculty of Management, University of British Columbia Okanagan campus, Kelowna, Canada

**Christian Tangkjær** is an Associate Professor at Copenhagen Business School, Copenhagen, Denmark

**Jesús M. Valdaliso** is a Professor and Head of the Department of Economic History and Institutions, University of the Basque Country, Bilbao, Spain

**James R. Wilson** is a Senior Researcher at Orkestra-Basque Institute of Competitiveness and faculty at Deusto Business School, University of Deusto, San Sebastián, Spain

# 1 Strategies for shaping territorial competitiveness

## An introduction

*Jesús M. Valdaliso and James R. Wilson*[1]

## Territorial strategy for competitiveness: a living concept in need of reflection

Competitiveness is essentially constructed from place. People, firms and other institutions all need the right environment to thrive, and yet it is they themselves that must create that environment in the places where they are based. In this sense, territories – nations, regions, cities, municipalities – are the critical building blocks for competitiveness and socio-economic development in the world economy. However, while it has long been common to analyse the strategies of firms, analysis of the strategies of territories has often been neglected. That is starting to change, as around the world today we see policy discourse dominated by territories looking to develop, implement and monitor the progress of distinctive strategies to boost their competitiveness.

The concept of territorial strategy for competiveness has come very much alive, therefore, and it is currently evolving through practice and dialogue in many different arenas. Yet there is a strong sense in which this practice is racing ahead of conceptual and empirical understanding in the academic sphere.[2] This provides the main premise of this book: that territorial strategy for competitiveness is a concept badly in need of rigorous academic reflection. Moreover, such reflection should build from and work with the wealth of evolving practice so as to support its ongoing development; we are at a moment when the academic and policy worlds need to collide more effectively so as to generate real improvements in how we 'do' territorial strategy for competitiveness.

The concept of 'strategy' for a territorial space (nations, regions, cities or municipalities) is not new in the academic literature. It can be traced to around the late 1950s, mainly linked to developing countries and regions (Hirschman, 1958; Robock, 1966) and to regional and city planning (Wannop, 1995). However, at this stage it didn't go beyond a broad presentation of priorities and policy actions, and it wasn't until the mid-1970s, and above all the 1980s, in the context of economic crisis, job destruction and increasing global competition, that governments in Western Europe and the United States became convinced of the need to have something akin to a strategy to cope with these challenges (Wannop, 1995; Stimson *et al.*, 2006). In Europe, the concept became intertwined with that of regional policy that had been launched by the European Commission in 1973 (Thomson, 1975) or with regional planning that had a much longer tradition (Wannop, 1995). In the United States, the 1980s saw the appearance of several commissions aimed at designing a new strategy to regain the 'productive edge', but as late as 1989 one of them reckoned that 'the United States is not used to designing national strategies' (Dertouzos *et al.*, 1989; Bloch, 1991). At the regional and even the county level, several plans were launched to cope with economic crisis and job losses (Stimson *et al.*, 2006: 71–5), and yet, as Sotarauta (2004: 8) has suggested, territorial strategy at that time was too much ado about almost nothing.

In the early 1990s, in the context of another economic recession combined with increasing globalisation, there was a further surge in demand for strategies for economic development and competitiveness at different territorial levels. There was a difference, however, in that demand for such strategies was boosted at the sub-national level by the ongoing worldwide trend towards decentralisation (Rodríguez-Pose and Tijmstra, 2009). The early 1990s, for example, saw the appearance of several regional plans and strategies in Europe, mostly focused in the field of science, technology and innovation (Morgan, 1997; Halkier, 2006; see also chapters 7 and 8 of this book). Michael Porter, who had been appointed in 1983 to President Reagan's Commission on Industrial Productivity, played a key role, in both academic and government circles, in generating recognition of places as shapers of competitiveness, having formulated a broad framework and agenda for tackling these issues in his seminal work on the competitive advantage of nations (Porter, 1990, 1998; Sölvell, 2012). Yet, still, at the beginning of the twenty-first century the concept of territorial strategy for competitiveness remained very fuzzy and under-conceptualised (Sotarauta, 2004; Stimson *et al.*, 2006; Navarro *et al.*, 2014).

As with corporate strategy, the central issue when it comes to constructing a territorial strategy is the choice around the type of socio-economic activities that should be developed, both now and in the future. In this regard there is widespread recognition that territories need to construct development strategies that are focused on shaping sustainable competitive advantages which draw upon their own unique resources, competencies and capabilities alongside intelligence on existing technological and market trends (Asheim *et al.*, 2006; Etkowitz and Klofsten, 2005; Porter, 1998; Aranguren *et al.*, 2012; Navarro *et al.*, 2014). In this sense, strategy and institutions are seen as the two wheels of the 'regional development bicycle' (Rodríguez-Pose, 2013), recognition of which has driven the current boom of popularity in territorial strategy-making.

Europe has played a particularly important role in the current debates, which have taken shape there around what are now called 'research and innovation strategies for smart specialisation' (RIS3). The RIS3 concept has its roots in the work of the knowledge for growth expert group established in 2005 by the European Commission to provide advice on the contribution of knowledge to sustainable growth and prosperity in the European Union. Based on analysis of the EU–US productivity gap, it was observed that R&D in Europe was fragmented along national lines and that there was a tendency for both countries and regions to try to emulate success elsewhere rather than explore original ideas. This led to an initial proposal for countries and regions to develop clear visions and strategies for a 'smart specialisation' of their activities (Foray and van Ark, 2008). These arguments were very rapidly adopted by the European Commission as a concept for guiding regional policy in the EU (European Commission 2010, 2011; Foray *et al.*, 2012), to the extent that Foray (2014) suggests that the passage from conceptualisation to general implementation has perhaps been too short (see also chapter 12 of this book). Nevertheless, as theoretical evolution and policy practice come together in the processes of regions developing their 'smart specialisation strategies', the debate around what constitutes a territorial strategy, and in particular how it should be constructed, is currently raging in Europe.

Whether we talk about smart specialisation in the European sense or about other related constructs, territorial strategy is fundamentally about making choices. In this sense, the debate around territorial strategy overlaps with literature on science and technology policy (see chapter 2 of this book) and with previous and currently re-emerging debates around industrial policy (Warwick, 2013). As with previous surges in interest in these debates, they have corresponded with a context of deep economic crisis in many parts of the world that renders making choices both more pressing and more difficult. Clark (2013), for example, argues that 'the dominant policy models of the last two decades privileged innovation and competition and in the process failed to provide a framework capable of strategically engaging a real decline in overall demand.'[3] In this sense the ongoing policy discussion in Western Europe and North America has turned towards job creation and retention, reindustrialisation and on-shoring, with resilience replacing growth (and to some extent even competitiveness) as the key focus for regional economies (Clark, 2013; Boschma, 2014; Porter and Rivkin, 2012). As happened previously in the 1980s and 1990s, therefore, governments, policy-makers and academics have been forced to rethink their discourses, rationales and practices about economic strategy and industrial policy in order to cope with pressing challenges.

Regardless of where policy priorities should be focused, there is strong recognition that territories do need to build strategies for sustainable economic development. Territorial strategies should address the multilevel and complex nature of each policy space, where different goals, agents and interests co-exist in mutual dependence; hence the necessity of taking systemic or holistic approaches (Bianchi and Labory, 2012; Magro and Wilson, 2013; Navarro *et al.*, 2014). In this regard, territorial strategy, and indeed 'new industrial policy', should not be about the articulation of choices 'top-down' from government. Rather, it should be the result of diffused processes carried out among different agents and organisations within the territory – what in the smart specialisation literature is referred to as processes of 'entrepreneurial discovery'. Yet there remains a large gap in understanding around how these processes take place and how they can be articulated towards coherent strategies capable of shaping competitiveness in the specific contexts of different territories.

## The contribution of this book

This book builds on a strong trajectory of research shared by several of the contributors in the 'living lab' of the Basque Country, one of Europe's leading regions with respect to the development of territorial strategies. Ongoing analysis of the Basque case originated a process of theoretical reflection that resulted in a conceptual holistic framework to analyse territorial strategies (Aranguren *et al.*, 2012; Navarro *et al.*, 2014). This conceptual framework is based around three core questions:

1. the '*what for*': the objectives of the strategy, usually centred on socio-economic and environmental goals;
2. the '*what*': the strategic positioning of the territory (the economic activities and/or the scientific and technological fields in which to compete, the relationship with other territories and external agents), its base of assets, resources and capabilities, and the agents that a strategy should target (firms, clusters, universities …);
3. the '*how*' and '*who*': the process of strategy formation and implementation (emergent or deliberate), its governance (hierarchical or participatory) and its leadership.

Now it is time to deepen this conceptual framework and to extend the analysis to other places. With that aim, we have brought together in this book a broad team of scholars with long experience in academic research on regional development and competitiveness from different perspectives and with different methodologies – some of them even directly engaged in the processes of territorial development analysed here.

The objectives of the book are threefold. First, to elaborate a holistic conceptual framework for the analysis of (past) territorial strategies, which at the same time may help policy-makers and other actors to design, implement and evaluate current and future territorial strategies for competitiveness. Second, to explore and contrast this theoretical framework through analysis of a series of empirical cases: four European regions (the Basque Country, Wales, Navarre and Murcia), one European cross-border region (Øresund), a Canadian region (Okanagan, in British Columbia) and a city in Argentina (Rafaela). And, finally, to offer further food for thought to readers interested in regional development through the specific lessons that can be learnt from each of the seven cases.

The book is divided into two parts – the first more conceptual and the second more empirical. Part I progressively develops key elements of the territorial strategy framework introduced briefly above. It is centred loosely on the core questions of 'what for', 'what' and 'how/who' and deals with questions concerning the prioritisations or choices inherent in any strategy, the processes and policies required to make and support these choices, and the evaluation requirements of a territorial strategy. The second part is then dedicated to exploring this conceptual framework through application to a series of cases from around the world that have been chosen for their unique or leading experiences in various respects. Each case offers something different and enables the framework to be thoroughly tested, generating concluding reflections that are the focus of the final chapter.

## Part I: the concept of territorial strategy

In Part I of the book, the first two chapters deal explicitly with the content of a territorial strategy – the question of 'what'. Mikel Navarro (in chapter 2) addresses this question from a perspective that integrates literature dealing with the identification of priorities from the fields of science and technology policy, economic development, economic geography and innovation systems. He defines the content of a territorial strategy as a group of actions to be undertaken in some specific areas so as to achieve the goals of the strategy. These actions require a set of different choices. Most obviously there are choices around the main economic, technological and scientific activities to be prioritised (*vertical priorities*) and around the capabilities (assets, resources, etc.) to be developed in support of those activities (*horizontal priorities*). Yet there are also choices, considered less often, around the *agents* (firms, universities, research centres, etc.) that a strategy should target, around the *external relationships* that a territory should develop with other territories, and around the *internal articulation* to take place within the territory itself. Navarro explores in turn the main debates surrounding each of these. While the context and specificities of each territory render impossible universal recommendations, the chapter arrives at a series of general messages with respect to defining the content of a territorial strategy and emphasises, above all, the interconnectedness between these different types of priorities.

In chapter 3 Christian Ketels provides a complementary perspective to Navarro that returns directly to the roots of the strategy concept in the field of business studies and which results in a different focus in its recommendations for the content of a territorial strategy. He begins by setting out the five questions that the business literature suggests should be answered by a strategy – ambition, markets served, value proposition, delivery of value proposition and support system – and then considers the translation of each in turn to the territorial level. This exercise highlights the fact that the translation of the strategy concept to the territorial level works only in part. While in both cases it is underlying capabilities that are critical to compete with others, the competitive dynamics themselves are different in various respects. In particular, Ketels's arguments point to the special significance at the territorial level of the business environment, which offers some parallels with Navarro's discussion of the relationship and balance between vertical and horizontal priorities. In the second part of the chapter Ketels explores whether the current practice of regional strategies reflects this conceptual framework. Here he is critical of much practice in various respects, arguing that, while the notion of strategy as implying 'choices' has become more accepted as a general idea, there is no clarity on the dimension in which choices should be made. In particular he maintains that most regional strategies focus their choices on the wrong dimension, given that places compete not in specific sectors/technologies but, rather, for the economic activities within these areas. As such, he proposes a change in focus for the content of many existing territorial strategies from choosing domains of activities (industries/technologies) to choosing a set of business environment qualities that would best support the activities in which the territory hopes to specialise.

The process of territorial strategy, or the question of 'how', is addressed by Mari José Aranguren and Miren Larrea in chapter 4. As was the case in the previous chapter, they build on the business strategy literature, drawing heavily on the distinction between ten different strategy schools made by Mintzberg *et al.* (1998) and guided by the lessons from their own experience in several projects on territorial development. While the focus of Ketels in chapter 3 corresponds with the so-called positioning school, Aranguren and Larrea argue the importance of the so-called learning, power and cultural schools for the processes underlying territorial strategy development. After exploring the relevance of each school, they seek to link their individual contributions to a series of other concepts that are already prevalent in the literature on regional development, with the overall aim of deepening our understanding of the subtle issue of 'how' territorial strategies are formed and implemented. They identify three key assets that territories should create and develop to make a strategy happen: social capital (as it creates dialogue spaces and supports the construction of a shared territorial vision among the different actors involved); shared leadership and new modes of networked governance; and three dynamic capabilities (to learn and innovate, to generate networks and relationships, and to generate vision and leadership). They conclude that, while these existing concepts can help us understand the 'how' of territorial strategy, the challenge is not in their definition but in putting them into practice in different territorial contexts and uncovering barriers in the real-life processes of strategy-making. For this they suggest that the concept of *praxis* is relevant; what is needed now to deepen our understanding of how territorial strategy takes place is a linking of thought and action.

Chapter 5, by Edurne Magro and Claire Nauwelaers, deals explicitly with one critical area of action in operationalising territorial strategy – that of public policy, and in particular competitiveness policy. Their analysis is premised on the argument that strategy and policy are different, although often confused. Specifically, while strategy is about setting goals and directions, public policy is about deploying public means to serve the strategy. However, Magro and Nauwelaers point to the risks of an implementation gap, given that most territorial strategy literature has a strong focus on design, simply assuming that good design will lead to straightforward implementation. The chapter offers a comprehensive analytical framework for understanding the challenges associated with this missing link between strategy and policy: clear concepts and definitions of both territorial strategy and competitiveness policies (and a very useful, sharp and accurate description of the complexity of policy domains, rationales, typologies and instruments), differences and overlaps between them, and challenges for an effective implementation. Governments, the authors conclude, should establish communication spaces the better to align policy and strategy, set up 'goal-oriented' policy mixes, and make a systematic evaluation of strategies and policies. Summing up, they recommend a sort of '3C tool' for governments and territories: more communication, more coherence and more coordination.

The missing link between territorial strategy and public policy is explored further by Edurne Magro and James Wilson in chapter 6, this time through the specific lens of evaluation. As with evaluating competitiveness policies, evaluating territorial strategy is something that is spoken about a lot but actually undertaken very rarely. As such, the chapter looks to bridge the gap between acknowledgements that evaluation should play an important role in territorial strategy and the practice that policy evaluations tend to remain isolated and not well linked to the strategy process at the territorial level. Magro and Wilson start from a reflection on the state of art in competitiveness policy evaluation, from which they highlight the differences between policy and strategy evaluation with regard to the three main questions of territorial strategy – the 'what for', the 'what' and the 'how'. In this sense, their analysis builds on the concepts and issues developed in the preceding chapters and offers valuable insights from the evaluation perspective. They propose a concrete evaluation framework that makes a clear distinction between evaluation at different levels (strategy and policy) and emphasises the powerful learning possibilities that can be uncovered through effectively linking these two levels (with what they term adequacy evaluation). Concluding that evaluation is a learning process that jointly co-evolves with the strategy and policies adopted, they also recognise limitations in time and resources, which points to a need for evaluation prioritisations.

## Part II: cases in territorial strategy

Chapters 7 to 12 deepen our understanding of different elements of the framework explored in the first part of the book through analysis of specific cases. These cases represent different territorial levels (regions, cross-border regions, cities), take on board different stages of the territorial strategy process, and focus their analysis on different elements of the strategy. Chapters 7 and 8 start by juxtaposing two old industrial European regions – the Basque Country and Wales – that have been in the vanguard of discussions around regional industrial policy for many years and which share many similarities (in their industrial structures and strong territorial identity, for example) but whose territorial strategy paths tell quite different stories.

The Basque Country, analysed by Jesús Valdaliso in chapter 7, is widely regarded as a success story of regional change. Following a discussion of polity, economy and industrial policy in the Basque Country as a context for regional strategy, the chapter tells this story by splitting thirty-five years of Basque regional development strategy into three periods: the 1980s, the 1990s and from 1999 onwards. The evolution of strategy through these periods is then analysed in terms of the 'what for', the 'what' and the 'how' (and 'who') questions. Led initially by a new regional government created almost from scratch in the early 1980s, strategy in the Basque Country has followed a clear political mission of strengthening self-government and autonomy. Valdaliso's analysis emphasises the strong government leadership in the early periods, which was important in clarifying the region's goals or ambitions (in the language used by Ketels in chapter 3) and its priorities, which were established around strengthening and building from existing industry. From the 1990s onwards, other actors were gradually engaged in this process of strategy and policy-learning and -making, which became increasingly path dependent over time. While path dependence often implied lock-in, the author argues that, in this case, lock-in was avoided by the continual addition of new organisations, agents and institutions, which at the same time has served to increase the complexity of the policy system, creating its own challenges. Strategy is presented here as following a natural evolution in which regional actors, on the one hand, built on the existing economic base to upgrade, broaden and even transform it and, on the other hand, learnt from the past and used that knowledge to adapt and/or gradually change their policies and their strategy for economic development. As time went by, strategy became increasingly formal and explicit, and the types of dynamic capabilities emphasised in chapter 4 emerged and developed in the region.

However, the case of Wales, as Robert Huggins and Rhiannon Pugh make clear in chapter 8, shows that increasing autonomy and a well-planned territorial strategy –Wales designed one of the earliest regional innovation strategies in Europe in the early 1990s – has not always led to higher rates of socio-economic development. Their chapter begins with a discussion linking regional competitiveness with innovation and entrepreneurship, in which they make clear that this triumvirate has been steadily raising concerns in terms of policy. They then track this policy evolution in the Welsh context, illustrating a fluctuating importance attached to the innovation agenda over the last twenty years. They argue that Wales has deep structural weaknesses in its economy which, because of the effects of economic lock-in and path dependence – and despite successive policy attempts that have been heavily influenced by the European Commission – it is still struggling to overcome. Although Wales has lacked the fiscal autonomy of the Basque Country, lack of funds did not account for this failure. Indeed, the authors suggest that Wales is a case in point of the so-called regional innovation paradox in which lagging regions are unable to utilise the spending made available through European Commission funding for innovation and entrepreneurship because they lack the absorptive capacity in both public and private sectors. Huggins and Pugh point for explanation instead to two salient features of polity and policy evolution in the region: a regional government that has undertaken a rent-seeking strategy devoted more to strengthen its powers ('interdepartmental wars') than to promote economic development, innovation and competitiveness; and a continuous change in the policy mix deployed by successive regional governments. In particular, there has never been a clear 'what for' formulated before policy design and implementation, and the absence of policy evaluation processes have left a vacuum for policy learning.

Chapter 9, by Pablo Costamagna, Mari José Aranguren and Miren Larrea, shifts the focus to another part of the world. The case of Rafaela is one of city strategy and planning that contains valuable lessons with regard to the 'how' of territorial strategy, and in particular for the development of the 'dynamic capabilities' identified in chapter 4 as one of the key assets that territories need to make a strategy happen. Rafaela, a city in the province of Santa Fe in Argentina, is an emblematic success story of Latin American local economic development that started in the 1990s. The authors take the explanatory approach developed in chapter 4, centred on the learning, cultural and power schools of strategy, to explore how this success has been achieved. While the conjunction during the 1990s of political change in the city council and a deep economic crisis acted as a shock that made change easier, the case really highlights the importance of creating dialogue spaces that eventually fostered trust and collaboration among public and private actors in the city. Over time this has resulted in the creation of critical dynamic capabilities that have become reinforcing. In this sense the authors argue that having a new approach to strategy formation in a territory is not about having the right solution ready to be implemented. The case of Rafaela demonstrates the importance first of social change and learning among all agents, from which more formal planning processes may later emerge. In particular, politics and politicians, as also happened for different reasons in the Basque Country and Wales, played a key role in Rafaela, and the case analysis suggests that it was their willingness to learn that was especially critical in laying the foundations for the development of dynamic capabilities. Other critical aspects for a learning approach to strategy identified here include political continuity, a time management that balances the need for short-term achievements within an essentially long-term vision, and the powerful roles of training, social research and international exchange of experiences in feeding reflection and learning spaces.

Christian Tangkjær and Ola Jonsson deal in chapter 10 with the design and implementation of strategies in cross-border regions. The Øresund region between Denmark and Sweden is well known, both as a leading case in cross-border collaboration initiatives and as one of the more innovative regions of Europe, and yet the authors tell a story of unfulfilled potential in territorial strategy. They start by setting up the contrasting notions of involutionary (a creative and experimental bringing together of heterogeneous things and people) and evolutionary (reproduction of routines and positions as an extension of the past into the future) strategy, either of which may be combined with bottom-up or top-down decision-making authority. This conceptual framework provides a specific lens for their case analysis, which is focused on the institutional processes behind cross-border regionalisation and thus builds on the previous chapter in deepening analysis of how territorial strategy is (or is not) constructed. As is the case in the three preceding chapters, the authors pursue a dynamic, historical analysis of the strategy over the last few decades, which they split into three distinct eras. The cross-border region gained rapid momentum during the 1990s because of the newness of the idea (that is, the lack of previous existing institutions and organisations), the influence of ideas of a Europe of the Regions and, most critically, the impetus of the decision to construct a fixed infrastructure link between Denmark and Sweden. The process in this era was led by policy entrepreneurs and a multitude of public–private partnerships that created many new cross-border institutions and organisations, each articulating elements of a strategy in what the authors characterise as its most involutionary stage. However, as strategy attempted to become more formalised during the years between 1997 and 2006, it drifted towards a more evolutionary approach, in which context the difficulties of cross-border strategy implementation began to appear as a result of the political division of the territory and the lack of political power of the cross-border organisations (and policy entrepreneurs) to influence the Danish and Swedish governments. In the current era, from 2007 onwards, it is suggested that there is no such thing as a common cross-border strategy, but separate city strategies instead. Politics and polity, in the last resort, made the difference, and Tangkjær and Jonsson suggest that there is a need to find a better balance between evolutionary and involutionary processes, with a strengthening of the latter.

If strategy implementation remains especially challenging in cross-border regions, how should territories that until now have limited experience of a 'strategy from within' first approach the issue? This is the question addressed in chapter 11 by Keith Culver, Nicky Dhaliwal, Malida Mooken and Roger Sugden for the Okanagan region in the interior of British Columbia, Canada. As the authors rightly point out, the key issue at stake here is how to initiate a process of strategy formation in a 'young' territory, defined in terms of its physical geography, but without a long history or a clear socio-economic identity, and with complex governance that lacks a unique administration – in short, quite a different scenario to the 'old' European regions of the Basque Country, Wales and Navarre dealt with in other chapters. Building on a detailed analysis of the social and economic development trajectory of the territory, the authors argue that the focal point for constructing a strategy in this context is to get the different stakeholders involved in a process of envisioning the region's future. They advocate a bottom-up process, with the engagement of local communities and the creation of public fora (dialogue spaces in Aranguren and Larrea's terms), and a method based on Dewey's (1938) concept of inquiry rather than on strategic planning. This proposed journey of inquiry nevertheless requires a starting point, for which Culver *et al.* suggest that (and illustrate how) the practice of scenario planning can provide a suitable catalyst. Their contribution highlights that, for 'young' territories such as the Okanagan region, and in contrast with the 'old' regions of Europe – even before the three general aforementioned questions of a territorial strategy – there is a prior 'when' question that needs to be addressed.

The final case chapter (chapter 12) returns to Europe, and indeed directly to the concept of RIS3 that we argued at the beginning of this introductory chapter has been so influential in fuelling the boom in territorial strategy-making. Mari José Aranguren, Mikel Navarro and James Wilson undertake a comparative analysis of the ongoing process of RIS3 development in three European regions, in what is one of the first available assessments of the current state of RIS3 in Europe. The Basque Country features here again, this time alongside Murcia and Navarre – three Spanish regions with quite different contexts and experiences with RIS3. The case analysis is structured around the six steps set out by the European Commission to guide regions in their RIS3 (Foray *et al.*, 2012), although the authors propose a prior analysis of two other more general elements that will condition the pursuit of these steps in practice: the context of the region, in particular in terms of features that influence governance complexity and political stability; and what is actually understood in the region by RIS3. Significant differences in how each of the steps are being approached are uncovered by the analysis, and the chapter concludes by reflecting that the 'state of practice' in territorial strategy in Europe echoes many of the concerns that were highlighted in the conceptual analysis of Part I regarding how territorial strategy is operationalised. In particular, the cases point to severe practical difficulties in setting actual priorities, in aligning policy to strategy and in establishing evaluation processes.

In the final chapter we bring together the analysis of both parts of the book by returning to the main questions that a territorial strategy should address – 'what for', 'what' and how/who' – and the practical challenges of implementation. Combining the conceptual arguments of Part I with the lessons revealed from the cases in Part II, we discuss some general propositions that can serve as a guide for taking analysis of territorial strategies for competitiveness further forward. This final chapter also sounds a call to arms for academics, politicians and practitioners to engage together in processes for change in their respective territories (Culver *et al.* in chapter 11 issue a similar call to academics). Indeed, following Albert Hirschman (Hirschman *et al.*, 1984: 110–11) – actually one of the first scholars who employed the term 'strategy for a given place' – our aim with this book is, first, to *persuade* by the arguments and ideas developed and, second, to *recruit* for joint work and collaboration in this exciting area of research and practice. After reading this book, it might be the case that, even if you do not agree with some of the arguments, or rather because you do agree with them, you join the ranks of those interested in this field. Then, go ahead!

## Notes

1 This work was supported by the Spanish Ministry of Economy and Competitiveness under Grant number HAR2012-30948 (Valdaliso); by the Basque Government Department of Education, Language and Culture under Grant numbers IT807-13 (Valdaliso) and IT629-13 (Wilson); and by the European Commission (FP7 SSH.2012.1.1-3) under Grant number 320131 (Wilson). Any errors are the responsibility of the authors.

2 Research is starting to emerge, particularly in the European context, where regional strategies for smart specialisation have received a strong impulse from the European Commission. See, for example the recent books by Thissen *et al.* (2013) and Foray (2014).

3 See also Hadjimichalis and Hudson (2014) for a critical view of regional development theories.

## References

Aranguren, M. J., Magro, E., Navarro, M., and Valdaliso, J. M. (2012) *Estrategias para la construcción de ventajas competitivas regionales: el caso del País Vasco.* Madrid: Marcial Pons.

Asheim, B., Boschma, R., Cooke, P., Dahlstrand-Lindholm, A., Laredo, P., and Piccauga, A. (2006) *Constructing Regional Advantage: Principles, Perspectives, Policies.* Brussels: European Commission.

Bianchi, P., and Labory, S. (2012) Conceptualisations, relationships and trends between innovation, competitiveness and development: industrial policy beyond the crisis. In Cooke, P., Parrilli, M. D., and Curbelo, J. L. (eds), *Innovation, Global Change and Territorial Resilience*. Cheltenham: Edward Elgar.

Bloch, E. (1991) *Toward a US Technology Strategy: Enhancing Manufacturing Competitiveness*. Washington, DC: National Academy Press.

Boschma, R. (2014) *Towards an Evolutionary Perspective on Regional Resilience*. Utrecht University, Papers in Evolutionary Economic Geography, 14.09.

Clark, J. (2013) *Working Regions: Reconnecting Innovation and Production in the Knowledge Economy*. London: Routledge.

Dertouzos, M., Lester, R., and Solow, R. (1989) *Made in America: Regaining the Productive Edge*. Cambridge, MA: MIT Press.

Dewey, J. (1938) *Logic: The Theory of Inquiry*. New York: Henry Holt.

Etkowitz, H., and Klofsten, M. (2005) The innovating region: toward a theory of knowledge-based regional development, *R&D Management*, 35(3), pp. 243–55.

European Commission (2010) *Communication from the Commission to the European Parliament, the Council, the European Economic and Social Committee and the Committee of the Regions COM(2010) 553 Final: Regional Policy Contributing to Smart Growth in Europe 2020*. Brussels: European Commission.

European Commission (2011) *Regional Policy for Smart Growth in Europe 2020*. Brussels: European Commission.

Foray, D. (2014) *Smart Specialisation: Opportunities and Challenges for Regional Innovation Policy*. Abingdon: Routledge.

Foray, D., and van Ark, B. (2008) Smart specialisation in a truly integrated research area is the key to attracting more R&D to Europe. In European Commission, *Knowledge for Growth: European Issues and Policy Challenges*. Brussels: European Commission.

Foray, D., Goddard, J., Goenaga, I., Landabaso, M., McCann, P., Morgan, K., Nauwelaers, C., and Ortega-Argilés, R. (2012) *Guide to Research and Innovation Strategies for Smart Specialisation*. Brussels: European Commission.

Hadjimichalis, C., and Hudson, R. (2014) Contemporary crisis across Europe and the crisis of regional development theories, *Regional Studies*, 48(1), pp. 208–18.

Halkier, H. (2006) *Institutions, Discourse and Regional Development: The Scottish Development Agency and the Politics of Regional Policy*. Brussels: Peter Lang.

Hirschman, A. O. (1958) *The Strategy of Economic Development*. New Haven, CT: Yale University Press.

Hirschman, A. O., Diaz-Alejandro, C., and Streeten, P. P. (1984) *A Dissenter's Confession: 'The Strategy of Economic Development' Revisited*. New York: Oxford University Press.

Magro, E., and Wilson, J. R. (2013) Complex innovation policy systems: towards an evaluation mix, *Research Policy*, 42(9), pp. 1647–56.

Mintzberg, H., Ahlstrand, B., and Lampel, J. (1998) *Strategy Safari*. New York: Free Press.

Morgan, K. (1997) The learning region: institutions, innovation and regional renewal, *Regional Studies*, 31(5), pp. 491–503.

Navarro, M., Valdaliso, J. M., Aranguren, M. J., and Magro, E. (2014) A holistic approach to regional strategies: the case of the Basque Country, *Science and Public Policy*, 41(4), pp. 532–47.

Porter, M. E. (1990) *The Competitive Advantage of Nations*. London: Macmillan.

Porter, M. E. (1998) Clusters and competition: new agendas for companies, governments, and institutions. In *On Competition*. Boston: Harvard Business School.

Porter, M. E., and Rivkin, J. W. (2012) The looming challenge to US competitiveness, *Harvard Business Review*, March.

Robock, S. H. (1966) Strategies for regional economic development, *Papers in Regional Science*, 17(1), pp. 129–41.

Rodríguez-Pose, A. (2013) Do institutions matter for regional development? *Regional Studies*, 47(7), pp. 1034–47.

Rodríguez-Pose, A., and Tijmstra, S. (2009) *On the Emergence and Significance of Local Economic Development Strategies*. Caracas: CAF Working Paper 2009/07.

Sölvell, O. (2012) The CAON story, paper presented in the 2012 MOC Faculty Workshop. Boston: Harvard Business School.

Sotarauta, M. (2004) *Strategy Development in Learning Cities: From Classical Rhetoric towards Dynamic Capabilities*. University of Tampere, Sente Working Papers 8/2004.

Stimson, R. J., Stough, R. R., and Roberts, B. H. (2006) *Regional Economic Development: Analysis and Planning Strategy*. 2nd ed., New York: Springer.

Thissen, M., Van Oort, F., Diodato, D., and Ruijs, A. (2013) *Regional Competitiveness and Smart Specialization in Europe: Place-Based Development in International Economic Networks*. Cheltenham: Edward Elgar.

Thomson, G. (1975) A regional strategy for Europe, address to the Chamber of Commerce and Industry, Nantes, 5 December; http://aei.pitt.edu/8570/ [accessed 7 October 2014].

Wannop, U. A. (1995) *The Regional Imperative: Regional Planning and Governance in Britain, Europe and the United States*. London: Jessica Kingsley.

Warwick, K. (2013) *Beyond Industrial Policy: Emerging Issues and New Trends*. OECD Science, Technology and Industry Policy Papers no. 2.

## Part I

# A framework for analysing territorial strategy

# 2 Territorial strategy

## Deepening in the 'what'

*Mikel Navarro*[1]

## Introduction

As has been presented in the introduction of this book, any territory that wants to develop a strategy has to work on the 'what for', or the objectives of development of the territory, the 'what', or the content of the strategy, and the 'how', or the process of strategy formation. The 'what for' has been treated in the introductory chapter and is reflected upon in several of the subsequent chapters. Analysis of the 'how' is provided in chapter 4 and then deepened in the cases of Oresund, Rafaela and the Okanagan (chapters 9 to 11) in particular. This chapter, alongside the next one by Christian Ketels, deals with the 'what'. While both are inspired by how Michael Porter (and, more broadly, the so-called positioning school of strategic management) conceptualises the strategy of a firm, their roots in fundamentally different literatures complement each other. Building on Navarro *et al.* (2012, 2014) and Aranguren *et al.* (2012), and rooted in literature on scientific and technological (S&T) policy, on economic development, on economic geography and on innovation systems, this chapter develops analysis around the following five questions that should be answered by the 'what' of a territorial strategy.

1. What are the main economic activities (industries or clusters) or scientific and technological fields in which the territory is meant to excel?
2. What are the unique assets or resources that the territory must possess or develop in order to succeed in those activities and scientific-technological fields?
3. What are the targeted actors of that strategy and the actors by means of which the strategy will be carried out?
4. What relationships is the territory developing with other territories and external agents?
5. What kind of internal articulation is sought in the territory?

The first two questions coincide more or less with questions 2 to 4 posed by Ketels in his analysis rooted in the literature of strategic management.[2] As we will see later on, they have been put forward also by the literature on S&T policy when discussing the pros and cons of thematic/vertical and functional/horizontal policies or, alternatively, of mission- and diffusion-oriented policies. While the other three questions (questions 3 to 5) have not been so conspicuous in the debate around economic and innovation policies and strategies, they have been considered crucial by some analyses to explain the economic and innovation success of certain territories. As a consequence, it is worth contemplating their inclusion among the questions to be addressed by the content of a territorial strategy.

Before going ahead, let's remember in a nutshell what distinguishes thematic and functional priorities, as well as what relationship they have with the distinction between mission- and diffusion- oriented policies proposed by Ergas (1986, 1987). Thematic (or vertical) priorities concern the S&T areas, clusters or industries considered crucial for competitiveness and development and correspond directly with the first of the five questions. Functional, structural or horizontal priorities concern the structures, functions or assets that are critical in the innovation or economic system, and thus correspond with the second question.

In market economies, the debate on thematic priorities has usually been marked by a divide between those authors or countries opposed to fixing priorities in S&T or industries in order to foster competitiveness and economic development (thinking predominant in the US) and those in favour of making those kinds of choices (thinking predominant in Europe and Japan, and with France a paradigmatic example). At the regional level, the debate on priorities appeared later on, with the revival or growth of the literature on economic geography, regional innovation systems (and learning regions), clusters and, more recently, smart specialisation strategies.

In this regard, the main contribution of economic geography comes from its debate on the advantages and effects stemming from the different types of agglomeration economies (Boschma and Martin, 2010). Along with its systemic approach, the literature on regional innovation systems (RIS) has paid more attention to structural/functional problems and priorities in the system than to thematic priorities (Asheim and Gertler, 2005; Tödtling and Trippl, 2005). Nevertheless, with regard to the kind of economic activity to be favoured, like the economic geography literature, the RIS literature is concerned with agglomeration economies (especially those giving 'related variety') and not so much with industries or clusters (Cooke *et al.*, 2007). Although biased in its practice towards high-tech activities, the cluster literature states that no kind of activity is intrinsically (or everywhere) better than others. Thus, starting from existing activities, cluster policies should try to affect and enhance the sophistication of the whole economy (Porter, 1998, 2003). Finally, research and innovation smart specialisation strategies (RIS3) advocate that territories should develop a specialised diversification and smart upgrading, by means of applications of general purpose technologies (GPT) or other innovation activities in the industries in which the region has comparative advantages (Foray *et al.*, 2012).

In parallel with this distinction between thematic and functional priorities, Ergas (1986, 1987) classified S&T policies applied in developed countries in two opposed categories: mission- versus diffusion-oriented policies. Mission-oriented priorities are those related to scientific and technological areas or industries that governments choose on account of their statutory responsibilities or desire to reach a specific goal. Diffusion-oriented policies, conversely, seek to provide a broad-based capacity for adjusting to technological change throughout the industrial structure, thus facilitating rather than directing change.

There is no coincidence among authors about what scope these mission-oriented priorities and policies should have. For instance, Ergas focuses his analysis on the priorities taken by a few countries (the US, the UK and France) in some fields highly related to defence (aerospace, electronic and nuclear energy, above all). Even if the support given by government in defence-related mission-oriented policies indirectly impinges heavily on the competitiveness and development of civil sectors, the main reason or rationale for that support is to gain international strategic leadership (Branscomb, 1995; Ergas, 1986, 1987). However, the support given to some S&T areas or activities linked to the responsibilities or missions of government ministries in other fields (health, environment, agriculture …) are also considered by many authors to be mission-oriented policies. The main reason for governments to give this support is not fundamentally the competitiveness or development of the economy. However, while in defence-related mission-oriented policies it is frequent to find profound differences among countries, all governments support R&D activities in health, agriculture, and so on, and thus the differences among countries are not outstanding (Lederman, 1987).

Some authors (for example, Mowery, 2009) go even further and include within mission-oriented policies government promotion of some technologies or activities with the aim of supporting industrial technology development (considering that this is also a government mission). Finally, more recently, the recognition of societal challenges such us climate change, ageing populations, scarcity of raw materials, mobility issues, and so on, and the need to respond to them with public strategies and policies, has led some authors and entities to speak about 'new mission-oriented' policies (Gassler *et al.*, 2008).

Some analysts (OECD, 1991; Gassler *et al.*, 2004, 2008) combine these two approaches in order to create a new one and, as a result, distinguish three main types of priority: mission-oriented, thematic and structural/functional. In our view it is preferable to work with only two main categories – thematic or vertical priorities, on the one hand, and functional, structural or horizontal priorities, on the other. However, this option doesn't rule out, in the particular analysis of thematic priorities, distinguishing among priorities established due to strategic leadership or the responsibility or missions of government in some fields (defence, health, environment …) and those more closely connected to competitiveness and economic development.

Anyway, returning to the five questions to be answered by the 'what' of a territorial strategy, it is worth highlighting that there are a lot of linkages between the issues posed in them. As a result the responses given to any one of them should take into account and be coherent with the answers given to the others. Just as the reality which they try to affect, the chosen strategy should present systemic features, and the responses given to the five questions must be interconnected.

In the second section of the chapter we will go deeper into the dilemmas related to thematic priorities (question 1), in the third section we will do the same with regards horizontal priorities (question 2), and in the fourth section we will group analysis of the main issues concerning priorities as regards targeted actors, outward relationships and internal articulation of the territory (questions 3 to 5). The chapter will end with a summary and some conclusions.

## Priorities in scientific and technological areas and activities

A territorial strategy for development can be seen as an economic transformation agenda (Foray *et al.*, 2012). In this sense, economic development is not just a quantitative matter (how much the economy grows) but also a qualitative one (how the production composition changes) (Neffke *et al.*, 2011). Therefore, it is not only about the pace but also about the direction of innovation (Foray, 2009). But change or move towards where? And what should be the way to move there?

### *Some dilemmas: specialisation/deepening versus diversification/shifting*

Regarding the direction of transformation in production, one of the traditional debates in economic geography has revolved around the advantages of being specialised or diversified. It has been argued since Alfred Marshall ([1890] 1920) that territorial specialisation in a few industries favours the development of a specialised labour force, suppliers, infrastructures and institutions, as well as knowledge spillovers (and, as a result, innovation and learning).[3] Location economies allow the exploitation of economies that are external to the firm but internal to the industry (Harmaakorpi, 2010). In favour of diversification, it has been argued since Jane Jacobs (1969) that, in addition to less vulnerability in the face of shocks and disturbances that affect one given activity or industry, a variety of activities and related knowledge make their combination and cross-fertilisation easier, and therefore fuel innovation.

This debate has been inconclusive for a long time. However, a growing consensus has emerged in recent decades in the sense that specialisation is preferable in mature industries (e.g., metal industries), whereas diversification is more preferable in young sectors (e.g., bio-industries). Additionally, a new alternative has recently appeared in the debate: so-called related variety. According to this new approach, cross-fertilisation and combination has a higher impact in innovation than specialisation, but with the proviso that the cognitive distance between activities or knowledge bases that are to be combined is not excessive. Otherwise, diversification could allow the reduction of vulnerability in the presence of particular shocks, but agents of one activity would not be able to make use of the knowledge spillovers coming to them from the surrounding activities or industries. Empirical analysis conducted in this regard confirms the proposals of this new approach, and the recent literature on territorial strategy advocates the transformation of the economy based on such related variety (see Frenken *et al.*, 2007; Boschma and Iammarino, 2009; Neffke *et al.*, 2011; Boschma *et al.*, 2012; Foray *et al.*, 2012; McCann and Ortega-Argilés, 2011; Delgado *et al.*, 2014).

In parallel to the debate about whether a territory should bet on moving towards a specialised or a diversified economy has been a related debate revolving around the pros and cons of engaging in either deepening or shifting strategies (Pontikakis *et al.*, 2009). Deepening strategies consist of focusing and specialising in those industries or activities in which the territory has comparative advantages, and arguably deepening strategies would be more related to specialisation. Shifting strategies, on the other hand, give preference to the ability to adapt to changes and reinvent oneself, and would be connected more with diversification. This dilemma between deepening and shifting is posed by Etzkowitz and Klofsten (2005) in terms of being a learning region or an innovating region: the learning region would aim at building on existing assets by processes of incremental innovation, while the innovating region would seek to create new assets linked to a research base.

Regarding this, Freeman (1997: 39, 42–3) states:

> The argument for preserving and even encouraging diversity may sometimes outweigh the shorter-term advantages of the scale economies ....
>
> A technological monoculture may be more dangerous than an ecological monoculture. Even when a technology matures and shows clear-cut advantages and scale economies it is important to retain flexibility and to nourish alternative sources of radically new technology and work organisation.[4]

***Ways to transform the production structure***

Accepting that strategies are transformation agendas and that the production structure should move towards specialised diversification and smart upgrading (McCann and Ortega-Argilés, 2011; Camagni, 2011), both the European Commission (2010) and Foray (2013) have categorised the main ways of doing so, categories that have been slightly modified by Navarro *et al.* (2012) and Aranguren *et al.* (2012). According to this adapted categorisation there are four main ways to transform the production fabric: modernisation, extending, radical foundation and cross-sectoral combination.

We speak of *modernisation* ('retooling', in the words of the European Commission, 2010) when upgrading occurs within an already existing industry. One of the most fruitful ways to transform and upgrade is to apply Key Enabling Technologies (KETs) to traditional sectors. For instance, nanotechnologies are being applied to the pulp and paper industry and biocomponents incorporated in some food products in the Basque Country in order to make them more competitive.[5]

*Extending* refers to a jump by firms from one activity or industry to another, on the grounds of synergies and commonalities existing between their knowledge bases. For example, the development of aeronautics in the Basque Country in the 1990s was rooted in already existing capacities in engineering, automobiles and machine tools (López *et al.*, 2012).

*Radical foundation* consists of the emergence of an entirely new niche or activity in the territory. A well-known and general example is the appearance of clusters of biofirms in a number of regions in developed countries. The incipient attempt to develop the wave and tidal energy industry in the Basque Country could be another example of diversification based on radical foundation.

Finally, as Schumpeter holds, sometimes innovation and new products arise from the combination of existing knowledge and products. This *cross-sectoral combination* is more and more frequent as a result of the increasing convergence of disciplines and knowledge domains. In fact, the biostrategy pursued by the Basque Country depends not so much on biotechnology (a field in which it is not particularly strong) as on the combination of this with a range of technologies and capabilities (engineering, micro-technology, electronics …) where the region has particular strengths (Navarro *et al.*, 2011).

### *Aggregation level of thematic priorities*

The thematic priorities incorporated in territorial development strategies typically refer to scientific domains as much as to technological fields, clusters, industries or economic activities. However, there is an increasing tendency to avoid defining thematic priorities in terms of industries. On the one hand, as a consequence of the unstoppable development of 'global production networks' and the parallel fragmentation or 'de-verticalisation' of production processes, it is more and more difficult nowadays to approach prioritisation and diversification in terms of complete industries or clusters. Instead, prioritisation should be approached in terms of given sets of activities (Breznitz, 2007), usually related by a shared set of skills or knowledge bases (Henning *et al.*, 2010). On the other hand, even when industries are chosen not as a result of 'picking winners'[6] but, instead, by taking into account the context and current or potential comparative advantages existing in the territory, analysts consider that the level of industry or cluster is too broad or aggregated.

More precisely, according to Foray (2013: 59):

> The relevant level at which to observe, detect and set priorities is of 'mid-grained' granularity – the level at which new activities/projects are involving a group of firms and other (research) partners aiming at exploring a new domain of (technological and market) opportunities; which has potentially a certain weight and is of a high significance relative to the regional economy (in terms of the kind of structural changes it is likely to generate).

In the end, priorities should be chosen by crossing the current and potential strengths of the territory in industries and clusters with the scientific and technological capabilities available that could support them, as well as taking into account the market possibilities opened by new societal challenges. One example of this way of choosing priorities is demonstrated by the Basque Country, whose process to define thematic priorities is shown in Figure 2.1. According to the relative strengths of its industries and clusters (reflected at the bottom of the triangle), scientific and technological capabilities (at the right side of the triangle) and the market opportunities opened by the societal challenges that are thought will have most impact on the region (at the left side of the triangle), three main meta-priorities (advanced manufacturing, energy and biosciences) and some opportunity niches linked to the territory have been chosen. In contrast to the three-pronged nature of this approach, many other regions have based their decisions on fewer criteria – usually a combination of the existing or potential strengths in industries and S&T.

## Horizontal priorities on functions and assets

Although vertical and horizontal priorities should be identified by means of an interlinked and mutually reinforcing process, for the sake of clarity we will assume that thematic priorities have already been determined, taking into account the territory's resources and capabilities. Now is the time to pay attention to the assets and functions in need of development or strengthening to be a successful territory in those vertical priorities and, even more, in the whole economy. Or, in the terms expressed by Christian Ketels in chapter 3, it is time for the strategy to define what value the region will provide and how it will be provided.

Porter claims that, similar to the fundamental choice between competing on costs or differentiation that a firm must undertake in order to determine what value it is going to provide, a territory ought to understand in which stage of competitive development it is immersed. According to the stage of development (competing mainly in factors, in efficiency or in innovation), the main assets, functions or structures to be developed will be of one type or another. The OECD (2011) has arrived at a similar proposal by identifying three main types of choice that regions face, with three corresponding families of strategies: catching up, supporting the socio-economic transformation (reconversion or new specialisation) and building on current advantages in science and technology. Not surprisingly, the three Porterian categories can be easily matched with those proposed by the OECD: competing mainly in factors could match with the catching-up strategy; competing in efficiency with supporting socio-economic transformation; and competing in innovation with building on current S&T advantages.[7]

Moving to the specific resources and capabilities that territories should develop in order to be successful in their competitive stage, two main dilemmas must be faced: 1) to work with a broad or narrow approach to competitiveness, innovation and their determinants; and 2) to focus on the core strengths or

The **selection** of the Basque Country´s main priorities has been **based on:**

- **The existence of a solid business base**, with capacity to pull and/or exploit innovations. Evaluated by economic weight and specialisation, exports (global share), technological intensity, growth, industry structure.

- The presence of **significant scientific and technological capabilities**. Evaluated by dimension of S&T agents, quality (publications, return in competitive programmes), applicability and likelihood of results exploitation (patents, number of projects with companies) …

- **The applicability** to areas of greatest (global) potential opportunity. Evaluated by potential impact on society, expected growth in priority markets, potential of high-value-added solutions …

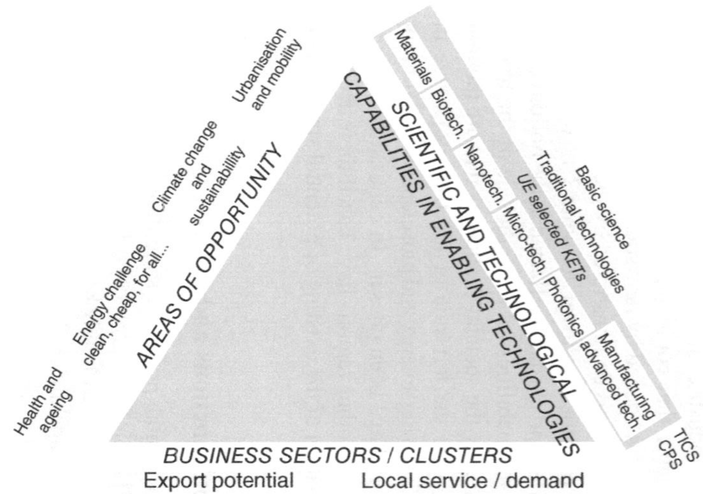


*Figure 2.1* Identification of thematic priorities by the R&D&i strategy of the Basque Country

Source: Basque Government (2014), RIS3 strategy.

capabilities existing in the territory or to seek a balance among the different types of assets or functions.

With regard to the first dilemma, apart from the choice about a broader or narrower 'what for' of the strategy, the territorial strategy could opt to focus only on R&D and innovation-related resources and capabilities or encompass all kind of factors that affect development and competitiveness. The recently launched smart specialisation strategies in the European Union, for example, are purposively focused on research and innovation. They expressly try to avoid the past tendency of many regions to expend most of the funding coming from European structural funds on physical infrastructures very weakly connected to innovation capabilities.

But, even with respect to R&D and innovation, the approach might be broader or narrower, as the debates between different developers of the innovation system concept show. For instance, in opposition to Nelson (1993), Etzkowitz and Leydesdorff (2000) or Niosi (2010), who support a narrow approach to the innovation system (that is, one focused only on R&D components and relationships), there is an array of authors (such as Lundvall, 1992; Edquist, 1997, 2005; Asheim and Gertler, 2005) in favour of a broader perspective in which all the components and relationships that affect any kind of innovation would have to be taken into account. The narrow approach could be designed and handled more easily, because it would contain many fewer components, and perhaps it would be a good fit for territories, such as Cambridge in the UK, which are very advanced in scientific knowledge. Yet clearly it would have a small impact on the competitiveness and innovation capability of less developed regions, whose modes of innovation and learning respond more to the so-called DUI model (learning by doing, by using and by interacting) than the STI model (science, technology and innovation).

The second dilemma is to what extent horizontal priorities should concentrate on the areas where the territory presents higher comparative advantage and try to turn them into unique strengths, or, conversely, whether they should have a more balanced approach and try to neutralise the weakest structures and functions of the region and combine different types of learning, innovation and knowledge bases. In the field of strategic management, Hansen and Birkinshaw (2007) have criticised those schools or authors that advocate focusing attention on the core capabilities of the firm, because it could entail undermining even further the most vulnerable parts of the system. Likewise, in the economics of innovation, Soete (2006) and Arundel and Hollanders (2008) claim that the mitigation or correction of the weakest points in the innovation system yields better results than the further development of the strongest points; therefore, territories shouldn't allow the existence of too large an imbalance among their different assets and competitive factors.

In the same vein, Lundvall and Lorenz (2010) and Jensen *et al.* (2007) hold that the best performance is achieved when innovation activities based on science are combined with those based on experience. Asheim (2009) states something similar when he stresses the benefits of combining different knowledge bases – analytical, synthetic and symbolic. In line with these conceptual arguments, Frenz and Lambert (2009) find that outcomes are better when different types of innovation (technological and non-technological) are combined, and Mairesse and Mohnen (2009) and Criscuolo *et al.* (2011) find that the organisations that combine and mix different sources of knowledge obtain better results. Wintjes and Hollanders (2010) come by analogous findings, but concerning European regions.

Even if territories should give priority to neutralising the weakest points of their systems and combining different types of innovation and learning, it does not mean that everyone should show the same mix of structures, functions or assets. Trying to be the best in everything and to develop all kinds of assets is a sign, precisely, of lack of strategy (Porter, 1996; Lafley and Martin, 2013).[8] On the contrary, the emphasis put on the diverse dimensions, modes or basis of the innovation process across regions can be different.

In particular, regarding innovation strategies, analysts have highlighted various aspects where different emphasis could be placed:

- the science, the technology or the innovation (technological, organisational, commercial …) side of the process (Morgan and Nauwelaers, 1999);
- the generation, absorption and diffusion of knowledge (OECD, 2011);
- the exploration, the development or the exploitation of knowledge (ibid.);
- the STI (science, technology and innovation) or the DUI (learning by doing, by using and by interacting) modes of innovation and learning (Jensen *et al.*, 2007);
- the analytical, the synthetic (or engineering) or the symbolic knowledge bases (Asheim, 2009).

For instance, in the Basque Country, innovation policies have been oriented towards technology development rather than towards science or innovation (see chapter 7). Policies have sought the generation and development of knowledge rather than its exploration, absorption, diffusion and exploitation. In this sense innovation policies have made a great effort to develop the STI model and the analytical knowledge base, even if the innovation system was based mainly on a DUI model and a synthetic knowledge base (Navarro, 2010).

## Priorities with regards targeted actors, external relationships and internal articulation

As has been argued previously, these kinds of priority are less usual in territorial strategies, which generally confine themselves to set vertical and horizontal priorities. This is quite evident in the so-called *RIS3 Guide* (Foray *et al.*, 2012), produced by the European Commission so as to help regions in the design of research and innovation strategies, which speaks only about vertical and horizontal priorities.

Certainly it is debatable if the issues concerning actors, external relationships and internal articulation of the territory should be included in the 'what' of the strategy rather than in the 'what for' or even in the 'how'. For instance, some people could be in favour of prioritising the development of small and medium-sized enterprises (SMEs) because these kinds of firm allow a more direct and democratic participation of workers in production and, therefore, lead to a more inclusive society (a 'what for' issue). But they could also be considered in the 'what' if the presence of this type of firm is particularly relevant in our territory or if we consider that their singular features could be better exploited and give us a competitive edge. Furthermore, it doesn't preclude taking SMEs into account in governance issues (i.e., in the 'how' of the strategy).

Similarly, the internal articulation and cohesiveness of the territory could be an objective in itself and, therefore, included in the 'what for' from a broad perspective. But, even when the goal of the strategy is restricted to economic development, it is undeniable that the sort of economic distribution prioritised in the territory and the agglomeration economies stemming from it affect economic output substantially. That is why the analysis of the content or 'what' of a territorial strategy should give thought to these issues as well.

### *Targeted actors*

In fact, there is a clear identification of the types of firm (large national champions versus SMEs; public, cooperative or purely private firms …) targeted by territorial strategies both in the first typologies of industrial districts and regional innovation systems (Markusen, 1996; Cooke, 1998; Asheim and Isaksen, 1997, 2002) and in the characterisation of the different development strategies of emerging countries (Breznitz, 2007) or S&T policies (Ergas, 1986, 1987; Branscomb, 1995).

It is not the same for a territory to be composed of a myriad of small and medium firms (like a Marshallian industrial district) or a combination of large companies and SMEs (as in some German *Länder*) or for a large part of the industrial fabric to be depending on one large company (as in the well-known 'hub-and-spoke' district described by Markusen, 1996). As Breznitz (2007) shows, the strategy of some of the most successful emerging countries differs in the size of the firms which are given preference (e.g., large companies or *chaebols* in Korea versus SMEs in Taiwan) or in the role fulfilled by private and state-owned companies (Israel versus Singapore). Likewise, a strong worker cooperative corporation such as the Mondragon group in the Basque Country (the biggest business group in this region and the seventh largest in Spain), apart from idiosyncratic reasons, has also to do with the policies that have fostered this type of firm in this region.

The priorities in terms of actors are more conspicuous when one looks at the components of the sub-system of generation and diffusion of knowledge in innovation systems. The weight of universities, public research centres, competence research centres, technological centres, knowledge intensive business services (KIBS), vocational education and training centres (VET), and the like, is very different from one territory to another (Niosi, 2010). The Basque Country (again, see chapter 7) is just a case in point: its sub-system of generation and diffusion of knowledge differs noticeably from that prevalent in the other Spanish regions (Sanz-Menéndez and Cruz-Castro, 2005; Navarro *et al.*, 2013), as it has given preference to technological centres, competence research centres and VET over the university, public research organisations and KIBS.

### *Priorities in external relationships*

Even if the practice of many of the territorial strategies applied in Europe is characterised by their inward-looking nature and by governments' attempts to keep all of the key components of their clusters or innovation systems within their territories, this approach is in fact not only unrealistic but even contrary to the aim of having strong and competitive clusters and innovation systems. This was clearly seen by the first analysts of industrial districts and regional innovation systems, who considered that one of the key elements that characterised the territory was its external connection (Markusen, 1996; Cooke, 1998; Asheim and Isaksen, 1997, 2002).

Some of the subsequent main contributors to the RIS literature (Kaufmann and Tödtling, 2000; Archibugi *et al.*, 1999) have consistently underlined that it would be not only impossible but also extremely inefficient and risky to base the development of regions upon their own knowledge and factors. Even more strongly, Bathelt (2003) has emphasised the need for regions to take into account and develop 'global pipelines' on top of 'local buzz'. In a similar way, the literature on S&T policies and priorities has highlighted that one of the main issues of these policies is the right combination of internal and external technology and international technology transfer (Tisdell, 1981).

Finally, the literature on the strategies followed by emerging countries shows that they differ according to the weight attributed to internal and external factors and, above all, to the role attributed to multinational firms (which build, manage and to some extent control global production networks). It is not the same for the territory if multinationals think about it as an assembler, a low-cost producer, a sophisticated producer or a knowledge hub (Breznitz, 2007). In addition, the territorial strategy should determine the type of relationships and role that the region will have with respect to other territories – neighbouring regions, the rest of the state and the geo-economic region in which they are located, or the global economy (Porter, 2011).

### *Priorities in internal articulation*

Regions are not homogeneous territories but, rather, are usually are made up of various 'places' that have distinctive features (Bathelt, 2003; Muscio, 2006; Uyarra, 2007; Uyarra and Flanagan, 2009; McCann, 2011). As Navarro and Larrea (2007) and Zubiaurre *et al.* (2009) show, even the Basque Country – a territory considered by the literature as a typical RIS with a strong identity – is made up of an array of counties or places with remarkably different innovation and competitiveness patterns.

In that sense, apart from non-economic reasons (e.g., to avoid the negative effect on the environment that could result from the depopulation of some areas), the agglomeration economies that might arise from one or another distribution of population and economic activity in space are very different. Certainly, that distribution can be strongly affected by the choices made by public policies on the provision of educational and health services, roads, and so on. Besides, the appropriate exploitation of the specific agglomeration economies existing in each place requires the tailoring of territorial policies to them. Therefore, the strategy should define the kind of internal structure and articulation that the territory is seeking – the degree of concentration, polarisation, specialisation, and so on.

## Conclusions

All territorial strategies must have a 'what for' or vision (a set of goals to be achieved), a 'what' or content (the definition of a group of actions to be undertaken in some specific areas so as to achieve the goals) and a 'how' or process (some kind of governance that allows the emergence of a shared vision and choice-making, as well as their materialising in policies and measures, duly monitored and assessed). Out of these three layers, this chapter has dealt basically with the second – with the 'what' or content of the strategy. More precisely, following the model of the strategic management school, in order to specify the 'what' of the territorial strategy, it has identified the key answers that ought to be addressed with regard to the latter's content. The essence of all strategy lies in making choices, and this chapter is designed to pinpoint the subjects on which choices have to be made. By means of an extensive review of the literature on scientific and technological (S&T) policy, on economic development, on economic geography and on innovation systems, five areas of prioritisation have been explored:

1 economic activities (industries or clusters) or scientific and technological fields in which the territory is meant to excel;
2 assets, resources or functions that the territory must possess or develop;
3 targeted actors of that strategy;
4 relationships with other territories and external agents;
5 internal articulation and distribution of activities sought in the territory.

Of these, the first two, referred to as thematic/vertical and functional/structural/horizontal priorities, have usually been dealt with by the literature on business and territorial strategy. However, as the literature on economic development and regional innovation systems shows, the actors, the connections with external agents and territories, and the internal articulation of the territory might be not only very specific, but also crucial for the economic development of the territory and the object of territorial choices.

We have brought to light the dilemmas or main debates existing around these five areas in the economic and innovation literature. As the literature on strategy and innovation unanimously acknowledges, the same strategy cannot be valid for everyone, and there is no best or optimal solution applicable everywhere. It is little wonder, therefore, that the review conducted here has not offered universal recommendations about which kinds of particular activities, functions, actors, external relationships and internal articulation should be pursued by territorial strategies. These choices must be made by taking into account the context of the territory and its aspirations. However, this doesn't imply that there are no general warnings emanating from the literature, and the analysis of this chapter has highlighted the following:

- the need not only to grow but also to transform the production structure;
- the advantages of fostering a specialised diversification based on related variety;
- the risk of following narrow deepening policies that do not develop shifting capabilities;
- the convenience of not defining very broad thematic priorities but, instead, trying to cross-fertilise industrial strengths with the opportunities opened up by technologies (especially Key Enabling Technologies) and markets;
- the necessity of understanding clearly the stage of competitive development of the territory, because this sets a general challenge for the kinds of resources and capabilities that the territory will have to develop;
- the desirability of not focusing only on the development of core capabilities but, rather, attending to the weakest points of the innovation system and avoiding profound imbalances in it;
- the desirability of combining different types of knowledge bases and innovation modes and not forgetting the absorption, diffusion and exploitation phases of the knowledge value chain;
- the danger of inward-looking development strategies that don't take into account economic globalisation and the need for operating with open innovation models.

Finally, it is important to highlight that these five sorts of priority shouldn't be faced independently of one another. As Pavitt (1984) showed, the pattern of innovation changes from industry to industry, and therefore the choices about the resources and capabilities to be prioritised cannot be taken in disregard of the choices made in vertical priorities. In turn, the firm's size is not independent of the type of industry and the innovation pattern, as the review by Cohen (2010) makes evident. The level of openness differs by industry, kinds of resources (natural resources, labour, capital and knowledge) and firm size. Last but not least, industries, innovation, firm openness and the agglomeration economies related to them vary hugely depending on the composition of a territory. What is called for is a strategy that is capable of integrating choices around these five questions in a coherent whole, something that in turn demands novel and efficient strategic processes. This will be addressed in subsequent chapters of the book.

## Notes

1 This work was supported by the European Commission (FP7 SSH.2012.1.1-3) under Grant number 320131. Any errors are the responsibility of the author.
2 According to our framework, the first question posed by Ketels (the region's ambition) deals with the 'what for' rather than the 'what'. Likewise, his fifth question (the support system the region needs) is included within our framework in the 'how'.
3 When firms are involved in the same activity or industry, the observation and comparison of the different trajectories and results of each one make it possible to select and imitate best practices (Maskell, 2001). Moreover, when firms are located in different stages of the value chain, the proximity of suppliers and users favours innovation and learning through interaction (Lundvall, 1992). Additionally, the specialisation and concentration of the firm in its core competences increases its innovation capability (Maskell, 2001).
4 Dalum *et al.* (1992) and Carlsson (1994) express a similar opinion.
5 Foray (2013) distinguishes between 'modernisation' (which brings about changes in terms of efficiency and quality in an existing sector) and 'transition' (the emergence of a new domain from the existing industrial commons). In our categorisation, as long as product innovation occurs within the boundaries of the existing industry and doesn't arrive at the creation of a new sector, it would be considered as modernisation, and not transition. If a firm's product innovation allows it to enter another existing industry, it would be considered as 'extending'. And if product innovation gives rise to a new industry or activity, we would speak of 'radical foundation'.
6 'Picking winners' policies consider that some industries or activities are preferable per se everywhere, regardless of the particular assets and context existing in the territory.
7 Rodríguez-Pose (2011) rightly criticises linear models, such as that of Rostow (1960), which imply that all territories should pursue similar policies and strategies, according to their stage of development and without consideration of their particular place and time context. Taking that for granted, it is also true that, depending on their level of development, territories face some common challenges that condition the setting in which their unique value proposition ought to be developed.
8 On this point, see the distinction made by Christian Ketels in chapter 3 between critical, hygiene and other regional qualities, and the different aims that territories should try to reach in each of them to generate value in the specific markets where they aim to compete.

## References

Aranguren, M. J., Magro, E., Navarro, M., and Valdaliso, J. M. (2012) *Estrategias para la construcción de ventajas competitivas regionales: el caso del País Vasco.* Madrid: Marcial Pons.

Archibugi, D., Howells, J., and Michie, J. (1999) Innovation systems in a global economy, *Technology Analysis & Strategic Management*, 11(4), pp. 527–39.

Arundel, A., and Hollanders, H. (2008) Innovation scoreboards: indicators and policy use. In Nauwelaers, C., and Wintjes, R. (eds), *Innovation Policy in Europe*. Cheltenham: Edward Elgar, pp. 29–52.

Asheim, B. (2009) La política de innovación regional de la próxima generación: cómo combinar los enfoques del impulso por la ciencia y por el usuario en los sistemas regionales de innovación, *Ekonomiaz*, 90, pp. 86–105.

Asheim, B. T., and Gertler M. S. (2005) The geography of innovation: regional innovation systems. In Fagerberg, J., Mowery, D. C., and Nelson, R. R. (eds), *The Oxford Handbook of Innovation*. New York: Oxford University Press, pp. 291–317.

Asheim, B., and Isaksen, A. (1997) Location agglomeration and innovation towards regional innovation systems in Norway, *European Planning Studies*, 5, pp. 299–330.

Asheim, B., and Isaksen, A. (2002) Regional innovation systems: the integration of local 'sticky' and global 'ubiquitous' knowledge, *Journal of Technology Transfer*, 27, pp. 77–86.

Basque Government (2014) *RIS 3 Euskadi: prioridades estratégicas de especialización inteligente de Euskadi*, April, https://www.irekia.euskadi.net/assets/attachments/4633/prioridades_estrategicas201404_ris3_gobierno_vasco.pdf?1400573225.

Bathelt, H. (2003) Geographies of production: growth regimes in spatial perspective (I): innovation, institutions and social systems, *Progress in Human Geography*, 27(6), pp. 763–78.

Boschma, R. A., and Iammarino, S. (2009) Related variety, trade linkages and regional growth, *Economic Geography*, 85(3), pp. 289–311.

Boschma, R., and Martin, R. (eds) (2010) *The Handbook of Evolutionary Economic Geography*. Cheltenham: Edward Elgar.

Boschma, R., Minondo, A., and Navarro, M. (2012) Related variety and regional growth in Spain, *Papers in Regional Science*, 91(2), pp. 241–57.

Branscomb, L. M. (1995) *Empowering Technology*. Cambridge, MA: MIT Press.

Breznitz, D. (2007) *Innovation and the State: Political Choice and Strategies for Growth in Israel, Taiwan and Ireland*. New Haven, CT, and London: Yale University Press.

Camagni, R. (2011) Local knowledge, national vision: challenges and prospects for the EU regional policy. In *Seminar on Territorial Dimension of Development Policies: Papers and Proceedings*, Ostróda, Poland, 18–19 July, pp. 57–63.

Carlsson, B. (1994) Technological systems and economic performance. In Dodgson, M., and Rothwell, R. (eds), *The Handbook of Industrial Innovation*. Cheltenham: Edward Elgar, pp. 13–24.

Cohen, W. M. (2010) Fifty years of empirical studies of innovative activity and performance. In Hall, B. H., and Rosenberg, N. (eds), *Handbook of the Economics of Innovation*, Vol. 1. Amsterdam: Elsevier, pp. 129–213.

Cooke, P. (1998) Introduction: origins of the concept. In Braczyk, H. J., Cooke, P., and Heidenreich, M. (eds), *Regional Innovation Systems: The Role of Governances in a Globalized World*. London: UCL Press, pp. 2–25.

Cooke, P., Laurentis, C., Tödtling, F., and Trippl, M. (2007) *Regional Knowledge Economies: Markets, Clusters and Innovation*. Cheltenham: Edward Elgar.

Criscuolo, P., Laursen, K., Reichstein, T., and Salter, A. (2011) Winning combinations: search strategies and innovativeness in the UK, paper given at the DRUID Conference, Copenhagen Business School, 15–17 June.

Dalum, B., Johnson, B., and Lundvall, B.-A. (1992) Public policy in the learning society. In Lundvall, B. A. (ed.), *National Systems of Innovation: Towards a Theory of Innovation and Interactive Learning*. London and New York: Pinter, pp. 296–317.

Delgado, M., Porter, M. E., and Stern, S. (2014) Clusters, convergence, and economic performance, *Research Policy*, 43, pp. 1785–99.

Edquist, C. (ed.) (1997) *Systems of Innovation: Technologies, Institutions and Organizations*. London and Washington, DC: Pinter.

Edquist, C. (2005) Systems of innovation: perspectives and challenges. In Fagerberg, J., *et al.* (eds), *The Oxford Handbook of Innovation*. Oxford: Oxford University Press.

Ergas, H. (1986) Does technology policy matter? In Guile, B., and Brooks, H. (eds), *Technology and Global Industry: Companies and Nations in the World Economy*. Washington: National Academy Press, pp. 191–245.

Ergas, H. (1987) The importance of technology policy. In Dasgupta, P., and Stoneman, P. (eds), *Economic Policy and Technological Performance*. Cambridge: Cambridge University Press, pp. 51–94.

Etzkowitz, H., and Klofsten, M. (2005) The innovating region: toward a theory of knowledge-based regional development, *R&D Management*, 35, pp. 243–55.

Etzkowitz, H., and Leydesdorff, L. (2000) The dynamics of innovation: from national sSystems and 'mode 2' to a triple helix of university–industry–government relations, *Research Policy*, 29, pp. 109–23.

European Commission (2010) *Commission Staff Working Document*, SEC(2010) 1183: *document accompanying the Commission Communication on Regional Policy contributing to smart growth in Europe 2020*.

Foray, D. (2009) Structuring a policy response to a 'grand challenge'. In *Knowledge for Growth: Prospects for Science, Technology and Innovation*. Selected papers from Research Commissioner Janez Potočnik's Expert Group, November; http://ec.europa.eu/invest-in-research/pdf/download_en/selected_papers_en.pdf.

Foray, D. (2013) The economic fundamentals of smart specialisation, *Ekonomiaz*, 83(2), pp. 54–78.

Foray, D., Goddard, J., Goenaga, X., Landabaso, M., McCann, P., Morgan, K., Nauwelaers, C., and Ortega-Argilés, R. (2012) *Guide to Research and Innovation Strategies for Smart Specialisations (RIS 3)*. Brussels: European Commission.

Freeman, C. (1997) The 'national system of innovation' in historical perspective. In Archibugi, D., and Michie, J. (eds), *Technology, Globalisation and Economic Performance*. Cambridge: Cambridge University Press, pp. 24–49.

Frenken, K., Van Oort, F. G., and Verburg, T. (2007) Related variety, unrelated variety and regional economic growth, *Regional Studies*, 41(5), pp. 685–97.

Frenz, M., and Lambert, R. (2009) Exploring non-technological and mixed modes of innovation across countries. In OECD, *Innovation in Firms: A Microeconomic Perspective*. Paris: OECD, pp. 69–110.

Gassler, H., Polt, W., Schindler, J., Weber, M., Mahroum, S., Kubeczko, K., and Keenan, M. (2004) *Priorities in Science & Technology Policy: An International Comparison*. Research Report no. 39-2004. Vienna: Institute of Technology and Regional Policy.

Gassler, H., Polt, W., and Rammer, C. (2008) Priority setting in technology policy: historical development and recent trends. In Nauwelaers, C., and Wintjes, R. (eds), *Innovation Policy in Europe: Measurement and Strategy*. Cheltenham: Edward Elgar, pp. 203–24.

Hansen, M. T., and Birkinshaw, J. (2007) The innovation value chain, *Harvard Business Review*, June, pp. 121–30.

Harmaakorpi, V. (2010) The 'regional development platform method' as a tool for innovation policy. In Eriksson, A. (ed.), *The Matrix: Post Cluster Innovation Policy*, VINNOVA Report VR 2010:10, www.vinnova.se/upload/EPiStorePDF/vr-10-10.pdf.

Henning, M., Moodysson, J., and Nilsson, M. (2010) *Innovation and Regional Transformation: From Clusters to New Combinations*. Malmö: Elanders.

Jacobs, J. (1969) *The Economy of Cities*. New York: Vintage.

Jensen, M. B., Johnson, B., Lorenz, E., and Lundvall, B.-Å. (2007) Forms of knowledge and modes of innovation, *Research Policy*, 36(5), pp. 680–93.

Kaufmann, A., and Tödtling, F. (2000) Systems of innovation in traditional industrial regions: the case of Styria in a comparative perspective, *Regional Studies*, 34(1), pp. 29–40.

Lafley, A. G., and Martin, R. L. (2013) *Playing to Win: How Strategy Really Works*. Boston: Harvard Business Review Press.

Lederman, L. L. (1987) Science and technology policies and priorities: a comparative analysis, *Science*, 237(4819), pp. 1125–33.

López, S., Elola, A., Valdaliso, J. M., and Aranguren, M. J. (2012) *El clúster de la industria aeronáutica y espacial del País Vasco: orígenes, evolución y trayectoria competitiva*. Donostia: Eusko Ikaskuntza; Instituto Vasco de Competitividad – Fundación Deusto.

Lundvall, B.-Å. (1992) *National Systems of Innovation: Towards a Theory of Innovation and Interactive Learning*. London: Pinter.

Lundvall, B.-Å., and Lorenz, E. (2010) El enfoque dui y de variedades relacionadas innovación y desarrollo de competencias en la economía del aprendizaje: implicaciones para las políticas de innovación. In Parrilli, M. D. (ed.), *Innovación y aprendizaje: lecciones para el diseño de políticas*. Zamudio: Innobasque.

McCann, P. (2011) *Notes on the Major Practical Elements of Commencing the Design of an Integrated and Territorial Place-Based Approach to Cohesion Policy*. Economic Geography Working Paper, June, Faculty of Spatial Sciences, University of Groningen.

McCann, P., and Ortega-Argilés, R. (2011) *Smart Specialisation, Regional Growth and Applications to EU Cohesion Policy*. Economic Geography Working Paper, Faculty of Spatial Sciences, University of Groningen.

Mairesse, J., and Mohnen, P. (2009) Innovation surveys and innovation policy, paper presented at Globelics 7th International Conference, 6–8 October.

Markusen, A. (1996) Sticky places in slippery space: a typology of industrial districts, *Economic Geography*, 72, pp. 293–313.

Marshall, A. ([1890] 1920) *Principles of Economics*. 8th ed., London: Macmillan.

Maskell, P. (2001) Towards a knowledge-based theory of the geographical cluster, *Industrial and Corporate Change*, 10(4), pp. 921–43.

Morgan, K., and Nauwelaers, C. (eds) (1999) *Regional Innovation Strategies: The Challenge for Less-Favoured Regions*. London: Routledge.

Mowery, D. C. (2009) What does economic theory tell us about mission oriented R&D? In Foray, D. (ed.), *The New Economics of Technological Policy*. Cheltenham: Edward Elgar.

Muscio, A. (2006) From regional innovation systems to local innovation systems: evidence from Italian industrial districts, *European Planning Studies*, 14(16), pp. 773–89.

Navarro, M. (2010) Retos para el País Vasco, tras tres décadas de desarrollo del sistema y de las políticas de innovación, *Ekonomiaz*, 25A, pp. 136–83.

Navarro, M., and Larrea, M. (eds) (2007) *Indicadores y análisis de competitividad local en el País Vasco*. Vitoria-Gasteiz: Servicio central de publicaciones del Gobierno Vasco.

Navarro, M., Aranguren, M. J., and Magro, E. (2011) *Smart Specialisation Strategies: The Case of the Basque Country*. Orkestra Working Paper Series in Territorial Competitiveness no. 2011-R07 (ENG); www.orkestra.deusto.es/.

Navarro, M., Aranguren, M. J., and Magro, E. (2012) Las estrategias de especialización inteligente: el caso del País Vasco, *Revista de Cuadernos de Gestión*, 12, pp. 17–50.

Navarro, M., Magro, E., Lorenz, U., Parrilli, M. D., Karlsen, J., and Egurbide, I. (2013) *Las infraestructuras de conocimiento: el caso vasco desde una perspectiva internacional*. San Sebastián: Cuadernos Orkestra.

Navarro, M., Valdaliso, J. M., Aranguren, M. J., and Magro, E. (2014) A holistic approach to regional strategies: the case of the Basque Country, *Science and Public Policy*, 41(4), pp. 532–47.

Neffke, F., Henning, M., and Boschma, R. (2011) How do regions diversify over time? Industry relatedness and the development of new growth paths in regions, *Economic Geography*, 87(3), pp. 237–65.

Nelson, R. (ed.) (1993) *National Systems of Innovation: A Comparative Study*. Oxford: Oxford University Press.

Niosi, J. (2010) *Building National and Regional Innovation Systems: Institutions for Economic Development*. Cheltenham: Edward Elgar.

OECD (1991) *Choosing Priorities in Science and Technology*. Paris: OECD.

OECD (2011) *Regions and Innovation Policy*, OECD Reviews of Regional Innovation. Paris: OECD.

Pavitt, K. (1984) Sectoral patterns of technical change: towards a taxonomy and a theory, *Research Policy*, 13, pp. 343–73.

Pontikakis, D., Chorafakis, G., and Kyriakou, D. (2009) R&D specialisation in the EU: from stylised observations to evidence-based policy. In Pontikakis, D., Kyriakou, D., and van Bavel, R. (eds), *The Question of R&D Specialisation: Perspectives and Policy Implications*. Luxembourg: Office for Official Publications of the European Communities, pp. 71–81.

Porter, M. E. (1996) What is strategy?, *Harvard Business Review*, November–December, pp. 61–78.

Porter, M. E. (1998) Clusters and the new economics of competition, *Harvard Business Review*, November–December, pp. 77–90.

Porter, M. E. (2003) The Economic performance of regions, *Regional Studies*, 37(6–7), pp. 549–78.

Porter, M. E. (2011) *Microeconomics of Competitiveness*. Institute for Strategy and Competitiveness, Harvard Business School.

Rodríguez-Pose, A. (2011) Spatially-blind strategies as place-based development strategies. In *Seminar on Territorial Dimension of Development Policies: Papers and Proceedings*, Ostróda, Poland, 18–19 July, pp. 85–9.

Rostow, W. W. (1960) *The Stages of Economic Growth: A Non-Communist Manifesto*. Cambridge: Cambridge University Press.

Sanz-Menéndez, L., and Cruz-Castro, L. (2005) Explaining the science and technology policies of regional governments, *Regional Studies*, 39(7), pp. 939–54.

Soete, L. (2006) Knowledge, policy and innovation. In Earl, L., and Gault, F. (eds), *National Innnovation Indicators and Policy*. Cheltenham: Edward Elgar.

Tisdell, C. A. (1981) *Science and Technology Policy: Priorities of Governments*. London: Chapman & Hall.

Tödlting, F., and Trippl, M. (2005) One size fits all? Towards a differentiated regional innovation policy approach, *Research Policy*, 34(8), pp. 1203–19.

Uyarra, E. (2007) Key dilemmas of regional innovation policies, *Innovation*, 20(3), pp. 243–61.

Uyarra, E., and Flanagan, K. (2009) From regional innovation systems to regions as innovation policy spaces, *Environmental Planning C: Government and Policy*, 28, pp. 681–95.

Wintjes, R., and Hollanders, H. (2010) *The Regional Impact of Technological Change in 2020: Synthesis Report*. Brussels: European Commission, DG Regional Policy.

Zubiaurre, A., Zabala, K., and Larrea, M. (2009) Capacidad local de innovación: una tipología de comarcas vascas, *Ekonomiaz*, 70(1), pp. 280–303.

# 3 What is regional strategy?

## Lessons from business strategy

*Christian Ketels*

## Introduction

A casual scan of European regions suggests that the notion of "regional strategy" has become significantly more popular in recent years. Much of that has been driven by demands (and financial support) from the European level. The European Commission has encouraged the development of regional innovation strategies (European Commission, 2007; Ortega-Argilés, 2012), and has now made smart specialization strategies a necessary condition for regions to be eligible for structural funds (European Commission, 2013a). Outside of Europe, too, some scholars have written about the 'advent of strategic management of places' (Audretsch, 2006). In practice, territorial strategies are often predominantly planning documents with a medium- to long-term view, designed to provide orientation for the annual activity plans and budgets governments regularly put forward. This chapter will focus on the content of these strategies, what the editors of this book call the "what" (Navarro *et al.*, 2014). Other parts of this book focus instead on the "how" and the "who," discussing the process and the involvement of different stakeholders.

For companies, strategy is about where and how to compete (Porter, 2000; Lafley and Martin, 2013). To deal with these two questions, companies identify market segments, analyze the industry dynamics on these markets, and then make their choice about how to design their business in a way that generates high profitability on the back of a compelling offer to customers. The academic literature and practice in this field has generated a robust array of tools and frameworks to support fact-driven decision-making on firm strategy.

But do these approaches translate into the realm of regional economies? This is the key question this chapter aims to explore. What are the markets in which regional economies compete, and with what purpose? How can they position themselves in these markets in ways that foster their ultimate objectives? And what types of tool might be available to regions as they aim to make these choices in line with an evidence-based policy approach? In tackling these questions, we conduct a review of the firm strategy literature to decompose the "what" of strategy into a number of key dimensions. These dimensions can then be put into the context of regional economies to outline how the "what" of their strategy would look if it followed the firm strategy literature. When contrasting this theoretical blueprint of regional strategy with current practice, we find a number of systematic "black spots" that existing regional strategies often fail to address. We argue that these omissions lead regions to fail in the creation of sustainable competitive advantages and hamper an effective implementation of meaningful actions.

The remainder of this chapter is organized in three main parts. First, it discusses how the content of strategy is described in the field of business studies. Second, it explores how these concepts can be translated in the context of public policy for regional economies. And, third, it contrasts these conceptual ideas with the current practice of regional economic strategies. A final section develops a few conclusions for theory and practice, and in particular for the ongoing work on smart specialization strategies throughout Europe.

## Strategy in the context of companies

While the term "strategy" has a longer tradition in management studies than in economics, here too there is no single definition that is applied consistently throughout the literature. Instead, there is a whole range of "schools" that have developed their own understanding of what strategy is (Mintzberg *et al.*, 1998). Our focus here is on the so-called positioning school, which is the one that deals most directly with the analytical process of making choices about the content of strategy (the "what"). In the next chapter Mari José Aranguren and Miren Larrea explore how several of the other schools might inform the "how" and "who" of territorial strategy.

The positioning school is concerned with tools that enable management to make an integrated set of choices that can tie the ultimate objectives of the company to its structure and its activities. The foundations of this work were laid in a number of publications by Michael Porter. *Competitive Strategy* provides managers with a toolkit for analyzing the nature of competition within a given industry (Porter, 1980, 2008). *Competitive Advantage* then developed an approach to think about activity systems and how they can support specific generic strategies based on low costs or differentiation (Porter, 1985). "What is strategy?" turned to how companies can develop unique strategies within these generic categories through creating trade-offs and integrated activity systems (Porter, 2000).

Importantly, the positioning school is based on an implicit underlying framework of how companies create economic value. This framework combines a conceptualization of the firm (the "value chain") with an industrial economics-driven conceptualization of markets (the "five forces"). The economics of the firm shape how much value, measured as customer benefit minus cost, is being created. The economics of the market define how much of that value is captured by the firm. Strategic positioning, then, is about the core choices firms face in order to achieve profitability given these underlying structures of firms and markets.

Porter is credited with creating the positioning school through his contributions since the 1980s and has had a unique impact among practitioners. His work sparked a still growing academic literature, and there is an ongoing debate about many elements of his framework (see, for a review, the relevant chapters in Huggins and Izushi, 2012). Some have suggested a different way to analyze industry dynamics (e.g., Nalebuff and Brandenburger, 1996). Others propose that firms should view resources (Wernerfelt, 1984) or capabilities (Prahalad and Hamel, 1990) as the core of delivering on their value propositions, not activities, and that the value chain does not apply equally well to all types of activities (Stabell and Fjeldstad, 1998). Arguments have been made that there is no trade-off between competing on low costs or high value (e.g., Kim and Mauborgne, 2004) or that firms should abandon competitive advantages and instead focus either on general best practices in management (e.g., Collins and Porras, 1994) or on flexibility to succeed in quickly changing markets (e.g., McGrath, 2013). Regardless of these debates, Porter's influence on issues of strategy and positioning among practitioners remains unrivalled (e.g., Magretta, 2011).

A key feature of the positioning school is the focus on choices and how those can be made in an analytical fashion. A recent practitioner-oriented application of the positioning approach gives a useful hands-on example of the key choices that firms face (Lafley and Martin, 2013). Together, these choices are described as an "integrated cascade"; they have a sequential nature with decisions on earlier choices setting the context for following ones, but also a feed-back loop where a later choice can lead to adjustments at earlier stages. The five key choices identified are set out in Figure 3.1 and then analyzed in turn.

*What is the firm's ambition?* In a sense, this is a simple question to answer for most companies. Their core goal is to achieve high levels of profitability through providing goods and services at a price level that is higher than their costs to the firm. An ambition marks the choice to narrow down the field in which the firm aims to reach high profitability. It is a statement of purpose that sets out in broad terms what activities the firm aims to engage in (sometimes called its "mission") and what outcome it aims to achieve (sometimes called its "vision").

*What market does the firm serve?* Within the scope given by its statement of purpose, a firm then needs to select the market(s) it aims to serve. This turns out to be a non-trivial task: before the company can choose a market, it needs to define the set of markets from which it can select. Market boundaries can shift as new technologies or other structural changes extend the range of rivals that offer competing solutions. Defining markets in the way that consumers experience them – i.e., capturing all offers that consumers consider to meet a specific need – is a critical foundation for successful strategic choices. Once an appropriately defined market has been chosen, a firm can consider the customers and rivals it will meet. The business literature has developed a range of tools to analyze the attractiveness and underlying dynamics of specific market segments. Porter's five forces framework has been mentioned above, as well as some of the alternative approaches.

*What value does the firm provide?* Within the target market, a firm then needs to make choices about is value proposition: What is the unique value that it will provide in serving specific needs of the selected customer base? Porter (1985) argued that firms can distinguish themselves either through low costs – i.e., providing

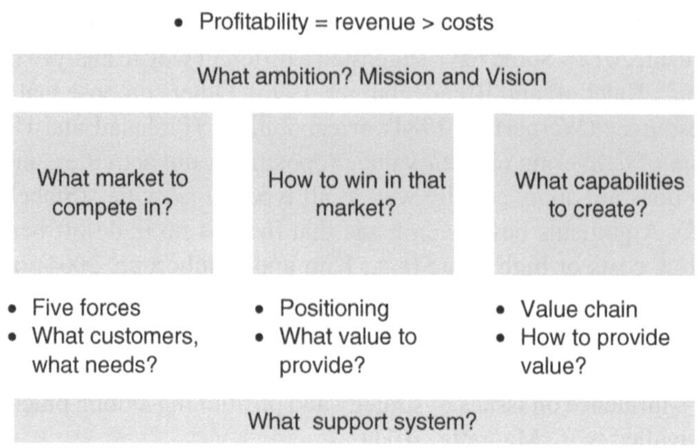


*Figure 3.1* Firm strategy

customers with the same value as others but at a lower price – or through differentiation – i.e., providing customers with a set of features and qualities that they don't get anywhere else. While price is a one-dimensional feature, differentiation can happen in many different ways depending on the market chosen.

*How does the firm provide this value?* The value proposition is a promise, and firms have to find ways to deliver on this promise while achieving their profitability targets. Some argue that firms should structure their thinking on how to deliver value around the choice of activity system to be created, while others suggest organizing the choice around the core competencies a firm needs to build. In either case, the answer to this question makes a strategy in the sense of the positioning school fundamentally different than purely setting out 'strategic' goals and ambitions. The distinction between strategy as theory and implementation as practice sometimes made is highly misleading strategy as discussed here is deeply action-oriented.

*What support system does the firm need?* Finally, there needs to be a management system in place with incentive structures, communication channels, and information tools that support the previous choices.

While there are different ways to organize these choices and to describe their content, this structure provides a useful background to think about how the notion of strategy can be applied to regions and economic policy.

## Regions and economic policy: lessons from business strategy

What are the key questions that a regional strategy has to answer? The discussion of business strategy suggests that we first need to think about the underlying economic model that might explain the drivers of regional prosperity. In a second step we then explore how the questions that make up the core of a firm's strategic choice apply to regions.

### *Drivers of regional prosperity*

Where firm strategy is based on a conceptual framework that explains profitability, economic strategy for a location is informed by a conceptual framework that explains prosperity levels. This understanding does not have to amount to a fully specified economic model but is, rather, a set of key assertions about the dynamics of economies that inform the policy choices made. Where the firm strategy literature looks at market dynamics and firm capabilities as key drivers of firm-level profitability, the economics literature looks at interregional/international competition and locational factors as drivers of prosperity.

A key difference between the two areas is the role of market dynamics. Firms compete with other firms, and the more intense this competition is, the lower profitability tends to be. Locations compete with other locations, but they also trade with them: they are both producers and consumers. The international trade literature has shown that economic interaction with other locations leads to (potentially sizable) prosperity gains, even when the other location is "more competitive" – i.e., productive – in all areas: the possibility to specialize according to comparative advantages offers benefits to both locations. The competitiveness literature arrives at similar results, concentrating more on the beneficial effects of cross-border rivalry on local productivity (Porter, 1990). While these models have focused on international exchange, their basic results translate to the competition between locations within national borders.

Despite the prosperity gains at the aggregate level, locations are also exposed to more traditional types of competition at the level of individual economic activities where not everyone will win. Locations do compete to attract specific economic activities and the (mobile) factors of production that perform them, just as firms do in product and service markets. Aggregate prosperity gains depend on a location's ability to allocate its resources to those activities in which it has an advantage. The new economic geography literature has studied the competitive dynamics in such markets under conditions of positive local externalities and factor mobility. Such models can lead to self-reinforcing concentration of economic activity, potentially driving even aggregate prosperity differences across locations (Fujita *et al.*, 2001). The cluster literature focuses on externalities among a narrower set of related industries, which is more likely to lead to regions specializing in different ways but not necessarily dominating each other in terms of overall prosperity.

Both types of model point out the difference between "traded" activities – i.e., those for which there is locational competition since the relevant markets can be served from different places – and "local" activities – i.e., those for which such competition does not exist since the market can only be served locally (Porter, 2003; Delgado *et al.*, 2014). These two parts of regional economies differ not only in their competitive dynamics but also in the economic potential that they have. Traded activities register higher productivity, wages, and rates of innovation. They are in their growth potential uninhibited by the size of the local market and thus turn out to be the critical engines of regional prosperity. Their true potential is realized when regions exhibit critical mass in strong clusters – i.e., groups of related traded activities (Porter, 2003; Delgado *et al.*, 2011, 2010; Ketels and Protsiv, 2013). Local activities are important as well; they account for a large share of jobs, and low productivity in these sectors hurts both prosperity and the traded activities that use them as inputs. But ultimately the local sector is subject to decreasing returns that reduces its potential for driving sustained prosperity growth.

The ability of locations to support high prosperity depends on underlying factors that drive productivity, similar to the capabilities discussed in the firm strategy literature. A large literature on prosperity differences between national economies provides valuable insights also for regions (e.g., Delgado *et al.*, 2012; Acemoglu and Robinson, 2012; McCord and Sachs, 2013). Geographic location and natural conditions, institutional qualities and social capital, a wide range of business environment conditions, especially skills (e.g., Glaeser and Saiz, 2004), and regional specialization patterns, especially cluster presence and diversification (Porter, 2003; Delgado *et al.*, 2011), have been discussed intensively. While there is significant disagreement on the relevant importance of individual factors, there is sufficient evidence to argue that all of them have some role to play. The literature on regional competitiveness has pointed out the need to acknowledge the breadth of, and often complex interaction between, these factors (e.g., Kitson *et al.*, 2004; Martin and Sunley, 2011; Ketels, 2013).

Within such a framework, policy is playing a role both in shaping those drivers of economic performance it can affect and in addressing market failures that arise in their provision or use (see also chapters 5 and 6). The regional innovation systems literature, for example, focuses on those areas where market failures in the innovation process might justify policy action (Cooke, 1992; Asheim and Gertler, 2005). A critical question is whether policies should be region-specific – i.e., set different priorities given local circumstances – or be region-"blind" – i.e., follow the same generic development path or even focus only on general policies across all regions (Barca *et al.*, 2012; Gill, 2010; OECD, 2009; World Bank, 2009). The region-specific approach argues that the impact of policies depends significantly on the local context in which they are applied, and that therefore different regions face different "optimal" policies. The region-"blind" approach argues that policies should be equal across locations, with the economic geography adjusting automatically to achieve the best overall outcomes.

In general, the basic tenants of the economic models underlying firm strategy translate only in part to the field of regional strategy. For both firms and regions, the underling capabilities – whether firm-specific competencies/activity systems or region-specific competitiveness fundamentals – are critical and drive the ability to win in competition with other firms/regions. However, the competitive dynamics are different. Firms face a largely zero-sum competition with other firms; the only way to soften rivalry is through a distinctive positioning that affords the firm some local market power. Regions face the same dynamics for traded activities, which are particularly important as the most productive parts of the regional economy. But regions are always both producers and consumers; while some producers might lose from interregional competition, consumers always win. Regions need thus to focus much more on the productivity benefits they can provide through their competitiveness fundamentals than on ways to soften the exposure to competition from other locations.

### *Core strategic choices for regions*

Applying the framework from business strategy to the realm of regions, we can now review the five key dimensions of strategic choices and discuss their relevance for regions. Again, these are set out in Figure 3.2 and discussed in turn below.

*What is the region's ambition?* For regions, the ultimate policy goal is to create an environment in which citizens can be prosperous and companies can successfully compete. Arguably this is a matter more of vision than of mission. Just like firms, regions can define an outcome they want to achieve – for example, reaching certain economic performance goals, taking a leading position in certain economic activities, and so on. This can be useful to mobilize action through an outcome objective that galvanizes the aspiration of firms and individuals, to provide a criterion that can be used when selecting specific activities, and as a benchmark as to whether a region and its policies have been successful. Unlike firms, however, regions do not need a distinct mission that provides a core idea underpinning their existence. Regions do exist and don't need a mission to justify their presence.

*What market does the region compete in?* As for firms, the first step is to define relevant markets in an appropriate way. Locations compete for specific sets of economic activity, not in the markets for products and services in which companies compete. They compete for what has been called above "traded" activities – i.e., those activities that can choose between locations from which to serve a given market.

*Figure 3.2* Regional strategy

There is not one market for traded activities but several markets for different sets of activities, defined by similar needs in terms of business environment conditions. The challenge for locations is then to figure out what exactly those markets are and what needs firms exhibit in each of them. This requires an understanding of the way that companies draw on the relevant activities as they compete in the market for products and services. Approaches such as cluster mapping, value-chain analysis, and network analysis aim to identify both the relevant groups of industries and the role of geographic proximity for the respective linkages between them. Tools such as the Cluster Observatories in Europe[1] and the US[2] provide the data that help regions to understand their relative position in terms of regional economic composition and specialization patterns versus other locations.

The definition of the relevant market is critical to understand both the customers – i.e., firms – and the competition – i.e., other locations: What are the relevant groups of firms, and what are their needs in terms of locational qualities? Who are the other locations that aim to attract the same type of economic activities, and what are the qualities that they can offer?

Regions are also in the market for mobile production factors, especially human and financial capital. These production factors do not directly create prosperity, but they contribute to the business environment that makes the location more or less attractive for the economic activities that do. Regions need to consider not only what makes them attractive for these factors. As importantly, they need to understand which production factors are most critical for the type of economic activities for which they are competing.

*What value does a region provide?* Regions provide value through the access they offer to markets, natural resources, and business environment conditions. These categories have been most widely discussed in the literature on foreign direct investment but also contribute a useful reference here.

Access to markets is particularly important in the competition for local industries, where companies have to be physically located in a region to serve its market. They can also influence the location of traded industries, but here proximity to, rather than presence within, the market is often sufficient. This still gives traded activities choices as to where they ultimately locate. Specific natural conditions, such as access to natural resources or a location at a major trading route, are critical to compete for economic activities such as mining or shipping that require them. But while such conditions reduce the list of locations that are relevant choices for these types of activities, they do not eliminate firms' ability to choose altogether: there are often many locations for mining a particular mineral and many harbors to serve a particular trading route.

Business environment conditions are particularly critical in the competition for traded industries that can choose the location that provides the most beneficial context for their activities. They include a broad range of factors, from access to specific skills, research capabilities, or physical infrastructure to the presence of clusters and sophisticated demand conditions. The "diamond" framework (Porter, 1990) provides a heuristic to organize the complex multitude of factors, many of which have been studied individually in the academic literature. Regions can draw on a wide range of tools providing data on different aspects of regional business environment quality – for example, the European regional competitiveness index (Annoni and Dijkstra, 2013), the regional innovation scoreboard (European Commission, 2013b), and many other more specialized tools focused on individual aspects of locational quality.

The particular value of these factors to individual firms depends on those firms' specific needs, driven by their respective activity systems. These needs are different by industry but potentially also influenced by firm-specific factors and strategies. Automotive companies focus on different aspects than biotech companies, but even BMW and Skoda might weigh the value of specific business environment qualities differently given their respective market positioning.

Two specific factors that are prominent in the applied business literature on locations are wages and taxation. Unlike the other dimensions of business environment quality, these two do not determine the productivity of economic activities but affect how economic value is shared between firms' owners and the location, both government and employees. In some ways, they are equivalent to the price that firms charge for their products and services. But there are also important differences: firms set their prices while wages are in most places set in a market process, not by (regional) fiat. The positioning choice for firms relates the price to the benefits its offering provides: low-cost providers offer similar benefits at a lower price, while differentiators offer more compelling benefits at the same price compared to rivals. For regions' value propositions, it makes sense to think about the same ratio: what matters is how high wages (and taxes as well as other local input costs) are relative to the productivity level that the competitiveness fundamentals allow companies to achieve (Delgado *et al.*, 2011), not the absolute level of wages.

*How does the region provide this value?* The creation of value is for companies rooted in the specific system of activities in which they are engaged and in the competencies on which these activities draw. For regions, some of the value is related to factors that can be influenced by policy, while others are the result of "given" legacy factors. Policy does not control natural resources, location, or market size. These factors are, however, important to take into consideration when making choices about where and how to compete. But policy-makers can influence many business environment conditions – some on their own, some in collaboration with other entities such as firms, universities, etc. The prioritization of specific business environment conditions is a core policy question that a regional strategy needs to address.

Regions need to decide which mix of business environment qualities can best support their target value proposition in their target market, relative to companies' needs and the conditions available in other locations. The choices here are many – there are a large number of business environment conditions and an even larger number of combinations among them. The key is to establish which (small) number of qualities is truly critical to generate distinct value in the market in which they aim to compete. Firms sometimes call these "business winning" properties – i.e., the qualities that in the end will determine whether the business goes to one firm (location) or the other. There are many others that can "lose" the business – i.e., will push the product/location from the list of relevant choices – if they are not in place. But they are in and of themselves not sufficient.

This approach can help regions to group qualities at three different levels:

- critical, business-winning qualities on which the region needs to outperform its rivals;
- hygiene qualities on which a region needs only to match its rivals or a generic lower level of quality that companies demand;
- other qualities that are not relevant for the type of value proposition and market in which the region is competing; these areas regions can and should downgrade in terms of priority.

What make this choice difficult are the likely interactions across the different qualities: offering a highly skilled workforce might, for example, be valuable only if the region also offers good infrastructure accessibility. If that accessibility exists, however, the availability of specific skills might be the true differentiator relative to peers. Regions thus need to think about the overall mix and interaction effects when analyzing the relative importance of individual qualities. The academic literature has aimed to develop analytical approaches to identify critical factors, or "binding constraints" (Hausmann *et al.*, 2005), but their empirical power for policy practice remains limited (e.g., Felipe and Usui, 2008).

*What support system does the region need?* Lafley and Martin (2013) then discuss the importance of putting systems in place that provide the capabilities, incentives and management information to ensure the effective operation of the activities selected. For regions, this raises the question of how the institutional architecture for supporting consistent competitiveness upgrading should look. While there is a general recognition in the literature that institutions matter (e.g., Dettori *et al.*, 2012), there is much less specific knowledge about how regions should organize themselves. The discussion of the "how" of strategy elsewhere in this book is related but does not cover this aspect head on. Regions need to think about the structure of institutions within government (e.g., an economic development agency) as well as in public–private collaboration (regional competitiveness efforts, cluster initiatives, etc.). At the national and EU level, this raises issues as to what type of information to provide (e.g., European Cluster Observatory) and what incentives to put in place for strategy development and execution (e.g., smart specialization strategy conditionality for structural funds).

## Confronting theory with practice: the nature of current regional economic strategies

The term "strategy" is used quite loosely in the practice of economic development policies. Often it means nothing more than "important" or "long-term." But more recently, especially in the context of smart specialization strategies in Europe, it has also become connected with the notion of "choice" (Foray, 2015; McCann and Ortego-Argiles, 2013). This focus on choice marks a significant departure from the previous policy consensus, which centered on general "framework conditions" and explicitly discouraged any region-specific "vertical" choices.

It also has a clear connection to the business strategy literature, where choice, as we have seen above, is a central concept. But, while choice has become more accepted as a general idea, there is no clarity on the dimension in which choices should be made.

Applying the framework borrowed from the business strategy literature discussed above, we can test how the diverse sets of choices evident in regional economic strategies relate to the five dimensions identified.

*What ambitions do regions state?* Many regional strategies now define an ambition – for example, being the most innovative region in Europe by 2020 (Skane, Sweden). This type of ambition is useful to set out a direction, both internally to guide implementation decisions and behavior and externally to communicate likely qualities of the region. It is also committing the region and its leaders to performance benchmarks, especially when they are formulated in a quantifiable way. However, the beneficial impact of quantifiable goals depends crucially on whether the region chooses targets that are good measures of their strategy's overall intent.

Arguably more problematic is the tendency to view the ambition and goals of the region as a mere translation of the broader European goals set out in the Europe 2020 strategy into the regional context. This type of ambition loses the context-specific dimension that, given the discussion in the previous chapter, is likely to be important for a successful strategy. While the Europe 2020 goals set a relevant context in terms of what Europe will do "on average" and of what the Commission will support with priority, it is not necessarily equivalent to what an individual region should aspire to. A region's ambition is likely more narrow – there is no reason why it should reflect the whole breadth of European priorities – but it could also go beyond the European goals where the region has interests that are different from those in other parts of Europe. Clarifying this balance between EU-level and regional-level strategic ambitions is important given the huge heterogeneity across Europe. This issue has some resemblance to the corporate versus business unit strategy discussion in the business literature. Regions need to think about how they can best leverage the assets provided at the European level, and the European level has its role in providing those assets that individual regions are not as well placed to provide themselves. But it also has clear differences: regions are not "owned" by the European institutions; rather (within the context of the nations of which they are part), they are their foundation.

*What markets do regions aim to compete in?* Many regions have started to talk significantly more about specific "vertical" choices in their strategy. As discussed by Mikel Navarro in the previous chapter, these choices are "vertical" in the sense of highlighting specific sectors, technologies, or activities as a regional priority.

This focus on specific parts of the economy puts such strategies into the context of the broader debate on a "new industrial policy" (Warwick, 2013). After the failed interventionist approaches of the 1970s, most OECD countries had switched to horizontal policies for improving the general "framework conditions" of the economy. But this consensus has eroded in recent years (Rodrik, 2007).

Academic research began to focus more on market failures specific to parts of the overall economy, and practical experience seemed to suggest that at least some countries with clear vertical policies were doing well while others with an entirely horizontal approach were falling behind (Studwell, 2013). In policy implementation it had also turned out that many horizontal policies, such as general R&D tax credits, had a highly heterogeneous impact across different vertical segments of the economy.

The new approach is significantly driven more by an interest in increasing the effectiveness of public policies than by the objective of the old industrial policies to create "champions" (European Commission, 2013a). This leads to differences both in theory and in practice. The theoretical argument for these policies is not driven primarily by economies of scale, the focus on generally more attractive sectors, and the zero-sum competition across locations to which this leads. It is instead founded on the economics of local linkages and spillovers within and across related industries, technologies, and activities that lead to regions specializing differently depending on their existing capabilities and economic base. In policy practice this leads to a focus on the concentration of quite traditional policy tools to enhance productivity and innovation in those parts of the economy where they can create the highest return based on the existing profile of the regional economy.

While many European regions do define industries, clusters, or technologies as priorities in their strategies, they often do not espouse the notion of the market in which they compete for them. There is only limited attention paid to the firms and economic activities that the regions aim to attract and the specific needs that they want to serve. And there is even less focus on their rivals and what their respective offerings are. The rhetoric of regions is often addressed to the importance of a specific sector to society at large, not its attractiveness as an economic activity in a specific location. Many of these arguments justify why a location should "consume" a certain product or technology but not why it should attract the economic activities that produce them. Regions in some cases act "as if" they would be companies – i.e., seeing themselves as competitors within the end markets in which these industries operate. But regions do not compete in the market for, say, wind energy – they compete in the market for economic activities in the production of wind energy-related products and services.

One practical challenge has been the conflict between the desire to choose vertical priorities and the political and economic dynamics that pull towards a more broad-based approach. All sectors push for support, and it is very difficult for political leaders to deny attention to part of their constituency. And all sectors contribute to prosperity, so concentrating all policy attention on a few is unlikely to generate sufficient impact. As a result, for many regions the process of choosing priorities unravels from the end: priorities are chosen so broad or in such large numbers that they can cover all activities already in place.

Another practical challenge has been the selection process itself. Should regions focus on those areas in which they already have a strong position? These areas are relatively easy to identify and usually form part of regional strategies, not least because there are incumbent interest groups that push for their inclusion.

Or should the strategy identify new areas in which the region aims to diversify? And, if so, what criteria should be used to identify these areas?

Many regions include such areas in their strategies as well, but here there seems to be greater heterogeneity among approaches. Some focus on enabling an "entrepreneurial discovery process" where firms identify areas in which the location can be an attractive base and the regional economy learns from their experience. While this is conceptually attractive, its dependence on entrepreneurs can seem risky for policy-makers; no one might emerge to engage in the discovery process, at least not in the short term. Others thus attempt to construct advantages for specific areas that they have identified as attractive (Boschma, 2013). Here the rationality of the political selection process stretches from efforts that merely respond to the perceived policy priorities at the European level to in-depth assessments of market opportunities and existing local capabilities. While the latter is clearly preferable, it still leaves the government in the uncomfortable situation of having picked the market. If no market success materializes, governments then face the trap of sticking to their prior investments, much as happened in the old industrial policy.

*What value do regions offer?* The identification of a specific value that a region offers to companies remains may be the most glaring weakness of many regional strategies. If value is discussed, it tends to be understood as the value of a specific sector or activity to the region or in addressing broader societal challenges. For companies, however, it is relevant to understand the specific value to them of locating in the region, given the type of economic activities in which they are engaged. Regions do discuss this sometimes as well, but mostly in their marketing material and in terms of generic qualities such as being centrally located, providing attractive costs, having a skilled workforce, etc. What is missing is the connection to vertical priorities and the integration into an overall positioning of the region.

These difficulties in defining a regional value proposition are to a large degree the consequence of the failure to answer appropriately the prior question of what market the region aims to compete in. Without a clear sense of what type of firms and economic activities a region aims to attract, and what needs it thus has to address, it is impossible to define and implement a clear value proposition. Regions then resort to marketing very general business environment qualities, from centrally located, to entrepreneurial, to low cost. While these qualities are meaningful, they are often not targeted sufficiently at specific groups of firms to be effective. Where regions have set clear priorities in terms of industries or clusters, the challenge often becomes a lack of specificity in how the location is going to be different from peers active in the same market. Partly this is driven by a lack of focus on the different needs companies have in a given market; partly it is the result of not analyzing the competition that exists among regions. The result is a me-too type of competition ("let's create another Silicon Valley …") in which only a very small number of locations will succeed.

Where a value proposition has been formulated as an ambition, a region needs to design and implement the specific policy actions required to create the business environment conditions promised. In fact, one of the key values of a regional value proposition should be just that: setting priorities among policy efforts and programs. In practice, and as highlighted by Edurne Magro and Claire Nauwelaers in chapter 5, there tends to be a considerable gap between the regional strategies formulated and the programs put into place. At best, there are a few new efforts launched in response to a strategy. But they tend to be drowned by the much larger number of activities already in place or going on in parallel. While this falls into the "how" of strategy implementation, it is a crucial part of "what" strategy is.

Although many of these challenges could be addressed through a more transparent choice of markets and value propositions, regional governments do face some challenges that firms do not have to worry about. For firms, one of the key aspects of strategy is choosing *what not to do*. For regions, this choice is much harder: while a region can decide to compete for a specific set of traded activities, it will always also be home to the full set of local industries with their respective needs. And while it can choose to focus on some business environment conditions as areas in which it aims to differentiate itself from competing locations, it will always have to address the full range of market failures and public-sector roles that it is constitutionally required to cover.

*What systems do regions put in place?* Here, too, there tends to be a significant gap. Regions do talk about the need for public–private collaboration. And some link their strategy to the allocations of responsibility and budget to specific agencies and programs. But it is hard to find examples in which regions systematically state which structure they intend to build in order to deliver on their value proposition. More often it is instead the existing institutional structure of ministries and specialized agencies that drives the way strategy is implemented or even designed. Some of these issues will be discussed elsewhere in this book under the notions of "who" and "how" of strategy, where the focus of analysis of several of the cases is more on implementation than on design (see in particular chapters 7 to 10).

## Conclusion

This chapter has discussed how the concepts developed in the literature on firm strategy can be translated to the realm of regional economies and has then explored whether the current practice of regional strategies reflects this conceptual framework. We find that the concepts of firm strategy do indeed provide some valuable perspective into the "what" of regional strategy. This value becomes most visible when looking at the current practice of regional strategies and where they run into problems.

Most regional strategies focus their choice on the wrong dimension: locations do not compete in specific sectors/technologies; they compete for the economic activities within these areas. And they compete with a distinct set of business environment qualities, not their specialization patterns alone. Changing the focus of regional strategies from choosing "domains" of either industries or technologies to choosing a set of business environment qualities would have a number of important advantages.

First, it would provide a much closer and less controversial link between strategic ambition and policy action. Selecting a domain easily leads to a discussion about the financial and other benefits that such a priority area should receive. The presence of the domain, not the value that it provides to the location, becomes the goal. There is a slippery slope towards traditional interventionist models of industrial policy. Selecting business environment conditions is less prone to these complications. There is a clear link to policy interventions that enhance the business environment in ways that do not interfere in the market but truly build the productive capacity of a location.

Second, it would overcome many of the political and economic pitfalls of focusing all policy attention on a few segments of the economy. While the targeted business environment qualities or improvements will by design benefit some segments more than others, they will provide improvements for all. This is important to alleviate political pressure from interest groups. But it is also important because a location's prosperity depends on the productivity of all parts of the economy, not only the key economic engines represented by its leading traded clusters.

These considerations are particularly important for emphasizing economic activities that do not exist in a significant way in a given location. Regions can decide to build up business environment qualities that might be useful for specific new economic activities. And these decisions can be informed by the needs of specific new activities. But whether or not these activities then materialize depends on the market success of entrepreneurs, not the region itself.

While regional strategies can benefit from applying the concepts of firm strategy, there are also important differences. First, locations are always both producers and consumers, while firms are primarily producers. For producers, competition is challenging, and strategy is one of the tools to reduce head-on competition. For consumers, however, competition is a significant asset. Locations thus need to ensure that their policies do not create attractiveness for producers at the expense of consumers.

Second, positioning and choice are for regions specifically relevant for the "traded" activities; a location needs to have a sense of what type of business environment conditions it aims to foster for what type of "traded" activities. But a region's prosperity also depends on the dynamism of its "local" activities that are not facing any real locational choice. For them, locations need to figure out which type of business environment improvements will generate the strongest productivity gains.

Third, while firm strategy is importantly about what *not* to do, governments have a public role that makes it much harder to neglect completely a specific part of the economy or a specific feature of the business environment shaped by policy. Regional strategy is much more about what, rather than what not, to focus on.

Transferring a conceptual framework from one knowledge domain to another is always fraught with difficulties. Many of the implicit reference points and assumptions do not travel well, and the subject matter itself reduces the applicability of models and approaches across domains. We have discussed some of these issues here as well; a simplistic use of strategy ideas from firms to regions is full of problems. But at the same time it is useful to reflect on the questions and tools developed in the firm strategy field for regions as well. Both at the conceptual and the practical level, much remains to be done to reach a more robust understanding and practice of regional economic strategies.

## Notes

1 European Cluster Observatory: www.clusterobservatory.eu.
2 US cluster portal: www.clustermapping.us.

## References

Acemoglu, D., and Robinson, J. A. (2012) *Why Nations Fail: The Origins of Power, Prosperity, and Poverty.* New York: Random House.

Annoni, P., and Dijkstra, L. (2013) *EU Regional Competitiveness Index*. JRC Scientific and Policy Reports, European Commission: Joint Research Center.

Asheim, B. T., and Gertler, M. S. (2005) The geography of innovation: regional innovation systems. In Fagerberg, J., Mowery, D. C., and Nelson, R. R. (eds), *The Oxford Handbook of Innovation.* Oxford: Oxford University Press, pp. 291–317.

Audretsch, D. (2006) Entrepreneurship policy and the strategic management of places. In Audretsch, D. (ed.), *Entrepreneurship, Innovation and Economic Growth*. Cheltenham: Edward Elgar.

Barca, F., McCann, P., and Rodríguez-Pose, A. (2012) The case for regional development intervention: place-based versus place-neutral approaches, *Journal of Regional Science*, 52, pp. 134–52.

Boschma, R. (2013) *Constructing Regional Advantage and Smart Specialization: Comparison of Two European Policy Concepts*, Papers in Evolutionary Economic Geography no. 13.22, Utrecht University.

Collins, J. C., and Porras, J. I. (1994) *Built to Last: Successful Habits of Visionary Companies*. New York: HarperBusiness.

Cooke, P. (1992) Regional innovation systems: competitive regulation in the New Europe, *Geoforum*, 23(3), pp. 365–82.

Delgado, M., Porter, M. E., and Stern, S. (2010) Clusters and entrepreneurship, *Journal of Economic Geography*, 10, pp. 495–518.

Delgado, M., Porter, M. E., and Stern, S. (2011) *Clusters, Convergence, and Economic Performance*, ISC Working Paper. Boston: ISC; www.isc.hbs.edu/pdf/DPS_Clusters_Performance_2011-0311.pdf.

Delgado, M., Ketels, C., Porter, M. E., and Stern, S. (2012) *The Determinants of National Competitiveness*, Working Paper no. 18249. Cambridge, MA: National Bureau of Economic Research.

Delgado, M., Porter, M. E., and Stern, S. (2014) Defining clusters of related industries, mimeo. Institute for Strategy and Competitiveness, Harvard Business School.

Dettori B., Marrocu, E., and Paci, R. (2012) Total factor productivity, intangible assets and spatial dependence in the European Regions, *Regional Studies*, 46(10), pp. 1401–16.

European Commission (2007) *Innovative Strategies and Actions: Results from 15 Years of Regional Experimentation*. Brussels: European Commission.

European Commission (2013a) *Proposal for a Regulation of the European Parliament and of the Council on the Structural Funds*, COM(2011) 615 final. Brussels: European Commission.

European Commission (2013b) *European Innovation Scoreboard*. Brussels: European Commission.

Felipe, J., and Usui, N. (2008) *Rethinking the Growth Diagnostics Approach: Questions from the Practitioners*, ADB Economics Working Paper Series, no. 132. Manila: Asian Development Bank.

Foray, D. (2015) *Smart Specialisation: Opportunities and Challenges for Regional Innovation Policy*. London: Routledge.

Fujita, M., Krugman, P., and Venables, A. (2001) *The Spatial Economy: Cities, Regions, and International Trade*. Cambridge, MA: MIT Press.

Gill, I. (2010) *Regional Development Policies: Place-Based or People-Centered?*, 9 October, www.voxeu.org/article/regional-development-policies-place-based-or-people-centred.

Glaeser, E., and Saiz, A. (2004) The rise of the skilled city, *Brookings-Wharton Papers on Urban Affairs*, 5, pp. 47–94.

Hausmann, R., Rodrik, D., and Velasco, A. (2005) *Growth Diagnostics*, Working Paper, John F. Kennedy School of Government, Harvard University.

Huggins, R., and Izushi, H. (eds) (2012) *Competition, Competitive Advantage, and Clusters: The Ideas of Michael Porter*. Oxfoord and New York: Oxford University Press.

Ketels, C. (2013) Recent research on competitiveness and clusters: what are the implications for regional policy? *Cambridge Journal of Regions, Economy and Society*, 6(2): 269–84.

Ketels, C., and Protsiv, S. (2013) *Clusters and the New Growth Path for Europe*, WWW for Europe Working Paper no. 14. Vienna: WIFO.

Kim, W. C., and Mauborgne, R. (2004) Blue ocean strategy, *Harvard Business Review*, 71, October.

Kitson, M., Martin, R., and Tyler, P. (2004) Regional competitiveness: an elusive yet key concept? *Regional Studies*, 38(9), pp. 991–9.

Lafley, A. G., and Martin, R. L. (2013) *Playing to Win: How Strategy Really Works*. Boston: Harvard Business Review Press.

Magretta, J. (2011) *Understanding Michael Porter: The Essential Guide to Competition and Strategy*. Boston: Harvard Business Press Books.

Martin, R., and Sunley, P. (2011) Regional competitiveness: clusters or dynamic comparative advantage? In Huggins, R., and Izushi, H. (eds), *Competition, Competitive Advantage and Clusters: The Ideas of Michael Porter*. Oxford and New York: Oxford University Press, pp. 239–58.

McCann, P., and Ortega-Argilés, R. (2013) Smart specialization, regional growth and applications to European Union cohesion policy, *Regional Studies*, 47, pp. 1–12.

McCord, G. C., and Sachs, J. (2013) *Development, Structure, and Transformation: Some Evidence on Comparative Economic Growth*, Working Paper no. 19512. Cambridge, MA: National Bureau of Economic Research.

McGrath, R. G. (2013) *The End of Competitive Advantage: How to Keep your Strategy Moving as Fast as Your Business*. Boston: Harvard Business Review Press.

Mintzberg, H., Ahlstrand, B., and Lampel, J. (1998) *Strategy Safari: A Guided Tour through the Wilds of Strategic Management*. New York: Free Press.

Nalebuff, B. J., and Brandenburger, A. M. (1996) *Co-opetition*. London: HarperCollins Business.

Navarro, M., Valdaliso, J. M., Aranguren, M. J., and Magro, E. (2014) A holistic approach to regional strategies: the case of the Basque Country, *Science and Public Policy*, 41(4): 532–47.

OECD (2009) *Regions Matter: Economic Recovery, Innovation and Sustainable Growth*. Paris: OECD.

Ortega-Argilés, R. (2012) *Economic Transformation Strategies: Smart Specialization Case Studies*. Seville: European Commission, Smart Specialization Platform.

Porter, M. E. (1980) *Competitive Strategy: Techniques for Analyzing Industries and Competitors*. New York: Free Press.

Porter, M. E. (1985) *Competitive Advantage: Creating and Sustaining Superior Performance*. New York: Free Press.

Porter, M. E. (1990) *Competitive Advantage of Nations*. New York: Free Press.

Porter, M. E. (2000) What is strategy? In *On Competition*, Boston: Harvard Business School Press, pp. 37–71.

Porter, M. E. (2003) The economic performance of regions, *Regional Studies*, 37, pp. 549–78.

Porter, M. E. (2008) The five competitive forces that shape strategy, *Harvard Business Review*, January.

Prahalad, C. K., and Hamel, G. (1990) The core competence of the corporation, *Harvard Business Review*, 68(3), pp. 79–91.

Rodrik, D. (2007) *Normalizing Industrial Policy*, Working Paper, John F. Kennedy School of Government, Harvard University.

Stabell, C. B., and Fjeldstad, Ø. D. (1998) Configuring value for competitive advantage: on chains, shops, and networks, *Strategic management journal*, 19(5), pp. 413–37.

Studwell, J. (2013) *How Asia Works: Success and Failure in the World's Most Dynamic Region*. New York: Grove Press.

Warwick, K. (2013) *Beyond Industrial Policy: Emerging Issues and New Trends*, OECD Science, Technology and Industry Policy Papers no. 2. Paris: OECD.

Wernerfelt, B. (1984) A resource-based view of the firm, *Strategic Management Journal*, 5(2), pp. 171–80.

World Bank (2009) *World Development Report 2009: Reshaping Economic Geography*. Washington, DC: World Bank.

# 4 Territorial strategy

## Deepening in the 'how'

*Mari José Aranguren and Miren Larrea*[1]

### Introduction

The previous chapters in this book have emphasised that territorial strategy differs in some aspects from firm strategy but should answer, as in the case of the latter, three main questions (Navarro *et al.*, 2014). What are the objectives, or the 'what for', of the strategy? What is the content, or the 'what', of the strategy? And what are the processes, or the 'how', of the strategy? This chapter will focus on the 'how' question. Moreover, when we talk about the 'how', we are by implication also considering the 'who', discussing the processes through which different stakeholders are involved in the strategy.

To deepen our understanding of the 'how', the approach to strategy chosen for this chapter, and also developed later in this book in the case of Rafaela (Argentina), has two main inputs. On the one hand, it is inspired by a process approach to strategy formation proposed by several authors from different perspectives (Albrechts, 2006; Sotarauta, 2004; Healey, 2004; Harmaakorpi, 2006; Aranguren *et al.*, 2012). On the other, it is based on the experience of the authors in various research projects on territorial development where the issue of strategy was approached.

The main argument of the chapter can be summarised using an anecdote from one such project, the Gipuzkoa Sarean, which was established to develop a participatory approach to territorial development in the province of Gipuzkoa in the Basque Country (Spain). The provincial government had decided to focus on a process approach to develop a territorial strategy. It had explicitly resolved not to formulate a plan but to embark on a learning process based on action research principles. Revealingly, the discussion became framed in terms of strategy only when the government was criticised for not having a strategy. A reflection process was then opened to find the right framework to communicate the strategy formation process inherent in the project. The authors who most influenced this discussion were Mintzberg and his colleagues (1998), with their proposal of ten different schools on strategy formation. The learning school was taken as the main approach in the project, but there was an awareness that there were two other schools that also made relevant contributions to the process perspective in practice – the power and cultural schools. The process perspective proposed in this chapter is inspired by the contributions of these schools, which are presented in more detail later.

We find that most approaches that have been significant in territorial development have had to do with strategic plans. This is a positive contribution but not enough to understand what it takes to have a territorial strategy, especially if we aim to understand the process perspective. Mintzberg *et al.* (1998) say that, for the most part, the teaching of strategic management has highlighted the rational and prescriptive side of the process, namely three schools (design, planning and positioning). Strategic management has commonly been portrayed as revolving around the discrete phases of formulation, implementation and control, carried out in progressive steps. They argue that this bias is heavily reflected in practice, particularly in the work of corporate and governmental planning departments, as well as of many consulting firms. To move away from this bias they present their ten schools, opening the perspective of what strategy is and how it can be developed.

The main contribution of this chapter is to try to bring the reflection that Mintzberg *et al.* (1998) make for business strategy to the field of territorial strategy, thus opening up the more traditional perspective based on planning to other perspectives that the experience in our research projects tells us are relevant in order to generate territorial development.[2] Alongside this we connect some of the concepts that have been integrated in mainstream literature on territorial development but have not often been considered as part of territorial strategy.

In order to achieve these goals, we first present three of the schools that give an interesting insight into territorial strategy from a process perspective. We then connect concepts and frameworks that are relevant in the territorial development field with these schools, showing that strategic plans are not the only way to construct territorial strategies. In particular we make links with the popular concepts and frameworks of social capital, new governance and territorial dynamic capabilities. These conceptual reflections on the 'how' of territorial strategy serve as a base for practice-informed case analysis within several of the later chapters in this book, most notably the case of Rafaela (Argentina).

## Changing the angle to look at strategy

The initial discussion in this section, which sets the framework for the rest of the chapter, is based on the contribution of Mintzberg *et al.* (1998). Their book analyses ten schools of thought which they consider contribute a unique perspective on one major aspect of the strategy formation process. They argue that each of these perspectives is, in one sense, narrow and overstated but at the same time interesting and insightful. Moreover, each school is considered as a different dimension of a single process. Three of them are prescriptive in nature (the design, planning and positioning schools), and six (the entrepreneurship, cognitive, learning, power, culture and environmental schools) focus more on describing how strategies are formulated. It is this focus on the *how* that makes them more interesting for the goals sought with this chapter. Finally, the tenth school, the configuration school, combines both aspects.

In order to understand the diversity of perspectives, there are some definitions and concepts used by Mintzberg *et al.* (1998) that need to be introduced. One of them is the distinction between intended strategy and realised strategy. The first relates to the plans of the organisation for the future, the second to the patterns of their past. The authors argue that the real world inevitably involves some thinking ahead as well as some adaptation en route. They also distinguish strategy as a position, which in the name of business strategy has to do with the locating of particular products in particular markets, and strategy as a perspective, an organisation's fundamental way of doing things. They argue that, whlie changing position within perspective may be easy, changing perspective, even while trying to maintain position, is not.

As we said in the introduction, we do not discuss all ten schools described by these authors but focus on what three of them might contribute to territorial strategy. The choice of these three has not been made by chance but responds to our reflection on the choices made in the context of various research projects with policy-makers in different regional governments. This does not mean that these schools are more relevant than others in all territorial development processes, but we do know that they have been significant for policy-makers developing territorial strategies in various contexts. Like Mintzberg *et al.* (1998), we consider each one on its own to be restricted. But we believe that considering them in this book on territorial strategy for competitiveness opens up existing debates in this area, which have focused largely on the planning school perspective, to other angles that might help see the same problems in a new light. In the following subsections we present what we find most relevant about each of the three schools and argue their contribution in territorial development.

### *The learning school*

According to this school, strategies emerge as people, sometimes acting individually but more often collectively, come to learn about a situation as well as about their organisation's capability of dealing with it. Through this learning, they eventually converge on patterns of behaviour that work. Following Mintzberg *et al.* (1998), the premises of the learning school are the following. Strategy-making must above all take the form of a process of learning over time, in which, at the limit, formulation and implementation become indistinguishable. While the leader must learn too, and can sometimes be the main learner, more commonly it is the collective system that learns. This learning proceeds in emergent fashion, through behaviour that stimulates thinking retrospectively, so that sense can be made of action. The successful initiatives create streams of experiences that can converge into patterns that become emergent strategies and, once recognised, may be made formally deliberate. The role of leadership is thus not to preconceive deliberate strategies but to manage the process of strategic learning, whereby novel strategies can emerge. Strategic management involves crafting the subtle relationships between thought and action, control and learning, stability and change. Accordingly, strategies appear first as patterns out of the past – only later, perhaps, as plans for the future – and, ultimately, as perspectives to guide overall behaviour.

Our main reflections to embrace a learning approach to territorial strategy come from the feeling that strategic plans for territorial development are seldom implemented (Sotarauta, 2004). One of the features of these processes is that a lot of energy is often used in the design of the plan, where different territorial actors are gathered to share perspectives and decide on goals. Once the goals are settled there is an assumption that now the plan 'just has to be implemented', as if it were a kind of recipe that meant the goals could be achieved just by following its instructions. But there are often unexpected difficulties that prevent the achievement of goals. We propose the learning school, where learning is understood as a continuous process, as a perspective that helps to overcome this chasm between design and implementation of territorial strategy. This is in contrast with what Mintzberg *et al.* (1998) describe as decades of tradition in strategic management, which has insisted that thinking must end before action begins and that formulation must be followed by implementation.

### *The power school*

Mintzberg *et al.* (1998) suggest that strategy formation in business goes under the label of policy-making in government (see also chapter 5 on this distinction). They characterise strategy formation following the power school as an overt process of influence, emphasising the use of power and politics to negotiate strategies favourable to particular interests. They argue that the intention of those writing in the power school has been to wake strategic management up to a basic reality of organisational life: that organisations consist of individuals with dreams, hopes, jealousies, interests and fears. From this perspective, strategy-making can be a process of bargaining and compromise among conflicting individuals, groups and coalitions. The power school suggests that the strategies that emerge from such a process will not necessarily be optimal but will reflect the interests of the most powerful groups in the organisation. In this context, strategy is the product not of a single architect but of various actors and coalitions that pursue their own interests and agendas. Indeed, Mintzberg *et al.* (1998) suspect that, when strategies do appear out of political processes, they tend to be more emergent than deliberate.

In a context where they are focused on business strategy, Mintzberg *et al.* (1998) use the term 'political' for behaviour that is not legitimately related to the way in which a commercial organisation competes 'legitimately' in an economic marketplace. For them, such political behaviour is illegitimate or a legitimate. When taking the concept to reflect on territorial development, we find that the features described previously in terms of different interests, bargaining and compromise fit with our experiences in territorial development. But we consider that, from a policy-making perspective, a political behaviour in terms of a continuous tension between representatives of different interests is legitimate when framed in a democratic system. There are of course cases when power can be used in an illegitimate way in a political process, but we understand that this is an exception and not the essence of politics.

Our main arguments for considering the power school are related to two elements underlined by Mintzberg *et al.* (1998). The first is that it hardly makes sense to describe strategy formation as a process devoid of power and politics. We consider that power affects learning in the territory, and unless continual bargaining and compromise are developed to create the necessary conditions for learning, the strategy formation process based on learning will stagnate. The second is that this perspective highlights the importance of politics in promoting strategic change, where established actors seeking to maintain a status quo have to be confronted. As we have argued, in democracy, politics can be a critical element of territorial development, especially when new frameworks need to be shared in order to generate development. Indeed, politics and polity play a key role, either positive or negative, in all the empirical cases explored in Part II of this book.

### *The cultural school*

When comparing the power and cultural schools, Mintzberg *et al.* (1998) argue that, while power takes the organisation and fragments it, culture knits a collection of individuals into an integrated entity called organisation. They say that culture represents the life force of the organisation, the soul of its physical body, and they suspect that much of it exists below the level of conscious awareness. They use the word 'ideology' to describe a rich culture in an organisation and define it as a strong set of beliefs, shared passionately by its members, that distinguishes a particular organisation from all others.

When used to reflect on territorial development and strategies, this perspective brings into focus the relevance of territorial identity, the sense of belonging of territorial actors that is related to their concepts of culture and ideology. These are critical elements in order to build a shared view of the future among territorial actors that can drive forward a territorial strategy.

Again following Mintzberg *et al.* (1998), the premises of the cultural school are that strategy formation is a process of social interaction, based on beliefs and understandings shared by the members of an organisation. An individual acquires these beliefs through a process of acculturation, or socialisation, which is largely tacit and non-verbal, although sometimes reinforced by more formal indoctrination. The members of an organisation can only partially describe the beliefs that underpin their culture, and strategy therefore takes the form of perspective, above all, more than positions, rooted in collective intentions (not necessarily made explicit). These premises can easily be translated to processes where strategy is formed in a territory and not in a company.

Culture and especially ideology, Mintzberg *et al.* (1998) say, do not encourage strategic change so much as the perpetuation of existing strategy. Strategy, then, is best described as deliberate, and there are two arguments in particular that explain why we propose the relevance of this school in a territorial context. One is that, for this school, strategy formation becomes the management of collective cognition, which is important to understand a territorial strategy based on a learning approach. The other is that it can help us understand a period of reframing, during which a new perspective develops collectively, and even a period of cultural revolution that tends to accompany strategic turnaround. These are features that we feel are helpful when trying to change the focus on territorial strategy from planning (focus on what) to learning (focus on how).

## Critical concepts and frameworks for a learning approach

In this section we revise contributions in the territorial development literature that help link a learning approach to strategy formation with territorial development. Among these contributions we focus on concepts such as social capital and collaboration, leadership and new modes of governance, and dynamic capabilities, linking them to the strategy schools discussed in the previous section. Figure 4.1 aims to be not an analytical framework but a synthesis of the discussion we undertake in this chapter. We argue that all these concepts are related to the learning school, but leadership is also associated with the power school and social capital with the cultural school.

### *Collaboration and social capital*

Collaboration and social capital are critical elements in debates around territorial development. Specifically, territorial development is conditioned by the capabilities of territories to be innovative, which is a social and interactive process that occurs between different actors. The evolution of the concept of innovation from a linear to a cooperative process underlines the relevance of social capital. Specifically, social capital increases the efficiency both of action (Nahapiet and Ghoshal, 1998) and of information diffusion (Burt, 1992), reduces the costs of monitoring processes and transactions, and encourages the cooperative behaviour necessary for innovation and value creation (Fukuyama, 1995). As such, it facilitates interaction and collaboration and is especially relevant for the concept of strategy-making according to both the learning and the cultural school.

For the learning school, the process of strategy-making takes the form of a process of learning over time, and commonly it is the collective system that learns. This happens in an interactive process among different actors, and social capital is a critical element that facilitates such collaboration and collective learning. For the cultural school, strategy formation is a process of social interaction, based on beliefs and understandings shared by the members of an organisation. So, strategy formation becomes the management of collective cognition, and social capital is also critical for this approach.

In essence, each organisation in a region has its own mission and objectives. These missions and objectives should follow a convergent evolution for the construction of a regional strategy. So, the first important ingredient of a territorial strategy is collaboration. In a territory, each actor or agent (a point in Figure 4.2) has its vision (each arrow in situation 1 in Figure 4.2). Through collaboration networks (relationship structures) in which people share and dialogue about its vision, a new shared vision is created. It will be easier to develop this vision if

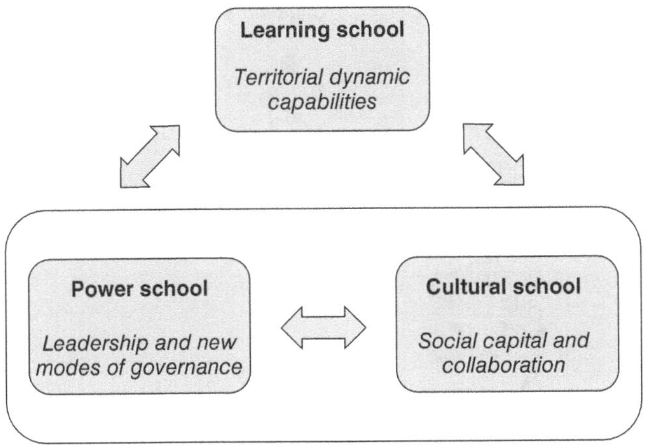


*Figure 4.1* An interpretation of possible connections between basic concepts on territorial development and the discussion on strategy schools

there are relations based on trust and reciprocity among people participating in the network (situation 2 in figure 4.2). If people participating in some networks collaborate with people participating in other networks, a shared vision is generated, which will be easier to develop if there are trust-based relations among people of different networks. In this way, a territorial shared vision is developed and a territorial strategy emerges.

According to Nahapiet and Ghoshal (1998) social capital is 'the sum of the actual and potential resources embedded within, available through, and derived from the network of relationships possessed by an individual or social unit'. They differentiate three dimensions of social capital that we consider are very relevant for the efficiency of the collaborative process in the construction of a regional strategy according to the perspective of cultural school: the *structural* (the structure of relationships and networks), the *relational* (relational actives, such as trust or reciprocity, connected with behaviours of people participating in the networks) and the *cognitive* (the generation of shared languages and visions that occur in these networks) dimensions.

1 The *structural dimension* refers to the overall pattern of connections between actors – that is, who you reach and how you reach them. Among the most important facets of this dimension is the presence or absence of network ties between actors, describing the pattern of linkages in terms of such measures as density, connectivity and hierarchy. In this dimension it is not only the existing networks at any moment that is important but also the capability to create new networks.
2 The *relational dimension* refers to the kind of personal relationship people have developed with each other through a history of interactions. This concept focuses on the particular relations people have, such as respect and friendship,

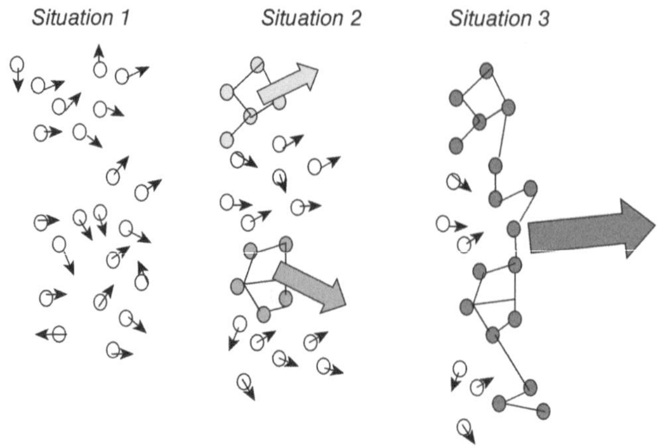


*Figure 4.2* Process of generation of a shared vision

Source: Aranguren *et al.* (2012).

that influence their behaviour. Among the key facets in this dimension are trust and trustworthiness, norms and sanctions, obligations and expectations, and identity and identification.

3 The *cognitive dimension* refers to those resources providing shared representations, interpretations and systems of meanings among parties. The generation of shared vision among different actors is critical in processes of territorial strategy development. The aim here is to achieve a major convergence among the various visions of different actors, who need to have both the desire and the ability to identify and share their collective objectives. This requires actors to adjust the expectations that each has from the other.

The three dimensions are both fundamental for the development of an efficient territorial strategy and reinforce one another. A sustainable economic territorial strategy requires that territorial leaders understand and accept the legitimacy of others' needs and objectives. Three points in particular are important.

- The creation of spaces or networks (*structural dimension*) for dialogue, to share information and experiences, and to exlpore existing consensus and conflicts is critical to generate shared vision and clarify the role of each actor in the territorial strategy.
- This process should facilitate the generation of a shared vision in which each territorial actor has their own role and resources (recognised by the rest of the actors) for the achievement of this vision (*cognitive dimension*).
- This shared vision has to be mutually beneficial, which is what guarantees sustainability. Trust, reciprocity and feelings of unity are very important assets to generate a shared vision in the dialogue spaces or existing networks (*relational dimension*).

Territorial strategy will emerge from these dialogue spaces, which should themselves have some continuity so that different territorial leaders (political leaders and leaders from other fields, such as intermediary institutions) have the opportunity to explore a diversity of existing territorial perspectives, experiences, projects, proposals and assets, combined with prospective exercises to detect new emergent socio-techno-economic opportunities (which will avoid lock-in situations and overcome actual knowledge and capability shortcomings). So, both collaboration and analysis are necessary to base the strategy on more promising opportunities, taking into account the strengths and weaknesses of the territory. If territorial strategy emerges through the collaboration of different actors, it is more likely to generate their commitment, as they have participated in the process of the strategy construction. That is, since they have participated in the decision-making, their actions will be more easily aligned with the reflection, and implementation will be much easier.

In this sense, it is important to share a story about the future of the territory (*cognitive dimension*). To share a story, different territorial actors have to transform their ways of thinking. For instance, in the case of firms, as Porter and Kramer (2011) underline, it is critical to assume the principle of *shared value*, which is intended to generate economic value in ways in which societal needs and challenges are answered and value for society is created. The concept of *shared value* refers not to personal values or to the redistribution of value created by firms but to the idea of expanding economic and social value together.

### *Leadership and new modes of governance*

Leadership and modes of governance are critical issues for a strategy based on the power school approach. From the power school perspective, strategy-making is a process of bargaining and compromise among conflicting individuals, groups and coalitions. So, leadership understood as an individual's capacity to influence others is an important consideration.

Leadership is also central to the learning school, given that learning happens in an interactive process among different actors, and the kind of leadership will affect how this interactive process develops (this is connected with what Healey (2004) calls the relational conception of space or place). A territory is a complex system, and in a complex system the knowledge necessary to overcome detected challenges is distributed not only among different territorial actors but at a global level. So the territorial strategy cannot be led by one individual. Rather, it is critical to develop a multiplicity of private–public partnerships that respond to different strategic challenges. Thus, in order to reinforce multiplicity of learning processes, the better kind of leadership is shared leadership.

According to Pearce and Conger (2003), 'shared leadership is a dynamic, interactive influence process among individuals and groups for which the objective is to lead one another to the achievement of group or organizational goals or both.' The key distinction between shared leadership and traditional models of leadership is that the former involves more than downward hierarchical influence on subordinates from an appointed or elected leader. It also involves influence being shared laterally among peers or proceeding upwards. In a territory, there is not a single leader at the apex of the hierarchy who holds power over subordinates, as is often the case in a firm. The generation of shared leadership capabilities is therefore key in a territory. In particular, in order to generate shared leadership, the following considerations are fundamental.

- Public and private actors have to develop new collaborative habits. This demands thinking and acting at territorial level and overcoming particular aims and worries that are not shared by others. Connected with this territorial leadership, Stough concludes that there is a tendency for local leader groups to emerge and cooperate to influence the economic future of the territory. He defines leadership as a 'tendency of a community to collaborate among sectors (different groups) in a sustainable and decided way to increase the economic outcome of a region' (Stough, 2001: 35).
- Different competencies are necessary at each stage of strategy development, and the same actor or organisation may not always have these competencies. That is why the role of each actor may change, and it could be necessary for the leadership to rotate.
- It is key that each actor identifies the moment when their role could be critical and assume their responsibilities. Indeed, sometimes the process of territorial leadership development has been compared with a relay race.

Very few regions have exhibited a process of formation of a leadership team with these habits of collaboration and analysis. It is not an easy task, and learning about leadership takes place through practice (doing and leading). It requires, therefore, learning in a dynamic way through doing – through reflecting on the process and improving.

Another critical issue for the development of a territorial strategy from the learning and power school perspectives is the issue of governance more generally. According to Sugden *et al.* (2006), the concept of governance is usually associated with the decisions and actions of the government, but its meaning is broader in its definition and implications. For instance, for Kooiman and Van Vliet (1993), the concept of governance means 'the creation of a structure or order that can't been imposed from outside'. It is the result of a continual interaction among different actors. Jessop (1998: 29) emphasises that, according to a broad definition, governance is 'any mode of co-ordination of interdependent activities'. However, in a narrower approach appropriate to apply to a territory, he defines governance as 'self-organisation modes or co-ordination' (heterarchy). These actors could be public institutions – such as different territorial level governments – but also autonomous but interdependent private institutions and individuals.

Different modes of governance can result in the achievement of different goals. As Bailey *et al.* (2006) affirm, any actor or territorial system has an explicit and/or an implicit development strategy, and conscious or unconscious decisions will affect that strategy. If the final goal of a territory is to achieve a better standard of welfare for its people, it is critical that the decisions of actors (firms, governments and others) reflect adequately the interests of different groups in society (Sugden and Wilson, 2002, 2005). So, decision-making processes (who participates and how this participation is articulated) are critical, and this is what Sudgen and Wilson (2002) understand basically by governance. Moreover, the fact that a multilevel approach is necessary to understand the decisions taken at different territorial levels, both inside and outside the territory, makes the concept of governance even more complex.

There can be different types of governance. Sacchetti and Sugden (2003), for example, distinguish among 'directed networks' and 'mutually dependent networks'. 'Directed networks' are characterised by asymmetry, authority and control-based relationships. However, 'mutually dependent networks' are based on shared frameworks for decision-making and co-responsibility. Johannisson (2008) also studies this issue and asks if the traditional modes of governance (market or hierarchy) fit with the network-based structure that today's economy asks for. This author underlines the necessity for interactive and relational control and for process-oriented governance modes based on dialogue or, even better, on a polylogue, since the conditions for development are defined jointly by a multitude of stakeholders. The type of governance corresponds essentially to the 'mutually dependent networks' defined by Sacchetti and Sudgen (2003) and the networks of interactive and relational control defined by Johanninsson (2008).

Garmann Johnsen *et al.* (2008) underline five aspects for the evolution of governance in order to respond to actual societal challenges. For this, they adapt Wallis's (2000) proposal concerning the elements essential to transit from old to new regionalism. Basically, and in line with earlier arguments, this consists of the change from hierarchical systems to network-based systems (see Table 4.1).

The first of the elements is the process approach rather than the structure approach. In systems based on hierarchy, the relevance is in the creation of structures, the delimitation of new territorial units and the formation of new authorities. In network- based systems, while sometimes new structures are created, the main focus is on processes such as vision generation, strategic planning, conflict resolution and consensus generation.

The second element is the level of openness. Systems based on hierarchy focus on the definition of frontiers and administrative boundaries and understand the region as a bounded territory. However, network-based systems accept that the frontiers of the region are open, fuzzy and elastic.

The third element is collaboration in network-based systems versus coordination in systems based on hierarchy. Coordination implies that there is an agent that, usually because of their position in the hierarchy, coordinates the activities of the actors. Collaboration is understood as a voluntary agreement among equals.

Trust in network-based systems and accountability in hierarchical systems form the fourth element. Coordination in hierarchical systems is accompanied by the need for some agents to account for others. Network-based systems emphasise trust as a cohesive element of different regional interests.

*Table 4.1* From hierarchy-based to network-based governance

| *Old approach to governance: system based on hierarchy* | *New approach to governance: network-based system* |
|---|---|
| Structure | Process |
| Closedness | Openess |
| Coordination | Collaboration |
| Accountability | Trust |
| Power | Empowerment |

Source: Based on Garmann Johnsen *et al.* (2008).

Finally, as the fifth element, hierarchical systems focus more on power while in network-based systems the key is in empowerment processes. These generate capabilities in different communities to enable them to engage in a constructive way in regional decisions. Empowerment also means engaging profit and non-profit organisations in decision-making that is generally understood as proper to public bodies.

Focusing more on the specific role of governments in the process of constructing a territorial strategy, the participation and involvement of supra-regional levels is important not only because their strategies and policies affect regions in a decisive manner (Uyarra and Flanagan, 2009) but also because, as Barca (2011) underlines, they can add new knowledge and value from abroad that might be crucial in overcoming frequent local government failures.

Finally, apart from the issue of administrative competence, governments' capabilities to use these powers are critical (Ismeri Europa and Applica, 2010; Walendowski *et al.*, 2011; OECD, 2011). As Breznitz emphasises, those capabilities are determined by the bureaucratic profile of the administration – that is, by 'the modes in which bureaucracy is constructed, the social origins and education level of its people and its capacity to make decisions' (Breznitz, 2007: 32). The type of bureaucracy will strongly determine the way in which governments interact with the other actors.

## *Territorial dynamic capabilities through learning*

For the learning school, the process of strategy-making takes the form of a process of learning over time. When individuals and collective systems learn, new capabilities are created in the territory. If this learning process is continued, new capabilities are constantly created and reconfigured by experience. So learning capability is one of the relevant elements that facilitates the generation of new territorial dynamic capabilities, and the two reinforce each other in a virtuous circle.

What are these critical territorial dynamic capabilities? We can distinguish among the critical capabilities for the formation of the strategy (capability to work in networks, visionary capability …) and those that the strategy should try to develop (innovation capability, capability of collaboration …). As the literature on dynamic capabilities emphasises, the territory has to be able to reinvent itself, which requires that it both knows its existing capabilities and develops new ones.

Possible trajectories of territorial strategy development are dependent on the history and previous development trajectories of the region (*path dependency*). In this sense a process of territorial strategy development is impossible without taking into account the assets and configuration of existing resources (Teece *et al.*, 1997). These capabilities need to be renewed constantly, and this is essentially what is meant by the concept of dynamic capabilities, which stresses that, for a competitive advantage to be sustainable, it has to be based on valuable, rare, inimitable and non-substitutive resources (Teece *et al.*, 1997; Eisenshardt and Martin, 2000). Also Sotarauta (2004) emphasises that, in order to create competitive advantage, it is key to have the skills for making good use of affordable resources and generating new resources and capabilities. This author argues that it is very important to create dynamic regional capabilities, embedded in a multiplicity of development processes that facilitate change. This is a long-term process but, once created, dynamic capabilities are very difficult to imitate.

Harmaakorpi (2004, 2006) transfers the idea of dynamic capabilities from the management sphere to the territorial sphere. Harmaakorpi (2006) defines regional dynamic capabilities as the ability to generate in interaction new competitive resource configurations in a turbulent environment. He distinguishes five regional dynamic capabilities: innovation capability, learning capability, networking capability, leadership capability and visionary capability. Sotarauta (2004) also, when transferring the concept of dynamic capabilities from the firm to the territory, highlights five dynamic capabilities: absorptive capability, combining capability, interpretative capability, strategic capability and exciting capability.

Critical dynamic capabilities in a territory are those that help in the development of a territorial strategy and in the continual ability to reinvent that strategy. These capabilities should help in the aspects analysed above: the development of networks (structural dimension); the development of trust and commitment-based relationships (relational dimension); and the generation of a shared vision (cognitive dimension). But the territory also needs continually to innovate and reinvent its strategy. Taking this into account, and departing from the dynamic capabilities that a territory should have according to Harmaakorpi (2006) and Sotarauta (2004), the following dynamic capabilities appear critical for the process of developing territorial strategy.

1 ***Capability to learn and innovate*** This is the ability of the regional innovation system to exploit and continually renew existing resource configurations in order to create a sustainable competitive advantage. It is essential for actors to be able to identify the external changes that are taking place and react in such a way that innovative activities generate a new frontier for the region. To do this they need to develop what Harmaakorpi (2006) calls regional *learning capability* – e.g., the ability to create and manage knowledge in a collective, interactive and accumulative learning process, leading to new settings of new resources, competences and skills. It also needs *absorptive capability*, defined

by Sotarauta (2004) as the ability to identify, assimilate and exploit knowledge from local and other contexts. At the territorial level, this includes, for instance, the ability to value, assimilate and apply new knowledge and to transfer vision and strategies into action.

2 ***Capability to generate networks and relationships*** Harmaakorpi (2006) defines this as the ability of a regional innovation system to build interactive networks, including field-specific creative social capital, leading to the effective utilisation of the resource configurations in the networks. It is essentially the ability to build collaborative networks for the development of the regional strategy. Combinative and interpretative capabilities are two of the critical dynamic capabilities for the development of networks and interactions (Sotarauta, 2004). *Combinative capability* is the capability to connect and combine knowledge and abilities of different actors in the system (even external knowledge and abilities) in order to create new regional knowledge and capacities. Sotarauta distinguishes three different types of combinative capability:

- *institutional capability:* the ability to create an institutional set-up that supports the promotion of urban (regional) competitiveness and facilitates the removal of institutional obstacles and bureaucratic rigidities blocking processes and networks;
- *networking capability:* the capability to forge trust, mutual dependency, loyalty, solidarity and reciprocal support-based horizontal cooperation between organisations and individuals. This includes a) the ability to involve people and empower them to act as a network; b) the ability to encourage people to reach joint and separate goals and renew them in an ongoing process; c) the ability to promote interactive processes serving as an intermediary in interaction between actors; and d) the ability to connect various actors to the knowledge pool from their own starting points;
- *socialisation capability:* the ability to build shared knowledge (often tacit) leading to social integration between agents that goes far beyond institutions and formal networks – thus the ability to network competently and efficiently by using informal relationships.

With regard to *interpretative* capability – the ability to understand different mental models and cognitive maps – it is also critical to build networks and relationships. The development of continual collaborative processes requires skills and competencies for network management, and, according to Sotarauta (2004), a critical element in these processes is the management of perceptions. Agents do not react directly to reality but rather to internally constructed perceptions of reality; they generally have different perceptions of problems, other actors, dependency relations and benefits and drawbacks of working together. These perceptions are very difficult to change but, in the long term, developing activities together could stimulate change. The management of perceptions should aim not to reach consensus, however, but to generate a common ground for joint decisions, respecting and accepting other perceptions. Openness and transparency are hence critical elements of interpretative capability.

3 ***Strategic capability: vision generation and leadership*** Harmaakorpi (2006) defines the *capability to build regional vision* as the ability to outline the possible potential development trajectories based on paths travelled and utilising the opportunities emerging through the changing techno-economic paradigm. It is what Sotarauta calls *strategic capability* – the ability to make decisions about what to focus on in economic development in long run, and thus to set the strategic direction for many development efforts. Strategic capability includes a) the ability to define strategies and visions for regional/urban development in a collaborative process; b) the ability to bring to the fore visions of different futures and to transform these visions into focused strategies and actions; c) the ability to transform crisis situations into something constructive; d) the ability to launch processes well and to manage and lead them consistently in different phases; and e) the ability to make decisions on time. Harmaakorpi defines a critical capability to build strategic capability and shared vision as *regional leadership*, which refers to the ability of the system to effect actions steering the processes and resources of the system in the desired direction and avoiding harmful lock-ins.

The processes of development of regional strategies are very difficult and require constructing all of these dynamic capabilities in the region. These are rooted in people, and thus people are always the starting point when trying to generate such territorial dynamic capabilities. People with these capacities are those able to communicate with all parts of the system and generate trust and social capital in partnerships. They have to facilitate and guide regional strategy development, combining analysis, collaboration and action. The generation of a common language and a proactive attitude among territorial actors (public and private) to develop these capabilities can be key elements to accelerate the construction of a territorial strategy. For this, it is necessary for people to be motivated. That is why Sotarauta (2004) defines another key dynamic capability, *excitement capability*, which refers to the ability to capitalise on the creative tension between the inspiration of key individuals and the dominant thought patterns and to excite agents to 'development rebellion'. This is facilitated if leaders are enthusiastic, known and respected people. It is critical to maintain the excitement in the process to combine some short-term with long-term results.

## Final reflections

In the introduction to this chapter we said that most approaches to strategy that have been significant in territorial development have had to do with strategic plans. We argue that, while this is a positive contribution, it is not enough to understand what it takes to have a territorial strategy. For that we also need to understand the underlying processes. Mintzberg *et al.* (1998) suggest that, for the most part, the teaching of strategic management has highlighted the rational and prescriptive side of the process, namely three schools (design, planning and positioning). Strategic management has commonly been portrayed as revolving around the discrete phases of formulation, implementation and control carried out one after the other. They argue that this bias is heavily reflected in practice, particularly in the work of corporate and governmental planning departments and many consulting firms. This supposes a clear separation among thinking and reflection on one side and action on the other.

Mintzberg *et al.* (1998) present ten strategy schools, offering a perspective of what strategy is and how it can be developed. In this chapter we have tried to bring the reflections of these authors for business strategy to the field of territorial strategy, opening the more traditional perspective based on planning to other contexts that the experience in our research projects tells us are relevant in order to generate territorial development. To deepen this analysis, we have sought to connect the three of these schools that are most relevant for understanding the process of territorial strategy – the learning, power and culture schools – to a number of key concepts from the literature on territorial development: social capital; shared leadership and new modes of governance; and territorial dynamic capabilities.

Our main concluding reflection from this analysis relates to idea that the concept of *praxis* could facilitate the dynamic combination of the diversity of perspectives on the concept of territorial strategy and make its processes more effective and efficient. Mintzberg *et al.* (1998) distinguish between intended strategy and realised strategy. The first relates to the plans of the organisation for the future (connected more with thinking and reflecting), the second to the patterns of their past (connected more with acting). In particular, these authors argue that the real world inevitably involves some thinking ahead as well as some adaptation *en route* and that there is a need to combine both the intended and the realised strategies. This is where the concept of *praxis* comes in, as it connects thinking and action as proposed in the learning school. According to Streck *et al.* (2012), *praxis*, following Freire (1978), can be understood as the close relationship between a way of interpreting reality and the consequent practice that results from this understanding, leading to a transforming action. It is a synthesis between theory–word and action, whereby there is a close tie between thinking–saying the word and acting.

Indeed, the concepts that can help us understand the 'how' of territorial strategy, building on the learning, power and cultural perspectives on strategy, already exist and are quite simple to explain. The challenge is not in their definition but in putting them into practice and in seeing what are the barriers in the process of strategy-making in different territorial contexts. This requires us to think and reflect on action and to act on what is thought: we need more *praxis* on territorial development.

## Notes

1 This work was supported by the European Commission (FP7 SSH.2012.1.1-3) under Grant number 320131. Any errors are the responsibility of the authors.

2 In this sense the chapter complements Ketels translation of the positioning school in the previous chapter.

## References


Albrechts, L. (2006) Bridge the gap: from spatial planning to strategic projects, *European Planning Studies*, 14(10), pp. 1487–500.

Aranguren, M. J., Magro, E., Navarro, M., and Valdaliso, J. M. (2012) *Estrategias para la construcción de ventajas competitivas regionales: el caso del País Vasco*. Madrid: Marcial Pons.

Bailey, D., De Propris, L., Sugden, R., and Wilson, J. R. (2006) Public policy for European economic competitiveness: an analytical framework and a research agenda, *International Review of Applied Economics*, 20(5), pp. 555–72.

Barca, F. (2011) Alternative approaches to development policy: intersections and divergences, *Seminar on Territorial Dimension of Development Policies, papers and proceedings*, Ostróda, Poland, 18–19 July, pp. 45–50; https://www.mir.gov.pl/english/Regional_Development/Presidency/event_shedule/Documents/Seminar_%20Papers_and_Proceedings.pdf

Breznitz, D. (2007) *Innovation and the State: Political Choice and Strategies for Growth in Israel, Taiwan and Ireland*. New Haven, CT, and London: Yale University Press.

Burt, R. S. (1992) *Structural Holes: The Social Structure of Competition*. Cambridge, MA: Harvard University Press.

Eisenshardt, K. M., and Martin, J. A. (2000) Strategic capabilities: what are they? *Strategic Management Journal*, 21, pp. 1105–21.

Freire, P. (1978) *Pedagogy in Process: The Letters to Guinea-Bissau*. New York: Seabury Press.

Fukuyama, F. (1995) *Trust: The Social Virtues and the Creation of Prosperity*. New York: Free Press.

Garmann Johnsen, H. C., Normann, R., Karlsen, J., and Ennals, R. (2008) Democratic innovation: addressing the comprehensive challenges in today's innovation policies: the case of Norway. In Nolan, T. P. (ed.), *Handbook of Regional Economies*. New York: Nora Science, pp. 397–450.

Harmaakorpi, V. (2004) *Building a Competitive Regional Innovation Environment: The Regional Development Platform Method as a Tool for Regional Innovation Policy*. Espoo: Helsinki University of Technology; http://lib.hut.fi/Diss/2004/isbn9512270110/isbn9512270110.pdf.

Harmaakorpi, V. (2006) Regional development platform method (RDPM) as a tool for regional innovation policy, *European Planning Studies*, 14(8), pp. 1085–104.

Healey, P. (2004) The treatment of space and place in the new strategic spatial planning in Europe, *International Journal of Urban and Regional Research*, 28(1), pp. 45–67.

Ismeri Europa and Applica (2010) *Distribution of Competences in relation to Regional Development Policies in the Member States of the European Union: Final Report*, http://ec.europa.eu/regional_policy/sources/docgener/studies/pdf/2010_distribution_competence.pdf).

Jessop, B. (1998) The rise of governance and the risks of failure: the case of economic development, *International Social Science Journal*, 50 (March), pp. 29–45.

Johannisson, B. (2008) Regional development as entrepreneurial networking: from rational choice to self-organizing. In Aranguren, M. J., Iturrioz, C., and Wilson, J. R. (eds), *Networks, Governance and Economic Development: Bridging Disciplinary Frontiers*. Cheltenham: Edward Elgar.

Kooiman, J., and Van Vliet, M. (1993) Governance and public management. In K. A. Eliassen and J. Kooiman (eds), *Managing Public Organisations: Lessons from a Contemporary European Experience*. 2nd ed., London: Sage.

Mintzberg, H., Ahlstrand, B., and Lampel, J. (1998) *Strategy Safari*. New York: Free Press.

Nahapiet, J., and Ghoshal, S. (1998) Social capital, intellectual capital and the organizational advantage, *Academy of Management Review*, 22(2), pp. 242–66.

Navarro, M., Valdaliso, J. M., Aranguren, M. J., and Magro, E. (2014) A holistic approach to regional strategies: the case of the Basque Country, *Science and Public policy*, 41(4), pp. 532–47.

OECD (2011) *Regions and Innovation Policy: OECD Reviews of Regional Innovation*. Paris: OECD.

Pearce, C. L., and Conger, J. A. (2003) *Shared Leadership*. London: Sage.

Porter, M. E., and Kramer, M. R. (2011) Creating shared value, *Harvard Business Review*, January–February.

Sacchetti, S., and Sugden, R. (2003) The governance of networking and economic power: the nature and impact of subcontracting networks, *Journal of Economic Surveys*, 17(5), pp. 669–92.

Sotarauta, M. (2004) *Strategy Development in Learning Cities: From Classical Rhetoric towards Dynamic Capabilities*, Sente Working Papers, 8. University of Tampere; http://people.uta.fi/~atmaso/verkkokirjasto/sotarauta_strategy.pdf.

Stough, R. R. (2001) Endogenous growth theory and the role of institutions in regional economic development. In Johansson, B., Karlsson, C., and Stough, R. R. (eds), Theories of Endogenous Regional Growth: Lessons for Regional Policies. New York: Springer.

Streck, D. R., Redin, E., and Zitkoski, J. J. (2012) *Paulo Freire Encyclopedia*. Lanham, MD: Rowman & Littlefield.

Sugden, R., and Wilson, J. R. (2002) Economic development in the shadow of the consensus: a strategic decision-making approach, *Contributions to Political Economy*, 21, pp. 111–34.

Sugden, R., and Wilson, J. R. (2005) Economic globalisation: dialectics, conceptualisation and choice, *Contributions to Political Economy*, 24, pp. 1–20.

Sugden, R., Wei, P., and Wilson, J. R. (2006) Clusters, governance and the development of economies: a framework for case studies. In Pitelis, C., Sugden, R., and Wilson, J. R. (eds), *Clusters and Globalisation: The Development of Urban and Regional Economies*. Cheltenham: Edward Elgar.

Teece, D. J., Pisano, G., and Shuen, A. (1997) Dynamic capabilities and strategic management, *Strategic Management Journal*, 18, pp. 509–33.

Uyarra, E., and Flanagan, K. (2009) From regional systems of innovation to regions as innovation policy spaces, *Environment and Planning C: Government and Policy*, 28(4), pp. 681–95.

Walendowski, J., Kroll, H., Wintjes, R., and Hollanders, H. (2011) *Innovation Patterns and Innovation Policy in European Regions: Trends, Challenges and Perspectives: 2010 Annual Report*. Project no. 0932 for the European Commission. Brussels: Technopolis.

Wallis, A. (2000) The New Regionalism, www.alternative-regionalisms.org/?p=980.

# 5 Reconciling territorial strategies goals and means

## Towards smart competitiveness policies

*Edurne Magro and Claire Nauwelaers*[1]

## Introduction

Faced with the lasting impacts of the financial crisis, added to pre-existing structural weaknesses, European economies, and regions in particular, need to deploy fresh policies to enhance their competitiveness. In this perspective, new strategies and new policies are being designed across the European Union, notably within the context of EU cohesion policy, which is currently placing a greater emphasis on growth-oriented strategies.

However, while a lot of effort is being devoted to drawing up strategies that include new visions and goals, many policies are not yet delivering the intended results. This chapter investigates a problem that lies behind this challenge: the disconnection, in general, between strategy and policy and, in particular, between territorial strategy and competitiveness policy. As has been highlighted in chapters 2 and 3, strategy is about setting goals and directions. Public policy, on the other hand, is about deploying public means to serve the strategy, and the risk is that the latter is not thought through and implemented in line with the former. This chapter discusses how to ensure that such a link is effective.

The first section discusses differences and convergence between the concepts of strategy and policy and their application to territorial strategy. In essence, policy, deployed by governments, should serve strategy, which is the product of stakeholders' interactions. Effective implementation requires an alignment between strategic goals and policy means. A wide range of 'competitiveness policies' are relevant when it comes to territorial strategies.

The second section investigates the rationales and components of policies for territorial strategy. Policies serving territorial strategies are place-based, focused on innovation and founded on a mix of 'market and systems failure' rationales, with a greater emphasis on the latter. These are complex policies, and the chapter analyses several dimensions of complexity arising from the widening and deepening of innovation policy, the multilevel and multilayer dimensions of policy, and the diversity of policy instruments. We also introduce the policy-mix idea, which calls for balance and synergies between individual policy instruments. Policy typologies are proposed to provide a broader picture of all instruments at play, something that is not easy in a fragmented policy environment. The discussion highlights the diversity in policy responses to strategies.

The conclusions focus on policy learning: this is needed to create the 'missing link' between strategy and policy. There is no optimal policy mix but only one that is adapted to the strategic goals: the design of this mix needs to be based on robust evidence and requires enhanced capacities of policy-makers.

## What is the link between territorial strategy and competitiveness policy?

Over the last few years there has been an adoption of the notion of strategy as a substitute for the policy concept. Evidence for this can be found in European Commission documents and policies, such as the Europe 2020 growth strategy or the recent work on Regional Innovation Strategies, which goes from the initial innovation strategies (RIS) to the concept of research and innovation for smart specialisation strategies (RIS3). However, a clear understanding of the differences between strategy at any territorial level and public policy is still missing, both in the literature and in practice. Indeed, smart specialisation strategies have been understood by a wide range of scholars and policy-makers as a new generation of innovation policies which aim at affect not only the intensity of innovation but also the direction of innovation efforts. This means that regions should not only focus on increasing R&D or innovation rates generally but also prioritise the areas with the largest potential for innovation. We argue in this chapter that strategy and policies are different concepts but should be interlinked for an effective strategy-making process.

### *Similarities and differences between territorial strategy and public policy*

Territorial strategy has borrowed concepts from the business field (Aranguren *et al.*, 2012; Navarro *et al.*, 2014; see also chapters 2–4 in this volume), where 'policies' refers to the guidelines and limits that help align the organisation to reach its strategic goals and objectives (Mintzberg and Quinn, 1991). Policies provide top-down guidance about how things should be done and facilitate strategy implementation (Thompson *et al.*, 2008). Thus, in both business and public policy fields, policies are there to serve a strategy.

Public policy has traditionally been defined as the actions that governments take to reach certain goals (Howlett *et al.*, 2009). From this definition differences and convergences between public policy and territorial strategy can be discussed. It will be shown that, while they are different in theory, the two concepts tend to converge in practice.

First of all, public policy has government as a key actor while territorial strategies involve a wider set of actors. Although there is a clear recognition of the importance of involving other actors in the different phases of the policy-making cycle, decisions on public policy are made by government (state, regional, local government) (Howlett *et al.*, 2009). On the other hand, territorial strategy involves government strategy or positioning but also includes other intended and realised strategies embedded in the territory (i.e., the strategies of individual firms, knowledge infrastructures, etc.) (Mintzberg, 2000; Aranguren *et al.*, 2012). In smart specialisation strategies, for example, government is seen as a facilitator or orchestrator of territorial strategies (Foray *et al.*, 2012) and has a key role in the strategic process. The wider recognition in the policy literature of the role of other stakeholders in policy-making processes brings the two concepts of policy and strategy closer to each other: 'policy actors', 'policy systems' and 'policy universes' are all terms that broaden participation in the policy-making process beyond government (Howlett *et al.*, 2009; Flanagan *et al.*, 2011). This gives complexity to implementation owing to lack of communication between actors involved in strategy and actors involved in policy.

Secondly, both concepts include an agenda or goal-setting phase, but their orientation can be interpreted differently. Whereas public policy goals have traditionally focused on a problem-solving framework (associated with either market or systemic failures or problems) (Howlett *et al.*, 2009) and therefore respond to certain rationales, strategic goals can be understood as the translation of the territorial vision, based on territorial assets. Therefore, territorial strategies might put more emphasis on reinforcing strengths and less on solving problems: this implies a proactive role for the government as it acts as catalyser of a vision and does not only react when a problem is already visible. However, these two approaches converge in practice, as policy could both target problems and strengthen the assets of a territory.

Another key characteristic in which territorial strategy differs from public policy in principle is the importance given to specific place or context. Whereas territorial strategy is place- and context-specific, we can distinguish between two types of public policy: those that are neutral from a territorial point of view – *spatially blind policies* – and those that take into account the territory in which they act – *place-based policies* (Barca, 2011; Rodríguez-Pose, 2011; McCann and Ortega-Argilés, 2013). These latter types of policy are therefore closer to territorial strategy, as they consider that places really matter for regional growth and development (McCann and Ortega-Argilés, 2013). There is a consensus in the innovation systems literature that territory or place matters: public policy has to be context specific – i.e., there is no single policy recipe (*one size doesn't fit all*) for all territories (even at the same level, such as regions). The place-based policy approach has similarities to territorial strategy, leading to blurred boundaries between strategy and policy. The entire generation of regional innovation policies and strategies that the literature and both EU and the OECD have been promoting belong to these last types of policy.

Another difference between the two concepts is that strategy defines goals while policy defines means. According to Porter (1996) and Navarro *et al.* (2014), strategy is mainly a prioritisation issue. It implies a basis in territorial assets but also taking into consideration weaknesses or problems. Policy is related to choices or options as well, but these concern the instruments or tools that could contribute towards solving a specific policy problem and/or reach a specific goal (Howlett *et al.*, 2009). But here too there is convergence between the two concepts: instruments are related to choices because public policy should be aligned to territorial strategy (Aranguren *et al.*, 2012) and deploy the means to serve it. Indeed, public policy can be understood as one of the possible means or instruments employed for implementing and operationalising territorial strategy. However, it is only one of the possible means, and it is directly related to the role of government in territorial strategy, which, as mentioned previously, is not the only role that can be identified within a territorial strategy. Other means could include actions realised by private actors – or 'private policies' – within a territory, which also constitute an important part of the strategy and need to be collectively articulated. Thus territorial strategies can be seen as the articulation of aims and objectives from a variety of private and public actors (Sugden and Wilson, 2002) where public policies are the government's means to implement these strategies.

In the public policy case, the main means are policy instruments or tools, which are usually defined as 'the actual means and/or devices governments have at their disposal for implementing policies, and among which they must select in formulating a policy' (Howlett *et al.*, 2009), but also as the 'techniques of governance that, one way or another, involve the utilisation of state authority or its conscious limitation' (Howlett, 2005). While the former definition shows a more instrumental way of understanding tools, the latter demonstrates that instruments and tools can be broadly understood and incorporate governance elements.

To conclude, territorial strategy and public policy can be understood differently, but their boundaries are blurred by overlaps and similarities (see Table 5.1). Moreover, when territorial strategy refers to government strategy and does not include other actors' strategies, the overlaps are even bigger; strategy could therefore be considered as a new generation of public policy, and some of the key characteristics and elements would thus be common to both strategy and policy. Strategy could be defined as 'a guiding pattern for the everflowing stream of single actions' (Sotarauta, 2004: 16) and so is considered as an 'umbrella', while policy often refers to delivering concrete actions or programmes.

### *Territorial strategy and public policy: the implementation question*

The above discussion makes clear that public policy and territorial strategy are not the same and that, in fact, policies are perhaps the most important means for operationalising territorial strategy. From this, it is important to understand what is meant by implementation in both concepts and what are the main challenges that both face with regard to implementation.

It is common to divide territorial strategy into several phases in the public policy cycle. These phases go from strategy design to implementation and evaluation, as in public policy literature. However, we argue that it is inaccurate to consider strategy or policy as linear processes: they should rather be seen as continuous or evolving processes in which some elements are continually reconsidered.

*Table 5.1* Main elements in territorial strategy and public policy

| *Territorial strategy* | *Public policy* |
|---|---|
| Strategic goals based on territorial assets and problem-solving | Goals oriented towards problem-solving and assets exploitation |
| Government as one of the actors | Government as the main actor |
| Territory oriented | Can be place-blind |
| Based on strategic choices | Based on policy options |
| Policies as one of the possible means | Instruments as means |

The linear conceptualisation of strategy is usually linked to the classical approach of strategy (Mintzberg, 2000). According to Whittington (2001), this approach is rooted in planning, and therefore several phases can be defined. First of all, there is a formulation stage, resulting from a conscious planning process. Action is not taking during this phase, and it is assumed that action and implementation will follow when the strategy is formulated (Mintzberg, 2000). There is no specific interest in how the implementation is carried out, as theoretically this approach considers that implementation will succeed if planning or strategy formulation is well done. However, territorial strategy implementation is not an easy task, as it is not only a duty of government but also implies the involvement of several other actors (Sotarauta, 2004). Strategy implementation following the classical approach may fail: as a consequence of the separation of these two stages and the lack of communication between people involved, it is difficult to operationalise strategic thinking into concrete or operative actions (Mintzberg, 2000; Sotarauta, 2004). Within this approach, evaluation and monitoring is not stressed as an important phase.

In the non-linear view, in contrast, strategy is seen as a 'communicative process, in which different aims and strategies of many actors are reconciled and various interests balanced and touching-points and concreted means between many objectives are constantly looked for and coordinated' (Sotarauta, 2004).

Here design and implementation are not separated. The linear approach offers analytical tools but lacks continuous communication spaces (beyond the planning phase) in which different actors can reflect, negotiate and enter into dialogue within the strategic process (see chapter 4). In order to reduce the implementation gap, learning and communicative processes should take place in a continuous strategic process. Therefore a more effective approach to strategy combines analytical tools from the classical school and communication spaces (Aranguren *et al.*, 2012). In this interactive approach, there is no clear distinction between strategic phases, so that the implementation gap in the classical approach is reduced.

In line with strategy literature, policy theory also considered the implementation phase unproblematic until the 1970s (Howlett *et al.*, 2009), though subsequently there has been a huge debate around two policy implementation approaches – top-down and bottom-up. The top-down approach assumes that implementation is effective when the implementation mechanisms are defined from the design stage, while the bottom-up approach defends the idea that implementation will be more effective when it takes into account the view of the agents that are affected by it. In addition, as Howlett *et al.* (2009) point out, implementation implies decisions dealing with the choice of instruments, which are intrinsically related to policy design. Policy science literature has evolved and has criticised the stages model of policy-making. Therefore, in policy science there is also recognition that design and implementation are not separated and that policy-making is an interactive process. However, stages models help to simplify the complex reality in which policy-making processes are embedded and form a useful tool for policy learning processes (John, 1998). In these models, the evaluation stage, which is recognised as a critical phase for policy-learning purposes, completes the design and implementation phases (Raines, 2002).

While in strategy development the communicative approach has arisen in opposition to the linear one, in policy sciences too there is an increasing recognition of the importance of stakeholders' involvement in policy-making processes. This is especially visible in the design and evaluation phases, with the use of more participatory approaches in both cases. However, policy implementation still lacks communication spaces and is considered in many territories as a mechanical issue in which only officials and policy-makers are involved.

To summarise, implementation in both strategy and policy-making needs to be connected more to design and should involve communication, dialogue and the participation of actors in the territory. The role of government is crucial, as it can act as an orchestrator and catalyser of actors' dialogue. There is a consensus among scholars that strategy and policy-making are not linear processes, which leads to blurred boundaries between phases. It is therefore preferable not to see implementation as a separate phase. In this chapter, we consider implementation as a concept that refers to the operationalisation of strategy (government-led) and leads to policy and policy instruments and how these are chosen and delivered. In this sense, taking into account that strategy and policy are interlinked, we focus on how strategic goals and policy means are reconciled.

## Policies for territorial strategy: policy complexity and policy mixes

Given that policy is intrinsically related to territorial strategy when this is led or facilitated by government, it is necessary to understand the main policy concepts, which means answering, among others, the following questions: How should policies be articulated to be in line with strategic goals and vision? Which policy domains are important for territorial strategy? What are the rationales behind these policies that justify their use? What types of policy instruments are the key elements for territorial competitiveness?

According to evolutionary theory, territorial competitiveness is linked to the behaviour of firms and the political and institutional environment in which they are embedded (Nelson and Winter, 1982). This theory has stressed the importance of knowledge and innovation for territorial competitiveness. Innovation therefore constitutes a key element that has been articulated through different theories, such as the innovation systems theories (national/regional) (Lundvall, 1992;

Nelson, 1993) that have been widely adopted in practice. These have led to the emergence of innovation policies at many territorial levels, including at regional level, especially among the European Union countries (OECD, 2011).

Innovation policy is not a new concept. The origins of science, technology and innovation (STI) policy can be found in the Second World War, when some countries such as the United States decided to foster certain science fields, such as defence and aerospace, as a national duty. The main policy aim was the rapid development of science, and the focus was mainly on scientific infrastructures. This stage of policy evolution, which was called policy for science, was followed in the 1970s by a *science in policy* stage (Gibbons *et al.*, 1994), centred on the development of key technologies and taking advantage of the previously established research infrastructures. In the 1980s innovation policy came onto the scene, along with the theoretical contributions of innovation systems theories (Edquist, 2001) and a new interactive conception of innovation. In the last decade, innovation policy has experimented with a process of widening and deepening (Borrás, 2009), which can be seen both in theory and in practice. Innovation policy widening is reflected in the fact that innovation policy is spread over several policy domains and not confined only to STI, whereas deepening refers to the sophistication of policy instruments, such as new forms of collaboration, partnership, demand side instruments, etc. This widening and deepening of innovation policy is at the core of the strategies adopted by international organisations, namely the European Union and the OECD (European Commission, 2010; OECD, 2010a). This phenomenon has led to a greater complexity in the design of innovation policies, which is also reflected in their implementation. But other trends are at play that contribute to the complexity of policy.

## *Policy complexity: four dimensions*

Four dimensions of policy complexity can be identified (Borrás, 2009; Flanagan *et al.*, 2011; Magro and Wilson, 2013; Magro *et al.*, 2014): the widening and deepening of certain policy domains, such as innovation; multilevel governance; multilayer context; and the policy-mix concept. These four elements are present in competitiveness policies and impact on territorial strategy.

Other policy domains beyond innovation policies *stricto sensu* are related to territorial competitiveness – e.g., internationalisation, cluster and entrepreneurship policies. Given the widening and deepening of innovation policies, most of them, and especially cluster and entrepreneurship policies, could be considered (and are in practice) included in or closely related to innovation policy.

Both innovation policy and cluster policy share the common objectives of enhancing productivity and innovation-driven strategies for competitiveness and fostering regional development (Ketels *et al.*, 2013). Although there is a broad literature stream that focuses on the specificities of clusters and cluster policy (Nauwelaers and Wintjes, 2008; Uyarra and Ramlogan, 2012; Ketels, 2013; Aranguren and Wilson, 2013), it is also acknowledged that the latter could be considered as a demand-side tool for fostering an interactive and systemic type of innovation (Georghiou *et al.*, 2003; Edler and Georghiou, 2007).

Entrepreneurship policy is another domain that could be individually analysed or, if we consider that corporate entrepreneurship is one of the possible innovation outputs within firms, included in a broader concept of innovation, as well as being part of context conditions for innovation. Therefore, while recognising its specificities, entrepreneurship policy shares innovation policy groundings.

Although it might seem that internationalisation and innovation in firms are disconnected issues, some studies have demonstrated that innovative firms have greater internationalisation activity, while the contrary effect does not seem to occur. That is to say, innovation and export activities in firms are related, but only in one direction, as firms do not experiment with a *learning-by exporting* that leads to innovations (Monreal-Pérez *et al.*, 2012). This implies that exports do not lead to a learning process and innovation but that innovative firms tend to export more. Other studies show evidence for a correlation between internationalisation and the type of innovation profile of firms: high-profile science- and research-based innovators tend to display greater internationalisation rates than low-profile innovators (Peeters *et al.*, 2004).

To summarise, innovation policy, understood in a broad sense, is the key policy area for territorial competitiveness, but on account of this broadness it brings complexity to the policy-making process.

The second dimension that gives complexity to policy is multilevel governance. This is a key issue especially for regions or sub-national units, as it refers to the situation in which, because of processes of both decentralisation and devolution, a given territory might be impacted by policies administered at different levels (Magro and Wilson, 2013; OECD, 2011). This gives complexity to policy-making processes and poses the challenge to government and policy-makers of setting their own strategy and policies while taking into account those that are being put in place at other territorial levels. This leads to greater challenges in coordination (Magro *et al.*, 2014).

The third dimension that gives complexity to policy-making processes is the existence, at each territorial level, of different policy layers (OECD, 1991; Boekholt *et al.*, 2002; Lindner, 2012) – political, administrative and operative. According to Magro *et al.* (2014), the political layer (governmental bodies) is in charge of policy definition and priority setting; the administrative layer is in charge of policy implementation and the management of programmes and instruments (research councils, public agencies, etc.); and the operational layer includes 'performing' actors involved in the translation of policy priorities into concrete action (firms, knowledge infrastructures, investors, etc.). This distribution does not facilitate the connectedness and dialogue among all the actors in view of reaching a communicative strategic and policy-making process and, in order to avoid misalignment between strategic goals and policy means, poses, once again, challenges to strategic and policy coordination.

Finally, probably the most important dimension of complexity relates to the policy-mix concept. Policy-mix has become a fashionable concept in the innovation policy debate in recent years (Nauwelaers *et al.*, 2009; OECD; 2010b; Flanagan *et al.*, 2011; Borrás and Edquist, 2013; Magro and Wilson, 2013).

However, it is a concept that was already used and applied in other policy fields and policy studies in general. Its origin could be dated in Mundell's (1962) contributions on the relationship between monetary and fiscal policy, and it is also a term that can be found in the public policy literature (Howlett *et al.*, 2009).

The policy-mix concept reflects the complexity of instrument choice in public policy and refers to the combination of instruments implemented by a government to respond to a specific problem or rationale. It is a useful concept for understanding innovation policy complexity, as it reflects both the processes of widening and deepening referred to earlier and their implications for implementation.

A useful definition of policy-mix is the one provided in Nauwelaers *et al.* (2009) referring to policy-mix for R&D, which defines the term as 'the combination of policy instruments which interact to influence the quantity and quality of R&D investments in public and private sectors'. Taking into account that policies for competitiveness might include other non-innovation-related domains and instruments, such as infrastructures and taxation, we could define the policy-mix for competitiveness as the combination of instruments that might alter the competitiveness conditions and/or performance of a territory. Most of them will target innovation, but others belong to other policy domains and impact on territorial competitiveness.

The policy-mix concept embodies the idea of interactions between different instruments from different policies. These interactions might bring positive, negative or neutral effects, but in any case have to be taken into account in the policy-making process, leading to higher complexity. They come from the combination of different instruments, corresponding to different types of policies responding to different rationales. These elements and their implications for policy implementation in territorial strategy are explained further below.

### *Rationales for competitiveness policies*

Rationales in economic theory are defined as the theoretical justification for government intervention. Two approaches are commonly used to justify policy intervention: neoclassical and evolutionary-systemic theory. They often appear as contradictory and mutually exclusive arguments, but in practice those rationales coexist in policy mixes or combinations of instruments (Flanagan *et al.*, 2011; Magro and Wilson, 2013).

In a neoclassical approach policy intervention can be justified only when market failures appear. Neoclassical theory assumes that markets are perfect, and any imperfections are labelled as market failures. These market failures could be a justification for innovation policy as well as for other policies important for territorial competitiveness. The most common market failures are information asymmetries, externalities, appropriability and indivisibilities (Arrow, 1962; Stiglitz, 1989). Other failures corresponding to this approach include more strategic questions and link to 'infant industry' justifications: strategic trade, competition policy and national missions (Niosi, 2010; Dasgupta, 1987).

Market failure arguments underpin some interventions in the policy fields related to territorial competitiveness, such as STI policy, internationalisation or cluster policy. In the first case, technology and innovation are made of knowledge, and therefore uncertainty and appropriability failures might appear as an inherent result of such innovation processes. Internationalisation policy might rely on information asymmetries and the uncertainty derived from those asymmetries, as well as indivisibilities associated with the size needed to start internationalisation activities. In addition, other policies important for territorial competitiveness, such as cluster policy, might respond to market failures such as externalities, and appropriability justifies a government's intervention in the promotion of firm agglomerations or clusters.

The neoclassical approach has been the main theory for justifying government intervention until recently, especially since the 1990s, when evolutionary and systemic approaches came onto scene. Learning plays a key role in evolutionary theory, and therefore this approach pays attention to learning processes that take place within different types of actors – public and private.

In the evolutionary approach, the key idea is that innovation is a collective action, and the focus is on the cognitive capabilities of the actors and on the key role of institutions in promoting interactions among them in order to facilitate collective learning. The systemic approach thus breaks with the linearity of neoclassical approaches and recognises the importance of (national and regional) territorial systems for innovation (Lundvall, 1992; Nelson, 1993). The regional approach for innovation is widely referred to by policy-makers in Europe. It acknowledges that a firm cannot have all the knowledge needed to innovate in-house and therefore maintains that connections with other agents, such as knowledge actors, should be promoted. In the same line, other SME-related policies, such as internationalisation or cluster policies, are based on these systemic rationales, especially those instruments associated with the promotion of firm agglomerations or alliances for certain activities such as internationalisation, diversification or training. Within this approach, proximity gains relevance, as partnerships and agglomeration might be more effective in geographical proximity, and so regional policy plays a key role in these policy fields.

There are several classifications of systemic failures for innovation policy, some of them directed specifically at regional policy (Smith, 2000; Edquist, 2001; Laranja *et al.*, 2008; Chaminade *et al.*, 2009; Malerba, 2010), but there is no general consensus about which are the main systemic failures. Chaminade *et al.* (2009) distinguish between failures regarding the components of the system (lack or failures of components), such as knowledge infrastructures or firms, and failures regarding interlinkages among these components. The most common failures that justify government intervention under this approach are network problems, institutional problems, transition or lock-in problems and learning problems.

In spite of the acceptance of theoretical rationales that justify policy intervention, in public policy literature this is considered as a deductive approach (Howlett, 2005), which has been rejected by policy scientists. These argue that theory rationales are not based on what policy-makers and politicians really do. Practitioners base their decisions on multiple factors, including political factors, context-related factors and decisions taken in the past. That leads to a situation where policy rationales (inductive approach) do not fit with theory rationales (Mytelka and Smith, 2002; Flanagan *et al.*, 2011). This would lead to challenges in policy implementation on account of the different interpretation of rationales and policy goals from different policy actors, and therefore strategic alignment would be affected.

### *Competitiveness policy typology*

It is useful to understand the contribution to strategy of several typologies of policy for competitiveness according to different criteria.

The first criterion is related to policy rationales. We distinguish between policies responding to market or systemic failures. Traditionally we can find in the literature the distinction made by Ergas (1987) between mission-oriented policies and diffusion-oriented policies. The former are characterised by high R&D investments in a few key technologies in an early development of the sector life cycle, whereas the latter emphasise promoting cooperation among actors within a scientific and technology system. At first sight, mission-oriented policies seem closer to neoclassical approaches and diffusion-oriented policies to evolutionary-systemic approaches (Cartner and Pyka, 2001; Bach and Matt, 2002). However, both types of policy are also recognised by the evolutionary theory (Niosi, 2010). Mission-oriented policies do not respond only to neoclassical failures, as their fundamentals are also based on looking for international strategic leadership (Ergas, 1987). Additionally, although these policies are focused on a few technologies, these could constitute the basis for developing cognitive capabilities and knowledge in firms, which is closer to an evolutionary framework (Bach and Matt, 2002).

Both mission-oriented and diffusion-oriented policies target the two different types of priority set out in chapter 2: thematic priorities and structural/functional priorities (Gassler *et al.*, 2004; Navarro *et al.*, 2014). The former refers to S&T areas, activities or industries that are crucial for territorial development and competitiveness, whereas the latter are related to the systemic failures or problems the policy wants to overcome. It is important in a strategy to have a combination of both thematic (vertical) and functional (horizontal) policy, as each has a different aim. In the regional innovation systems approach there was a prioritisation of horizontal policies, which are useful for 'building the system', but the lack of vertical priorities has been one of the weaknesses that smart specialisation strategies are trying to overcome. Smart specialisation strategies emphasise the combination of types of policy, assuring that it is important not only to affect the innovation climate (perhaps by promoting R&D investment) but also to alter the direction of innovation (i.e., subsidising research centres oriented to biosciences) in a certain region or territory.

For example, in a less-developed territory in which there is lack of knowledge infrastructures, policies directed at building the innovation system would have to be stressed over policies oriented towards certain activities, such as cluster policies or mission-oriented policies. This is in fact the option taken in the Czech Republic smart specialisation strategy, which combines horizontal priorities to support the innovation system as a whole with vertical priorities that are domains with growth potential and specific assets in the country. Examples of policies in the first group include the introduction of pro-innovation support schemes to strengthen cooperation between research organisations and the corporate sector (innovation vouchers, mobility support schemes between the triple-helix spheres, technology transfer) and human capital enhancement and accumulation specifically in technical fields. Examples of supported domains in the second group are transport, engineering industries, ICT and automation and health-care instrumentation. In contrast, in a more advanced region such as Flanders, the focus of the smart specialisation strategy is more heavily on vertical themes, such as 'nanotechnology for health' and 'sustainable chemistry', as the infrastructure is already well developed.

Some authors (Gassler *et al.*, 2008; Edquist and Zabala-Iturriagagoitia, 2012) have been referring to this phenomenon as a return to the so called mission-oriented policies – the 'new mission-oriented policies'. However, more than new mission-oriented policies, they do not deny inputs from previous streams and combine them into a new approach. In smart specialisation strategies, for example, it is common to find references to selecting and promoting activities in a region (vertical/thematic priorities), which is related to mission-oriented policies, but also to capacity building (horizontal/functional priorities), which is closer to evolutionary-systemic approaches.

Also interesting are the policies that follow the narrower view of 'one policy – one domain' or that take into consideration that one policy might be influenced by several domains (broader view). If we take the innovation policy case, the narrower view would consider STI policy domains (Lundvall and Borrás, 2005) as the only ones of relevance for policy intervention in these areas. The broader view considers that innovation policy is a systemic and holistic framework that might affect and be affected by interventions that traditionally 'belong' to other policy domains, which was called 'third generation innovation policy' (Remoe, 2008). In this case it implies recognising that a huge range of policy fields in a certain territory influence the direction of innovation and therefore territorial competitiveness. This not only happens in the innovation field, as has been characterised by some authors such as Nauwelaers *et al.* (2009), but is something that it is also applicable to other policies which are highly relevant for territorial competitiveness, such as education policies, environmental policies or internationalisation policies.

This broader view gives complexity to the strategic process at all stages, but especially at the implementation and evaluation stages. Practitioners acknowledge the need for an integrated and holistic view for setting a strategic vision or objective, and even for policy design, according to the settled strategic objectives. Governments have started to include all departments or ministries in their agenda setting, and even other actors and stakeholders from the territory are included in this task. However, one of the most common mistakes is to leave implementation (and also evaluation) as the duty of each ministry or department, assuming that it is a straightforward task. It is therefore common to find situations in which strategies and policies are defined and discussed following a broad and holistic view, but the action and policy implementation is left to officials from different domains without putting in place the necessary corresponding coordination mechanisms across the different layers (political and administrative) and domains. In Table 5.2 there is an attempt to classify key policies for territorial competitiveness directed towards thematic or functional priorities in different policy domains.

In addition to these distinctions, policies can be categorised according to their target group. Here, we can distinguish among *framework policies*, *mixed policies* and *blanket policies* (Lipsey and Carlaw, 1998). Framework policies are horizontal policies with no specific target group, mixed policies are directed at a certain technology or industry, and blanket policies are a hybrid type directed at a specific group of firms.

### *Types of instruments for competitiveness policy*

Several taxonomies of policy instruments have been proposed, either from the public policies perspective or specific to innovation policies.

Some of the best-known approaches in public policy literature differentiate between regulatory instruments, economic or financial instruments and soft instruments (Bemelmans-Videc *et al.*, 2003; Borrás 2009). Regulatory instruments refer to legal and binding regulations, such as the regulation of intellectual property rights or competition policy, etc. Economic and financial instruments are the most commonly implemented in some policy arenas, such as STI (Borrás; 2009), examples being tax incentives, grants, loans, etc. Soft instruments are voluntary and non-coercive measures that provide information and recommendations and offer contractual agreements; the most commonly used are the international or national standards, partnership agreements and public communications.

*Table 5.2* Policy domains and instruments for territorial strategy

| *Policy domains* | *Thematic priorities* | *Functional priorities* |
|---|---|---|
| Innovation domain | Sectoral innovation policies<br>Strategic innovation arenas | General innovation policies (direct business innovation support, innovation vouchers schemes, etc.) |
| Science and technology domain | Sectoral and GPT-based policies, including support to certain sectoral-oriented research centres, such as competence centres | Human resources policies related to science<br>Science and technology policy (funding of basic science and technology infrastructure – science and technology parks, etc.) |
| Industrial domain | Cluster policies | Human resources policies related to industry<br>Internationalisation policies |
| Financial domain | | Macro-economic policies<br>Fiscal policies |

Source: Based on Nauwelaers *et al.* (2009).

Another useful classification is the one provided by Howlett (2005), who divides policy tools into two types. The first is composed of the substantive instruments, which are those that affect the nature, type, quantities and distribution of goods and services (loans, grants, regulation, etc.) and the second consists of procedural instruments (treaties and political agreements). The most interesting assumption in this approach is that these two types do not constitute a dichotomy of policy instruments but tend to be implemented together. Several classifications are adapted to the specific arenas of STI policy or to specific policy levels (i.e., regional level). In the STI policy field, Georghiou *et al.* (2003) and Edler and Georghiou (2007) provide a taxonomy which differentiates between supply-side instruments (grants for R&D, tax incentives, support for research infrastructures) and demand-side instruments (innovative public procurement). In fact, this is a simplistic picture, as there are some instruments, such as cluster policies, that can work on both the supply and the demand side and which have been referred to in the literature as systemic instruments (Edler and Georghiou, 2007). A more extended typology is the one provided by the European Commission (2013), which gives an exhaustive list of policy instruments according to different objectives. Additionally, we can mention the categories provided by the OECD (2011) and Foray *et al.* (2012) referring to STI policy or strategy field at the regional level. These include traditional (i.e., R&D grants), emerging (i.e., vouchers) and experimental instruments (i.e., cross-border research centres).

The distinction between policies oriented to firms and policies oriented to the system made by Nauwelaers and Wintjes (2002) is also useful. It is important, first, to have a clear view of the target group of the policy in order to choose the relevant policy instruments and, second, to assess whether there is a gap in terms of instruments and policies, as it is necessary to include both types of measure when implementing a territorial strategy. This typology can be combined with one that distinguishes orientations as focusing either on thematic or vertical priorities, on the one hand, or on horizontal or functional priorities, on the other, as mentioned in the previous section (see Table 5.3).

### *Policy-mix composition and instruments choice*

There are a lot of documents and guides available that provide insights into the instruments from which governments can choose for designing policy mixes (OECD, 2011; European Commission, 2012; 2013). However, these do not solve the issue of choice – i.e., which combination of instruments might be most effective for solving certain problems or rationales.

One reason for this is that instrument choice is context specific, and therefore it is impossible to provide a recipe applicable for all territories (one size does not fit all). For example, establishing technology centres in less-developed regions including only firms with little absorptive capacity for new technology might result in 'cathedrals in the desert' rather than in the creation of growth poles. Likewise, the creation of hubs for entrepreneurs in e-mobile business is a good instrument in Estonia, which is booming with such personnel and provides

*Table 5.3* Examples of policy instruments according priorities and level of support

| *Target of support* | *Thematic priorities* | *Functional priorities* |
|---|---|---|
| Firm oriented | R&D grants for firms in specific sectors<br>Investment in sectoral-based knowledge infrastructure<br>Public procurement for innovation focused on specific sectors | Training and mobility programmes<br>Science parks<br>Incubators<br>Innovation vouchers |
| System oriented | Cooperative schemes research–industry<br>Cluster policies<br>Network policies | Training and mobility programmes between industry and academia |

Source: Based on Nauwelaers and Wintjes (2002).

a favourable demand context for such innovations, but such hubs might remain empty houses in more traditional environments which lack such dynamism and openness to new ICT applications.

Another reason is that one instrument might be responding to different failures. For example, the creation of cluster associations in order to promote cooperation within a sector responds to both market and systemic failures, as its aim is to overcome networking failures or problems but also externalities failures. The same would happen with R&D subsidies to collaborative projects that respond both to market failures (indivisibilities, uncertainties and externalities) and to system failures (networking failures). It is therefore not possible to assign one instrument to a specific type of failure or problem. This is in line with the argument that alternative instruments could be employed to achieve the same objective (Landry and Varone, 2005; Nauwelaers and Wintjes, 2003). However, we can also find some instruments that try to overcome only one type of failure, as for example tax incentives to R&D, which are related only to market failures.

There may be a good understanding of the functioning of individual policy instruments from a technical point of view, but it is often forgotten that instrument choice takes place in a certain political context, and the best technical solution might therefore not be the optimum one from a political point of view (Peters, 2005). For example, cross-border applied research centres are being established between Flanders and the neighbouring Dutch region, but such an initiative is much more difficult to implement between Belgian regions, where the political context does not favour such cooperation.

In addition, there are other important factors that affect instrument choice. One of these is path dependence, which refers to the importance of past decisions on the present ones. Path dependence affects public policy processes in general and instrument choice in particular, as it is a source of continuity of some policy instruments whatever the goals of public policy of strategy are. However, path dependency can also be a source of change in an institutional context, as Martin (2010) and Valdaliso *et al.* (2014) argue. In this literature, path dependence is seen as a source of change, especially through three different mechanisms: layering (the creation of new rules, instruments or actors, which are added to the old ones), conversion (the reorientation of an existing institution towards new roles) and recombination (new institutions and organisations are introduced while old ones are removed from the system). The first two are responsible for incremental changes in a system, while the last is related more to radical breakthrough. These three mechanisms are applicable also to instrument choice.

Another important factor highlighted by Peters (2005) is legitimacy. Some instruments are more legitimate in some territories than in others, which is also a sign of how much context matters and how this affects instrument choice. An example of this can be seen in Europe, where vouchers or innovative public procurement are instruments more commonly accepted in Northern and Central than in Southern countries. Other dimensions important for instrument choice include economic factors (for example, in budget constraint situations or financial crises, financial instruments might be restricted), administrative elements or even ethical features.

Given the complexity of policy systems, a combination of instruments needs to be designed to form a policy-mix, as there is no best instrument for each situation, problem or context (Peters, 2005). Hence, it is not only difficult to provide guidelines for individual instrument choice (Nauwelaers *et al.*, 2014) but also almost impossible to provide a recipe for policy-mix choice. In fact, in a recent study made by the European Commission (2013), there is recognition that there is not an optimum policy-mix model.

## Conclusions

Territorial strategy and public policy are different concepts that are often mixed and used interchangeably, both in literature and in practice. Even if their definition and conceptual backgrounds differ, in practice the boundaries between the two concepts are sometimes fuzzy. In a nutshell, public policy is there to serve strategy and therefore is one of the possible means to reach the strategic goals and vision set for a territory.

Territorial strategy relies on the individual strategies of a range of actors. If these are disconnected there is no 'territorial strategy': a strategy exists when the various agendas/strategies are placed in synergy. Working towards such synergies is a key role for the public actor as orchestrator, not as top-down organiser. In addition, public policies are to provide the right incentives and correct the market and systemic failures that act as barriers to the achievement of a territorial strategy once it is emerging.

Most of the literature and documentation studying strategy have a stronger focus on design, assuming that a good design will lead to a straightforward implementation, and therefore that policies defined and implemented to reach the strategic goals will be perfectly aligned with them. This is not the reality for several reasons, which we have tried to identify in this chapter, all of them related to complexity.

Competitiveness policies (those with more influence on territorial competitiveness and strategy) are complex, both in their definition (rationales, domains and instruments) and in their governance. Complexity is not only seen in the different levels under which policies are administered; what it is more important for strategic purposes is that policies are designed and implemented by different and usually disconnected policy actors (at different layers). One of the main challenges that governments have to face is therefore how to establish communication spaces to align public policy and strategy better.

The missing link between strategies and policies consists in 'goal-oriented' policy mixes – i.e., sets of interacting instruments which together are able to influence conditions and actors in a territory to reach the goal of the strategy.

Taking a policy-mix approach implies combining different types of policy, covering horizontal and vertical priorities, involving several levels and layers of government and following different theoretical rationales, which might be seen by some practitioners and academics as contradictory. In addition, policy path dependency and inertia make the change in instruments difficult and lead to greater challenges to manage policy mixes associated with specific strategic goals. Hence it is important to include evaluation tools and exercises in the design and implementation of strategies and policies, as they will help to assess the complementary effects of all types of policy and provide intelligence in the process, a theme that is taken up in the next chapter.

Government capacities and capabilities to overcome these challenges form the key issue for providing policy and strategy coherence. In addition, it is necessary to see implementation and policies not at stages following policy design but as integral components of the whole strategic process.

In conclusion, to tackle the implementation gap between strategy and policy, there is a need for more communication, more coherence and more coordination.

## Note

1 This work was supported by the European Commission (FP7 SSH.2012.1.1-3) under Grant number 320131. Any errors are the responsibility of the authors.

## References

Aranguren, M. J., and Wilson, J. R. (2013) What can experience with clusters teach us about fostering regional smart specialisation?, *Ekonomiaz*, 83, pp. 126–45.

Aranguren, M. J., Magro, E., Navarro, M., and Valdaliso, J. M. (2012) *Estrategias para la construcción de ventajas competitivas regionales: el caso del País Vasco*. Madrid: Marcial Pons.

Arrow, K. (1962) The economic implications of learning-by-doing, *Review of Economic Studies*, 29 (June), pp. 155–73.

Bach, L., and Matt, M. (2002) Rationale for science & technology policy. In Georghiou, L., Rigby, J., and Cameron, H. (eds), *Assessing the Socio-Economic Impacts of the Framework Programme*. University of Manchester, PREST.

Barca, F. (2011) Alternative approaches to development policy: intersections and divergences, *Seminar on Territorial Dimension of Development Policies, papers and proceedings*, Ostróda, Poland, 18–19 July, pp. 45–50; https://www.mir.gov.pl/english/Regional_Development/Presidency/event_shedule/Documents/Seminar_%20Papers_and_Proceedings.pdf.

Bemelmans-Videc, M.-L., Rist, R. C., and Vedung, E. (eds) (2003) *Carrots, Sticks & Sermons: Policy Instruments & their Evaluation*. London: Transaction.

Boekholt, P., Arnold, E., Deiaco, E., McKibbin, S., Simmons, P., Stroyan, J., and Mothe, J. (2002) *The Governance of Research and Innovation: An International Comparative Study: Synthesis Report*, http://in3.dem.ist.utl.pt/master/03itt/lec_2_4.pdf.

Borrás, S. (2009) *The Widening and Deepening of Innovation Policy: What Conditions Provide for Effective Governance?*, CIRCLE Electronic Working Paper Series, no. 2009/02, University of Lund.

Borrás, S., and Edquist, C. (2013) The choice of innovation policy instruments, *Technological Forecasting and Social Change*, 80(8), pp. 1513–22.

Cartner, U. and A. Pyka (2001) Classifying Technology Policy from an Evolutionary Perspective. *Research Policy* 30(5): 759.

Chaminade, C., Lundvall, B.-Å., Van, J., and Joseph, K. J. (2009) Designing innovation policies for development: towards a systemic experimentation-based approach. In Lundvall, B-Å., Joseph, K. J., *et al.* (eds), *Handbook on Innovation Systems and Developing Countries: Building Domestic Capabilities in a Global Setting*. Cheltenham: Edward Elgar.

Dasgupta, P. (1987) The economic theory of technology policy: an introduction. In Dasgupta, P., and Stoneman, P. (eds), *Economic Policy and Technological Performance*. Cambridge: Cambridge University Press.

Edler, J., and Georghiou, L. (2007) Public procurement and innovation: resurrecting the demand side, *Research Policy*, 36, pp. 949–63.

Edquist, C. (2001) Innovation policy: a systemic approach. In Archibugi, D., and Lundvall, B.-Å. (eds), *The Globalizing Learning Economy*. Oxford: Oxford University Press.

Edquist C., and Zabala-Iturriagagoitia, J. M. (2012) Public procurement for innovation as mission-oriented public policy, *Research Policy*, 41(10), pp. 1757–69.

Ergas, H. (1987) The importance of technology policy. In Dasgupta, P., and Stoneman, P. (eds), *Economic Policy and Technological Performance*. Cambridge: Cambridge University Press.

European Commission (2010) *Communication from the Commission to the European Parliament, the Council, the European Economic and Social Committee and the Committee of the Regions: Regional Policy Contributing to Smart Growth in Europe 2020*, COM(2010) 553 final.

European Commission (2012) *Guide to Research and Innovation Strategies for Smart Specialisation (RIS3)*, March, Smart Specialisation Platform, EU Regional Policy Series.

European Commission (2013) *Lessons from a Decade of Innovation Policy: What can be Learnt from the INNO Policy TrendChart and the Innovation Union Scoreboard.*

Flanagan, K., Uyarra, E., and Laranja, M. (2011) Reconceptualising the 'policy mix' for innovation, *Research Policy* 40(5), pp. 702–13.

Foray, D., Goddard, J., Goenaga, X., Landabaso, M., McCann, P., Morgan, K., Nauwelaers, C., and Ortega-Argilés, R. (2012) *Guide to Research and Innovation Strategies for Smart Specialisations (RIS 3)*, European Commission.

Gassler, H., Polt, W., Schindler, J., Weber, M., Mahroum, S., Kubeczko, K., and Keenan, M. (2004) *Priorities in Science & Technology Policy: An International Comparison.* Research Report no. 39–2004. Vienna: Institute of Technology and Regional Policy.

Gassler, H., Polt, W., and Rammer, C. (2008) Priority setting in technology policy: historical development and recent trends. In Nauwelaers, C., and Wintjes, R. (eds), *Innovation Policy in Europe: Measurement and Strategy*. Cheltenham: Edward Elgar, pp. 203–24.

Georghiou, L., *et al.* (2003) *Raising EU R&D Intensity: Improving the Effectiveness of Public Support Mechanisms for Private Sector Research and Development: Direct Measures*, EUR 20716.

Gibbons, M., Limoges, C., Nowotny, H., Schwartzman, S., Scott, P., and Trow, M. (eds) (1994) *The New Production of Knowledge: The Dynamics of Science and Research in Contemporary Societies*. London: Sage.

Howlett, M. (2005) What is a policy instrument? Policy tools, policy mixes, and policy-implementation styles. In Eliadis, P., Hill, M., and Howlett, M. (eds), *Designing Government: From Instruments to Governance*. Montreal: McGill–Queens University Press.

Howlett, M., Ramesh, M., and Perl, A. (2009) *Studying Public Policy: Policy Cycles & Policy Subsystems*. 3rd ed., Oxford: Oxford University Press.

John, P. (1998) *Analysing Public Policy*. London: Pinter.

Ketels, K. (2013) Recent research on competitiveness and clusters: what are the implications for regional policy? *Cambridge Journal of Regions, Economy and Society*, 6(2), pp. 269–84.

Ketels, C., Nauwelaers, C., J. Harper, G., Lubicka, B., and Peck, F. (2013) *The Role of Clusters in Smart Specialisation Strategies*, Expert Group Report for DG Research, European Commission.

Landry, R., and Varone, F. (2005) Choice of policy instruments: confronting the deductive and the interactive approaches. In Eliadis, P., Hill, M., and Howlett, M. (eds), *Designing Government: From Instruments to Governance*. Montreal: McGill–Queens University Press.

Laranja, M., Uyarra, E., and Flanagan, K. (2008) Policies for science, technology and innovation: translating rationales into regional policies in a multi-level setting, *Research Policy*, 37(5), pp. 823–35

Lindner, R. (2012) Cross-sectoral coordination of STI policies: governance principles to bridge policy-fragmentation. In Fraunhofer ISI (ed.), *Innovation Systems Revisited: Experiences from 40 years of Fraunhofer ISI Research*. Stuttgart: Fraunhofer, pp. 275–87.

Lipsey, R., and Carlaw, K. (1998) Technology policies in neoclassical and structuralist-evolutionary models, *Science, Technology and Industrial Review*, 22, pp. 31–73.

Lundvall, B-Å. (1992) *National Systems of Innovation: Towards a Theory of Innovation and Interactive Learning*. London: Pinter.

Lundvall, B-Å., and Borrás, S. (2005) Science, technology, innovation and knowledge policy. In Fagerberg, J., Mowery, D., and Nelson, R. (eds), *The Oxford Handbook of Innovation*. Oxford: Oxford University Press.

Magro, E., and Wilson, J. R. (2013) Complex innovation policy systems: towards an evaluation mix, *Research Policy*, 42(9), pp. 1647–56.

Magro, E., Navarro, M., and Zabala-Iturriagagoitia, J. M. (2014) Coordination-mix: the hidden face of STI policy, *Review of Policy Research*, 31(5), pp. 367–89.

Malerba, F. (2010) Increase learning, break knowledge, lock-ins and foster dynamic complementarities: evolutionary and system perspectives on technology policy in industrial dynamics. In Foray, D. (ed.), *The New Economics of Technology Policy*. Cheltenham: Edward Elgar.

Martin, R. (2010) Rethinking regional path dependence: beyond lock-in to evolution, *Economic Geography*, 86(1), pp. 1–27.

McCann, P., and Ortega-Argilés, R. (2013) Smart specialisation, regional growth and applications to EU cohesion policy, *Regional Studies*, doi: 10.1080/00343404.2013.799769.

Mintzberg, H. (2000) *The Rise and the Fall of Strategic Planning*. London: Prentice Hall.

Mintzberg, H., and Quinn, J. B. (1991) *The Strategy Process: Concepts, Contexts, Cases*. Englewood Cliffs, NJ: Prentice Hall.

Monreal-Pérez, J., Aragón-Sánchez, A., and Sánchez-Marín, G. (2012) A longitudinal study of the relationship between export activity and innovation in the Spanish firm: the moderating role of productivity, *International Business Review*, 21, pp. 862–77.

Mundell, R. A. (1962) The appropriate use of monetary and fiscal policy for internal and external stability, *IMF Staff Papers*, 9(1), pp. 70–79.

Mytelka, L., and Smith, K. (2002) Policy learning and innovation theory: an interactive and co-evolving process, *Research Policy*, 31, pp. 1467–79.

Nauwelaers, C., and Wintjes, R. (2002) Innovating SMEs and regions: the need for policy intelligence and interactive policies, *Technology Analysis & Strategic Management*, 14(2), pp. 201–15.

Nauwelaers, C., and Wintjes, R. (2003) Towards a new paradigm for innovation policies? In Asheim, B., Isaksen, A., Nauwelaers, C., and Tötdling, F. (eds), *Regional Innovation Policy for Small-Medium Enterprises*. Cheltenham: Edward Elgar.

Nauwelaers, C., and Wintjes, R. (2008) Innovation policy, innovation in policy: policy learning within and across systems and clusters. In Nauwelaers, C., and Wintjes, R. (eds), *Innovation Policy In Europe: Measurement and Strategy*. Cheltenham: Edward Elgar.

Nauwelaers, C., Boekholt, P., Mostert, B., Cunningham, P., Guy, K., Hofer, R., and Rammer, C. (2009) *Policy Mixes for R&D Europe*. European Commission, Directorate-General for Research.

Nauwelaers, C., Periañez-Forte, I., and Midtkandal, I. (2014) RIS3 Implementation and Policy Mixes, *JRC Policy Briefs* no. 07/2014, European Commission.

Navarro, M., Valdaliso, J. M., Aranguren, M. J., and Magro, E. (2014) A holistic approach to regional strategies: the case of the Basque Country, *Science and Public Policy*, 41(4), pp. 532–47.

Nelson, R. R. (ed.) (1993) *National Innovation Systems: A Comparative Analysis*. Oxford: Oxford University Press.

Nelson, R. R., and Winter S. G. (1982) *An Evolutionary Theory of Economic Change*. Cambridge, MA: Harvard University Press.

Niosi, J. (2010) *Building National and Regional Innovation Systems: Institutions for Economic Development*. Cheltenham: Edward Elgar.

OECD (1991) *Choosing Priorities in Science and Technology*. Paris: OECD.

OECD (2010a) *OECD Innovation strategy*, Paris: OECD.

OECD (2010b) *OECD Science, Technology and Industry Outlook 2010*. Paris: OECD.

OECD (2011) *Regions and Innovation Policy*. Paris: OECD.

Peeters, L., Swinnen, G., and Tiri, M. (2004) *Patterns of Innovation in the Flemish Business Sector: A Multivariate Analysis of CIS-3 Firm-Level Data*, IWT Studies, no. 47.

Peters, B. G. (2005) The future of instruments research. In Eliadis, P., Hill, M., and Howlett, M. (eds), *Designing Government: From Instruments to Governance*. Montreal: McGill–Queens University Press.

Porter, M. E. (1996) What is strategy?, *Harvard Business Review*, November–December, pp. 61–78.

Raines, P. (2002) The challenge of evaluating cluster behaviour in economic development policy, paper presented at the International RSA Conference: *Evaluation and EU Regional Policy: New Questions and Challenges*, European Policies Research Centre, University of Strathclyde.

Remoe, S. O. (2008) Innovation governance in dynamic economies: lessons from the OECD MONIT project. In Nauwelaers, C., and Wintjes, R. (eds), *Innovation Policy In Europe: Measurement and Strategy*. Cheltenham: Edward Elgar.

Rodríguez-Pose, A. (2011) Spatially-blind strategies as place-based development strategies. In *Seminar on Territorial Dimension of Development Policies: Papers and Proceedings*, Ostróda, Poland, 18–19 July, pp. 85–9; www.mrr.gov.pl/english/Presidency/Main/event_shedule/Documents/Seminar_%20Papers_and_Proceedings.pdf.

Smith, K. (2000) Innovation as a systemic phenomenon: rethinking the role of policy, *Enterprise & Innovation Management Studies*, 1(1), pp. 73–102.

Sotarauta, M. (2004) *Strategy Development in Learning Cities: From Classical Rhetoric towards Dynamic Capabilities*, Sente Working Papers 8/2004, University of Tampere.

Stiglitz, J. E. (1989) Markets, market failures, and development, *American Economic Review*, 79(2), pp. 197–203.

Sugden, R., and Wilson, J. R. (2002) Economic development in the shadow of the consensus: a strategic decision-making approach, *Contributions to Political Economy*, 21(1), pp. 111–34.

Thompson, A. A., Strickland, A. J., and Gamble, J. E. (2008) *Crafting and Executing Strategy: The Quest for Competitive Advantage*. 16th ed., Boston: McGraw-Hill.

Uyarra E., and Ramlogan, R. (2012) *The Effects of Cluster Policy on Innovation: Compendium of Evidence on the Effectiveness of Innovation Policy Intervention*. Report for the National Endowment for Science, Technology and the Arts (NESTA).

Valdaliso, J. M., Magro, E., Navarro, M., Aranguren, M. J., and Wilson, J. R. (2014) Path dependence in policies supporting smart specialisation strategies: insights from the Basque case, *European Journal of Innovation Management*, 17(4), pp. 390–408.

Whittington, R., (2001) *What is Strategy – and Does it Matter?* London: Thomson Learning.

# 6 Evaluating territorial strategies

*Edurne Magro and James R. Wilson*[1]

## Introduction

The monitoring and evaluation of public policies has garnered increasing attention over recent years for two fundamentally different reasons. Most obviously, the scarcity of public resources characterising many economies since the 1997 financial crisis has provided a strong stimulus for public administrations to ask more searching questions around their policies. As such, policy-makers increasingly need to justify the impacts or 'return on investment' of the policies that they implement to ensure future funding in an era of austerity. Alongside these concrete pressures, however, there has been a second, less obvious force at work in pushing forward the evaluation agenda. This concerns the centrality of evaluation for processes of policy learning. While the two are of course related – evaluation for accountability purposes can also help us learn about policy – a policy learning imperative takes us in a different direction. In particular, in the systemic context in which today's public policies are designed and implemented, the boundaries between policy-makers and policy recipients are increasingly fuzzy.[2] Thus it is not only the so-called policy-makers who are the focus of this policy learning but, rather, the whole collective of stakeholders in the policy process (Bennett and Howlett, 1992; Nauwelaers and Wintjes, 2008). In this context it is widely recognised that monitoring and evaluation can play a critical role in fostering learning as an integral and ongoing part of the policy process (Sanderson, 2002; Howlett *et al.*, 2009; Aranguren *et al.*, 2013; Aragón *et al.*, 2014).

Unsurprisingly, there is also strong acknowledgement that evaluation should play an important role in territorial strategies for shaping competitiveness. In the European context, for example, the European Regional Development Fund has played a part in spreading monitoring practices among the regions, and the combination of 'monitoring and evaluation' are explicitly recognised by Foray *et al.* (2012) as the 'sixth step' in developing research and innovation strategies for smart specialisation (RIS3). Despite this, it remains the case that evaluation is something that is spoken about a lot, and with great agreement on its importance, but actually done very little. Combining this with the rapid translation into practice of the smart specialisation concept, we shouldn't be surprised that there is very little research on how territorial strategies should be evaluated in practice. While it is logical to argue that a core part of any strategy should be the mechanisms that enable evaluation of its success (or lack of it) and facilitate learning to generate improvements, we need to understand more about the type of monitoring and evaluation that is most appropriate for territorial strategies. Indeed, as highlighted in previous chapters in this book, much of the novelty in the current focus on territorial strategy is based on the underlying processes of entrepreneurial discovery that might lead to better ways of prioritising certain activities over others. This would suggest a *priori* an evaluation focus that is dynamic rather than static, that is learning focused, and that can therefore contribute to and help shape these underlying processes.

While there is a strong relationship between policy evaluation and strategy evaluation, they are not the same thing. As suggested by Magro and Nauwelaers in chapter 5, territorial competitiveness strategy can be seen as a framework, within which policies and policy mixes are designed and implemented to give impetus to the overall direction. In the European context, therefore, the key relationship is between research and innovation strategies at the territorial level (RIS3) and the mix of science, technology and innovation policies that are implemented within the territory (the 'policy-mix' step in Foray *et al.*, 2012). It is this relationship that is our focus here. In particular, we aim to bridge the gap between acknowledgements that evaluation should play an important strategic intelligence role in territorial strategy processes and the practice that policy evaluations tend to remain isolated and not well linked to the strategy process at the territorial level. Building on analysis of the 'what', 'what for' and 'how' of territorial strategy in previous chapters, and in particular on the policy complexity issues raised in chapter 5, we bring together perspectives on competitiveness policy evaluation, policy learning and competitiveness benchmarking. This leads to a learning-centred framework that makes a clear distinction between evaluation at different levels (strategy and policy) and emphasises the powerful learning possibilities that can be uncovered through effectively linking these two levels.

In the next section we explore the current state of the art in competitiveness policy evaluation, which we argue is characterised today by the need to deal with increasing policy complexity and to be learning focused. This leads us in the following section to explore the differences between competitiveness policy evaluation and territorial strategy evaluation with reference to the 'what for', 'what' and 'how' questions that should be answered by a territorial strategy. Building from these reflections, we propose an evaluation framework that articulates the relationships between the evaluation of territorial strategy and the evaluation of the competitiveness policies designed to give that strategy impetus. In the final section we make some concluding comments, highlighting the likely challenges in moving towards a coherent and learning-focused evaluation of territorial strategy.

## Competitiveness policy evaluation: complexity and dynamism

Public policy in the economic sphere has traditionally been strongly related to the concept of market failure. Mainstream economics analysis builds on the seminal work of Arrow and Debreu (1954) in taking as a starting assumption the existence of a complete set of perfect markets that will deliver an efficient allocation of resources to different activities within the economy. As such, market failure was first defined as 'the failure of a more or less idealized system of price–market institutions to sustain "desirable" activities or to stop "undesirable" activities' (Bator, 1958: 351). Under this still dominant perspective, government intervention in the economy is seen to be justified only in cases where markets fail to provide an optimal outcome, which they may do for a number of reasons, including the existence of externalities, public goods, indivisibilities, information asymmetries and market (or monopoly) power (Arrow, 1962; Greenwald and Stiglitz, 1986; Tirole, 1988). Furthermore, the notion that governments also fail is widely accepted, especially but by no means exclusively in the context of less developed countries (Datta-Chaudhuri, 1990; Krueger, 1991). This provides a further caveat to the mainstream view of policy intervention: it should take place only when the market fails and the government is capable of improving the situation.[3]

Unsurprisingly, this dominant perspective on the case for government intervention in the economy has marked the practice of evaluating public policies for competitiveness. The mainstream focus on 'failure' to provide an 'optimal' outcome has given birth to the neoclassical concept of 'additionality', whereby public policy interventions are judged on their 'additional' effect (in input and/or output) over that which would have occurred without the intervention. This approach generally takes place *ex post* and with the aim of evaluating past interventions in terms of their correction (or not) of a market failure, hence providing accountability and supporting long term decision-making around future interventions. Moreover, this focus understandably puts a premium on the quantifiable impacts of policy in order to demonstrate additionality, and as such evaluations are usually carried out at the level of individual programmes. It commonly results, for example, in much demanded (by politicians) and easy to interpret 'return on investment' statistics of the type 'for each € invested in policy intervention X, the additional impact on Y is …'.

To give an example from one key area of competitiveness policy, the typical neoclassical rationale for innovation policy intervention is rooted in markets failing to provide for optimal knowledge creation given externalities and appropriability concerns. Essentially, firms invest less than is optimal for society in R&D because they cannot capture all of the societal benefits from their investments, and therefore the associated innovation outputs are sub-optimal for society. A common public policy response, therefore, is to intervene to correct this failure by boosting firm-level investment in R&D inputs, using instruments such as subsidies or tax credits for firms that conduct R&D. This leads to an evaluation of such subsidy or tax credit programmes that seek to determine (i) whether firms have in fact invested more in R&D than they would have done without the intervention or whether government spending has in fact 'crowded out' existing firm spending (input additionality); and (ii) the extent to which the intervention has had an impact on the desired innovation outcomes, however these might be measured (output additionality).[4]

While these types of programme-based evaluations remain commonplace, there are two important trends that have been changing how we approach the evaluation of competitiveness policy: (i) the emergence of evolutionary alternatives to the linear, market failure rationales of neoclassical analysis; and (ii) a large increase in policy complexity such that competitiveness policies increasingly overlap in rationales, domains, space and time. These trends are interrelated, and in combination they provoke challenging technical questions for competitiveness policy evaluation as well as suggesting a more fundamental need for evaluation to be much more learning focused.

The rise of evolutionary rationales is closely associated with policy interventions that respond to 'system problems' inhibiting the creation and transfer of knowledge within 'innovation systems' (Metcalfe, 1995; Smith, 2000; Edquist, 2001; Laranja *et al.*, 2008).[5] This trend has strong relevance for the whole range of competitiveness policies given the recognised centrality of knowledge and innovation to competitiveness and following a broad conception of the innovation system.[6] Most importantly, however, these rationales represent a marked difference from the linearity of neoclassical rationales for policy intervention in that they are not concerned with reaching an 'optimum state' in terms of an input and/or an output. Rather, they are based on the centrality of system relationships for innovation and economic development and the possibility that there are barriers to the flourishing of such relationships that justify policy support. As such they don't replace neoclassical rationales based on market failure but have emerged alongside them in a 'policy mix' (Flanagan *et al.*, 2011). Indeed, the policy complexity highlighted by Magro and Nauwelaers in the previous chapter is a result of this process, combined with others such as the increasing significance of multiple geographical scales of policy governance and multiple operational layers of policy decision-making (Magro and Wilson, 2013; Magro *et al.*, 2014).

In terms of implications for the evaluation of competitiveness policies, the emergence of new policy rationales has necessitated the application of different techniques. While traditional quantitative evaluation tools easily fit rationales that are relatively linear, they are more difficult to apply to systemic innovation policies on account of the difficulty of capturing complex cause–effect relationships and intangible benefits. As a consequence, 'softer' policies such as networking or cluster policies have tended to be approached using qualitative, case-based analysis (Aranguren *et al.*, 2008; Borrás and Tsagdis, 2008; Konstantynova and Wilson, 2014; Pitelis *et al.*, 2006).

There have also been more fundamental changes in approach to evaluation associated with the appearance of new concepts. In particular, different approximations of additionality have emerged to reflect the changes in behaviour among agents in a system that policies under evolutionary rationales are trying to provoke. Commonly grouped together under the broad concept of 'behavioural additionality' (Buisseret *et al.*, 1995), several different interpretations have been employed, ranging from an extension of input additionality to cover scale, scope, acceleration, and the like, to changes in the general conduct of the firm (Gok and Edler, 2012). While the growing use of this concept, particularly in the innovation policy field, demonstrates the importance being attached to understanding and measuring the changes in behaviour sought by today's competitiveness policies, Gok and Edler maintain that it remains a fuzzy concept with both theoretical and methodological shortcomings. In particular, their analysis of its use in a large number of innovation policy evaluations finds that 'the methods used are not appropriate and the multiple dimensions of behaviour and the cascade effects of changes in behaviour on innovation performance and management more generally are not conceptualised' (ibid.: 315).

This fuzziness and these methodological challenges are unsurprising given that, when policy seeks explicitly to change certain types of behaviour in a systemic context, the necessary engagement between the policy and the agents of the system fundamentally blurs the line between policy and its evaluation. As Arnold (2004: 14) suggests, 'evaluation, like the policy-making process, becomes increasingly *evolutionary*, no longer seeking an overall optimum' and 'in a certain sense less rigorous (because it is less complete) as we move to higher levels'.

Today's evaluation challenges are also accentuated by the fact that policy systems typically include both neoclassical and systemic instruments targeted at the same group of agents – for example, targeted R&D subsidies alongside generic networking or cluster policies. Thus an overall understanding of the functioning of the policy system requires the integration of different approaches to additionality (input, output and behavioural) (Bach and Matt, 2002). This implies an underlying approach that appreciates the systemic context of innovation policy alongside a triangulation of the evaluation methods appropriate for different elements of the policy mix (Diez, 2002; Magro, 2012; Aranguren *et al.*, 2014). In this regard there is emerging consensus on the need for better understanding of policy interactions and their impacts through, for example, systemic evaluations (Arnold, 2004; Molas-Gallart and Davies, 2006; Edler *et al.*, 2008). Magro and Wilson (2013), for instnace, propose an evaluation mix protocol as a series of steps designed to take on board the different elements of complexity in arriving at a connected set of evaluations.

In summary, we find ourselves at an interesting juncture in the evaluation of competitiveness policies. Greater demand for evaluation is emerging at a time when there is also increasing policy complexity that makes evaluation more challenging. In this context, evaluations are evolving from being static pieces of information about the effectiveness of individual policies towards being integrated, dynamic learning processes which themselves interact with policy-making practices.[7] In the next section we turn to consider how this scenario relates to the challenges of evaluating territorial strategies.

## From policy evaluation to strategy evaluation: exploring the differences

As argued in chapter 5, strategy and policy are not the same. While strategy concerns the goals and vision of a territory, public policy is an important means to support that strategy and arrive at those goals. There should therefore be a strong link between the two, although in practice there is often either a disconnection or an unconscious assumption that both concepts are the same. When thinking about the evaluation of territorial strategy, therefore, we should expect differences with respect to the evaluation of competitiveness policy, but we should also expect them to be interconnected. To understand this relationship it is useful to turn to the general framework introduced and deepened in the preceding chapters, which conceives territorial strategy with respect to three core questions: 'what for', 'what' and 'how'. We can ask ourselves how evaluation relates to each of these questions, with the aim of drawing a picture of the relevance of evaluation to territorial strategy as a whole.

### *Evaluating the 'what for'*

The first of these questions, the 'what for', must be at the core of territorial strategy evaluation because it represents the ultimate goals of the strategy. If a territory is not progressing towards these ultimate goals, then what value does the strategy have? In chapter 3 Ketels talks about the *ambition* of the region as akin to the ambition of the firm in the business strategy literature. In the regional context he associates this with creating an environment in which citizens can be prosperous and companies can successfully compete, and he suggests that this should be context specific, not simply reflecting an average European ambition, for example. We would strongly echo this. The 'what for' of a territorial strategy must be context specific because it should reflect the underlying socio-economic development objectives of the people within a territory; if it does not, then resulting processes and activities will move the territory in an erroneous direction, generating socially inefficient outcomes (Sugden and Wilson, 2002; Bailey *et al.*, 2006). These objectives are likely to be multiple and to be evolving slowly over time, and, while they will have many common elements, it is impossible to imagine that they will be the same across different territories. In this sense, the very notion of the 'prosperity' or 'type of competitiveness' sought will differ from place to place (Branston *et al.*, 2006; Wilson, 2008).

Given the balance of different objectives likely to characterise the desired development of a territory, evaluating the 'what for' of the strategy is very much related to the concept of competitiveness benchmarking, which typically takes on board a range of different elements (Niosi, 2002; Iurcovich *et al.*, 2006). In this sense, there are essentially three benchmarking approaches that could be followed by a territory seeking to evaluate how well it is progressing towards the objectives of its strategy (Edquist, 2008; Navarro *et al.*, 2014). First, the territory can be compared to itself over time, tracking the evolution of a set of indicators that reflect the 'what for' of the strategy. Second, the performance of the territory in this set of indicators can be compared with a set of specific targets that the strategy establishes as part of its ambition. Finally, progress in this set of indicators can be compared against that of other territories.

The last of these approaches is problematic given the difficulty of finding territories for which it makes sense to make such a comparison – i.e., territories that share both similar characteristics *and* similar strategic goals. Nevertheless, if such comparisons are carried out intelligently, with a careful selection of reference regions, they can offer learning opportunities in terms of the identification of competitive advantages, the mapping of international context, the search for examples to learn or mark a difference from, and setting the basis for policy benchmarking (Navarro *et al.*, 2014; Iurcovich *et al.*, 2006). The most powerful benchmarking approach for evaluating the 'what for' of territorial strategy, however, is likely to be a combination of the first two options: a benchmarking of the territory itself over time in indicators that reflect defined objectives of the strategy, combined with evaluating the achievement of desired targets within the evolution of those indicators.

Although not linked to an explicit territorial strategy, one of the most striking examples of a self-benchmarking exercise in areas that explicitly reflect the underlying development aims of a territory can be found in the Canadian Index of Wellbeing (Michalos *et al.*, 2011). This composite index – itself a set of composite indices in different domains – was first published in 2011 following over a decade of discussions, interaction and research into what really matters to Canadians for their wellbeing.[8] It is built around eight domains of life (community vitality, democratic engagement, education, environment, healthy populations, leisure and culture, living standards, and time use), each of which is the subject of detailed analysis resulting in a composite indicator that is tracked over time. It purports to 'measure what matters' to Canadians and to provide evidence to steer Canada in the right direction, and we would suggest that much can be learned from it for territories that are seeking to evaluate progress towards the objectives that mark the 'what for' of their territorial strategy.

### *Evaluating the 'what'*

While achieving the 'what for' of a strategy must be linked to the overall objectives that a territory seeks to move towards, progress in the 'what' is fundamentally linked to the policy choices that are made to support the priorities (or content) identified and being pursued in that strategy (see chapters 2 and 5). It must be the case, therefore, that evaluating the 'what' is closely related to ongoing practices of policy evaluation. However, one thing is evaluating policies for their own effectiveness, and another is evaluating them in terms of their alignment to the content of the strategy that they are supporting (and ultimately linking this to the benchmarking of objectives reflected in the 'what for' of that strategy). In particular, we need to question what the evaluation of policies and their constituent programmes tell us about the ability to support the priorities identified in the strategy. How well are they aligned? How can we adjust this alignment? How might these policies be interacting with the strategic process, leading to changes in the strategy over time?

In this sense, while evaluating the 'what for' is about evaluating (or benchmarking) *desired strategy outcomes*, evaluating the 'what' is about evaluating *desired policy outcomes*, where these policy outcomes are linked to the content of the strategy itself. One of the main failures that might occur in strategy evaluation is to assume that policies have to be evaluated in terms of their own effectiveness and to forget their evaluation in terms of their contribution to the prioritisations identified in the strategy. It is important to do both in order to reach a true understanding of whether policies are actually supporting what is set out in the strategy. Moreover these two questions should also link back to the evaluation/benchmarking of the 'what for', because the achievement of desired policy outcomes must ultimately contribute to desired strategy outcomes, which themselves may be slowly evolving with the interactions between agents that are part of the strategy and policy processes. This complex scenario poses challenges to policy evaluation in two ways: first, how effectiveness can be evaluated alongside alignment, and in an evolving context; and, second, and maybe more challenging, how it can be ensured that the results of this evaluation feed into the strategic process and provide intelligence for the ongoing evolution of the strategy.

As argued in the previous section, policy evaluation has traditionally taken place for accountability purposes, with a strong emphasis on effectiveness and on demonstrating the existence of different types of additionality. Without denying that much of this evaluation, such as impact evaluation, might be useful for strategic purposes, it is clear that it is not the most adequate for evaluating policy in a dynamic context. In particular, to conduct a good impact evaluation it is normally important to consider a time lag between the policies implemented and the analysis of the results, especially in areas such as innovation in which results take time to flourish. This time lag makes it difficult for impact evaluations to play a role in a strategy that is 'alive' and constantly evolving. While it is not valid to discard such impact evaluations from our considerations of how to evaluate territorial strategy – we know that they can provide results that support learning in policy and potentially also in strategy – this limitation does mean that we have to be careful in how we interpret the results of impact evaluations for a fundamentally dynamic context. In line with our arguments in the preceding section, it further suggests that quantitative impact-type evaluations should be complemented with other more qualitative approaches that are more useful in changing contexts. A triangulation of evaluation techniques – bringing in case-based analysis and participatory approaches – can help in understanding better the reasons behind the impacts and to capture the more intangible elements present in the policy–strategy interface.

Participatory approaches are likely to be particularly important in strategy evaluation because they rely on the involvement of different stakeholders and, as such, respond directly to the challenges associated with both the alignment of policy to strategy content and the dynamism of strategic processes. They might be applied in a continuous way, and alongside more traditional impact evaluations, in order to conduct a continuous policy evaluation that could monitor alignment and feed intelligence on what is working and how into the strategy process. This would be a break from much traditional practice, where policy evaluation has tended to be seen as a process or a task that involves external experts and programme managers as opposed to the whole collective of agents implicated in the policy. As highlighted in chapter 5, the separation between policy-makers and programme managers, for example, might generate an implementation gap, one that is likely to be exacerbated in the case of evaluation given its common association with accountability. Participatory approaches can help to reduce this gap by establishing policy evaluation as a tool both for policy learning and for strategy learning, and most importantly as a route to understanding the links between them.

### *Evaluating the 'how'*

Evaluation of the 'how', like the 'what', is also strongly linked to policy, given that policy seeks to impact on 'how' the strategy is developed and articulated as well as the actual substance of the strategy. Most critically, and as we have argued when addressing evaluation of the 'what', evaluation itself cannot be separated from the strategy process. The entrepreneurial discovery process that is at the core of a territorial strategy is a process that is alive and evolving, involving a wide range of stakeholders from the so-called quadruple helix of business, government, research and civil society. Through this process the activities that form the content of the strategy are first identified, then explored/developed, and then likely altered as new knowledge emerges from ongoing interactions. In chapter 4 of this book, Aranguren and Larrea highlight three dynamic capabilities that appear critical for this process of developing territorial strategy: capability to learn and innovate; capability to generate networks and relationships; and strategic capability for vision generation and leadership. This focus on the 'how' in learning and relationships (and the vision and leadership associated with these) is strongly consistent with the changes in policy evaluation practice that we have suggested is starting to take place. As evaluations evolve from being static pieces of information about the effectiveness of individual policies towards being integrated, dynamic learning processes which themselves interact with policy-making practices, they become more consistent with what is required for the 'how' of territorial strategy.

In other words, the question is not really how we should evaluate the 'how' of territorial strategy but, rather, about seeing evaluation as an integral part of that 'how'. Territorial strategy is not a linear process, and in consequence evaluation cannot be an afterthought. It has to be integrated in a continuous process that feeds the strategy and in which learning becomes the core element of the evaluation task. But learning about what? In the last sub-section, where we mentioned that learning was important for evaluating the 'what' of territorial strategy, we were referring mainly to learning about what has worked and what has not worked, in terms of effectiveness and in terms of the alignment of policy to priorities. This is associated most closely with the concepts of input and output additionality. But learning about processes, learning about the 'how', means going beyond inputs and results and puts the focus on what happens throughout the strategic process in terms of changes in behaviour. It thus implies both a greater focus on the concept of behavioural additionality and recourse to qualitative evaluation methods and tools that help us to capture the more intangible effects of the strategy process.

Seeing evaluation as an integral part of 'how' a territorial strategy takes place also implies a continuous evaluation of the involvement of different agents in the strategy process. This is a very complicated task. Even employing the participatory evaluation techniques suggested in the previous sub-section, it is almost impossible and very time- and cost-inefficient constantly to involve all of the key strategic stakeholders in such processes. Moreover, overkill and/or badly organised processes can stifle participation. The key, therefore, is in finding the right balance; understanding when and how to involve different agents in evaluation exercises; and, above all, knowing how to combine evaluation with other strategic processes core to entrepreneurial discovery so that they fit together in ways that create benefits for participants without taking too much time. In this way, evaluating the 'how' will complement and support the evaluation of the 'what for' and the 'what' in a seamless fashion. All of this implies that the best evaluation is a combination of evaluating the three elements, which will actively contribute to strategic learning processes.

## A learning-centred territorial strategy evaluation framework

In the previous section we argued some principles around the evaluation of the different questions of a territorial strategy – the 'what', the 'what for' and the 'how' – and suggested the need to integrate these in a comprehensive and balanced way. In this section we bring these arguments together in a *territorial strategy evaluation framework* that we propose as useful for understanding the links between the different evaluation elements and therefore as a guide for the evaluation of territorial strategies in practice. It is important to stress that, following the well-accepted principle of territorial policy that 'one size does not fit all' (Tödtling and Trippl, 2005), there is no unique valid recipe for evaluating territorial strategy. What we propose here is designed as a guide for territorial strategy evaluation to be adapted to the specificities of different contexts.

In order to establish a sound evaluation framework that can be adapted to different specific territorial realities, it is important first to make some assumptions about the hierarchy of elements that exist within a territorial strategy. As illustrated in Figure 6.1, there are four levels that are likely to be important when considering how to evaluate territorial strategy. The top two levels make a subtle distinction between a *general strategy* and more *specific strategies*. A general strategy is built around the overall ambition of the territory and the corresponding strategic goals. As such, it reflects what we have talked about above in terms of the 'what for' question, the answer to which must be in line with the underlying socio-economic development objectives of the people that live in the territory. There is a sense in which this is quite an abstract concept, and in many cases it will be easier to see territorial strategy come alive in more specific strategies that focus on certain domains. In the European regional context, for example, this is clear in the development of 'research and innovation strategies for smart specialisation' (RIS3), as promoted by the European Commission, and we can also imagine other domains where more specific strategies might be developed (environment, energy or health, for example). These specific strategies make concrete the general ambition of the region and corresponding strategic goals in certain domains, thus presenting a more focused response to the 'what for' question.

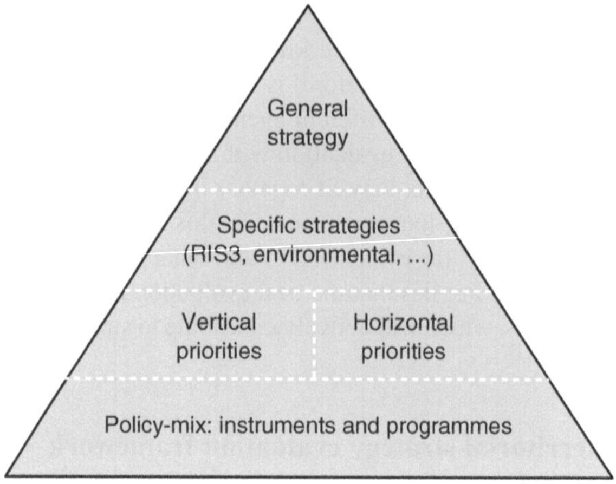


*Figure 6.1* Hierarchy of elements in territorial strategy

The bottom two levels move into the concrete operational aspects of the territorial strategy process – into the 'what' and the 'how' questions. Sitting below the specific strategies are the priorities that are established within each strategy – the priorities established within an RIS3, for example. Following Navarro's analysis in chapter 1, we can distinguish here between *vertical priorities* (the main economic, technological and scientific activities to be prioritised) and *horizontal priorities* (the capabilities of the territorial system as a whole to be prioritised). In both cases, these priorities are related to the 'what' question; they refer to the content of the strategy. In turn, and following the analysis in chapter 5, these priorities are normally articulated through policy instruments and programmes. We refer to the concrete policy measures that support the content of the strategy as the *policy mix*. This mix of instruments can be related to both the 'what' and the 'how' questions of the territorial strategy. The policy mix must be oriented towards the priorities identified in the strategy and therefore aligned with the 'what'; and the way in which the policy mix works in pushing the territories towards these priorities is a core element of the 'how'.[9]

Having established this hierarchy of elements, we can draw a clearer picture of how the different evaluation principles discussed above might fit together in working towards a holistic evaluation of a territorial strategy. Figure 6.2 sets out our proposed framework. Following from the discussion in the previous sections, the central concept is learning. In particular we distinguish two types of learning: learning at the strategy level, or *strategy learning*, and learning at the policy level, or *policy learning*. Each of these types of learning is closely linked with a certain type of evaluation (*strategy evaluation* and *policy evaluation*), although the most critical element of the framework concerns the links between these two levels of evaluation and learning.

The strategy evaluation at the top of the framework refers essentially to the 'what for' of the strategy – to understanding whether the territory is moving

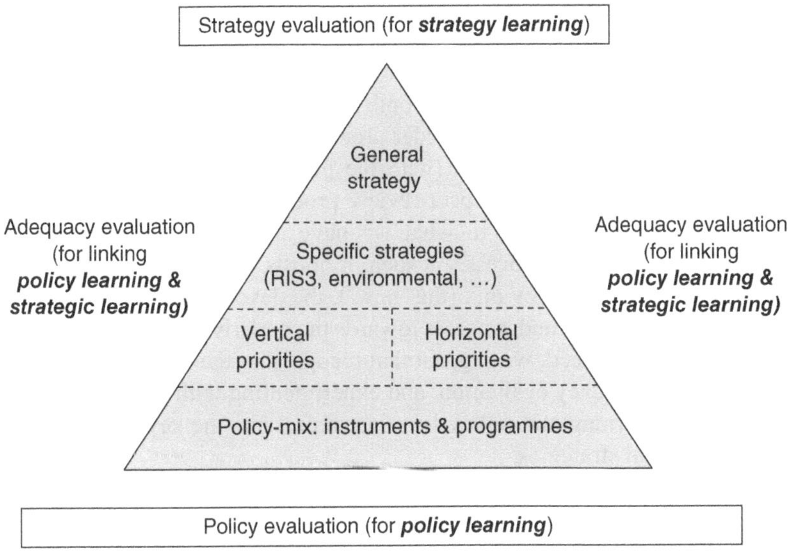


*Figure 6.2* Evaluation framework for territorial strategy

towards its underlying socio-economic development objectives. The policy evaluation at the bottom of the framework refers to both the 'what' and the 'how' of the strategy – to understanding the workings of the policy mix that is being employed to give impetus to the direction of the strategy. As such, strategy evaluation relies on the benchmarking techniques discussed in the previous section – on identifying a set of indicators that best reflect the underlying objectives of the general strategy and/or of the specific strategies and benchmarking these over time (and potentially also in comparison with others where relevant comparators can be found). In contrast, policy evaluation relies on the triangulation of techniques identified as important in previous sections – on weaving together quantitative studies geared at evaluating different types of additionality (input, output, behavioural), with other methods (case-based, participatory, meta-evaluations) better suited to understanding certain more intangible elements and/or capable of bringing a more systemic and dynamic perspective to understanding the policy mix.

The key contribution of this framework, however, is to emphasise the link between these two levels of evaluation, in what we have termed *adequacy evaluation*. This refers to the need to understand, on the one hand, how well the policy mix is aligned with both the content and the objectives of the strategy and, on the other, how it interacts with the evolution of the content and objectives of the strategy over time. As such, it brings together the 'what for', the 'what' and the 'how' and constitutes the central arena for learning in the territorial evaluation sphere.

While strategy evaluation in isolation can lead to some strategy learning, this will be limited to learning around whether or not the territory is progressing towards its objectives, not how this is happening. Likewise, while policy evaluation in isolation can lead to some policy learning, this will be limited to understanding the policies in their own right and at most how different policies interact among themselves, not how they are contributing to the strategy of the territory and how the evolving strategy in turn shapes them. Bringing the two together unlocks a powerful new level of both strategy and policy learning. Based fundamentally on participative stakeholder processes that are built around inputs from policy and strategy evaluation (with the potential also to inject external knowledge through, for example, peer-review processes), adequacy evaluation brings dynamism in evaluation to what we have argued is a fundamentally dynamic territorial strategy process. As such, it boosts our understanding of the interactions between the policy mix (the 'how'), the development of the content of the strategy (the 'what') and progress towards the underlying aims of the strategy (the 'what for'). Indeed, we suggest that recognising the need for processes that support such adequacy evaluation, and experimenting with them so as to tie together strategy learning and policy learning, represents the key challenge for evaluating territorial strategies.

## Concluding remarks

In this chapter we have sought to bridge the gap between the acknowledgement that evaluation should play an important strategic intelligence role in the territorial strategy processes that are so *en vogue* today and the practice that policy evaluations tend to remain isolated and not well linked to the strategy process at the territorial level. Policy evaluation in the innovation field, for example, typically focuses on the evaluation of specific policies per se, or at most their combination in a policy mix. Evaluating territorial strategies, however, implies more than the evaluation of the effectiveness of policy portfolios; these are just one part of the territorial strategy process and must fit together with the content and the objectives of the strategy, both of which are evolving over time.

Rooted in an analysis of the state of the art in competitiveness policy evaluation, our proposed framework has identified what we call *adequacy evaluation* as a critical gap between the fairly prevalent practices of competitiveness policy evaluation and strategy benchmarking. Most territories already evaluate some of the policies that are put in place to boost competitiveness, and most also carry out some form of benchmarking of their progress with respect to a set of core socio-economic outcomes. On the one hand, we are suggesting here that improvements are necessary in each of these to make them more suitable for serving the dynamic, evolving, stakeholder-centred discovery processes that are at the core of a territorial strategy. But, most critically, we are suggesting that they need to be woven together in order to unleash a new set of learning possibilities in the context of the territorial strategy process.

In making these arguments, however, it is important to recognise the limitations of evaluation, which apply as much to strategy as they do to policy or to any other process. In particular, often the desire for a perfect answer is simply unrealistic. Rigorously carrying out a full range of impact evaluations or establishing an ideal set of socio-economic indicators that reflect the objectives of the territory requires large amounts of resources, and in many cases a partial coverage or imperfect analysis is the best that can be hoped for. Likewise, the processes that we have highlighted in this chapter as critical for linking together policy and strategy evaluation and generating powerful new learning opportunities require the ongoing involvement and time of many stakeholders.

Just as prioritisation is a core principle of territorial strategy, therefore, it is also required in the evaluation of territorial strategy. It is impossible to do everything. In this sense we suggest that our territorial strategy evaluation framework, and the arguments contained in this chapter, can help in supporting this prioritisation and in finding an appropriate balance in each specific case. It is important to understand when and how to involve different agents in evaluation exercises, and here many synergies are possible with other strategic processes that are core to territorial entrepreneurial discovery processes. The key is in seeing evaluation as an integral part of the strategic process at the territorial level. Rather than putting all of our evaluation focus on impact studies or on benchmarking, for example, this means prioritising elements of adequacy evaluation alongside these often existing elements.

## Notes

1 This work was supported by the European Commission (FP7 SSH.2012.1.1-3), under Grant number 320131. Any errors are the responsibility of the authors.
2 Indeed, while it remains common to refer to 'policy-makers' as a distinct group of agents responsible for designing public policies, the blurred boundaries between politicians, policy technicians, policy administrators and a whole range of other agents that may be involved in the policy design process, including beneficiaries, mean that the notion of there being a unique 'policy-maker' is inappropriate.
3 That the market–government failure perspective still dominates public policy debate can be seen clearly in responses to the 2007 financial crisis, which has been analysed almost exclusively in terms of market failures and corresponding regulatory (or government) shortcomings that have failed to address or have exacerbated these failures (Branston *et al.*, 2012).
4 In practice it is very difficult to arrive at complete and objective measures of innovation outcomes. See Klette *et al.* (2000) for a critical review of several evaluation studies and reflections on the analytical difficulties in making these evaluations. See also Streicher *et al.* (2004), Cerulli and Potí (2008) and Magro (2012) for a selection of more recent innovation policy evaluation studies in the Austrian, Italian and Basque Country (Spain) contexts.
5 In the context of these evolutionary rationales, Edquist (2008) pleads for a substitution of the term 'failure' for 'problem', arguing that failure is a neoclassical concept.
6 Highlighting the scope of the innovation system concept, Lundvall (2007: 1–2) has argued: '*Without a broad definition of the national innovation system encompassing individual, organizational and inter-organizational learning, it is impossible to establish the link from innovation to economic growth.* A double focus is needed where attention is given not only to the science infrastructure, but also to institutions/organisations [*sic*] that support competence building in labour markets, education and working life.'
7 This is reflected in the growth of popularity of theory-based evaluation approaches (Chen and Rossi, 1983; Chen, 1990), including realist evaluation (Pawson and Tilley, 1997), which seek to understand the intervention logic of policies alongside the real-life mechanisms and processes that determine their effective implementation in practice.

8 For more information, see https://uwaterloo.ca/Canadian-index-wellbeing/.

9 We should note that the policy mix reflects only the governmental interventions that steer towards territorial priorities and leaves apart the actions of other stakeholders; this is why we suggest that it is only part of the how, albeit a very significant part.

## References

Aragón, C., Aranguren, M. J., Iturrioz, C., and Wilson, J. R. (2014) A social capital approach for network policy learning: the case of an established cluster initiative, *European Urban and Regional Studies*, 21(1), pp. 128–45.

Aranguren, M. J., De La Maza, X., Parrilli, M. D., and Wilson, J. R. (2014) Nested methodological approaches for cluster policy evaluation: an application to the Basque Country, *Regional Studies*, doi:10.1080/00343404.2012.750423.

Aranguren, M. J., Iturrioz, C., and Wilson, J. R. (2008) *Networks, Governance and Economic Development*. Cheltenham: Edward Elgar.

Aranguren, M. J., Magro, E., and Wilson, J. R. (2013) La evaluación como herramienta para transformar las políticas de competitividad, *Economía Industrial*, 387, pp. 159–68.

Arnold, E. (2004) Evaluating research and innovation policy: a systems world needs systems evaluations, *Research Evaluation*, 13(1), pp. 3–17.

Arrow, K. (1962) The economic implications of learning-by-doing, *Review of Economic Studies*, 39 (June), pp. 155–73.

Arrow, K. J., and Debreu, G. (1954) Existence of an equilibrium for a competitive economy, *Econometrica*, 22(3), pp. 265–90.

Bach, L., and Matt, M. (2002) Rationale for science & technology policy. In Georghiou, L., Rigby, J., and Cameron, H. (eds), *Assessing the Socio-Economic Impacts of the Framework Programme*. University of Manchester, PREST.

Bailey, D., De Propris, L., Sugden, R., and Wilson, J. R. (2006) Public policy for economic competitiveness: an analytical framework and a research agenda, *International Review of Applied Economics*, 20(5), pp. 555–72.

Bator, F. M. (1958) The anatomy of market failure, *Quarterly Journal of Economics*, 72(3), pp. 351–79.

Bennett, C. J., and Howlett, M. (1992) The lessons of learning: reconciling theories of policy learning and policy change, *Policy Sciences*, 25(3), pp. 275–94.

Borrás, S., and Tsagdis, D. (2008) *Cluster Policies in Europe: Firms, Institutions and Governance*. Cheltenham: Edward Elgar.

Branston, J. R., Rubini, L., Sugden, R., and Wilson, J. R. (2006) The healthy development of economies: a strategic framework for competitiveness in the health industry, *Review of Social Economy*, 64(3), pp. 301–29.

Branston, J. R., Tomlinson, P. R., and Wilson, J. R. (2012) 'Strategic failure' in the financial sector: a policy view, *International Journal of the Economics of Business*, 19(2), pp. 233–53.

Buisseret, T. J., Cameron, H. M., and Georghiou, L. (1995) What difference does it make? Additionality in the public support of R&D in large firms, *International Journal of Technology Management*, 10, pp. 587–600.

Cerulli, G., and Potí, B. (2008) *Evaluating the Effect of Public Subsidies on Firm R&D Activity: An Application to Italy using the Community Innovation Survey*, CERIS-CNR Working Paper no. 9/2008. Rome: CERIS-CNR.

Chen, H.-T. (1990) *Theory-Driven Evaluations*. Thousand Oaks, CA: Sage.

Chen, H.-T., and Rossi, P. H. (1983) Evaluating with sense: the theory-driven approach, *Evaluation Review*, 7(3), pp. 283–302.

Datta-Chaudhuri, M. (1990) Market failure and government failure, *Journal of Economic Perspectives*, 4(3), pp. 25–39.

Diez, M. A. (2002) Evaluating new regional policies: reviewing the theory and practice, *Evaluation*, 8(3), pp. 285–305.

Edler, J., Ebersberger, B., and Lo, V. (2008) Improving policy understanding by means of secondary analyses of policy evaluation, *Research Evaluation*, 17(3), pp. 175–86.

Edquist, C. (2001) Innovation policy: a systemic approach. In Archibugi, D., and Lundvall, A. A. (eds), *The Globalizing Learning Economy*. Oxford: Oxford University Press.

Edquist, C. (2008) *Design of Innovation Policy through Diagnostic Analysis: Identification of Systemic Problems (or Failures)*, CIRCLE Electronic Working Paper 2008/06, University of Lund.

Flanagan, K., Uyarra, E., and Laranja, M. (2011) Reconceptualising the 'policy mix' for innovation, *Research Policy*, 40, pp. 702–13.

Foray, D., Goddard, J., Goenaga Beldarrain, X., Landabaso, M., McCann, P., Morgan, K., Nauwelaers, C., and Ortega-Argilés, R. (2012) *Guide to Research and Innovation Strategies for Smart Specialisation*. Brussels: European Commission.

Gok, A., and Edler, J. (2012) The use of behavioural additionality in innovation policy making, *Research Evaluation*, 21(4), pp. 306–18.

Greenwald, B., and Stiglitz, J. (1986) Externalities in economies with imperfect information and incomplete markets, *Quarterly Journal of Economics*, 101(2), pp. 229–64.

Howlett, M., Ramesh, M., and Perl, A. (2009) *Studying Public Policy: Policy Cycles & Policy Subsystems*. 3rd ed., Oxford: Oxford University Press.

Iurcovich, L., Komninos, N., Reid, A., and Pierrakis, Y. (2006) *Mutual Learning Platform: Blueprint for Regional Innovation Benchmarking*. Luxembourg: Innovation Regions in Europe Secretariat.

Klette, T. J., Moen, J., and Griliches, Z. (2000) Do subsidies to commercial R&D reduce market failures? Microeconomic evaluation studies, *Research Policy*, 29, pp. 471–95.

Konstantynova, A., and Wilson, J. R. (2014) *Comparing Cluster Policies: An Analytical Framework*, Working Paper no. 2014-R01. San Sebastian: Orkestra.

Krueger, A. O. (1991) *Government Failures in Development*, Working Paper no. 3340. Cambridge, MA: National Bureau of Economic Research.

Laranja, M., Uyarra, E., and Flanagan, K. (2008) Policies for science, technology and innovation: translating rationales into regional policies in a multi-level setting, *Research Policy*, 37(5), pp. 823–35.

Lundvall, B.-Å. (2007) *Innovation System Research: Where it Came from and Where it Might Go*, Working Paper Series no. 2007–01, www.globelicsacademy.org/2011_pdf/Lundvall_(post%20scriptum).pdf.

Magro, E. (2012) Evaluation in a systemic world: the role of regional science and technology policy, PhD thesis, University of Deusto.

Magro, E., and Wilson, J. R. (2013) Complex innovation policy systems: towards an evaluation mix, *Research Policy*, 42, pp. 1647–56.

Magro, E., Navarro, M., and Zabala-Iturriagagoitia, J. M. (2014) Coordination-mix: the hidden face of STI policy, *Review of Policy Research*, 31(5), pp. 367–89.

Metcalfe, J. S. (1995) Technology systems and technology policy in an evolutionary framework, *Cambridge Journal of Economics*, 19(1), pp. 25–46.

Michalos, A. C., Smale, B., Labonté, R., Muharjarine, N., Scott, K., Moore, K., Swystun, L., Holden, B., Bernardin, H., Dunning, B., Graham, P., Guhn, M., Gadermann, A. M.,

Zumbo, B. D., Morgan, A., Brooker, A. S., and Hyman, I. (2011) *The Canadian Index of Wellbeing: Technical Report 1.0*. Waterloo, Ontario: University of Waterloo.

Molas-Gallart, J., and Davies, A. (2006) Toward theory-led evaluation: the experience of European science, technology and innovation policies, *American Journal of Evaluation*, 27(1), pp. 64–82.

Nauwelaers, C., and Wintjes, R. (2008) Innovation policy, innovation in policy: policy learning within and across systems and clusters. In Nauwelaers, C., and Wintjes, R. (eds), *Innovation policy in Europe: Measurement and Strategy*. Cheltenham: Edward Elgar.

Navarro, M., Gibaja, J., Franco, S., Murciego, A., Gianelle, C., Hegyi, F. B., and Kleibrink, A. (2014) *Regional Benchmarking in the Smart Specialization Process: Identification of Reference Regions based on Structural Similarity*, S3 Working Paper Series no. 03/2014. Seville: European Commission, Joint Research Centre.

Niosi, J. (2002) National systems of innovations are 'x-efficient' (and x-efective): why some are slow learners, *Research Policy*, 31, pp. 291–302.

Pawson, R., and Tilley, N. (1997) *Realistic Evaluation*. London: Sage.

Pitelis, C., Sugden, R., and Wilson, J. R. (2006) *Clusters and Globalisation: The Development of Urban and Regional Economies*. Cheltenham: Edward Elgar.

Sanderson, I. (2002) Evaluation, policy learning and evidence-based policy making, *Public Administration*, 80(1), pp. 1–22.

Smith, K. (2000) Innovation as a systemic phenomenon: rethinking the role of policy, *Enterprise and Innovation Management Studies*, 1(1), pp. 73–102.

Streicher, G., Schibany, A., and Gretzmacher, N. (2004) *Input Additionality Effects of R&D Subsidies in Austria*. Vienna: Austrian Institute for Economic Research.

Sugden, R., and Wilson, J. R. (2002) Economic development in the shadow of the consensus: a strategic decision-making approach, *Contributions to Political Economy*, 21, pp. 111–34.

Tirole, J. (1988) *The Theory of Industrial Organization*. Cambridge, MA: MIT Press.

Tödtling, F., and Trippl, M. (2005) One size fits all? Towards a differentiated regional innovation policy approach, *Research Policy*, 34(8), pp. 1203–19.

Wilson, J. R. (2008) *Territorial Competitiveness and Development Policy*, Working Paper no. 2008–02. San Sebastian: Orkestra.

# Part II

# Cases in territorial strategy

# 7 The Basque Country

## Past trajectory and path dependency in policy- and strategy-making

*Jesús M. Valdaliso*[1]

### Introduction

This chapter deals with the strategies for competitiveness implemented in the Basque Country, an autonomous region of Spain, between 1980 and 2012. The Basque case is particularly interesting for several reasons. First, it epitomises the experience of old industrial European regions that, ravaged by the economic crisis of the 1970s, were able successfully to transform their industrial and productive structures and to achieve significant progress in terms of economic and social development (Birch *et al.*, 2010; Aranguren *et al.*, 2012a). Second, it is a region with exclusive jurisdiction in many policy matters and with a complex and multilevel policy system, thus representing the dual process that has taken place in Europe involving top-down decentralisation and the transfer of powers from national governments to supranational institutions. In fact, there is no region within the EU than enjoys more political autonomy (Cooke and Morgan, 1998; Morgan, 2013). Third, it provides a good example of the application of the new regional policy that has been evolving in the EU since the 1980s. Analysis of the development of regional strategy over time is uncovered within the framework of the three questions emphasised in the first part of the book: what for, what and how (and who).

History matters when it comes not only to explaining the trajectory of regional development but also to implementing new strategies for a given territory; hence the necessity of adopting a dynamic or historical perspective or of employing historically based explanations (Woolcock *et al.*, 2009; Breznitz, 2010; Martin, 2011; Valdaliso, 2013). Public policies and regional strategies are path dependent – that is, previous regional economic development shapes and conditions the sectors, assets, capabilities and even actors available. Besides, institutions and key regional actors are shaped by their experiences: positive evaluations of the past trajectory will become a source of self-reinforcement in the design and implementation of strategies and policies, while negative ones will have the opposite effect, becoming a source of change. The existence of learning and coordination effects and adaptive mutual expectations among the agents involved in this process and the intrinsic degree of organisational inertia in political institutions is also another source of path dependence (Valdaliso *et al.*, 2011a, 2014). Regional actors, therefore, must 'learn from the past' (Morgan, 2013) before implementing new strategies.

In the first part of the chapter I present the context for the regional strategy implemented in the Basque Country, with particular attention to the salient features of the economy and to the characteristics of the political system and the dynamics of policy-making over this period of more than thirty years. In the second part I analyse the regional strategies in terms of the three aforementioned questions. Finally, I attempt to emphasise the main conclusions that may be inferred from this case.

## The context for regional strategy: polity, economy and industrial policy in the Basque Country

The Basque Country is a small autonomous region located on the north coast of Spain and divided into three historical territories or provinces (Alava, Biscay and Gipuzkoa). It is home to 2.1 million people – about 4.7 per cent of the population of Spain – but since the mid-1990s has accounted for more than 6 per cent of Spain's GDP (OECD, 2011; Aranguren *et al.*, 2012a). In 2008 the region ranked among the top forty European regions in terms of GDP per capita, significantly higher than that of both Spain (34 per 100) and the EU-27 (37 per 100). With educational levels, R&D expenditure and patenting activity much higher than the Spanish average, the Basque Country notably outperformed the rest of Spain in terms of GDP per capita, growth and employment rates both during the economic growth of 1995 to 2007 and from 2008 to 2012 in the context of the current economic crisis (Aranguren *et al.*, 2012a). According to the OECD, the Basque case 'is a regional transformation success story' (OECD, 2011: 14).

From early modern times the Basque Country had a manufacturing and business tradition centred on iron, firearms, the maritime trade and shipping, and related industrial activities such as shipbuilding. Modern industrialisation from 1840s onwards was led by these sectors, along with some new related industries that were appearing in a process of related diversification built on the regional base of knowledge and capabilities: metal products and machinery, transport equipment, electrical goods and equipment, machine tools and consumer goods. Economic growth in the 1950s and 1960s reinforced Basque specialisation in metal-based manufacturing, which was concentrated on the highly protected Spanish market (Valdaliso *et al.*, 2011a; Valdaliso, 2013).

Around 1975 the Basque Country faced a sharp political and economic crisis. First, the death of Franco and the beginning of a political transition in Spain opened up a new period of democratisation and political decentralisation, which had significant consequences on both the political system and the articulation of regional governance in the country. Second, like other European regions that were industrialised early and came to specialise in heavy industry (North Rhine-Westphalia, Northeast England, Wales and Scotland, among others) the Basque Country was particularly hard hit by the economic crisis of the late 1970s and early 1980s. As a result of job losses in industry and the building sector, the unemployment rate rose from 3 per cent in 1975 to 24 per cent in 1986. Basque businessmen had to cope with growing labour militancy and suffered from extortion by ETA, an extreme-left terrorist group that sought the independence of the Basque Country. The existence of ETA terrorism, moreover, reduced the possibility of attracting foreign direct investment to the region.[2] This led to a significant reduction in the region's GDP per capita, which between 1975 and 1980 fell behind the EU-15 average, from 99 to 74 per cent, and a major industrial reconversion in several sectors (Aranguren *et al.*, 2012a: 143–5; Porter *et al.*, 2013).

The harsh economic and business climate, along with the momentum of political change in those years, acted as a kind of external jolt that shook up the region's actors, paved the way to a radical breakthrough with the past, and made institutional and economic change easier (Aranguren *et al.*, 2012a; Valdaliso *et al.*, 2011a; Valdaliso, 2013). The new constitution of 1978 granted considerable autonomy to Spain's autonomous communities in general and to the Basque Country in particular. By the Statute of Autonomy for the Basque Country, approved in 1979, the Basques were allowed to elect their own government, which became responsible for providing some services formerly provided by the national government (education, health, economic development, infrastructure); it also renewed and updated the old system of economic agreements between the three Basque provinces and Spain, which gave their respective provincial councils full authority to set tax rates and collect taxes (Aranguren *et al.*, 2012a: 147–50; Zubiri, 2010).

From 1980 onwards, as a result of a parallel process, on the one hand, of transferring competences from the Spanish national government to the regional one and, on the other, the creation of a new regional and local administration (the Basque government and the three provincial councils) with powers and competences to design, fund and develop their own policies, a policy space with multilevel governance has emerged in the Basque Country (see Table 7.1). As Magro *et al.* (2014) have stated, 'the Basque region is a good example of multi-level policy complexity due to the coexistence in the same region of policies from at least five different administrative levels: European, Spanish, Basque, the three sub-regional provinces and the county/municipality level.' The new regional administration was created almost from scratch, without the inertia or routines inherited from the past. For example, the Department of Industry started with a small team of high government officials recruited from the private sector and very close to industry. Both characteristics gave government action a high degree of flexibility. According to the first minister of industry, the Basque government in those early years was managed like a private firm (Aranguren *et al.*, 2012a: 149).

The first regional government was constituted in 1980, headed by the Basque Nationalist Party, which, either alone or in coalition with other political parties, ruled successive regional governments until 2009. Between 2009 and 2012 the Basque Socialist Party was in office, and it was followed by another government led by the Basque Nationalist Party. Throughout this period, but particularly during the 1980s and 1990s, the Basque government, through its Department of Industry, played an outstanding leading role in the regional strategy for economic

*Table 7.1* Multilevel policy governance in the Basque Country

| *Level of government* | *Powers* | |
|---|---|---|
| European Union | Development (structural funds)<br>Monetary policy<br>Tariffs and currency | Economic regulation (competition, environment, etc.)<br>Common agricultural policy |
| Spanish government | Defence and foreign policy<br>Economic regulation (education, labour relations, energy, financial system)<br>Social security (retirement pensions) and assistance (unemployment subsidies) | Large transport infrastructure (highways, ports, railways)<br>Payments to EU administration<br>Customs, prisons |
| Basque government | Health<br>Education and training<br>Law & order and police<br>Social assistance and welfare<br>Economic promotion and development: agriculture and fishing, industry, commerce and tourism, transport, environment | R&D, STI policy<br>Labour and employment, lifelong training<br>Railways (regional), underground system and small ports<br>Housing and urbanism<br>Culture |
| Provincial councils (*Diputaciones*) | Treasury and tax collection<br>Roads, transport and hydraulic infrastructure<br>Economic promotion and development<br>Agriculture and forestry | Social assistance and welfare<br>Urbanism<br>Culture |
| Municipalities (*Ayuntamientos*) | Sports and culture<br>Housing and urbanism<br>Public health | Public safety<br>Urban transport<br>Social services |

Source: Aranguren *et al.* (2012a: 148).

development. This was the result of the weak position of the regional business elite, which since the early nineteenth century had traditionally assumed that role, the strong impact of the economic crisis of the early 1980s and 1990s, and the persistence of ETA terrorism (Azua, 2006; Ardanza, 2011; Porter *et al.*, 2013; Valdaliso, 2013). In fact, the widespread perceived need felt by most of regional actors to counteract the negative image and effects of ETA terrorism allowed for broad-based agreement on industrial policy plans across most of the political parties (Aranguren *et al.*, 2012a: 205, 391).

The Basque economy enjoyed a recovery in the second half of the 1980s. Then, after a short crisis from 1991 to 1993, came a long period of sustained growth that lasted until 2007. From 1994 to 2007 the economy experienced higher rates of growth than the EU-15 average and that of Spain; the GDP per capita of the Basque Country moved up in the ranking of European regions (NUTS2) to reach a position in the top forty (Aranguren *et al.*, 2012a: 150–60). According to several indicators of economic performance, economic structure and innovation, at the end of this period the region compared well with Catalonia and Navarre in Spain, North-Rhine Westphalia and Baden Württemberg in Germany, Emilia-Romagna and Lombardy in Italy, and the West Midlands in the United Kingdom (Navarro *et al.*, 2011).

In accordance with a range of different quantitative and qualitative indicators,[3] four distinct stages can be perceived in the evolution of industrial policies in the Basque Country between 1980 and 2012:

- the 1980s, when a new regional administration was created and when the main challenge was to cope with the severe economic crisis in the region and to carry out a substantial industrial reconversion in many sectors;
- the 1990s, when the regional government attempted to deal with the economic crisis early in the decade and at the same time introduced fresh policies to face new challenges related to the advent of the single European market and to promote the internationalisation of the economy;
- the 2000s, when a booming economy (and budget) allowed for ambitious programmes aimed at fostering the internationalisation and science-driven diversification of the economy; and
- the years from 2008 onwards, when the economic recession resulted in increasing pressures for fiscal consolidation and the government's priorities, although continuing to be centred on internationalisation and innovation, also incorporated help for firms to cope with and survive the crisis.

In the first period, the reconversion programmes absorbed most of the Department of Industry's budget and efforts. In the 1990s, most of the budget was consumed by the technology and internationalisation programmes, although other horizontal policies (competitiveness and business change) began to be developed. From 1999 to 2008 the innovation and internationalisation programmes accounted for the great part of the budget. The Department of Industry continued the broad policy lines of the 1990s governments, but with a stronger emphasis on the internationalisation of Basque firms and on the diversification of the economy towards science-driven sectors. The same holds true for the last period analysed, in spite of the increasing financial restraints resulting from economic recession (Aranguren *et al.*, 2012a: 357–84).

Over time, Basque industrial policy has shown an increasingly path dependent trajectory for several reasons. First, there has been striking political continuity in the Basque government and in the team of policy-makers in charge of the Department of Industry and its main agencies (SPRI – the Society for Industrial Promotion and Reconversion – and EVE – the Basque Energy Board) since the early 1980s. This continuity, along with the positive outcomes and evaluation of the first policy plans and the sheer institutional inertia that tends to appear in every organisation, reinforced a widespread rule of thumb in the Industry Department of 'building on what already exists'. This in turn accounted for the long-term perspective of many of the policy plans, programmes and institutions. It also eventually brought about self-reinforcing learning and coordination effects and adaptive mutual expectations among the policy-makers, high-government officials and main socio-economic agents,

*Table 7.2* Stages, actors, problems and challenges of the Basque industrial policy, 1980–2012

| | *Policies to cope with the crisis (1980–90)* | *Transition policies (1991–8)* | *Policies for competitiveness and growth (1999–2008)* | *Policies for competitiveness and against the recession (2009–12)* |
|---|---|---|---|---|
| *Political constituencies (and presidents and parties)* | I–II (C. Garaikoetxea, PNV)<br>II–III (J. A. Ardanza, PNV) | IV–V (J. A. Ardanza, PNV) | VI–VII–VIII (J. J. Ibarretxe, PNV) | IX (P. López, PSE) |
| *Ministers of industry (and political party)* | Javier García-Egocheaga (PNV)<br>Juan C. Isasti (PNV)<br>José I. Arrieta (PNV)<br>R. González-Orús (PSE) | Jon Azua (PNV)<br>Javier Retegui (PNV) | Josu J. Imaz (PNV)<br>Ana Aguirre (PNV) | Bernabé Unda (PSE) |
| *Economic context, policy problems, and challenges* | Crisis and industrial restructuring<br>Scarce technological infrastructure<br>Transition problem (*lock-in*) | Crisis (1991–3) and growth<br>Single European market<br>Global competition and internationalisation | Growth<br>Internationalisation<br>Diversification<br>'Second Great Transformation' | Depression<br>Fiscal consolidation<br>Internationalisation<br>Diversification |
| *Main fields* | Industrial restructuring and promotion (sector and firms) | Industrial restructuring and promotion (sector and firms)<br>Competitiveness (clusters)<br>Business change (horizontal) | Innovation and internationalisation<br>Competitiveness (clusters)<br>Business change (horizontal) | Innovation and internationalisation<br>Competitiveness (clusters)<br>Openness |
| *Types of policies and government role* | Top-down (design and implementation)<br>Sector and firm focused | Top-down (design and implementation)<br>First horizontal policies (design)<br>Sectors and clusters | Top-down (implementation)<br>Horizontal policies (design, implementation and first steps of evaluation) | Horizontal policies (design, implementation and evaluation)<br>Cross-department policies |

| | | | | |
|---|---|---|---|---|
| *Instruments* | Financial | Financial<br>Soft | Financial<br>Soft | Financial<br>Soft |
| *Coordination problems and/or challenges* | Government–firms<br>Government–technology centres and state agencies<br>Basque government–provincial councils | Government–technology centres and state agencies<br>Government–firms and cluster associations<br>Firms–cluster associations | Different government departments (Industry and Education)<br>Government–state agencies, technology centres and cluster associations<br>Technology centres–universities and other PROs<br>Firms–cluster associations | Different government departments (presidency, Industry, Education and Health)<br>Basque government–provincial councils<br>Government–state agencies, technology centres and cluster associations<br>Technology centres–universities and other PROs<br>Firms–cluster associations |
| *Additionality* | Input and output | Input and output<br>Behaviour | Input and output<br>Behaviour | Input and output<br>Behaviour |
| *Milestones* | PRE<br>PET<br>Energy Policy Plan 1982–90 | General economic policy plans<br>Plan 3R<br>Competitiveness programme<br>PTI-PCT<br>Plan 3E2000 & 3E2005 | PIPE & PCEIS (Euskadi 2015)<br>PESI & Agenda Digital, Agenda Digital 2015<br>PCTI 2001–4 & 2010 | PCE (2010–13)<br>PCTI 2015<br>Strategy 3E2020<br>EcoEuskadi 2020 |

Source: Updated from Aranguren *et al.* (2012a: 186), Navarro *et al.* (2014: table 1) and Magro *et al.* (2014).

Notes: PNV: Basque National Party; PSE: Basque Socialist Party. The acronyms quoted within Milestones cells refer to the initials (in Spanish) of the most important industrial policy plans.

thus making their joint alignment around a shared vision and strategy for regional development easier.

Policy path dependence in this case did not lead to a situation of lock-in as a result of three mechanisms: the addition of new organisations, actors and institutions to the regional policy system; greater resort to horizontal rather than sector and vertical policies; and the subsequent creation of a regional policy network increasingly autonomous of the political change in the Basque government and the provincial councils (Navarro *et al.*, 2014; Valdaliso *et al.*, 2014). Yet these changes also made the regional policy system more complex, resulting in some coordination and duplicity problems both between different institutions, agents and organisations and across the three policy layers – political (government, parliament, provincial councils), administrative (public agencies, STI council, cluster associations) and operational (firms, knowledge infrastructures, investors) (Morgan, 2013; Magro *et al.*, 2014; see Table 7.2).

## Regional strategies for economic development

The strategies for economic development implemented in the Basque Country over this period co-evolved with the socio-economic context, the stages of economic development, and the dynamics of polity and policy-making in the region (Breznitz, 2007; Aranguren *et al.*, 2012a: 388–90). Three distinct strategies for regional development can be observed throughout the period under analysis that broadly correspond with the same stages identified for industrial policy:

- the 1980s, defined by the creation of a new regional government and administration (self-government) and the need to carry out a substantial and comprehensive industrial restructuring of the economy;
- the 1990s, when a new strategy for competitiveness based on clusters and efficiency was explicitly formulated; and
- the period from 1999 onwards, when the successive governments implemented a long-term sustained strategy focused on innovation and science-driven industrial diversification (see Table 7.3).

Throughout this period, as happened in other leading European regions (Walendowski *et al.*, 2012: 11), strategy followed a political mission that in the Basque case consisted of strengthening self-government and autonomy – an underlying but at the same time very clear objective of the Basque Nationalist Party, which ruled the region between 1980 and 2008.

Regarding the *what for*, three types of strategic objectives may be distinguished: economic, social and environmental. In the 1980s, the main government goals were to stop the industrial decline and reduce the gap in per capita GDP with leading European nations; to fight unemployment and social unrest and cope with severe pollution problems; and to build up, almost from scratch, a regional government with increasing powers and competences. In the 1990s, the goal was to converge with the leading European nations in terms of per capita GDP and other indicators of social development and innovation. For the first time, a unique value proposition was coined, centred on competitiveness (based on productivity and quality), solidarity (based on employment opportunities and inclusiveness) and environmental sustainability. Successive regional governments from 1999 onwards attempted to upgrade that strategy, driving the Basque Country to a new stage of economic development – science and knowledge-based – that would allow the region to maintain its parity within the EU and even increase its level in terms of per capita GDP and productivity, while at the same time achieving the social and environmental indicators envisaged in the Lisbon strategy (see Table 7.3).

With regard to the *what*, the Basque government's clear priority from the very beginning centred on industry and related sectors such as energy and knowledge-intensive business services. In the 1980s, efforts were directed towards industrial reconversion of sectors in crisis (such as iron and steel, metal products and machinery, shipbuilding and transport equipment, appliances, machine tools) and the technological upgrading and modernisation of existing industries through the diffusion of micro-electronics. According to the first Ministry of Industry, 'the first thing we did with the traditional industry was not to let it die. The key issue was to keep on doing what we already did, but doing it better … which meant changing everything except the markets' (Bizkarguenaga, 2001: 169; Ardanza, 2011: 174).

In the 1990s, a new cluster-based strategy of upgrading was initiated, along with the first attempts to promote industrial diversification into new sectors, such as the aeronautics industry, telecommunications and ICTs, or creative industries linked to Bilbao's transformation driven by the Guggenheim Museum. The successful development of the aeronautics industry, in particular, can be regarded as a smart specialisation strategy of extending existing firms from sectors and markets in crisis (special steels, automotive) to new high-tech sectors and more dynamic markets (Aranguren *et al.*, 2012a: 197–201; Aranguren *et al.*, 2012b; Porter *et al.*, 2013).

In the first years of the twenty-first century, and building on the successful experience of the aeronautics industry, the Basque government embarked on a smart diversification strategy around high-tech and science-based sectors (bios, nano-sciences, advanced manufacturing, renewable energies), operationalised by strong support for the creation of a scientific infrastructure (Aranguren *et al.*, 2012a: 208–16; Aranguren *et al.*, 2012b). In any case, industry has remained a key priority of successive Basque governments. According to the last industrialisation plan (2014–16) approved by the Basque government: 'the Basque Country is a country with an industrial history and an industrial present, and we believe that our future will be based on industry too, as a driver of wealth and welfare' (Gobierno Vasco, 2014: 3).

This strong bet on industry and related sectors was combined with serious efforts to develop and improve physical, technological and, later on, knowledge infrastructure. During the 1980s and 1990s, technology centres and technology parks concentrated on developing technological and engineering capabilities to make easier the massive process of upgrading and modernisation required by Basque industry. Since the 2000s, and in line with the new

*Table 7.3* Regional strategies in the Basque Country, *c.* 1980–2012

| | *1980–90*<br>*Self-government and industrial restructuration* | *1991–8*<br>*Clusters and efficiency- driven competitiveness* | *1999–2012*<br>*Towards R&D-based innovation and diversification* |
|---|---|---|---|
| *Goals* | Stop the decline and reduce per capita GDP gap with EU-15<br>Fight against high unemployment and social unrest (reactive)<br>Fight against severe pollution problems (reactive) | Converge with EU-15 in per capita GDP<br>Solidarity and social welfare (based on employment opportunities and education and health services)<br>First explicit goals on quality of the environment | Per capita GDP well above the EU-15<br>Social and environmental objectives adapted to the Lisbon strategy: in the social field the emphasis moves from employment to more ambitious welfare and social objectives; adoption of a formal strategy towards more sustainable growth |
| *Unique value proposition* | Self-government, industrial restructuring (cost competitiveness), building up fundamentals for economic development and solidarity | Clusters, quality and efficiency-based competitiveness | Diversification and competitiveness (based on R&D) and solidarity, more systemic and shared by different stakeholders |
| *Economic sectors*<br>*Scientific and technological areas* | Restructuring and upgrading of traditional industry | Restructuring and upgrading of traditional industry<br>Industrial diversification: aeronautics, ICTs, creative and cultural industries | Traditional industry: size (tractor groups) and location, cluster development<br>Smart industrial diversification: bios, nano-technologies, advanced manufacturing, renewable energies, tourism, etc. |
| *Assets/innovation*<br>*Assets/people*<br>*Assets/physical infrastructure*<br>*Assets/institutions and social context* | Technological infrastructure<br>Educational infrastructure<br>Physical, energy, and finance and investment infrastructure<br>New institutions (Basque government and *diputaciones*) with high level of self-government (progressive transfer of powers from national government)<br>Terrorism, social unrest and bad public image of entrepreneurs | Technological infrastructure<br>Human capital improvement<br>Physical, energy, and finance and investment infrastructure<br>Transfer of powers stopped until 1996<br>Terrorism, but increasing social appreciation of entrepreneurship | Technological and scientific infrastructure<br>Qualified human capital<br>Physical, energy, and finance and investment infrastructure<br>Transfer of powers in R&D, employment and others from 2010 onwards<br>Decreasing social support and power of terrorism (which ceased in 2011) |
| *Main actors: private/ public* | Firms and sectors | Sectors, clusters and business associations<br>Urban regeneration | Sectors, social capital based on cooperation within and across clusters and local networks, socially shared challenges (innovation, international branding *Made in Euskadi*)<br>Embryonic technological platforms |

| | | | |
|---|---|---|---|
| *Main actors/ type of firm* | Traditional industry: big firms involved in national government restructuring programmes; restructuring and upgrading of SMEs | Traditional industry: big firms less involved in national programmes; restructuring and upgrading of SMEs | Policies to foster cooperation to increase SMEs' competitiveness<br>Support for creation of tractor business groups |
| *Innovation agents* | Technological centres | Technological centres, KIBS | CICs and BERCs |
| *Relationship with other territories (regional, national, global)* | Lack of cooperation with neighbouring regions<br>Spain: transfer of powers and industrial policy coordination, friction until 1984, then agreement; to diminish the dependence on the Spanish market<br>EU: integration and increasing economic relations<br>Rest of the world: beginning of a slight openness | Lack of cooperation with neighbouring regions<br>Spain: collaboration but friction (on taxation policy); to diminish the dependence on the Spanish market<br>EU: integration and increasing economic relations<br>Rest of the world: internationalisation into Latin America | Lack of cooperation with neighbouring regions<br>Spain: friction and increasing political conflict; to diminish the dependence on the Spanish market<br>EU: integration and increasing economic relations<br>Rest of the world: internationalisation into Latin America, Eastern Europe and Asia |
| *Relations between sectors, areas and actors* | Sectors (to implement plans and get support) and territories (concentration of Mondragon group; birth of local development agencies) | Sectors and clusters (competitive upgrading) and territories (strengthening of local development agencies; divisional restructuring of Mondragon group)<br>Support to associations and networks (Euskalit, Saretek, etc.) | Strengthening of sector and cluster relations and relations between the different territories<br>Increasing support to institutions aimed at fostering networking between different agents (Basque STI Council, Innobasque, Innovanet) |
| *Participation of stakeholders, degree of social and political consensus, and degree of formalisation* | Social conversations with social and economic agents (labour unions and business associations), but clear governmental leadership<br>Political consensus on industrial policy (explicit from 1987)<br>Lack of a strategic plan: strategy as a result of different policies | Social dialogue with businessmen but governmental leadership; friction with labour unions<br>Explicit political consensus on industrial policy<br>Strategic plan, classic approach, *top-down* | Increasing participation in policy design, but still need of improvement in policy learning<br>Improvements in shared leadership and vision<br>Non-explicit political consensus on industrial policy<br>Strategic plan, classic ('future can be created') and process approach |

Source: Updated from Aranguren *et al.* (2012a: 394–5) and Magro *et al.* (2014).

smart and science-driven diversification strategy, there has been a gradual change towards the creation of a scientific infrastructure and the development of capabilities in science and basic research (with the setting up of cooperative research centres –CICs – and Basque excellence research centres – BERCs). The long-sustained priority given to technology over science in the Basque STI policy had resulted in a workforce technically well trained and equipped, but with some weaknesses and shortages in knowledge of foreign languages and transversal competencies (Navarro, 2010, 2013; OECD, 2011).

The main business actors targeted were large and medium enterprises, business groups and cooperatives (notably the Mondragon group). In particular, the regional government tried to promote the creation of large companies and business groups able to compete in the global market (Valdaliso, 2010). The successful development of several cluster initiatives in the 1990s gradually changed the government's approach from a sector-based perspective to a cluster-based one, with an increasing emphasis on transversal and horizontal programmes aimed at fostering intercluster and intersector cooperation (clearly visible in the smart specialisation strategies launched since the early 2000s). With regard to the regional innovation system, technology and research centres, rather than universities, were prioritised. This was due, on the one hand, to the strong stake in technological upgrading and modernisation of existing industry in the 1980s and 1990s and, on the other, to the sheer weaknesses of Basque universities in R&D capabilities. From 2004 onwards, however, universities began to play a more important role within this innovation system, and their links with technology centres and firms have been strengthened. Nevertheless, there is still room for improvement on these issues (Olazarán *et al.*, 2009; Navarro, 2010, 2013).

With regard to the relationship between the Basque Country and other territories at different levels, a long-sustained priority of successive governments has been to overcome its economic dependency on the Spanish market and to forge and strengthen relationships (in the 1980s and 1990s) with the rest of Europe and (since the 2000s) countries in Latin America and Asia. Internationalisation efforts were focused on promoting exports and the establishment of commercial and manufacturing facilities for Basque companies worldwide, and were reinforced from 2008 onwards to counter the severe recession in the Spanish economy. However, the priority has, so far, been more in facilitating firms and people to go abroad than in attracting foreign firms and talent to the Basque Country, although some new institutions and programmes have appeared with this aim, such as Ikerbasque (2007) and Bizkaia Talent (2005).

Until the 2000s, there were very few initiatives related to the internal structure and articulation of the region, either top-down or bottom-up, such as local development agencies. This was due, first, to the strong priority given by the Basque government to self-government and the tensions with the national government on the transfer of powers and on some industrial policies and programmes; and, second, to the coordination problems and even disputes that appeared between the Basque government and those of the provincial councils in some constituencies.

As to the process, the *how*, there is a clear trend towards increasingly formalised, deliberate and even proactive strategies over time. There was no such a thing as a formal and deliberate – e.g., on paper – strategy in the 1980s. Rather, it emerged from the different programmes and plans of the regional government, although there was a staff group of shadow advisers responsible for designing some key priorities. From 1991 onwards, successive governments designed and implemented strategies for regional development, highly formalised, and with a classical top-down approach until the early years of the twenty-first century (Aranguren *et al.*, 2012a: 390–93).

The Basque government played a clear leading role in this process in the 1980s on account of the weak position and poor public image of the business elite (suffering heavily from an economic crisis and its accompanying social costs), which was also affected by the extortion activities of the ETA terrorist group (Azua, 2006; Ardanza, 2011; Aranguren *et al.*, 2012a). Strong government leadership continued in the 1990s and in the early 2000s, although the business sector became involved in several public–private initiatives, still top-down designed and launched (cluster initiatives, Euskalit), and there was greater policy coordination between the regional government and the provincial councils (although there was still room for improvement here).

Since 2004, with the creation of a 'Competitiveness Forum' bringing together over one hundred people from the business sector, academia, trade unions, political parties and the government,[4] there was a clear shift towards a more horizontal and participative approach to policy design and implementation, with greater emphasis on the process. New organisations aimed at fostering networking between different agents were created in this period, such as the Basque STI Council, Innobasque and the Innovanet Network (all in 2007), as well as an academic institution, the Orkestra-Basque Institute of Competitiveness (2006), conceived as a research centre to give academic support and advice to regional agents in the field of competitiveness. Policy coordination between the regional government and the provincial councils improved. Further, the continuity of policy programmes and institutions such as cluster associations aimed at promoting cooperation, along with the existence of learning and coordination effects and adaptive mutual expectations among the socio-economic agents of the regional policy network, not only reinforced policy path dependency but also resulted in higher levels of social capital (Valdaliso *et al.*, 2011b; Aragón *et al.*, 2012; Aranguren *et al.*, 2013). It was in this latter stage when a common alignment of the different stakeholders around shared goals (innovation, international positioning through the brand *Made in Euskadi*), a shared strategy, and even vision about the future of the region began to be seen in the three different layers of the policy-making system – political, administrative and operational. However, both the increasing complexity of the regional policy system and the attempt to implement more systemic and holistic policies brought about new coordination problems and even rivalries between and within different government departments and levels, state agencies and other agents (Magro *et al.*, 2014).

In any case, strong government leadership along with the progressive strengthening of self-government over more than three decades seems to have resulted in the creation of a well-qualified bureaucracy very close to industry interests (Breznitz, 2007) and, more broadly, in the creation of substantial administrative capabilities in both policy- and strategy-making (Walendowski *et al.*, 2011, 2012). Over time, the long trajectory of policy and strategy learning, together with the increasing resort to horizontal and more participatory institutions, allowed the Basque Country to develop dynamic capabilities (of the sort described in chapter 4 of this book) critical to reshape or reinvent its strategy for economic development and to help the region to broaden the scope of alternatives or paths to be taken in the near future.

## Conclusions: history lessons for regional development

This chapter has analysed the industrial policies and the strategies for economic development designed and implemented in the Basque Country from circa 1980 to 2012. The Basque experience is particularly interesting for regional development literature for several reasons: as an old industrial European region that managed successfully to cope with the economic crisis of the 1980s and to transform itself into a knowledge-based economy and grow; as providing a good example of the dual process of political decentralisation in Europe and of multilevel policy complexity; and as a case for testing the so-called new regional policy that was adopted in the EU in the 1980s.

The Basque Country faced radical political and institutional change around the late 1970s in the middle of a harsh economic crisis. Its industrial policy in the 1980s was the outcome, on the one hand, of a new administration and a new government, with a clear political mission that assumed the leadership of the region and implemented new industrial policies, and, on the other, of an industrial legacy (conforming to the existing regional base of knowledge and capabilities) on which the new path of economic modernisation was built. Over time, both policy- and strategy-making in the Basque Country became increasingly path dependent for several reasons: the striking political continuity in the regional government, the Department of Industry (in charge of such issues) and its main agencies, and even in the team of policy-makers in control; the long-term perspective of most of the policy plans, programmes and institutions created throughout this period; the gradual appearance of self-reinforcing learning and coordination effects and adaptive mutual expectations among the regional agents; and the sheer institutional inertia that usually appears in every organisation. Path dependence, however, did not lead the region to a lock-in situation because of the continual addition of new organisations, agents and institutions, which has served to increase the complexity of the policy system. And the same holds true for the region's economic evolution, thanks to a process of technological modernisation in the existing industries and of economic diversification into new high-tech industries and knowledge-intensive business sectors.

With regard to regional competitiveness and STI policies, the Basque Country has always been at the forefront of innovative policies in Europe, from the first STI policies of the 1980s, to the cluster policy of the 1990s, to the RIS3 policies of the late 2000s. While the region had strong leadership from the government, with a clear political mission, over time the private sector became increasingly involved in many joint initiatives, policies became less top-down and vertical and more bottom-up and horizontal, and the regional administration developed strong capabilities in policy- and strategy-making. However, the greater complexity of the policy system resulted in new coordination problems and/or challenges.

The regional strategy co-evolved with the socio-economic context, the stages of economic development, and the dynamics of polity and policy-making in the region in a systemic way that makes it very difficult to distinguish between causes and consequences. There was no formal strategy for economic development in the 1980s, although there was something akin to a strategy for the region designed by a shadow group of advisers of the ruling political party. Since the 1990s, strategies have become more planned and formalised, with clear economic, social and environmental goals (*what for*) and with the development of a unique value proposition and even a shared vision for the region. Thus, regional strategy has become increasingly explicit over time.

From the very beginning, and mostly on account of the negative impact of terrorism, it was pretty clear that the Basque Country could attract little foreign direct investment and had to rely on its own resources and capabilities. Building on the existing regional industrial fabric, the government made a clear bet on manufacturing and related sectors – energy and knowledge-intensive business services – upgrading these in the 1980s, extending and diversifying them in the 1990s and 2000s, and with an increasing emphasis on innovation and internationalisation as drivers of industrial growth. According to this evolving '*what*', government resources were allocated to physical, educational and knowledge infrastructure (technological in the 1980s and 1990s, scientific in the 2000s) and to large and medium enterprises, cooperatives and business groups (increasingly internationalised).

Last, but not least, regardless of the ups and downs of the economic cycle, the divergent economic interests of the actors involved in this process, and even the political confrontation among the political parties about the relationship between the Basque Country and Spain, the regional trajectory of economic development shows that a certain basic consensus seems to have developed among the main socio-economic and political agents as to the fundamental strengths of the region and its sources of prosperity and as to which sectors enjoy distinctive competitive advantages (Valdaliso, 2013). This has been the result, somehow, of a process of 'self-discovery' (Hausmann and Rodrik, 2003), or policy learning by doing, and experience very similar to the 'entrepreneurial discovery process' suggested by the RIS3 literature (Foray, 2013).

What are the 'ultimate' lessons to be learnt from the recent history of Basque regional development? Put simply, I would say that, first, institutions and politics – the art of 'creating, choosing between, and acting on, different alternatives' (Breznitz, 2007: 10) – matter for regional development, as they make choices, set up priorities and create paths for development. And, second, and more broadly, history matters in the explanation of regional economic and institutional change and evolution. Coming from an economic historian, these conclusions are hardly surprising, but they are in line with the emergent discipline of evolutionary economic geography (Boschma and Frenken, 2006; Martin and Sunley, 2006; Martin, 2010). To quote one of the outstanding authors in this field, 'the role of history and historicity in regional economic development should be an integral part of regional policy analysis' (Martin, 2011: 207).

## Notes

1 Financial support from Ministerio de Economía y Competitividad of Spain (HAR2012-30948) and the Basque government (IT807-13) is acknowledged. This chapter has benefited from the comments of Edurne Magro, Mikel Navarro and James Wilson. Any errors are the responsibility of the author.
2 Between 1976 and 1980, ETA killed twenty-six businessmen and managers and kidnapped another twenty-nine. An unknown but presumably much larger number paid ETA's 'revolutionary tax' (see Aranguren *et al.*, 2012a: 144). Abadie and Gardeazabal (2003) estimated that ETA terrorism reduced Basque GDP per capita growth by ten percentage points during the 1980s and 1990s.
3 On the budget distribution of the Department of Industry, the political constituencies, the economic situation of the region and the main external challenges envisaged by the Basque government, see Aranguren *et al.* (2012a), which gives further and more detailed references.
4 See Foro de Competitividad Euskadi 2015, at www.politicaindustrialvasca.net/.

## References

Abadie, A., and Gardeazabal, J. (2003) The economic costs of conflict: a case study of the Basque Country, *American Economic Review*, 93(1), pp. 113–32.

Aragón, C., Aranguren, M. J., Iturrioz, C., and Wilson, J. R. (2012) A social capital approach for network policy learning: the case of an established cluster initiative, *European Urban and Regional Studies*, doi: 10.1177/0969776411434847.

Aranguren, M. J., Magro, E., Navarro, M., and Valdaliso, J. M. (2012a) *Estrategias para la construcción de ventajas competitivas regionales: el caso del País Vasco*. Madrid: Marcial Pons.

Aranguren, M. J., Magro, E., and Valdaliso, J. M. (2012b) Estrategias de especialización inteligente: el caso del País Vasco, *Información Comercial Española*, 869, pp. 65–80.

Aranguren, M. J., de la Maza, X., Parrilli, M. D., Vendrell-Herrero, F., and Wilson, J. R. (2013) Nested methodological approaches for cluster policy evaluation: an application to the Basque Country, *Regional Studies*, doi: 10.1080/00343404.2012.750423.

Ardanza, J. A. (2011) *Pasión por Euskadi: Memorias*. Barcelona: Destino.

Azua, J. (2006) Política industrial y competitividad: el caso del País Vasco, *Boletin Informativo Techint*, 321, pp. 49–67.

Birch, K., Mackinnon, D., and Cumbers, A. (2010) Old industrial regions in Europe: a comparative assessment of economic performance, *Regional Studies*, 44(1), pp. 35–53.

Bizkarguenaga, I. (2001) *Historia del Gobierno Vasco contada por sus Consejeros (1980–1998)*. Oñati: IVAP.

Boschma, R., and Frenken, K. (2006) Why is evolutionary economic geography not an evolutionary science?, *Journal of Economic Geography*, 6, pp. 273–302.

Breznitz, D. (2007) *Innovation and the State: Political Choice and Strategies for Growth in Israel, Taiwan and Ireland*. New Haven, CT: Yale University Press.

Breznitz, D. (2010) Slippery paths of (mis)understanding? Historically based explanations in social science. In Schreyögg, G., and Sydow, J. (eds), *The Hidden Dynamics of Path Dependence: Institutions and Organizations*. New York: Palgrave Macmillan.

Cooke, P., and Morgan, K. (1998) *The Associational Economy: Firms, Regions, and Innovation*. Oxford: Oxford University Press.

Foray, D. (2013) The economic fundamentals of smart specialisation, *Ekonomiaz*, 83, pp. 55–82.

Gobierno Vasco (2014) *Plan de Industrialización 2014–2016*. Consejo de Gobierno, 29 April.

Hausmann, R., and Rodrik, D. (2003) Economic development as self-discovery, *Journal of Development Economics*, 72, pp. 603–33.

Magro, E., Navarro, M., and Zabala-Iturriagagoitia, J. M. (2014) Coordination-mix: the hidden face of STI policy, *Review of Policy Research*, 31(5), pp. 367–89.

Martin, R. (2010) Rethinking regional path dependence: beyond lock-in to evolution, *Economic Geography* 86(1), pp. 1–27.

Martin, R. (2011) Regional economies as path-dependent systems: some issues and implications. In Cooke, P. (ed.), *Handbook of Regional Innovation and Growth*. Cheltenham: Edward Elgar.

Martin, R., and Sunley, P. (2006) Path dependence and regional economic evolution, *Journal of Economic Geography*, 6, pp. 395–437.

Morgan, K. (2013) The regional state in the era of smart specialisation, *Ekonomiaz*, 83, pp. 102–25.

Navarro, M. (2010) Retos para el País Vasco, tras tres décadas de desarrollo del sistema y las políticas de innovación, *Ekonomiaz*, 25A, pp. 136–83.

Navarro, M. (ed.) (2013) *Las infraestructuras de conocimiento: el caso vasco desde una perspectiva internacional*. San Sebastián: Cuadernos Orkestra.

Navarro, M., Gibaja, J. J., Franco, S., and Murciego, A. (2011) *Indicadores de innovación y benchmarking: reflexión y propuesta para el País Vasco*. Zamudio: Orkestra-Innobasque.

Navarro, M., Valdaliso, J. M., Aranguren, M. J., and Magro, E. (2014) A holistic approach for regional strategies: the case of the Basque Country, *Science and Public Policy*, 41(4), pp. 532–47.

OECD (2011) *OECD Reviews of Regional Innovation: Basque Country, Spain 2011*. Paris: OECD.

Olazarán, M., Albizu, E., and Otero, B. (2009) Technology transfer between technology centres and SMEs: evidence from the Basque Country, *European Planning Studies*, 17(3), pp. 345–63.

Porter, M. E., Ketels, C., and Valdaliso, J. M. (2013) *The Basque Country: Strategy for Economic Development*. Boston: Harvard Business School, Case 9-705-432.

Valdaliso, J. M. (2010) Treinta años de cambios en las empresas vascas: un estudio exploratorio y descriptive, *Ekonomiaz*, 25A, pp. 172–99.

Valdaliso, J. M. (2013) Las estrategias de desarrollo económico del País Vasco: una perspectiva histórica, *Ekonomiaz*, 83, pp. 146–73.

Valdaliso, J. M., Elola, A., Aranguren, M. J., and López, S. (2011a) Origins and development of industrial clusters in the Basque Country: path-dependency and economic evolution. In Ayestarán, S., and Barrutia, J. (eds), *Behavior and Organizational Change*. Reno, NV: Center for Basque Studies.

Valdaliso, J. M., Elola, A., Aranguren, M. J., and López, S. (2011b) Social capital, internationalization and absorptive capacity: the electronics and ICT cluster of the Basque Country, *Entrepreneurship & Regional Development*, 23(9–10), pp. 707–33.

Valdaliso, J. M., Magro, E., Navarro, M., Aranguren, M. J., and Wilson, J. R. (2014) Path dependence in policies supporting smart specialization strategies: insights from the Basque case, *European Journal of Innovation Management*, 17(4), pp. 390–408.

Walendowski, J., Kroll, H., Wintjes, R., and Hollanders, H. (2011) *Innovation Patterns and Innovation Policy in European Regions: Trends, Challenges and Perspectives: 2010 Annual Report*. Project no. 0932 for the European Commission. Brussels: Technopolis.

Walendowski, J., *et al.* (2012) *Governance, Policies, and Perspectives in World-Class Performers, Industrial, and Service-Oriented Regions: 2011 Annual Report*. Project no. 0932 for the European Commission. Brussels: Technopolis.

Woolcock, M., Szreter, S., and Rao, V. (2009) *How and Why Does HistWory Matter for Development Policy?*, Working Paper no. 68. University of Manchester, Brooks World Poverty Institute.

Zubiri, I. (2010) *The Economic Agreement between the Basque Country and Spain: Principles, Characteristics and Economic Implications*. Bilbao: Ad Concordiam.

# 8 Regional competitiveness and Schumpeterian development

## Policy evolution in Wales

*Robert Huggins and Rhiannon Pugh*

### Introduction

Changing patterns of economic activity and their consequential impacts on rates of development have brought competitiveness to the top of many political and policy-making agendas. Ensuring that regional competitiveness is retained and enhanced is a common concern across the globe, although the nature of these concerns may differ according to past histories and future expectations (Huggins *et al.*, 2014a). Changing patterns of global trade and development have made the resilience of competitiveness in European regions a core concern of the European Union and the governments of constituent nation-states, as well as of aspiring members (Reiner, 2010; Koschatzky and Stahlecker, 2010). The Lisbon Strategy, for instance, emphasised the importance of confronting the structural problems faced by European regions in their bid to increase productivity growth (Denis *et al.*, 2005; European Commission, 2010a).

Concerns about the loss of regional competitiveness moved further up the agenda of European governments with the onset of the financial crisis in 2007 and the recession that followed (European Commission, 2010b). Structural problems and the direct exposure of banking systems to the US sub-prime mortgage market have resulted in European economies suffering not only deeper and longer recessions than other national economies but also weaker recoveries (Claessens *et al.*, 2010, Yurtsever, 2011). Competitiveness disparities within European nations mean that the capability to withstand and overcome shocks is likely to vary across regions.

These concerns, however, are associated not only with more recent downturns but also with the changing patterns of economic activity experienced in the latter half of the twentieth and into the twenty-first century (Huggins *et al.*, 2014a). Through the case of Wales in the UK, which for a number of years has had significant political and policy autonomy, this chapter explores the notion of regional competitiveness from the perspective of policies relating to innovation and entrepreneurship that are aligned with the knowledge-based or Schumpeterian notion of development. This Schumpeterian development is central to the concept of regional competitiveness, which equates such development to the inputs, outputs and outcomes of effective processes of endogenous growth.

The study finds that policy evolution relating to innovation- and entrepreneurship-driven competitiveness in Wales is mediated by two key institutions: first, the regional Welsh Government, which has considerable policy autonomy in these fields; and, second, the European Commission, which, through its regional policy programmes, has exerted significant influence in shaping the nature of government intervention. Unfortunately, there is little evidence that policy intervention has impacted positively upon the Welsh economy. Rather, the policy agenda has swung between different approaches over time. It is concluded that the complex nature of multilevel governance within which Wales now finds itself, along with the potential rent-seeking tendencies of its emerging regional government, has worked against the development of a more innovative, entrepreneurial and, subsequently, competitive regional economic environment.

The next section outlines the key theoretical underpinnings of the concepts of regional competitiveness and Schumpeterian development. This is followed by an overview of the polity and economy of Wales and a critique of the evolution of relevant policy in the region. The penultimate section discusses the relationship between policies, governance mechanisms and regional competitiveness, and is followed by the conclusions reached.

## Regional competitiveness, innovation, and entrepreneurship

The competitiveness of a region generally refers to the presence of conditions that both enable firms to compete in their chosen markets and allow the value those firms generate to be captured (Begg, 1999; Huggins, 2003; see also chapter 3 in this volume). Regional competitiveness, therefore, is considered to consist of the capacity of a particular region to attract and maintain firms with stable or rising market shares in an activity, while maintaining stable or increasing standards of living for those who participate in it (Storper, 1997).

While the competitiveness of regions is intrinsically bound to their economic performance, there exists a growing consensus that it is best measured in terms of the assets of the regional business environment (Malecki, 2004, 2007). These include the level of human capital, the degree of innovative capacity, and the quality of the local infrastructure – all of which affect the propensity to achieve competitive advantage in leading-edge and growing sectors of activity. The influence these assets and other externalities can have on firm competitiveness, such as the ability of regions to attract creative and innovative people or provide high-quality cultural facilities, are all important features of regional competitive advantage (Kitson *et al.*, 2004). In other words, competitiveness is increasingly concerned with creativity, knowledge and environmental conditions rather than being based purely on accumulated wealth (Huggins, 2003).

As Martin (2005) outlines, concern with competitiveness has filtered down to the regional, urban and local levels, particularly in the shape of place-based policy interventions targeted at improving the economic fortunes of regions and city-regions. In many advanced nations, these interventions form part of a strategic framework to improve productive and innovative performance.[1] From this policy perspective, the key driver of regional competitiveness is usually considered to consist of the enhancement of knowledge and creativity through clusters (Porter, 1998) or networks (Huggins and Izushi, 2007) of firms and complementary organisations.

Malecki (2004) usefully distinguished between low-road and high-road competition. As he pointed out, regions may compete on the basis of low wages, docile labour and low taxes, but such low-road competition will simply perpetuate an inability to upgrade to an economic base of higher skills and higher wages. Conversely, competition on the high road involving, for example, knowledge policies aimed at promoting entrepreneurship and knowledge-based economic development can lead to positive-sum outcomes that bring benefits to all local economic and social activities (Leborgne and Lipietz, 1988; Malecki, 2004). Consistent with this, Krugman (2003) suggests that regions compete in terms of their ability to provide sufficiently attractive wages and/or employment prospects and a return on capital. For regions, therefore, it is important that competitiveness not only leads to increasing market shares in a particular industry but also raises, or at least maintains, the standard of living, as this should be the end goal of competitive activity (Aiginger, 2006; Storper, 1997). In general, regional development concerns the upgrading of the economic, institutional and social base, with innovation and entrepreneurship that is able to unlock wealth being a prime source of development (Amin, 1999).

Some commentators have suggested that, although policy-makers everywhere are appropriating the term 'regional competitiveness', it remains 'complex and contentious', and 'we are far from a consensus on what is meant by the term' (Kitson *et al.*, 2004: 992). Nevertheless, entrepreneurial, knowledge and innovation capacity is generally considered to be a key factor underpinning the future economic development and growth trajectory of regions. It is the link, therefore, between the entrepreneurial, knowledge and innovation bases of regions and their growth capacity and capability that is at the heart of the concept of competitiveness. In this respect, regional competitiveness concepts are strongly tied to the lineage of Schumpeterian theory (Schumpeter, 1934) – or 'Schumpeter's competitiveness', as it has been termed (Beugelsdijk and Maseland, 2011) – as well as to more contemporary theories relating to the endogenous nature of economic growth.

Both competitiveness and endogenous growth theory are rooted in the notion that the sources of high rates of economic performance and subsequent growth stem from the role played by the production, distribution and use of knowledge within and across economics (Antonelli *et al.*, 2011; Grossman and Helpman, 1994; Harris, 2001; Ibert, 2007; Vaz and Nijkamp, 2009; Zucker *et al.*, 2007). The knowledge-based economy is generally considered to consist of the sphere and nexus of activities and resources centred on, and geared towards, innovation (Romer, 2007). The innovation systems literature, in particular, pinpoints the flow of knowledge across organisations as a crucial factor for effective innovation (Andersson and Karlsson, 2007; Cooke, 2004; Cooke *et al.*, 2011; Freeman, 1987, 1994; Harris, 2001; Lundvall, 2010).

In relation to both competitiveness and endogenous growth theories, knowledge refers to the cumulative stock of information and skills concerned with connecting new ideas with commercial values, developing new products and processes, and therefore doing business in a new way. This may be called knowledge for innovation or innovative knowledge. Whereas innovation is a process, knowledge consists of the recipes and the ingredients to be processed (Romer, 2007). Therefore, as illustrated by Figure 8.1, the relationships between the concepts of knowledge, innovation and competitiveness are closely associated and interlinked.

In general, it is widely observed that the location where innovation occurs is evolving, with the stock of knowledge and knowledge-based resources constantly shifting, reflecting ever changing contexts for new and more advanced knowledge requirements (Dicken, 2007). Furthermore, the sources of regional productivity and growth are increasingly based on the role that knowledge plays within and across regional economies (Capello and Nijkamp, 2009). As a result, the concept of the knowledge-based economy has emerged to aid a better understanding of how the effective production, distribution and use of knowledge underpin innovative and competitive modern economies (Huggins and Izushi, 2007). As indicated above, the concept of regional innovation systems, for instance, is recognition of the role of knowledge for growth through innovation (Cooke, 2004). Innovation systems theory views an economy as an interlinked systemic network of components facilitating innovation (Freeman, 1987; Lundvall, 1992).

Endogenous growth theory has clearly placed knowledge at the centre of economic development (Romer, 1986, 1990), but, while endogenous growth can be considered the desired outcome of knowledge-based development and innovation, it is the process of endogenous development that underpins the growth trajectories of economies (Vázquez-Barquero, 2007). In particular, regions are increasingly considered to be key territorial units within which endogenous forms of development flourish through their innovative milieu – variously referred to as 'technopoles' (Castells and Hall, 1994), 'industrial districts' (Capello, 1999) or 'clusters' (Porter, 1998) – facilitating knowledge flow and new knowledge creation. Implicit is the contention that regional development and growth is best promoted through bottom-up activity focused on the enhancement of local production systems, rather

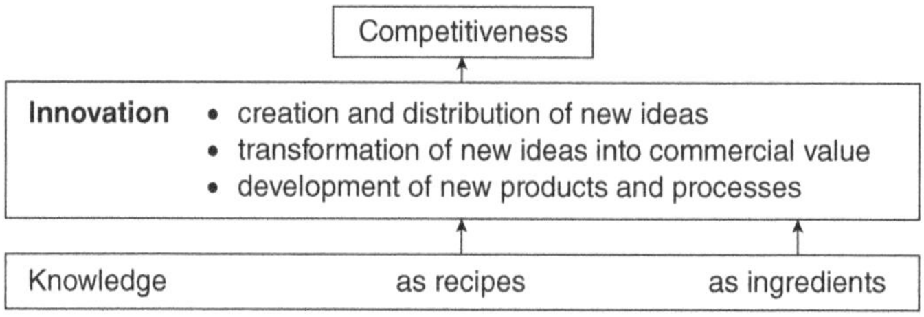


*Figure 8.1* The relationship between competitiveness, innovation and knowledge

Source: Huggins *et al.* (2014a).

than via top-down processes of exogenous development that seek to redistribute resources from elsewhere (Maillat, 1998a, 1998b; Garofoli, 2002).

Cooke (2004), for instance, suggests that regional innovation systems form a vital component of regional economic development, while others have concentrated on the notion of clusters as the focus of regional economic theory and policy, with the underlying tenet being that competitiveness is determined by the strength of key concentrations of specific industries (Porter, 1998; Huggins and Izushi, 2011). The innovative milieu of urban settings, and in particular metropolitan regions, means that they are singled out by scholars such as Maillat (1998b), Fischer *et al.* (2001), Revilla Diez (2002) and Vázquez-Barquero (2007) as being key territorial units within which endogenous forms of development flourish.

The principles of the endogenous development school of regions are rooted in the role that factors such as collective learning and cooperative behaviour play in the establishment of an innovative milieu. As Garofoli (2002) argues, endogenous development primarily concerns the capacity to innovate and produce 'collective intelligence' in a localised environment, which explicitly recognises the relevance of the spillover, diffusing, accumulating, creating and internalising of knowledge. In this sense, the region itself acts as an organisational form of coordination facilitating sustainable competitive advantage (Courlet and Soulage, 1995; Maillat, 1998a; Lawson and Lorenz, 1999; Garofoli, 2002).

Endogenous development theories make clear that differences in rates of economic development across regions are at least partly a function of differentials in rates of entrepreneurship and enterprise development (Fritsch and Mueller, 2004; Mueller *et al.*, 2006; Malecki, 2007). Furthermore, regional entrepreneurship differentials emerge because of the spatial and place-based nature of three underlying factors driving entrepreneurship: the nature of markets (Kirzner, 1973; Baumol, 1990; Huggins and Williams, 2009); the nature of innovation systems (Lundvall, 1995; Freeman, 1987, 1994; Cooke, 2004); and the nature of place-based cultures and communities and the institutions they establish (Storper, 2005; 2008; Rodríguez-Pose, 2013; Huggins and Thompson, 2014a).

Spatial economics which does not incorporate entrepreneurship factors may fail to understand and identify key sources of regional development (Andersson, 2005), with regions that are open and creative able to attract human capital and enjoy more dynamic entrepreneurship (Benneworth, 2004; Lee *et al.*, 2004). In a competitive environment, entrepreneurs will be alert to opportunities and contribute to regional economic growth (Audretsch and Keilbach, 2004). However, changes in levels of entrepreneurship and contributions to regional economic development will take time to emerge, and, as such, any effects may be seen only in the long term (Huggins and Johnston, 2009; Huggins and Williams, 2009). Alternatively, regions can be uncompetitive and lack entrepreneurial dynamism because they do not have the key strengths that allow leading regions to prosper and develop (Benneworth and Charles, 2005; Chaston, 2009; Huggins, 1997; Huggins and Johnston, 2009; Huggins and Williams, 2011; Lagendijk and Lorentzen, 2007; North and Smallbone, 2000; Virkkala, 2007).

Regional entrepreneurship is associated particularly with the effective or failing nature of regional innovation systems, with the flow of knowledge across organisations considered a crucial factor for effective innovation (Lundvall, 1995; Freeman, 1987, 1994; Cooke, 2004; Andersson and Karlsson, 2007; Cooke *et al.*, 2011; Harris, 2001). A key feature of the innovation system discourse has long concerned the role within the innovation process of both formal and informal networks of spatially proximate and co-located external organisations, such as universities, R&D labs and other firms or individuals (Keeble *et al.*, 1999; Brown and Duguid, 2001; Cooke *et al.*, 2004; Huggins and Izushi, 2007; Mattes, 2012).

It is generally through the networks underpinning systemic innovation processes that firms access knowledge that they do not, or cannot, generate internally based on their own capabilities (Meagher and Rogers, 2004; Lichtenthaler, 2005; Sammarra and Biggiero, 2008; Tomlinson, 2010; Bergenholtz and Waldstrøm, 2011; Huggins and Thompson, 2014b). Audretsch and Lehmann (2005) refer to entrepreneurs as a filter addressing the gap between new knowledge and economic or commercialisable knowledge (Arrow, 1962), which requires intentional and often complex efforts to access and assimilate. Successful economies are associated with efficient innovation systems and knowledge filters resulting from high levels of entrepreneurship, while weaker economies are those with failing innovation systems and low levels of entrepreneurship (Huggins *et al.*, 2014a, 2014b).

Policy-making is deemed necessary when entrepreneurial firms are considered to be vulnerable to 'market failures' compared with larger businesses, and when such market failures are likely to be permanent unless steps are taken to address them (Audretsch *et al.*, 2007). Despite this traditional emphasis on entrepreneurial firms and market failure, enterprise policies have become more pervasive, and there is increasing interest in promoting entrepreneurship in its broader context – that is, not simply in terms of business start-ups or small-business growth. This has meant less concern with imperfections in the market, with specific firms and with 'picking winners' and more interest in individuals, rather than businesses, and in long-term measures such as school-level education (Audretsch *et al.*, 2007; Stevenson and Lundstrom, 2001; Huggins and Williams, 2009, 2011).

Innovation systems failure occurs in regions because of the lack of coordinating and governance mechanisms underlying effective regional entrepreneurship and innovation-driven economies (Cooke, 2004). Mechanisms such as networks and clusters, which in more entrepreneurial regions are formed through the organic and evolutionary interdependency emerging between entrepreneurs and other economic agents, appear to be less apparent in entrepreneurially weak regions (Cooke, 2004; Porter, 2003; Desrochers and Sautet, 2004; Huggins *et al.*, 2014b).

## Wales: economy and polity

Located on the western edge of Britain, Wales is a country with a population of some 2.9 million people (5 per cent of UK citizens). The economy has traditionally depended upon industries such as farming, mining and quarrying, and steel-making, which have declined in significance over a number of years. This decline has given rise to a more diverse economy, although the region is still emerging from a fundamental restructuring of its economic base. Overall, the performance of the Welsh economy lagged behind that of the UK as a whole over the latter part of the twentieth and into the twenty-first century (Chatterji and Dewhurst, 1996; Jones and Henley, 2008). In 2001, the gross value added (GVA) per head in Wales was 77.1 per cent of the UK average, and this had fallen further, to 74.3 per cent, by 2009. This pattern is evident in labour market measures, including economic activity and unemployment rates. There is also greater relative employment in the public sector in comparison with the more prosperous regional economies of the UK, suggesting a reliance on the state to compensate for a weaker indigenous business community.

Over the last two centuries, Wales has shifted from a mainly agrarian economy to one that was at heart of the industrial revolution, largely on account of the exploitation of its reserves of natural resources, principally coal (Morgan, 1997, 2012). From the latter part of the 1800s onwards, large extractive industries, along with the manufacture of steel, began to dominate the Welsh economy, creating large numbers of new jobs and attracting significant numbers of migrant workers (Jones, 1984; Williams, 1950). However, the subsequent decline of these industries and the deindustrialisation occurring across the UK as whole left the Welsh economy with deep structural weaknesses, which, because of the effects of economic lock-in and path dependence, it is still struggling to overcome.

Administratively, Wales is one of the twelve government office regions of the UK. In recent years, alongside Scotland and Northern Ireland, it has achieved a degree of political autonomy from the UK government through the process of devolution. The National Assembly for Wales was established in 1999 following a referendum in which the people of the region voted for a degree of self-governance.

There were numerous cases for devolution – administrative, economic and cultural – but the main driving force was political (McAllister, 2003; Morgan and Mungham, 2000). The key rationale behind the devolution movement was the perception of a 'democratic deficit' arising from the power of the London-administered Welsh Office and its perceived lack of accountability. When the National Assembly for Wales became operational, its elected government became responsible for developing economic policies within the context of central UK policy frameworks, giving policy-makers in Wales more autonomy than previously. However, the fiscal powers of the Welsh Government are limited, as it has no major tax-raising powers and public finance continues to be provided via a block grant from Westminster.

Over time the Welsh Assembly and government have gained more powers and capabilities. Similarly, recent political and academic discourse concerning devolution has tended to stress the economic advantages of the transfer of power from national to sub-national institutions, characterised as the 'economic dividend' of devolution (Rodríguez-Pose and Gill, 2005). Unfortunately for Wales, however, despite political devolution it remains largely trapped in a vicious cycle that continues to erode its competitiveness and to lower the standard of living of its citizens.

Although in recent years Wales has had a growing degree of autonomy to establish policies tailored to creating interventions best suited to catalysing economic development, as yet there is little evidence of any economic returns. Compared with many other regions, Wales barely engages in the global economy (Huggins and Kitagawa, 2012). The percentage of Welsh firms that export goods is the lowest of any UK region, and well below the UK average (Huggins and Prokop, 2014). Furthermore, it is estimated that only twenty-five Welsh firms are listed on any public stock market, accounting for a mere 0.8 per cent of the UK's total market capitalisation. This is significantly below the approximately 5 per cent that might be expected given the size of the Welsh economy using a proportionate per capita estimation model. Overall, Wales has one of the lowest number of firms quoted on public markets across all developed nations in Europe; also the average company capitalisation of firms located in London is approximately nine times greater than it is in Wales (Huggins and Prokop, 2014).

More generally, devolution has not been able to address the underlying problems of the economy to any great extent, with Wales continuing to experience low levels of innovation and entrepreneurial activity in comparison with other UK regions (Robinson *et al.*, 2012). It has the lowest level of GVA per capita, coupled with levels of pay, productivity, employment and economic activity that are all significantly below the UK average. Overall, the Welsh economy persistently underperforms in relation to that of the UK as a whole: from 2000 to 2006 annual GDP growth was 3.93 per cent, compared with 4.3 per cent for the UK, leaving Wales at the bottom of GDP growth tables with a level of economic inactivity 4 per cent above the UK average. Some see this as a result of 'serious and persistent structural deficiencies' in the Welsh economy, caused in large part by structural adjustments in the 1980s whereby industry declined and was replaced by employment in services – in particular, relatively poorly paid public services and back-office functions (Thomas and Henderson, 2004).

There are a number of differing reasons for this underperformance, most of which relate to entrenched problems with the structure of the regional economy, in particular the lack of private-sector dynamism and an overreliance on the public sector for employment (Ball, 2008; Cooke and Clifton, 2005). There are few truly innovative and R&D-performing firms in Wales, and Welsh SMEs are usually involved in relatively low-value economic activity (Thomas and Henderson, 2004). The general business culture is seen to be weak, and a culture of entrepreneurship and innovation is lacking across the SME base; this can be attributed to past overreliance on branch plants and foreign direct investment (FDI) rather than building up indigenous capacity and capabilities (Ball, 2008).

## Policy evolution

The policy autonomy achieved by the devolved regions of the UK in areas relating to both entrepreneurship and innovation form part of processes referred to as the 'hollowing out' of the state (Jessop, 2004), with growing significance given to issues of place and spatial proximity in economic development and innovation processes (Huggins and Izushi, 2007). The power structures within which relevant institutions interact necessarily affect how economic and innovation systems operate regionally and nationally (Kitagawa, 2007; Huggins and Kitagawa, 2012). The structures and strategies of devolved economic governance are often interrelated in a complex way (Jones *et al.*, 2005), shaped by patterns of intergovernmental interaction and existing governance structures between supranational, national and sub-national actors. For instance, when comparing economic development financing and devolved state action across the UK, Cooke and Clifton (2005) identify emerging and different 'institutional structures of economic governance'.

The part of the Welsh Government currently responsible for innovation and economic development is the Department of Business and Economy (formerly known as Business, Enterprise, Technology and Science and Economy and Transport) under the minister for economy, science and transport. Before this, the innovation agenda was within the remit of the Welsh Development Agency (WDA), which was amalgamated with the Welsh Government in 2006. The WDA was established in 1976, which meant that, 'for the first time, Wales had a body capable of promoting strategic economic development.' Despite never producing an actual economic plan, it did have a tacit sector strategy to intensify inward investment (Cooke, 2004: 4). While the WDA was relatively successful in attracting FDI into Wales in the form of branch plant factories, which created jobs in needy areas, this was not a sustainable strategy in the longer term (Morgan and Rees, 2001). Whereas its role began as one focused largely on supplying hard infrastructure and inward investment, this later shifted to one of a 'regional animateur', seeking to develop a soft infrastructure of business services, skills and social capital (Morgan, 1997).

The WDA has an interesting and contested legacy in Wales. There have recently been calls for it to be resurrected in light of the perceived failure of the Welsh Government to improve the fate of the economy. Indeed, Morgan (1997: 90) argues that 'the economic situation in Wales would have been that much worse were it not for the endeavours of the WDA over the past 20 years.' According to Osmond (2012), the WDA was 'a brand to die for … and the failure to remedy that act of vandalism [its abolition] has been a black mark against every Economic Development Minister over the last 8 years.' Morgan (2012) questions the decision to amalgamate the WDA with the Welsh Government, arguing that the current system is actually less accountable than the independent body was. He maintains that the future for Welsh innovation policy is fairly bleak because of the lack of institutional capacity to engage with the cutting edge of new regional innovation policy ideas emerging from the European Union.

This apparent lack of capacity is worrying given that Wales was originally one of the first regions in Europe to develop its own innovation strategy, the Regional Technology Plan, in 1994 (WDA, 1998). Alongside this, there have to date been two further innovation strategies (Welsh Assembly Government, 2002a; Welsh

Government, 2013). Innovation has also featured in economic policies throughout the period since devolution (Welsh Office, 1998; Welsh Assembly Government, 2002b, 2005, 2010a), but also in specific sector, education, science and spatial policies, as well as in general strategy documents. Innovation is a key theme in policies relating to higher education in Wales, which are concerned with enhancing the economic role of Welsh universities. Indeed, universities are key to the Welsh Government's innovation agenda and are relied upon as drivers of innovation and economic growth (Huggins *et al.*, 2008; Huggins and Kitagawa, 2012).

The innovation agenda in Wales has varied in importance relative to other policy areas. In the early period following devolution, innovation was a key policy sphere, relating to three strategies – the Regional Technology Plan (RTP), the Innovation Action Plan (IAP) and the Entrepreneurship Action Plan (EAP) (Welsh Assembly Government, 2002b; WDA, 1998, 2000) – that take an explicitly systems- and entrepreneurship-based approach to innovation. In a second period, principally between 2003 and 2009, the innovation agenda became weaker, with policy focusing more on sustainability and social spheres. During these years, in the absence of a specific innovation strategy or a strong innovation element in economic policy, the innovation agenda was driven largely by higher education regional policy (Huggins and Kitagawa, 2012). The practical result of this policy direction was a strengthening of the triple helix approach to innovation (Huggins *et al.*, 2008). Since 2010, however, there has been a resurgence of innovation as an important element on the Welsh Government's agenda, and a new innovation strategy has been published for the first time in over ten years (Welsh Government, 2013). This recent period is characterised by sector-based policies and the move towards smart specialisation, which has resulted in a 'cluster' approach to innovation and economic development.

Following devolution, a distinctive approach to innovation emerged, with the role of the EU in driving the Welsh agenda being an important component of developments (Thomas and Henderson, 2004). The EU Objective One programme (2000–06) introduced a new style of bottom-up policies focusing on entrepreneurship and skills, which was a departure from the top-down inward investment focus of the pre-Assembly period (Brooksbank *et al.*, 2001). For Cooke and Clifton (2005), Welsh innovation policy follows the EU's standard approach of 'innovation push' and promotes knowledge transfer, entrepreneurship, venture capital and incubation, designed to absorb European Union funding. Because of European requirements, Welsh innovation policy and programmes have undergone frequent evaluations and reviews, but Thomas and Henderson (2004) find that the results of these are not always fed back into the policy process, so lessons and recommendations are not always accounted in for future policy formulation.

Nevertheless, in the aftermath of devolution, innovation was a central and important feature of the policy landscape. It was high on the Welsh Government's agenda, as evidenced by the two dedicated innovation strategies (WDA, 1998; Welsh Assembly Government, 2002a) and the increasing centrality of innovation to economic policy (Welsh Assembly Government, 2002b). However, after this initial interest, innovation lost its privileged position among the various policy priorities. Following the Innovation Action Plan there was no innovation policy for a decade, until the publication of *Innovation Wales* (Welsh Government, 2013).

Overall, the approach to innovation policy in Wales post-devolution was predominantly systemic in nature, viewing innovation in a broad fashion, in line with thinking at the European level. The initial impetus behind the RTP–EAP–IAP suite of interventions was to respond to the European Commission's requirement that regions develop individual innovation strategies. The other key policy during this period was *Science Policy for Wales* (Welsh Assembly Government, 2006). This was the first science policy published by the Welsh Government (it was subsequently updated and replaced in 2012) and sees great economic potential for science and research, asserting that intellectual property created in Welsh businesses, universities and the public sector needs to be protected and commercialised; the policy seeks to address this through providing funding and advisory services for such activities.

Wales has traditionally been viewed as having a less entrepreneurial economy than other areas of the UK (Welsh Assembly Government, 2005): there is a lack of positive perceptions of entrepreneurship among the general public, little incentive for encouraging entrepreneurial behaviour, limited entrepreneurial education, and only fragmented and short-term support for new businesses (WDA, 2000). Fostering increased levels of entrepreneurship is therefore of central importance to the Welsh economy (Brooksbank *et al.*, 2001; Welsh Assembly Government, 2005).

To improve levels of entrepreneurship, the Entrepreneurship Action Plan was developed with the vision of 'a bold and confident nation where entrepreneurship is valued, celebrated and exercised throughout society'. It stated that 'within a generation Wales must establish itself as one of the most entrepreneurial nations in Europe' (WDA, 2000: 19) and contained the target of reaching the UK start-up rate of VAT registrations by 2006, equivalent to an increase of 50 per cent, from 6,300 to 9,300 per annum (WDA, 2002). Since then, the overall rate of business start-ups has declined in the UK, but in Wales performance has improved (ERS, 2011; Huggins *et al.*, 2014b). The Welsh Government has more recently stated that 'there remains a role for Government in encouraging entrepreneurship – it is vital for developing a strong economy and therefore crucial for our future prosperity' (Welsh Assembly Government, 2010a: 43). This policy approach emphasises the need to focus on high potential start-ups, on self-employment related to participation, and on young people and graduates specifically (ERS, 2011; Huggins *et al.*, 2014b).

As indicated above, following the initial post-devolution burst of policy development and activity, in relative terms there was an overall absence of innovation policy in the period 2003 to 2009, although at this time a sector-based approach to economic policy emerged. However, three important policies have been published since 2010 that have had an important impact on the Welsh innovation agenda: the *Economic Renewal* programme (Welsh Assembly Government, 2010a), *Science for Wales* (Welsh Government, 2012a) and *Innovation Wales* (Welsh Government, 2013). These all have innovation as a strong theme, and restore it as a key priority within the Welsh Government's wider approach. The main concepts introduced by these publications are the sector-based approach currently underpinning economic and innovation policy with a cluster rationale; city regions as a new form of spatial planning; and a return to a wider and more systemic conceptualisation of innovation. The recent period has also seen the introduction of some important infrastructure strategies, such as the *Wales Infrastructure Investment Plan* (Welsh Government, 2012b) and *Delivering a Digital Wales* (Welsh Assembly Government, 2010b).

In terms of entrepreneurship policy, the Welsh Government has also signalled a move away from previous mechanisms where support was provided to any and all businesses, stating that 'we should not try to second-guess the action of markets at the level of individual businesses and therefore we will reduce substantially our direct business support' (Welsh Assembly Government, 2010a: 7). Alternatively, it states that it will focus resources on where the most value can be added, 'acting as an enabler for the economy as a whole rather than a significant direct deliverer of services to individual businesses' (ibid.: 36). As part of this strategy, it is the sector-based approach that is being utilised to target support where policy-makers see the greatest potential gains (Welsh Assembly Government, 2010a; Huggins *et al.*, 2014b).

As a result, entrepreneurship policy in Wales has gradually become more centralised. Despite a new focus on city regions, there has been a shift away from the more local interventions of the past, which means that policy may be less likely to be able to account for uneven geographies of entrepreneurship and local economic conditions. However, it is clear that the new governance arrangements of devolution are facilitating the evolution of enterprise policy. Furthermore, within the Welsh Government there is a strong perception that there are high levels of latent untapped entrepreneurship potential among young people in the region. In particular, a Youth Entrepreneurship Strategy has been established which contains a commitment to fostering and engendering interest through investment in entrepreneurship education from primary through to further and higher education (ERS, 2011).

More critically, it is has been suggested that governance structures are preventing effective enterprise policy development and the administration of support (Huggins *et al.*, 2014b). It has further been argued that, while the *Economic Renewal* plan (Welsh Assembly Government, 2010a) makes mention of entrepreneurship, it does not contain sufficient emphasis on it, and that the focus on sector-level development is at the expense of specific policies supporting entrepreneurial development – with the acknowledged exception of the Youth Entrepreneurship Strategy (Huggins *et al.*, 2014b).

Following the publication of *Economic Renewal* (Welsh Assembly Government, 2010a), the Welsh Government economy department was restructured into teams based around nine key sectors, with respective sector panels made up of external stakeholders to advise the Welsh Government. Business support is also delivered through Finance Wales, which is an independent company owned by the Welsh Government that provides commercial funding to Welsh SMEs; it essentially plays a venture capital role. Finance Wales invests both private and public funds, including EU funds, but its future is uncertain following a review into its activities (Jones-Evans, 2013a, 2013b).

The introduction of sector-specific strategies occurred in two stages, with the first six sector teams being set up in 2010 and an additional three added a year later. These sector teams are ICT, energy and environment, advanced materials and manufacturing, creative industries, life sciences, and financial and professional services, to which were added construction, tourism, and food and farming. The apparent policy rationale for the selection of these sectors was to focus support on those firms and activities seen as having the most growth potential and where policy intervention could add the most value. This outcome was the introduction of a sector-based rationale to delivering innovation support, and the individual teams have set up their own dedicated funds for businesses in their sector – e.g., a Life Sciences Investment Fund to promote the growth of life science businesses and a Digital Development Fund to meet the needs of creative industries. Each sector team has dedicated strategies and actions, although the level of alignment across priority sectors is not particularly clear.

The most recent innovation policy – *Innovation Wales* – presents four 'grand challenge areas' that are explicitly aligned with the concept of smart specialisation (Foray *et al.*, 2009, 2011) and was established as a direct response to the European Commission's requirement that regions produce RIS3 strategies before the next round of structural fund allocations. Innovation Wales is explicitly aligned with 'smart specialisation methodology' (Welsh Government, 2013: 8) and was submitted to the EC Smart Specialisation Platform for review. This is clearly part of a wider trend observed in Wales, stretching back to the original RTP in the 1990s, whereby the innovation agenda has been strongly driven by developments at the European level.

The interpretation of smart specialisation in Wales differs from the initial conceptualisation of the European Commission (see European Commission, 2010c, 2011; Foray *et al.*, 2009, 2011) in two main ways: first, it has been interpreted as a strongly cluster-based approach; and, second, the entrepreneurial discovery process has not been followed and the rationale behind the sectors chosen is not entirely clear. In essence, the Welsh approach revolves around the geographical co-location of firms in key sectors, and there is little evidence of the entrepreneurial discovery process at its heart.

## Discussion

Despite significant policy intervention and development, Wales continues to remain uncompetitive compared with a host of comparator regions. Research suggests that Wales and its constituent localities are among the least economically competitive places in the UK (Huggins and Thompson, 2010, 2014a). A recent study ranking its global competitiveness finds that it lags behind many advanced regions around the world on economic output and outcomes measures such as productivity and earnings (Huggins *et al.*, 2014a). It further finds that rates of investment in innovation by both the public and the private sector remain below what would be expected for a region within an advanced national economy. It is, perhaps, this lack of input investment that is of the greatest concern with regard to future economic competitiveness. The lack of public-sector investment had led some to some commentators claiming that, 'by seeking to develop a Knowledge Economy "on the cheap", the Assembly Government risks losing out to competitor economies across Europe and within the UK' (HEW, 2008: 8).

More generally, a benchmarking of the competitiveness of the Welsh economy continues to make dismal reading. In the area of human capital development, the economy has a relatively stagnant and low skills base typified by a lack of knowledge workers and a weak labour market. Along with the low density of public- and private-sector engagement in innovation, there are below average (national) rates of entrepreneurship, relatively low rates of business network formation, a lack of opportunity to access entrepreneurship, and a lack of strong industry clusters. These factors are coupled with often weak and dated infrastructure.

The inability of lagging regions to utilise effectively the spending made available through, for example, the European Commission for innovation and entrepreneurship has been termed the regional innovation paradox. It is argued that such regions lack the absorptive capacity in both public and private sectors to make good use of such funding (Oughton *et al.*, 2002). In other words, there is a pre-existing lack of the skills, expertise, technology and knowledge required to invest available funding in a manner that is likely to generate significant economic returns. To our minds, Wales is a clear case in point of a region that is suffering from such an innovation paradox. However, what is less clear is why this situation seems have become even further entrenched after fifteen years of devolved government that was set up precisely to equip the country with higher rates of absorptive capacity. We conclude that another paradox is play here, whereby the introduction of regional government has itself stifled and hampered the capability of the economy to become more competitive through enhanced levels of innovation and entrepreneurship.

We contend that the introduction of the National Assembly for Wales is likely to be providing an economic and political climate that encourages rent-seeking, in particular rent-seeking undertaken by government itself. Government rent-seeking in this instance can be considered to consist of politicians and public officials, principally in terms of the time they give to certain activities (Vasilev, 2013), allocating resources to compete for control of a larger share of public funds. Such rent-seeking is manifest in the resources that are used to maintain or further develop existing interests, to engage in policy and political turf wars and, more generally, to enhance political capital. In the case of devolution in Wales, key examples of government rent-seeking include the resources devoted to intra-political lobbying within the National Assembly for Wales and Welsh Government by its bureaucrats in the pursuit of certain vested agendas, as well as the political lobbying the Assembly has undertaken as a whole to increase its power base. Clearly, some form of lobbying is natural and necessary within political circles and forms part of the politicking associated with government activity. However, when such activity is neither in the public interest nor creating public value, it can be said to be rent-seeking in nature.

In general, the bigger the size of the public sector within an economy, the more scope there is for rent-seeking activity that results in economic inefficiencies (Gelb, 1991). Of particular pertinence to the Welsh example is the finding that government rent-seeking is especially harmful to innovation-related activities, which in turn hampers economic growth and competitiveness (Murphy *et al.*, 1993). Economies with a significant public-sector wage premium and high public-sector employment are significantly more likely to be engaged in government rent-seeking that results in inefficiencies through non-productive activities (Vasilev, 2013). Recent research has consistently suggested that the growth and bloating of the public sector can lead to increased economic inefficiency through rent-seeking behaviour (Persson and Tabellini, 2000; Vasilev, 2013).

In some ways, such behaviour can be expected to a certain degree within a new government institution such as the Welsh Government. At the outset there is likely to be interdepartmental and inter-official competition, whereby each has a vested interest in seeking to grow the status and significance of the political and policy areas within their jurisdiction (Von Mises, 1944; Parkinson, 1957; Niskanen, 1971; Warwick, 1975; Tinbergen, 1985; Box, 2004; Vasilev, 2013). Nevertheless, this behaviour may well have led to significant rent-seeking time being spent, resulting in wasted resources and an erosion of regional competitiveness.

It is to be hoped that this potential paradox of regional devolution is a relatively temporary phenomenon that equates to the 'start-up' costs of new government, which are partly the result of a historical cultural environment in Wales based on extractive institutions that were not best suited to producing a ready-made infrastructure for self-rule (Huggins and Thompson, 2014a). These cultural factors have led to a system of regional governance that has evolved in post-devolution years through a process of learning-by-doing, which will hopefully bear fruit in the coming years. Clearly, breaking a path-dependent economic trajectory that has been downward for many years is no easy matter, even with additional political autonomy, with positive change likely to become visible and transparent only after a significant period of time.

## Conclusion

In conclusion, it can be seen that, in Wales, the policy agenda has swung between different approaches over time. This has often resulted in programmes ending quite suddenly, often without being replaced, meaning that cumulative gains and experiences are lost. One of the probable causes of this is the lack of a clear and transparent 'what for?' question being answered before policies are formulated.

This has been compounded by a lack of the type of evaluation processes discussed by Magro and Wilson in chapter 6 being set in place to understand whether or not policies have made a difference. This said, it is possible to identify an evolution of policies and priorities that characterise the strategy: from attracting FDI, as was manifest in the period when the Welsh Development Agency played a central role, through to a focus more on horizontal priorities fostering innovation and entrepreneurship, and then to vertical sector-based policies in the most recent period.

The establishment of the Welsh Government and increased regional political autonomy have been at the heart of these processes. However, despite a governance environment that it was hoped would stimulate economic development and increased competitiveness, continuing institutional issues and a lack of political absorptive capacity has resulted in a policy mix that has been in almost constant fluctuation since devolution. In future, more consistency in the Welsh Government's approach would allow knowledge and experience to accumulate from the strategies implemented, with other stakeholders being better able to plan for and undertake activities in a more stable policy environment. Rather than swinging between different approaches, a more consistent, yet still mixed, approach would provide the framework for policies that are more amenable to promoting long-term economic growth and development.

Overall, the chapter suggests that systemic and cultural approaches to regional competitiveness based on the promotion of innovation and entrepreneurship are difficult to implement because of their broad and all-encompassing nature, and that, while they may make good policies, it is a challenge to translate these into implementable actions. As Driver and Oughton (2008) argue with specific regard to innovation, the important task for public policy is to characterise accurately the 'interplay of causal factors in innovation expenditure', although 'identifying the nature of what is required (or how to intervene) is methodologically difficult'. In other words, there are unlikely to be any easily identifiable wins, especially given the complexity of the devolution process and the potential conflicts of interest across the various actors involved, as well as the differences in legitimacy they share. In particular, the interests of regional, national and European governments, and the balance of influence across the three, will depend upon the relative strength or, in political terms, legitimacy of each tier of government (Rodríguez-Pose and Gill, 2005).

In the case of Wales, a clear and significant role has been played by the European Commission in seeking to drive forward the innovation agenda, most recently through the smart specialisation approach. In general, weaker regions are likely to be more dependent on Europe for funding innovation activities than their competitive counterparts and so must meet the European Commission's requirements, making them more susceptible to changes in trends and direction at the European level. This could be problematic if it requires a restructuring of governance structures, as in the case of Wales. From a practical perspective, this may be both costly and time consuming and may lead to policies being changed or dropped before they have reached fruition, resulting in a compounding of any resources wasted through rent-seeking. To this extent, the European Commission needs to be careful to ensure that it does not cause a diversion of scarce resources into governance restructuring and policy compliance that could be better spent directly on competitiveness support activities in weaker regions.

Finally, from a more theoretical perspective, this chapter has sought to suggest that the concept of regional competitiveness has evolved beyond those studies and measures that previously regarded it as consisting simply of the ability to compete with other regions for export markets, often relying on labour productivity alone as a measure of competitiveness differentials. It is now recognised that, while regions compete, the main competition between them is not only in terms of attracting and nurturing highly productive firms but also in the productive knowledge stemming from the attraction and nurturing of the creative knowledge-based workers and entrepreneurs who underpin the innovative capacity of regional firms.

## Note

1 The relationship between competitiveness policy and territorial strategy is treated in detail by Magro and Nauwelaers in chapter 5 of this book.

## References


Aiginger, K. (2006) Competitiveness: from a dangerous obsession to a welfare creating ability with positive externalities, *Journal of Industry, Competition and Trade*, 6(2), pp. 161–77.

Amin, A. (1999) An institutionalist perspective on regional economic development, *International Journal of Urban and Regional Research*, 23(2), pp. 365–78.

Andersson, D. E. (2005) The spatial nature of entrepreneurship, *Quarterly Journal of Austrian Economics*, 8(2), pp. 21–34.

Andersson, M., and Karlsson, C. (2007) Knowledge in regional economic growth: the role of knowledge accessibility, *Industry and Innovation*, 14, pp. 129–49.

Antonelli, C., Patrucco, P., and Quatraro, A. (2011) Productivity growth and pecuniary knowledge externalities: an empirical analysis of agglomeration economies in European regions, *Economic Geography*, 87, pp. 23–50.

Arrow, K. J. (1962) Economic welfare and the allocation of resources for invention. In Nelson, R. (ed.), *The Rate and Direction of Inventive Activity*. Princeton, NJ: Princeton University Press.

Audretsch, D. B., and Keilbach, M. (2004) Entrepreneurship and regional growth: an evolutionary interpretation, *Journal of Evolutionary Economics*, 14(5), pp. 605–16.

Audretsch, D. B., and Lehmann, E. E. (2005) Does the knowledge spillover theory of entrepreneurship hold for regions?, *Research Policy*, 34, pp. 1191–202.

Audretsch, D. B., Grilo, I., and Thurik, A. R. (2007) Explaining entrepreneurship and the role of policy: a framework. In Audretsch, D. B., *et al.* (eds), *The Handbook of Research on Entrepreneurship Policy*. Cheltenham: Edward Elgar, pp. 1–17.

Ball, J. (2008) *A Strategy for the Welsh Economy*. Cardiff: Institute of Welsh Affairs.

Baumol, W. J. (1990) Entrepreneurship: productive, unproductive and destructive, *Journal of Political Economy*, 98(5), 892–921.

Begg, I. (1999) Cities and competitiveness, *Urban Studies*, 36(5–6), pp. 795–810.

Benneworth, P. (2004) In what sense 'regional development'? Entrepreneurship, underdevelopment and strong tradition in the periphery, *Entrepreneurship and Regional Development*, 16(6), pp. 439–58.

Benneworth, P., and Charles, D. (2005) University spin-off policies and economic development in less successful regions: learning from two decades of policy practice, *European Planning Studies*, 13, pp. 537–57.

Bergenholtz, C., and Waldstrøm, C. (2011) Inter-organizational network studies: a literature review, *Industry and Innovation*, 18, pp. 539–62.

Beugelsdijk, S., and Maseland, R. (2011) *Culture in Economics: History, Methodological Reflections and Contemporary Applications*. Cambridge: Cambridge University Press.

Box, R. (2004) *Public Administration and Society: Critical issues in American Governance*. London: M. E. Sharpe.

Brooksbank, D. J., Clifton, N. C., Jones-Evans, D., and Pickernell, D. G. (2001) The end of the beginning? Welsh regional policy and Objective One, *European Planning Studies*, 9(2), pp. 255–74.

Brown, J. S., and Duguid, P. (2001) Knowledge and organization: a social practice perspective, *Organizational Science*, 12, pp. 198–213.

Capello, R. (1999) Spatial transfer of knowledge in high technology milieux: learning versus collective learning processes, *Regional Studies*, 33, pp. 353–65.

Capello, R., and Nijkamp, P. (eds) (2009) *Handbook of Regional Growth and Development Theories*. Cheltenham: Edward Elgar.

Castells, M., and Hall, P. (1994) *Technopoles of the World: The Making of the Twenty-First Century Industrial Complexes*. London: Routledge.

Chaston, I. (2009) Entrepreneurs, intuition, and small-business performance, *JCC: The Business and Economics Research Journal*, 2(1), pp. 37–45.

Chatterji, M., and Dewhurst, J. H. L. (1996) Convergence clubs and relative economic performance in Great Britain: 1977–1991, *Regional Studies*, 31(1), pp. 31–40.

Claessens, S., Dell'Ariccia, G., Igan, D., and Laeven, L. (2010) Cross-country experiences and policy implications from the global financial crisis, *Economic Policy*, 25(62), pp. 267–93.

Cooke, P. (2004) Regional innovation systems: an evolutionary approach. In Cooke, P., Heidenreich, M., and Braczyk, H.-J. (eds), *Regional Innovation Systems: The Role of Governance in a Globalised World*. 2nd ed., London: Routledge, pp. 1–18.

Cooke P., and Clifton, N. (2005) Visionary, precautionary and constrained 'varieties of devolution' in the economic governance of the devolved UK territories, *Regional Studies*, 39, pp. 437–51.

Cooke, P., Heidenreich, M., and Braczyk, H. (eds) (2004) *Regional Innovation Systems: The Role of Governance in a Globalised World*. London: Routledge.

Cooke, P., Asheim, B., Boschma, R., Martin, R., Schwartz, D., and Tödtling, F. (eds) (2011) *Handbook of Regional Innovation and Growth*. Cheltenham: Edward Elgar.

Courlet, C., and Soulage, B. (1995) Industrial dynamics and territorial space, *Entrepreneurship & Regional Development*, 7, pp. 285–307.

Denis, C., McMorrow, K., Röger, W., and Veugelers, R. (2005) *The Lisbon Strategy and the EU's Structural Productivity Problem*, European Commission Directorate-General for Economic and Financial Affairs Economic Papers, no. 221.

Desrochers, P., and Sautet, F. (2004) Cluster-based economic strategy, facilitation policy and the market process, *Review of Austrian Economics*, 17(2–3), pp. 233–45.

Dicken, P. (2007) *Global Shift*. 5th ed., New York: Guilford Press.

Driver, C., and Oughton, C. (2008) Dynamic models of regional innovation: explorations with British time-series data, *Cambridge Journal of Regions, Economy and Society*, 1, pp. 205–17.

ERS (2011) *Mid Programme Evaluation of the Start Up Service: Final Report*. Bristol: ERS.

European Commission (2010a) *Lisbon Strategy Evaluation Document*. Brussels: European Commission.

European Commission (2010b) *Europe 2020: A Strategy for Smart, Sustainable and Inclusive Growth*. Brussels: European Commission.

European Commission (2010c) *Investing in Europe: Fifth Cohesion Report on Economic, Social and Territorial Cohesion*. Brussels: European Commission.

European Commission (2011) *Research and Innovation Strategies for Smart Specialisation*. Brussels: European Commission.

Fischer, M. F., Revilla Diez, J., Snickars, F., and Varga, A. (2001) *Metropolitan Systems of Innovation: Theory and Evidence from Three Metropolitan Regions in Europe*. Berlin: Springer.

Foray, D., David, P., and Hall, B. (2009) *Smart Specialisation: The Concept*. Knowledge Economists Policy Brief no.9, European Commission.

Foray, D., David, P., and Hall, B. (2011) *Smart Specialisation: From Academic Idea to Political Instrument, the Surprising Career of a Concept and the Difficulties Involved in its Implementation*. Lausanne: Management of Technology & Entrepreneurship Institute.

Freeman, C. (1987) *Technology, Policy, and Economic Performance: Lessons from Japan*. London: Pinter.

Freeman, C. (1994) The economics of technical change, *Cambridge Journal of Economics*, 18, pp. 463–514.

Fritsch, M., and Mueller, P. (2004) The effects of new business formation on regional development over time, *Regional Studies*, 38, pp. 961–76.

Garofoli, G. (2002) Local development in Europe: theoretical models and international comparisons, *European Urban and Regional Studies*, 9, pp. 225–39.

Gelb, A., Knight, J. B., and Sabot, R. H. (1991) Employment, rent seeking and economic growth, *Economic Journal*, 101, pp. 1186–99.

Grossman, G. M., and Helpman, E. (1994) Endogenous innovation in the theory of growth, *Journal of Economic Perspectives*, 8, pp. 23–44.

Harris, R. G. (2001) The knowledge-based economy: intellectual origins and new economic perspectives, *International Journal of Management Reviews*, 3, pp. 21–40.

HEW (Higher Education Wales) (2008) *Universities Driving the Emergence of the Knowledge Economy in Wales: Final Evidence to the National Assembly's Enterprise & Learning Committee*. Cardiff: HEW.

Huggins, R. (1997) Regional competitive specialization: development agency sector initiatives in Wales, *Area*, 29(3), pp. 241–52.

Huggins, R. (2003) Creating a UK competitiveness index: regional and local benchmarking, *Regional Studies*, 37(1), pp. 89–96.

Huggins, R., and Izushi, H. (2007) *Competing for Knowledge: Creating, Connecting, and Growing*. London: Routledge.

Huggins, R., and Izushi, H. (eds) (2011) *Competition, Competitive Advantage, and Clusters: The Ideas of Michael Porter*. Oxford: Oxford University Press.

Huggins R., and Johnston A. (2009) Knowledge networks in an uncompetitive region: SME growth and innovation, *Growth and Change*, 40, pp. 227–59.

Huggins, R., and Kitagawa, F. (2012) Regional policy and university knowledge transfer: perspectives from devolved regions in the UK, *Regional Studies*, 46, pp. 817–32.

Huggins, R., and Prokop, D. (2014) Stock markets and economic development: the case for regional exchanges, *International Journal of Innovation and Regional Development*, 5(3), pp. 279–303.

Huggins, R., and Thompson, P. (2010) *UK Competitiveness Index 2010*. Cardiff: Centre for International Competitiveness, UWIC.

Huggins, R., and Thompson, P. (2014a) Culture and place-based development: a socio-economic analysis, *Regional Studies*, doi: 10.1080/00343404.2014.889817.

Huggins, R., and Thompson, P. (2014b) A network-based view of regional growth, *Journal of Economic Geography*, 14, pp. 511–45.

Huggins, R., and Williams, N. (2009) Enterprise and public policy: a review of Labour government intervention in the United Kingdom, *Environment and Planning C: Government and Policy*, 27, pp. 19–41.

Huggins, R., and Williams, N. (2011) Entrepreneurship and regional competitiveness: the role and progression of policy, *Entrepreneurship and Regional Development*, 23(9–0), pp. 907–32.

Huggins, R., Jones, M., and Upton, S. (2008) Universities as drivers of knowledge-based regional development: a triple helix analysis of Wales, *International Journal of Innovation and Regional Development*, 1(1), pp. 24–47.

Huggins, R., Izushi, H., Prokop, D., and Thompson, P. (2014a) *The Global Competitiveness of Regions*. London: Routledge.

Huggins, R., Morgan, B., and Williams, N. (2014b) Regional entrepreneurship and the evolution of public policy and governance: evidence from three regions, *Journal of Small Business and Enterprise Development*, forthcoming.

Ibert, O. (2007) Towards a geography of knowledge creation: the ambivalences between 'knowledge as an object' and 'knowing in practice', *Regional Studies*, 41, pp. 103–14.

Jessop, B. (2004) Hollowing out the nation-state and multilevel governance, in Kennett, P. (ed.), *Handbook of Comparative Social Policy*. Cheltenham: Edward Elgar, pp. 11–25.

Jones, G. E. (1984) *Modern Wales: A Concise History*. Cambridge: Cambridge University Press.

Jones, M. K., and Henley, A. (2008) Welsh economic performance: recent experience and future challenges, *Contemporary Wales*, 21(1), pp. 150–73.

Jones M., Goodwin, M., and Jones R. (2005) State modernization, devolution and economic governance: an introduction and guide to debate, *Regional Studies*, 39, pp. 397–403.

Jones-Evans, D. (2013a) *Access to Finance Review: Stage 1 Report*, http://wales.gov.uk/docs/det/publications/130625accesstofinanceen1.pdf.

Jones-Evans, D. (2013b) *Access to Finance Review: Stage 2 Review*, http://wales.gov.uk/docs/det/publications/131121accesstofund2en.pdf.

Keeble, D., Lawson, C., Moore, B., and Wilkinson, F. (1999) Collective learning processes, networking and 'institutional thickness' in the Cambridge region, *Regional Studies*, 33, pp. 319–32.

Kirzner, I. M. (1973) *Competition and Entrepreneurship*. Chicago: University of Chicago Press.
Kitagawa F. (2007) The regionalization of science and innovation governance in Japan? *Regional Studies*, 41, pp. 1099–114.
Kitson, M., Martin, R., and Tyler, P. (2004) Regional competitiveness: an elusive yet key concept? *Regional Studies*, 38, pp. 991–9.
Koschatzky, K., and Stahlecker, T. (2010) A new challenge for regional policy-making in Europe? Chances and risks of the merger between cohesion and innovation policy, *European Planning Studies*, 18(1), pp. 7–25.
Krugman, P. (2003) *Growth on the Periphery: Second Wind for Industrial Regions?* Glasgow: Fraser Allander Institute.
Lagendijk, A., and Lorentzen, A. (2007) Proximity, knowledge and innovation in peripheral regions: on the intersection between geographical and organizational proximity, *European Planning Studies*, 15(4), pp. 457–66.
Lawson, C., and Lorenz, E. (1999) Collective learning, tacit knowledge and regional innovative capacity, *Regional Studies*, 33, pp. 305–17.
Leborgne, D., and Lipietz, A. (1988) New technologies, new modes of regulation: some spatial implications, *Environment and Planning D: Society and Space*, 6, pp. 263–80.
Lee, S. Y., Florida, R., and Acs, Z. J. (2004) Creativity and entrepreneurship: a regional analysis of new firm formation, *Regional Studies*, 38, pp. 879–91.
Lichtenthaler, U. (2005) External commercialization of knowledge: review and research agenda, *International Journal of Management Reviews*, 7, pp. 231–55.
Lundvall, B.-Å. (ed.) (1992) *National Systems of Innovation*. London: Pinter.
Lundvall, B.-Å. (ed.) (1995) *National Systems of Innovation: Towards a Theory of Innovation and Interactive Learning*. New ed., London: Pinter.
Lundvall, B-Å. (2010) *National Systems of Innovation: Toward a Theory of Innovation and Interactive Learning*. New ed., London: Anthem Press.
Maillat, D. (1998a) Innovative milieux and new generations of regional policies, *Entrepreneurship and Regional Development*, 10, pp. 1–16.
Maillat, D. (1998b) Interactions between urban systems and localized productive systems: an approach to endogenous regional development in terms of innovative milieu, *European Planning Studies*, 6, pp. 117–29.
Malecki, E. J. (2004) Jockeying for position: what it means and why it matters to regional development policy when places compete, *Regional Studies*, 38, pp. 1101–20.
Malecki, E. J. (2007) Cities and regions competing in the global economy: knowledge and local development policies, *Environment and Planning C: Government and Policy*, 25(3), pp. 638–54.
Martin, R. (2005) *Thinking about Regional Competitiveness: Critical Issues*. Nottingham: East Midlands Regional Development Agency.
Mattes, J. (2012) Dimensions of proximity and knowledge bases: innovation between spatial and non-spatial factors, *Regional Studies*, 46, 1085–99.
McAllister, L. (2003) Plaid Cymru. In Osmond, J., and Jones, J. B. (eds), *The Birth of Welsh Democracy: The First Term of the National Assembly for Wales*. Cardiff: Institute of Welsh Affairs.
Meagher, K., and Rogers, M. (2004) Network density and R&D spillovers, *Journal of Economic Behavior and Organization*, 53, pp. 237–60.
Morgan, K. (1997) The learning region: institutions, innovation and regional renewal, *Regional Studies*, 31, pp. 491–503.

Morgan, K. (2012) Path dependency and the state: the politics of novelty in old industrial regions. In Cooke, P. (ed.), *Re-Framing Regional Development: Evolution, Innovation and Transition*. London: Routledge.

Morgan, K., and Mungham, G. (2000) *Redesigning Democracy: The Making of the Welsh Assembly*. Bridgend: Seren.

Morgan, K., and Rees, G. (2001) Learning by doing: devolution and the governance of economic development in Wales. In Chaney, P., Hall, T., and Pithouse, A. (eds), *New Governance, New Democracy*, Cardiff: University of Wales Press.

Mueller, P., Van Stel, A., and Storey, D. J. (2006) *The Effects of New Firm Formation on Regional Development Over Time: The Case of Great Britain*, Max Planck Institute Discussion Papers on Entrepreneurship, Growth and Public Policy, no. 2046.

Murphy, K., Shleifer, A., and Vishny, R. (1993) Why is rent seeking so costly to growth?, *American Economic Review, Papers and Proceedings*, 83, pp. 409–14.

Niskanen, W. N. (1971) *Bureaucracy and Representative Government*. Chicago: Aldine-Alberton Press.

North, D., and Smallbone, D. (2000) Innovative activity in SMEs and rural economic development: some evidence from England, *European Planning Studies*, 8, pp. 87–106.

Osmond, J. (2012) A Welsh brand to die for, *The Welsh Agenda*, 30 April.

Oughton, C., Landabaso, M., and Morgan, K. (2002) The regional innovation paradox: innovation policy and industrial policy, *Journal of Technology Transfer*, 27(1), pp. 97–110.

Parkinson, C. Northcote (1957) *Parkinson's Law, or the Pursuit of Progress*. London: John Murray.

Persson, T., and Tabellini, G. (2000) *Political Economics: Explaining Economic Policy*. Cambridge, MA: MIT Press.

Porter, M. E. (1998) *On Competition*. Boston: Harvard Business School Publishing.

Porter, M. E. (2003) The economic performance of regions, *Regional Studies*, 37, pp. 545–6.

Reiner, C. (2010) Brain competition policy as a new paradigm of regional policy: a European perspective, *Papers in Regional Science*, 89(2), pp. 449–61.

Revilla Diez, J. (2002) Metropolitan innovation systems: a comparison between Barcelona, Stockholm, and Vienna, *International Regional Science Review*, 25, pp. 63–85.

Robinson, C., Carey, J., and Blackaby, D. (2012) Firm performance in Wales: an analysis of productivity using company accounts. Cardiff: WISERD.

Rodríguez-Pose, A. (2013) Do institutions matter for regional development?, *Regional Studies*, 47, 1034–47.

Rodríguez-Pose, A., and Gill, N. (2005) On the 'economic dividend' of devolution, *Regional Studies*, 39, pp. 405–20.

Romer, P. M. (1986) Increasing returns and long-run growth, *Journal of Political Economy*, 94(5), pp. 1002–37.

Romer, P. M. (1990) Endogenous technological change, *Journal of Political Economy*, 98(5), pp. S71–S102.

Romer, P. M. (2007) Economic growth. In Henderson, D. (ed.), *The Concise Encyclopedia of Economics*. Indianapolis: Liberty Fund, pp. 128–31.

Sammarra, A., and Biggiero, L. (2008) Heterogeneity and specificity of inter-firm knowledge flows in innovation networks, *Journal of Management Studies*, 45, pp. 800–29.

Schumpeter, J. A. (1934) *The Theory of Economic Development*. Cambridge, MA: Harvard University Press.

Stevenson L., and Lundstrom A., (2001) 'Entrepreneurship policy for the future', Swedish Foundation for Small Business Research, Stockholm, http://eng.entreprenorskaps forum.se/b/.

Storper, M. (1997) *The Regional World: Territorial Development in a Global Economy*. New York: Guilford Press.

Storper, M. (2005) Society, community, and economic development, *Studies in Comparative International Development*, 39(4), pp. 30–57.

Storper, M. (2008) Community and economics. In Amin, A., and Roberts, J. (eds), *Community, Economic Creativity, and Organization*. New York: Oxford University Press, pp. 37–68.

Thomas, M., and Henderson, D. (2004) Learning through strategy making: the RTP in Wales. In Morgan, K., and Nauwelaers, C., *Regional Innovation Strategies: The Challenge for Less-Favoured Regions*. London: Routledge.

Tinbergen, J. (1985) *Production, Income and Welfare: The Search for an Optimal Social Order*. Brighton: Wheatsheaf.

Tomlinson, P. (2010) Co-operative ties and innovation: some new evidence for UK manufacturing, *Research Policy*, 39, pp. 762–75.

Vasilev, A. (2013) *On the Cost of Rent-Seeking by Government Bureaucrats in a Real-Business-Cycle Framework*, SIRE Discussion Paper, SIRE-DP-2013-84. Edinburgh: Scottish Institute for Research in Economics.

Vaz, T. D., and Nijkamp, P. (2009) Knowledge and innovation: the strings between global and local dimensions of sustainable growth, *Entrepreneurship and Regional Development*, 21, pp. 441–55.

Vázquez-Barquero, A. (2007) Endogenous development: analytical and policy issues. In Scott, A. J., and Garofoli, G. (eds), *Development on the Ground: Clusters, Networks and Regions in Emerging Economies*. London: Routledge, pp. 23–43.

Virkkala, S. (2007) Innovation and networking in peripheral areas: a case study of emergence and change in rural manufacturing, *European Planning Studies*, 15(4), pp. 511–29.

Von Mises, L. (1944) *Bureaucracy*. New Haven, CT: Yale University Press.

Warwick, D. (1975) *A Theory of Public Bureaucracy: Politics, Personality and Organization in the State Department*. Cambridge, MA: Harvard University Press.

WDA (Welsh Development Agency) (1998) *Wales Regional Technology Plan: An Innovation and Technology Strategy for Wales: Review and Update*. Cardiff: WDA.

WDA (Welsh Development Agency) (2000) *Entrepreneurship Action Plan for Wales*. Cardiff: WDA [www.wda.co.uk/resources/ent_actionplan_en.pdf].

WDA (Welsh Development Agency) (2002) *Implementation Plan for Entrepreneurship: Making It Happen*. Cardiff: WDA.

Welsh Assembly Government (2002a) *Wales for Innovation: The Welsh Assembly Government's Action Plan for Innovation*. Cardiff: Welsh Assembly Government.

Welsh Assembly Government (2002b) *A Winning Wales*. Cardiff: Welsh Assembly Government.

Welsh Assembly Government (2005) *Wales: A Vibrant Economy*. Cardiff: Welsh Assembly. http://webarchive.nationalarchives.gov.uk/20060715141954/http://new.wales.gov.uk/docrepos/40382/4038231141/403821124153/wave_en.pdf?lang=en.

Welsh Assembly Government (2006) *Science Policy for Wales*. Cardiff: Welsh Assembly.

Welsh Assembly Government (2010a) *Economic Renewal: A New Direction*. Cardiff: Welsh Assembly; http://wales.gov.uk/docs/det/report/100705anewdirectionen.pdf.

Welsh Assembly Government (2010b) *Delivering a Digital Wales*. Cardiff: Welsh Assembly.
Welsh Government (2012a) *Science for Wales*. Cardiff: Welsh Government.
Welsh Government (2012b) *Wales Infrastructure Investment Plan*. Cardiff: Welsh Government.
Welsh Government (2013) *Innovation Wales*. Cardiff: Welsh Government.
Welsh Office (1998) *Pathway to Prosperity*. London: HMSO.
Williams, D. (1950) *A History of Modern Wales*. London: John Murray.
Yurtsever, Ş. (2011) Investigating the recovery strategies of European Union from the global financial crisis, *Procedia: Social and Behavioral Sciences*, 24, pp. 687–95.
Zucker, L. G., Darby, M. R., Furner, J., Liu, R. C., and Hongyan, M. (2007) Minerva unbound: knowledge stocks, knowledge flows and new knowledge production, *Research Policy*, 36, pp. 850–63.

# 9 Reflecting on 'how' territorial strategies form

## The case of Rafaela, Argentina

*Pablo Costamagna, Mari José Aranguren and Miren Larrea*

### Introduction

There are different angles from which to reflect on territorial strategy. Chapter 4 in this volume focused on a process perspective in an attempt to understand "how" strategies form and proposed thinking in terms of emergent processes rather than prescriptive plans. In order to do so, the chapter adopted a learning approach, complemented by power and culture as critical elements that shape such an emergent strategy (Mintzberg *et al.*, 1998).

In this chapter we use this approach to analyze the case of Rafaela, a city in Santa Fe, Argentina (Costamagna and Gariboldi, 1997; Worcel and Ascúa, 1991). It is a case that has been considered a reference point for local development processes in Latin America (Aghón *et al.*, 2001; Alburquerque *et al.*, 2008). The city has shown a better performance in terms of traditional economic indicators than other cities that might initially be considered similar. It also shows an interesting development of institutions, interpreted both as organizations focused on the development of the city and its surrounding region and as specific rules that shape the behavior of local actors related to development processes. Our main argument is that the case of Rafaela shows a complex combination of approaches to strategy formation, where strategic plans, developed prescriptively, have played a role but are not sufficient to understand long-term development. Indeed, the learning proposed in chapter 4, together with elements of power and culture, help to appreciate the situation far better than analysis of formal planning processes.

As has been stressed throughout the first part of the book, territorial strategies require the participation of many actors. In this chapter we focus mainly on the perspective of a determined group of elected politicians. We also focus on a particular moment in time – the moment when these politicians initiated a process to change the way in which territorial development was undertaken, which had direct consequences on how territorial strategy was subsequently formed. Our analysis begins in the 1990s with the policy developed during two terms by the city council. We will argue that some processes initiated during this period have shaped territorial development in the long term and have influenced some of the capacities that Rafaela exhibits today.

From a methodological point of view, the authors of the study come from two different positions. One of them, Costamagna, is an insider to the process (Herr and Anderson, 2005): as the city councillor in charge of industrial development between 1991 and 1995, he was one of the territorial actors in Rafaela during the key period. The other two authors, Aranguren and Larrea, are outsiders. The research process was initiated with a discussion between insider and outsiders as to the relevant features of how territorial strategy had formed in Rafaela. Once these issues were agreed, the insider wrote an initial draft based on his experience and other relevant documents. This was then further documented, discussed and rewritten in successive cycles by all three authors after several visits made by the outsiders to Rafaela to participate in teaching and research activities. One exception to this is the reflection on social research in Rafaela, where the first draft was written by one of the outsiders after some fieldwork teaching the Maestría en Desarrollo Territorial (master's degree in regional development) in the city.

We start by giving a general overview of the main features of Rafaela, to introduce the motivation for initiating a different approach to territorial development in the city. We then describe the process of strategy formation, examining the process of change both in the municipal government and in the pattern of relationships between the government and other territorial actors. As an example of the latter, a section is dedicated to the change in the pattern of relationship between the government and the association representing business interests. After looking at how the process of strategy formation emerged, we describe how it was institutionalized and the role in that institutionalization played by research. We continue by analyzing two specific elements of strategy formation: the role of training and the role of internationalization. The chapter ends with concluding reflections.

## The main features of Rafaela

The city of Rafaela is located in the Department of Castellanos, in the central-west part of the Province of Santa Fe in Argentina. It is about 90 kilometers from the provincial capital and about 540 kilometers from Buenos Aires. The city has around 100,000 inhabitants.

The configuration of industry in Rafaela is closely linked to the arrival of immigrants from the Piedmont region in Italy and Swiss-German immigrants, who mainly developed the farming sector. After the 1920s a manufacturing sector emerged, initially centered on the transformation of local primary products and machinery for the agricultural sector. These manufacturing activities developed over the following decades, and Rafaela today has a diversified manufacturing sector composed mainly of automotive components, cooling equipment, food-processing machinery and a strong food sector.

Following Carmona (2003), Yoguel and Moori-Koenig (1999), Kantis *et al.* (2000) and Costamagna (2011), Rafaela is considered a success story in the field of territorial economic development from the perspective of business competitiveness, but also from the perspective of business atmosphere. We concentrate mainly on this second perspective.

It is often argued that Rafaela is a good case to analyze not because it has fewer problems than other territories, but because it has greater capacity to solve problems. We will examine the process of how some basic conditions were created in the 1990s to foster such capabilities, and how territorial development nowadays is still shaped by some of the decisions made then. Consequently, the experience of Rafaela is the result of a long historical process of institutional development. The ability of different organizations in Rafaela to work in an articulated way has been studied, among others, by Ferraro and Costamagna (1999) and Valle (2008).

Politics in Rafaela has been critical in fostering communication between the various actors involved. The process was not conceived as a simple instrument for territorial development but as a social construction process that would be continuous and dynamic, leading to long-term results. In order to play their role the municipality went through a process of learning and change (Mirabella, 2002). Until the beginning of the 1990s the municipality was somewhat isolated from the productive sector of the city, developing only traditional activities and without participating actively in discussions on economic, educational and institutional issues. But in the 1990s Rafaela took a qualitative step forward, characterized by two main factors: the role played by the local public administration and a shared effort among the different actors to define and execute development policies (Costamagna, 1999). Many of the features of Rafaela today can be considered as long-term results of this process.

As stated by Costamagna (2011), the economic performance of firms has been accompanied by the dynamism and capabilities of the municipal government and other public and private organizations such as associations, technology centers and the university (see also Quintar *et al.*, 1993). The articulation of a local network of organizations and the joint action of the municipal government and other organizations (mainly private firms) has created an atmosphere that has led to the development of innovative policies for territorial development. At the beginning the process was led mainly by the government and the private sector. But in the last decade there has also been active involvement by the scientific and technological sector.

Ferraro and Costamagna (1999) concluded that one of the important features in Rafaela's development of public–private cooperation is that all organizations involved achieved the recognition of the other actors and their place in the local structure was known and respected. This place is directly linked to the capabilities that each organization developed over time. Other features that have been emphasized are the clear pursuit of continuous rethinking of the region through policy design, including observation of best practices, and a continuous dialogue with international experts. An element that complements this perspective is the style of leadership, which has allowed actors to keep communication going among different organizations and reach consensus for joint action. This has helped solve conflicts, developing the capability of different organizations to listen to each other. The leadership style that has emerged in the region as a consequence is one that reflects a shared vision of local economic development. This was the political goal of territorial actors rather than the result of market forces. It is no doubt a dynamic process that requires continuous work.

The main argument that we will develop throughout this chapter is that the change process initiated in the 1990s has shaped the features of Rafaela and has given the city the ability to solve problems. We will argue that this process and its subsequent impact over the following decades make sense when interpreted as a learning approach to strategy formation.

## The motivation to initiate a different approach to strategy

In this section we focus on how the decisions and engagement of a government can form an important element that initiates a process of change, which in turn shapes strategy in a territory. We describe the process that started in 1991 and what the members of the municipal government at that time thought and felt about it.

A new administration arrived at the city council of Rafaela in 1991. It consisted of a young team, with little experience in public management but who were willing to make changes in the city. In their opinion, the council was not prepared for some issues that the rapid changes of context required; what was needed was a flexible organization that could adapt to new times – or, as they termed it, "to manage a complex reality". In retrospect, this awareness of the complexity of territorial development is at the core of the learning approach to strategy formation.

Argentina was in a deep economic crisis, and there was a belief that "less state and more market" was the key to development (Rubinzal, 2010; Kosacoff and Ramos, 2001; Kosacoff and Mercado, 2009). What citizens expected from government was mainly the traditional services. At the same time, neoliberal approaches, arguing for decentralization, pushed some services that had previously been provided by the central government to the municipalities – for instance, employment, support to SMEs and preventive health care. This took place in part to ease the central government's external debt, but it was done without providing local governments with the necessary resources. All of these elements added complexity to the challenge of the municipal government to find its own way in territorial development.

But this did not discourage the team, who believed it was necessary to reorganize public administration, to work with balanced budgets, to professionalize public-sector agents and to improve the processes and services offered by the council. Their goal was that different territorial actors individually, and various organizations and the region collectively, should develop new capabilities to work on development and inclusion issues. This focus was another critical element for the development of a learning approach.

The government believed that public administration should have a key place in society. This formed part of their political vision, which was neither a mainstream position nor the main one shared in the media. Besides, if they wanted to propose and promote changes, they needed to have management capacity and respond to the pressure from citizens to solve problems at the local level. Thus strategy for the territory emerged as the result of two main influences: the political stance of the incoming municipal government and the pressure they felt from citizens.

To put it in a nutshell, we might say that an awareness of the complexity of territorial development, the focus on individual and collective capabilities, and the combination of the position of the government and the requirements of its citizens are the critical elements. In turn, and over time, they have shaped an approach to strategy formation with a strong component of learning.

## First steps towards change: changes inside the government

The first changes in the development of a learning approach to strategy formation affected mostly members of government and civil servants in the municipality. Regarding structures, for instance, they reinforced the social policy area and created a specific sector that would deal with economic issues.

Regarding more intangible elements, a discourse of openness, dialogue and high commitment was adopted and transmitted transversally through all areas. This discourse emphasized the values that the political leaders considered should be at the core of management: transparency, honesty, participation and quality. Such an effort to focus on values connects with analysis in chapter 4 of the significance of culture for developing territorial strategy processes. Having a new approach to strategy formation in a territory is not about having the right solution ready to be implemented; it is about social change and requires working on the principles, attitudes and behavior taken for granted by all involved.

During the first few years after the new team took office, firms were considered to be the most innovative organizations in the region, since they were rethinking processes and developing many training activities. The city government started learning from companies: they thought that such innovations would contribute to the performance of the city council, providing flexibility and efficiency, and leading to more trust in relationships both with other territorial actors and with citizens. They needed trust in order to develop their strategy, and they knew that in order to build trust they had to work efficiently and show that they could fulfill their promises.

Bearing in mind that they needed to learn in order to generate the trust that the change process required, the city mayor took the political decision of empowering some administrative teams. Empowerment and trust are critical elements of social capital and new modes of governance presented in chapter 4 (Jessop, 1998; Nahapiet and Ghoshal, 1998). One of these teams had the specific aim of improving internal public administration. It was no easy task, for the culture of the administration had erected strong barriers against change. In other words, the new discourse of the political leaders had not yet had time to take root.

Nevertheless there was a lot of energy among some politicians to push the process forward, and in the medium term it led to a reduction in administrative times, a cutting of the costs of several services, and an improvement in transparency and in dealing with citizens, all of which enhanced the public image of the administration. This first phase ended in 1995 with the National Prize of Quality, which was awarded to the council by the national government. The award contributed towards increasing the public credibility of the council. One of the main lessons learnt during this phase was that, in order to be able to lead a process such as this, it is necessary to devote time and effort and to have teams that will continuously drive the process forward, overcoming resistance to change.

The working routines of the politicians became the core of the learning approach to strategy. The members of the municipal government met each Friday evening and Saturday morning with the aim of training themselves, discussing politics, searching for a common language and vision, and considering and agreeing work programs. They were aware that others needed to be trained but also those in charge of policies and those leading the design and execution of different programs. After some time, these spaces for learning evolved and transformed into spaces for coordination among different council departments and those in charge of them. This contributed towards solving a problem that is frequent in public administration – compartmentalization.

Within a short period of time, in addition to their training in Rafaela, all members of the cabinet received training outside Argentina. This was a challenge, as agendas made travelling abroad difficult. But in retrospect it was highly positive, as it not only strengthened the technical capabilities of individual politicians but also allowed them to gain a better and more open perspective on processes of change. As one of the government members said, "We started to understand better what was happening in the world."[1] The possibility of travelling was also considered as recognition of the effort that they were making.

The main aspect we would like to highlight in this section is the government's choice to develop a learning approach starting with its own learning. As discussed in chapter 4, social capital and trust are critical to develop a learning approach to strategy formation. If a government tries to foster a territorial strategy based on learning by instructing others or by generating the conditions for others to learn, but do not involve themselves in the learning process, it makes it very difficult to generate the social capital that these processes require.

## Changing outwards: involving territorial actors in the strategy formation

One of the results of the reflection and learning process for members of the government and public administration was their awareness that the strategy for territorial development should be designed and coordinated together with the rest of society. There was a will to search for collective strategies; they began to understand that development is not an exclusive competence of the administration and that it was necessary to open participation to others. This generated deep debates about the role of the administration and also created the need to generate new capacities and abilities – this time not only in the government and administration but also among territorial actors. This is an example of what was discussed in chapter 4 in terms of dynamic territorial capabilities and also relates to the learning-centered approach to strategy evaluation set out in chapter 6.

Although it was clear that there were different interests – sometimes in conflict – in the region, the political team considered it was necessary to strengthen dialogue among territorial actors. This led to a reflection on who these actors were and whether they were articulated or not in order to share their perspective on the development issues. In practical terms, the members of the public administration decided to work with business associations, but also with other companies that were outside that system.[2] As a result of this approach, they began to forge a new type of relationship with firms, business associations, the university, technology centers, training centers and citizens' organizations, among others.

Work commissions – for example, for the promotion of culture, for issues related to people with disabilities, and for sports – were formed with citizens' organizations to discuss policies. They received public funds, and a dialogue was initiated to set up working routines. In the beginning the discussions were only about budget distribution, but over time participation became deeper and more fruitful and a culture for exchanges was reinforced.

The processes developed in these commissions had a learning dimension but also a dimension focused on negotiation. In chapter 4 it was argued that, together with the learning school, the power school helps understand how strategy can emerge as a result of continual negotiation among territorial actors. We understand this as complementary to other approaches to strategy formation, but we examine it in the next section with a concrete example of how strategy emerged in Rafaela.

## Public–private cooperation: complementing learning with negotiation

Reality was telling the political team that the public administration could not build development in isolation, and that dialogue, participation and public–private collaboration were important capacity-building mechanisms. It was important to have an attitude and a will for shared work, and it was necessary to build new spaces with other organizations. As a response they developed an "outdoors" management policy: getting out of the office, getting to know and meet people, talking, being available on the telephone, and building active listening processes were clear instructions to the political team.

An example of this approach was the implementation of the Program for Micro and Small Enterprises, which worked with more than ninety companies that did not have any link with a business association. Because they were small they suffered from a lack of information and reduced management capacity. This was a sector that had "no institutionalized voice" in the region. Politicians started to visit the companies one by one, to show that they were not only collecting their taxes but were trying to help solve their problems.

This approach meant literally "knocking on the door of each company", listening to problems about how the system failed to respond to their financial problems and trying to visualize other relevant issues (costs, innovation, networks, etc.). Action was then generated jointly by firms and politicians to improve competitiveness levels: more visits were made to companies, information was supplied, training courses were set up, and marketing was undertaken through fairs and missions both inside and outside the country. After several months in dialogue with businessmen, these activities resulted in a new organization – the Cámara de Pequeñas Industrias de la Región (CAPIR; Chamber of Small Industries in the Region) – which was established at the headquarters of the local business association in the Commercial and Industrial Center.

But it would be misleading to tell this story without making reference to the relationship between the municipal government and the board of directors of the Commercial and Industrial Center, representing the larger firms. At first, they feared that this new approach to help smaller firms was a "trick" to weaken the private sector. The council explained that it was a strategy to strengthen the territory; they asked the association to give them time to prove their intentions and proposed that they join forces. The association trusted the council and gave them that chance. Thus the initial conditions to let the process emerge had to be negotiated before a shared vision of the future could be constructed to create the conditions for further collaboration. If we reflect on this using the frameworks presented in chapter 4, in order to learn together it is necessary to negotiate and form a shared vision.

One innovative idea was the way in which teams were built, which brought young people to the council through the university's internship program. Some politicians suggested that the students brought a "freshness" to the public administration, and a link between university and companies was later expanded, giving the council greater capacity to reach the private sector.

Another critical element in the learning process was evidence that the new spaces created for companies to undertake training led to the generation of new businesses or solutions to problems. But it was not only formal learning spaces that were relevant; more relaxed informal spaces also contributed to the process. For example, "*asados*" (barbecues) consolidated the team and opened new perspectives for the long term.

The business sector began to form a different impression of the public administration. They saw it not only as a collector of taxes but also as an actor that could help them achieve their goals. Meeting people who were working in the public sector and realizing that they wanted to bring change brought a reduction in prejudice concerning bureaucracy and politics in the business sector.

It is important to highlight a publication evaluating the process: *Industrial Policy at the Local Level: Evaluation of the Policy of the Municipality for the Promotion of Business Partnerships in Small Industrial Companies in Rafaela* (CEPAL, 1996). This was a document prepared by ECLAC (The Economic Commission for Latin America) and Rafaela City Council and showed that the companies which were associated with CAPIR had demonstrated increased capabilities in making changes. They also had a more systematized knowledge about how to use the resources made available by different policy programs. The municipal policies had contributed to the incorporation of new issues on the agendas of businesses, mostly related to modernization and competitiveness – issues that most of the companies concerned would have been unable to face in isolation. The document also demonstrated the awareness among territorial actors that behind these achievements there was a process of trust building.

## Institutionalizing the learning approach

Chapter 4 proposed that the learning, power and cultural schools of strategy-making are approaches that are not alternatives but complementary to planning. While plans are prescriptive, their approach is emergent. In this section we reflect on the complementary relationship between emergent and prescriptive approaches in the case of Rafaela, showing that the strategic plans of the city came to institutionalize some of the features of the emergent processes generated by a learning approach.

In 1996 the citizens and organizations of Rafaela participated widely in drawing up a strategic plan. One of the results of this was the creation, at the end of 1997, of the Instituto de Capacitación y Estudios para el Desarrollo Local (ICEDeL; Institute of Training and Studies for Local Development), with the aim of supporting changes and transformation in the local community. It focused on training, the strengthening of interaction between the public administration and local actors, and the transformation of local government. The establishment of the institute meant the institutionalization and legitimization of ideas that had been developed previously. Action, participation, consensus and leadership to solve new situations and problems were considered as key elements.

### *Research as a source for learning "how"*

Another critical element that we see in the case of Rafaela is the explicit awareness of the government of the relevance of "how" in strategy. This dimension, which could also be described as a process perspective, is one of the elements that make this case particularly interesting from the perspective proposed in chapter 4. During the 1990s there was a will to improve the communication between territorial actors. The government was aware that this was not easy. "How to do it" was the key issue because it dealt mostly with intangible topics. Initially the government worked in an intuitive way, but the need to systematize the approach became clear. This led them, together with the ECLAC office in Buenos Aires, to start building up a research methodology that would allow them to enter into dialogue with the main organizations in the region. They were interested in this research as a "product", but also in the "process" itself that would produce learning.

The methodology helped improve the identification of support organizations for business development and the connection with key informants. The government made a map of all the organizations in the system by approaching the actors with two goals: one was to obtain general information concerning the organization's structure (number of employees, goals, management capacity, perceptions about the context); the other was to sound out the opinion of different actors on the research process itself as a method of working together. In this sense, research was an instrument not only to analyze the relationships in the region but also to build them.

For some of the government members, who worked in teams together with researchers from ECLAC, it was very important to have contact with other actors. They could establish a dialogue with a broader scope than was the case in their day-to-day work. This ended up being an important learning experience.

Later they developed more fieldwork with interviews. The results were analyzed by the researchers, government members and those who had been interviewed. With these inputs they carried out a deep reflection on the productive model of Rafaela, holding workshops involving high levels of participation. Issues covered were, among others, information flows and public–private cooperation.

This process is interesting not only for its results as a specific research project, but for the learning process generated among policy-makers together with territorial actors. This led to the institutionalization of a pattern of relationships based on dialogue among the different constituents in order to analyze situations and generate action to respond together to challenges.

### *Reflecting on the results of learning "how"*

One of the relevant results of the project described above was the contribution to government learning. It helped them to formulate a working plan that allowed them to reflect and work on development topics over a longer time scale, beyond the urgencies of their daily activities. Combining theoretical discussions on leadership with actually contacting leading personnel in the various public and private fields helped them realize that there was not only one type of leadership that was required in the strategy formation process. One of the lessons learnt for members of the government that is considered relevant in retrospect is that approaching business and educational leaders and understanding their ideas and visions helped them to develop a more flexible approach to the territorial development process. The government acknowledged, together with these other actors, the need to identify those who were active in the generation of proposals and initiatives in the region and hold discussions with them in a constructive way; this helped articulate a new approach to participation that was more open than previously and led to some consensus as to policy. This way of proceeding, which at the beginning was considered experimental, was later extended and consolidated as an approach to public–private cooperation in Rafaela.

Another lesson learnt in this process of systematizing "how" development took place in Rafaela was that training became consolidated as a core activity. Training generated spaces for discussion, which led to action, and the more the different public and private actors worked together, the stronger the relationships of trust among them became. This generated better conditions for more ambitious projects.

One challenge that was faced in the process and became one of the critical features of the model was the need for a new communication system. The project generated the context for territorial actors to share their perceptions that information was not flowing adequately. This led to specific action to improve the communication system. For instance, those in the educational system, who had previously been excluded from territorial development projects, were systematically included.

Another relevant element was analysis of the barriers to cooperation, among them individualism, lack of human resources, and political interests. The necessary actions to overcome these were also discussed. One of the main obstacles identified was the lack of coordination between different organizations. There was a clear demand for more professionalism and for the development of trust. The fact that territorial actors had identified their own weakness in this respect made the solution much easier to implement.

One more important issue was time management. Working on these topics requires patience, and it was necessary to eliminate the idea that "we want everything now". The private sector tended to view matters in the short term, but the process allowed them all, public and private actors, to see the necessity of keeping a long-term perspective. However, they also kept in mind the need to achieve short-term goals that would allow them to show results and to keep building trust.

## The role of training in strategy formation

One of the specificities of the case of Rafaela is the way training has been interpreted as a critical element for territorial development, and how it has been designed and implemented closely linked to the priorities that were detected not only by the private sector but also by policy-makers. This, as we have said, is something that was not planned as such but emerged as a process that has been consolidated over the years.

It was realized early on that many well-trained people are needed to generate development in a region, not only within the public administration but also in society in general. The strength of this idea led to an approach to training in Rafaela that combined formal and informal spaces where capabilities were developed following the needs detected in various fields. The many meetings, courses, workshops and training trips developed throughout the years are characteristic of Rafaela's process, all these constituting also tools for participation, networking and shared vision building, as people met, listened to each other, and influenced one another.

Although this policy has never been evaluated, the effort to keep training at the core of the process has been maintained over time and by different governments (though the same political party) for more than twenty years. The activities that have taken place range from workshops and seminars on critical issues relating to innovation and productivity, on the one hand, to a master's degree in territorial development being taught at the time of writing, on the other. Those in Rafaela who participate in these training processes are also varied: civil servants, local development agents, businessmen and agents of the regional technology system (mainly university and technology centers). The formal programs are designed in such a way that they respond directly to the development model of the city. As one of the deans in a local university said when opening the master's degree, "Territorial development implies a change in management. It is not possible to achieve it with the same attitudes as usual; we need to make a big effort in capacity building."[3]

According to the words of the Italian expert Patrizio Bianchi, as a result of this focus on training, a body of executive agents has been created that work not only in local public administration but also in business associations, universities, research centers, and international organizations. The creation of this body of agents is one of the key factors for the success of the territorial development policy. The focus on these spaces where they all meet to share training, visions and critics is characteristic of this region.

The experience of Rafaela shows the relevance of training, but not just any approach to training. A feature of this case is that training has been linked to action. The city's territorial development model was not designed or planned first in theory and then implemented. It is an emergent model that was slowly institutionalized and where learning and action were very much connected. Those developing the model became involved in learning processes to support their action. They then generated learning spaces to reflect on their action and to learn collectively as to the next steps. It is this collective capacity to combine learning and action that is a feature of Rafaela's approach to strategy formation.

## Social research in strategy formation

These last sections deal with features of the model related to past events but which are reaching new stages of development. In particular, this section is based on the reflection process developed by the authors, which was complemented by a shared reflection with the students of the master's degree in territorial development in Rafaela in 2014 using an action research approach. These students came largely from local firms, the university, research centers, and the municipality.

If we take a traditional perspective of a regional innovation system and its three sub-systems (production, knowledge and policy) (Karlsen and Larrea, 2014), we might look for social research at university and related institutes and might rapidly conclude that there is no strong approach to social research linked to territorial development. But a closer look at the processes going on in Rafaela shows there are nuances related to this interpretation.

In a discussion with the students about social research in Rafaela, we realized that they unexpectedly located social researchers in the three sub-systems. We say "unexpectedly" because we anticipated that they would locate them in the knowledge generation sub-system – that is, the university, related institutes and technology centers. This led us to define Rafaela's approach to social research as diffuse compared with the more centralized approaches we had met in other cases, notably in the Basque Country, where we found that social researchers were found mainly in research organizations. Though the university in Rafaela has recently developed the degree in territorial development, its focus remains largely on the technological field, while social research on territorial development has traditionally been undertaken in organizations of the production and political sub-systems, which require new knowledge to develop their processes and undertake research on their own organizations.

There is a clear feeling among the territorial actors in Rafaela that there is social research going on and being integrated into the territorial development process, but it took time for the two authors of this chapter who were outsiders to the system to realize that the social research capabilities were not concentrated exclusively in the university but distributed more widely.

One of the features of social research in territorial development in Rafaela is that there are local social researchers who do not have a formal relationship with the university and are located in other organizations, mainly connected to the municipality and business associations. And even if they are linked to the university, they rarely work full time there. Their profile is mixed, often with responsibilities both in the university and in other organizations related to territorial development, mostly the municipality or a local development agency. This helps strengthen the connections between these organizations and contributes to the diffusion of social research in the system.

Another feature that characterizes social research in Rafaela is the high number of international social researchers who, without having lived there, are linked to the city and its development process. Their connection has often materialized through actors in the political sub-system, mainly the municipality, in the context of cooperation projects developed at local, national and international levels. A paradigmatic case is that of Francisco Alburquerque, a Spanish expert in territorial development who has considerable influence in Latin America, who was made an honorary citizen of Rafaela.

A third feature of social research in Rafaela is a very strong link with multilateral organizations such as ECLAC (a United Nations organization), which participated in reflection processes, and FOMIN (the Multilateral Investment Fund of the Inter-American Development Bank), which funded projects to support SMEs and also generated spaces for learning. This has created again the context for the participation of social researchers in Rafaela's development process, with a stronger link often to the municipality than to the local university.

Our hypothesis when analyzing the case is that this diffuse model of social research in 2014 responds to the framework that has been evolving, based among other trends, as a result of the decisions made in the 1990s. More specifically, social research has developed to support the learning processes of territorial actors. Such learning processes were led at the beginning by the political sub-system, mainly the municipality. That is why social research has developed in the spaces for dialogue and learning among territorial actors and not concentrated in the university environment, as in other places. We consider that this to be another feature of an approach to strategy formation based on an emergent process linked to learning.

## The role of internationalization in strategy formation

Up to now we have analyzed mainly the local dimension of strategy formation in Rafaela. But it would be impossible to understand the learning approach in the city without understanding international relationships that also contributed to such learning.

In the 1990s, companies in Rafaela were developing internationalization processes with good insertion in global markets. In coordination with the business sector – especially the chamber of commerce – the public administration developed some programs to support the construction of relationships between firms and new markets. It also started working on a new concept of internationalization of the economy that would go beyond the commercial dimension and include production, education, social and cultural issues. They developed region-to-region links with a network approach.

For instance, a scholarship and students' exchange program was set up with Baden- Württemberg (Germany), in which the business sector and education and cultural organizations participated. Through this program, German students completed internships in Rafaela for six months and students from Rafaela enjoyed similar experiences in Germany.[4] In 1996 Rafaela signed a twinning agreement with Fossano (Italy) to strengthen cultural ties and to establish cooperation and exchange mechanisms, among them cultural programs, a project to cross-breed Piedmontese and Holando Argentina cattle, the implementation of a student exchange program, and technical assistance in several firms.

The Japan International Cooperation Agency (JICA), Inasmet/Tecnalia (Basque Country), Columbus Networks and other organizations have a presence in the region. Local actors have been active in establishing contacts with international organizations. There has been a public–private approach and a key role for education –two of the main features of the process that had begun in the 1990s.

Currently, the cooperative actions taking place with the aim of the city's internationalization are based on knowledge management. The idea is to move from a company-focused perspective to one where the region learns by connecting to the rest of the world. Though some of the results mentioned were formalized, most of the work was done in informal spaces that required a high level of compromise among those who were leading the process. This is one of the main reasons why we consider this internationalization process to be also part of the learning approach to strategy formation in Rafaela. Below is an extract from an email exchanged in 1995 between some of the leaders of the internationalization process which shows the spirit of the way in which they worked:

> the process with the group is priesthood. The profile of the people we are approaching is oriented more to action than to strategy formulation … They get more easily involved in tangible things. But we need more than just voluntarism on their side: their organizations don't prioritize what they are doing, don't give them the spaces to work on these issues or don't listen to them when they bring news. At the moment the group is a space to validate processes and gather needs and challenges; we must not be too ambitious in the beginning. In which direction should we advance? We should keep bringing them together, not stop: analyze with them how their organizations can create the spaces to work through these issues, understand their logic,

> help them face topics which they feel uncomfortable with. At some point we should have a solid group, let's not slow down.

These efforts brought results that the participants had not foreseen in the beginning: some of the students in the exchange programs created new businesses, knowledge was exchanged in industry, and small investments from Rafaela were made overseas. It produced a myriad of new ties with a complex and changing world that helped open up the city. These elements were not foreseen because there was not a planning approach to strategy by which it was first designed and then executed. But this does not mean that they were not actively sought. There was a conscious effort to foster collaboration and learning, knowing that new actions would follow that could not be planned in advance. This is why we consider Rafaela to be a good case study as to how a learning approach to strategy formation develops in an emergent manner. As we have previously argued, these emergent strategies often develop in a territory together with strategic plans that at times collide and at others reinforce each other.

## Conclusions

The main goal in the chapter has been to share with the reader a case on strategy formation that emphasizes a process perspective by focusing on a learning approach instead of the much more generalized planning approach to strategy formation. As we argued, however, this does not mean that the planning approach has not been relevant in Rafaela.

The first conclusion is that the learning approach must depart from an understanding of the complexity of territorial development. The learning approach has to do with the actors in a region, who hold a diversity of perspectives and ideological positions. The process must consider this diversity and start by creating the spaces where these actors can meet and get to know each other. We saw the relevance of the process of trust building in this respect.

But how to proceed in these spaces where actors meet? What Rafaela shows is that training can play a key role. It creates environments where different problematic issues can be approached and analyzed and possible solutions discussed. It generates spaces where trust is built. It contributes to the development of collective capabilities, which means that it is not only individuals that learn, but that there can be a collective dimension of learning that provides a territory with the capacity to solve problems more efficiently. Training is linked to social research, which can help conceptualize an approach to territorial strategy. Finally, training can have an international dimension that can help open up a territory.

Public–private cooperation is another critical feature of this case. Learning as the engine of strategy formation cannot be undertaken by some and then transferred to others. It must be a collective process, and so cooperation is needed. But the picture of cooperation in Rafaela includes another critical concept: negotiation. This is very much related to the power school in strategy formation, which clearly complements the learning school in this case.

Another lesson learnt in Rafaela is related to the time span of strategy. Strategies based on a learning approach must show results in the short term in order to survive but generate change in the long term. As we saw, some of the features of Rafaela today are the result of a learning approach that was initiated in the 1990s, so we can clearly see how the decisions made more than twenty years ago are having an effect at the present time.

Our main conclusion after studying the case of Rafaela is the relevance of developing analytical frameworks in territorial strategy that complement the more traditional ones based on strategic planning. The learning approach, which has been the main approach studied in this chapter, can make a contribution in this respect. The case of Rafaela shows that there are features of the development process made visible by the learning approach that are important in understanding "how" strategy is formed.

## Notes

1 A comment from a local civil servant made in the workshop evaluations.
2 For much of the 1990s only 40 per cent of industrial companies were members of the business association.
3 Oscar David, dean of Universidad Tecnológica Nacional, Regional Department of Rafaela, speech inaugurating the master's degree in regional development.
4 Up to November 2002, forty-nine German students and twenty-six from Rafaela had taken part in the program (Mirabella, 2002).

## References


Aghón G., Albuquerque F., and Cortés, P. (2001) *Desarrollo económico local y descentralización en América Latina: un análisis comparativo*. CEPAL – GTZ.

Alburquerque, F., Costamagna, P., and Ferraro, C. (2008) *Desarrollo económico local, descentralización y democracia*. UNSAM.

Carmona, R. (2003) *Fomento productivo, entorno institucional y desarrollo económico local: análisis de casos en el escenario argentino*. Universidad Nacional de General Sarmiento.

CEPAL (1996) *Política industrial a nivel local: evaluación de la política de la municipalidad para la promoción de la asociatividad empresarial en pequeñas empresas industriales de Rafaela*. Municipalidad de Rafaela y CEPAL.

Costamagna, P. (1999) *Iniciativa de desarrollo económico local: la articulación y las interacciones entre instituciones: el caso de Rafaela, Argentina*. CEPAL–GTZ.

Costamagna, P. (2011) *El caso Rafaela 1991–1995: los primeros años de una experiencia de largo plazo: reflexiones para Gipuzkoa Sarean*. País Vasco: Orkestra.

Costamagna P., and Gariboldi, J. (1997) *Políticas de desarrollo local: el intento de la ciudad de Rafaela*. Documento de Trabajo.

Ferraro, C., and Costamagna, P. (1999) *Ambiente, entorno institucional y desarrollo: la articulación y las interacciones entre las instituciones de soporte técnico al desarrollo empresarial: el caso Rafaela*. CEPAL.

Herr, K., and Anderson, G. L. (2005) *The Action Research Dissertation*. Thousand Oaks, CA: Sage.

Jessop, B. (1998) The rise of governance and the risks of failure: the case of economic development, *International Social Science Journal*, 50 (March), pp. 29–45.

Kantis, H., Carmona, R., and Ascúa, R. (2000) *El estudio de las redes empresariales en el diagnóstico del desarrollo local: elementos metodológicos y su aplicación al caso Rafaela*. Córdoba: Red PyMEs MERCOSUR-IEF.

Karlsen J., and Larrea, M. (2014) *Territorial Development and Action Research: Innovation through Dialogue*. Farnham: Gower.

Kosacoff, B., and Mercado, R. (eds) (2009) *La Argentina ante la nueva internacionalización de la producción: crisis y oportunidades*. Buenos Aires: CEPAL–PNUD.

Kosacoff, B., and Ramos, A. (2001) *Cambios contemporáneos en la estructura industrial argentina, 1975–2000*. Bernal: Universidad Nacional de Quilmes.

Mintzberg, H., Ahlstrand, B., and Lampel, J. (1998) *Strategy Safari*. New York: Free Press.

Mirabella, R. (2002) Estrategias de desarrollo económico en el marco de la cooperación público-privada: la experiencia de la cuidad de Rafaela. ICEDeL (mimeo).

Nahapiet, J., and Ghoshal, S. (1998) Social capital, intellectual capital and the organizational advantage, *Academy of Management Review*, 22(2), pp. 242–66.

Quintar, A., Ascúa R., Gatto F., and Ferraro C. (1993) *Rafaela: un cuasi-distrito italiano "a la argentina"*. Documento de Trabajo no. 35, CEPAL.

Rubinzal, D. (2010) *Historia económica Argentina 1880–2009: desde los tiempos de Julio Argentino hasta Cristina Fernandez de Kirchner*. Bernal: Universidad Nacional de Quilmes.

Valle, Judith (2008) Análisis del entramado institucional rafaelino. Tesis de maestría. Universidad de Bologna.

Worcel G., and Ascúa, R. (1991) *Dinamismo empresarial y cooperación institucional: el caso de las pymes de Rafaela*. Doc. no. 24, CFI/CEPAL.

Yoguel, G., and Moori-Koenig (eds) (1999) *Los problemas del entorno de negocios: el desarrollo competitivo de las PyMEs argentinas*. UNGS–FUNDES.

# 10 Cross-bordering strategies for the Øresund region

## Different eras and territorial strategies, but unrevealed potential

*Christian Tangkjær and Ola Jonsson*

### Introduction

In this chapter our aim is to discuss the history of the Øresund region in order to understand how different territorial strategies support different cross-bordering strategies. We focus on how local actors and policies (both public and private) aim to create and transform institutions that foster the conditions for cross-border regional spaces. Having this focus means that we are interested first and foremost in institutional processes behind cross-border regionalisation, related to the 'how' of territorial strategy as explored in chapter 4 and in several of the other cases in this book. However, our interest in this chapter is also to reflect more critically on cross-border regions (CBRs) and to take a normative position.

In our research on CBRs we are basically interested in the different territorial strategies that are being followed, and from our research on the Øresund region it seems that several such strategies have been adopted during the last twenty years. As such, Øresund seems an excellent case for understanding different cross-bordering strategies.

### Being and becoming in-between spaces

CBRs are highly varied, and it is probably difficult to compare them because of institutional, political and economical characteristics. However, we believe that they share some fundamental characteristics, principally that of being a space in-between two or more nation-states. Anthropologists have studied such in-between spaces or borderlands for the formation of specific cultural practices or border cultures. For instance, Löfgren (1999) wonderingly examines the pedagogical settings in borderlands and how they prescribe different cultural practices of border crossing. Alvarez (1995) even calls specifically for making an *anthropology of borderlands* that could produce knowledge on the paradoxical, on the contradictory, and on the conflicts of cultural practices and identity in present society. In this chapter we focus our attention on the potentiality of these cross-border spaces.

From his research, Rottenburg (2000) concludes that borderlands are transitory spaces or, referring to a term from the anthropology of performance (Turner 1969, 1982, 1987), liminal space-times. In such transitory spaces symbols have the potential to move and change, because such space-times are a storehouse of possibilities. According to Turner (1982: 28), liminal space-times are the settings in which new models, symbols, paradigms, etc., arise; they are in fact the seedbeds of cultural creativity. Rottenburg's (2000) use of Turner's comparative symbology enabled him to catch symbols in their movement and to look at their ludic capacity (Turner, 1982: 23) – their capacity for variation and experimentation (ibid.: 29).

Every new state form and political power in general introduces its own particular way of partitioning space; it introduces its own administrative classification of discourse about space and about things and people in that space (Lefebvre, 1991: 281). A CBR represents territorial strategies and political powers and particular ways of partitioning spaces of things and people. We understand cross-border spaces as extraordinary spaces of becoming, and we believe that these extraordinary spaces are spaces of possible new movements, anxiety, conflicts, experimentations, new experiences, new agencies and structures (e.g., Alvarez, 1995; Smouts, 1998; Church and Reid, 1999; Blatter, 2003; Carmin *et al.*, 2003; Kramsch and Hooper, 2004; Löfgren, 1999, 2008). CBRs are not something fixed and completed; they do not have 'institutional thickness' (Amin and Thrift, 1995) but are outside national and regional 'thick' institutional systems. They are characterised by heterogeneity and institutional complexity and they are by nature non-institutionalised spaces, although nation-state bureaucracies of course try to institutionalise and control them in terms of their nature as 'border machines' (rules, regulation, identification, etc.). CBRs are expressions of both de-territorialisation and reterritorialisation (Hillier, 2013).

By definition CBRs are betwixt and between. They are in the midst of different bureaucratic national institutional systems, sometimes in the midst of cultural systems, sometimes in the midst of linguistic systems, and sometimes in the midst of different economic systems of production. This means that a CBR is a mid-space that risks separating rather than connecting, and this is especially true when national bureaucratic systems and their border machines enter cross-border spaces with a logic of reproducing or expanding existing bureaucratic rationalities in an institutional power game. However, being in the middle also means that these spaces have the capacity to combine culture, language, policy, knowledge and experience. This capacity should not be understood from a teleological point of view and as one that might be managed in a hierarchical structure; rather, is it a capacity that accelerates existing order in new directions and confronts it from different positions and perspectives.

## Four different territorial strategies for cross-bordering

From our research we have identified different territorial strategies that have been followed or have emerged. In our theoretical framework we will use the term 'involutionary' as a concept for thinking and organising that represents the more ludic and experimenting nature of territorial strategy. According to Deleuze and Guattari (1988: 238) involution is fundamentally about being creative, and an involutionary strategy is a *rhizome* that brings heterogeneous things and people into play. Deleuze and Guattari (1988: 21) further argue that a rhizome is made of plateaus that are middles rather than beginnings and ends. Hillier (2013: 105) stresses that a rhizome 'can challenge and transform structures of reified, fixed and static (territorialised) thought into a space of continuous transformation, composed of causal and/or chance connections'. She argues that the rhizome as metaphor can reveal the multiple ways of connecting and assembling thoughts and actions in always incomplete processes of emergence.

Rhizomes are liminal space-times as settings in which new models, symbols, paradigms, etc., arise. The anthropologist Victor Turner (1982) argues that 'these new symbols and changes feed back into the "central" economic and politico-legal domains and arenas, supplying them with goals, aspirations, incentives, structural models and raison d'être'. He borrows the term 'flow' from Mihaly Csikszentmihalyi to signify that liminality is about creative experience and experimentation having a flow quality (1982: 55–8).

In opposition to this, we define an evolutionary way of thinking and organising strategy. An evolutionary approach reproduces routines and positions as an extension of the past into the future. Nigel Thrift (2001) distinguishes between two different modes of learning, namely those of reproduction of routine and production of emergence. Reproduction of routine represents a linear and incremental way of organising. A territorialised space builds on an evolutionary logic and is stabilised upon routinised practices. One well-known organisational model obviously representing such an ordinary and evolutionary logic is that of bureaucracy. Bureaucracy is rule following, and actions in these systems are basically about documentation of past experiences and standards. Novelty in these systems of thought and practice threatens order, and novelty is often excluded or translated into the existing schemes of interpretation in terms of reterritorialising movements and powers. These mechanisms have, for instance, been discussed in terms of how CBRs become extended versions of national bureaucracies fighting for control and influence in these mid-spaces (e.g., Nilson, 1997). To Normann (2001: 181–2), an evolutionary logic is one anchored in rational functions found within rules and principles of the past, and we might add that an evolutionary approach argues that organising deals with causal processes and rests on a belief in directionality.

To sum up our conceptual framework, we distinguish between two different approaches –evolutionary and involutionary. An involutionary approach deals with extraordinary practices, experimentation and creativity, whereas an evolutionary approach extends the past and therefore the ordinary by controlling the reproduction of routines and positions. We will combine these two approaches with two different governance approaches –bottom-up and top-down. Some strategies have perhaps emerged as bottom-up strategies while others are based on top-down decisions and organisations. A bottom-up approach means that there is no institutional actor that has the authority and legitimacy to organise and develop strategy, and a top-down approach means that there is an institutional authority with the legitimacy to act and to take responsibility for organising and for strategy design.

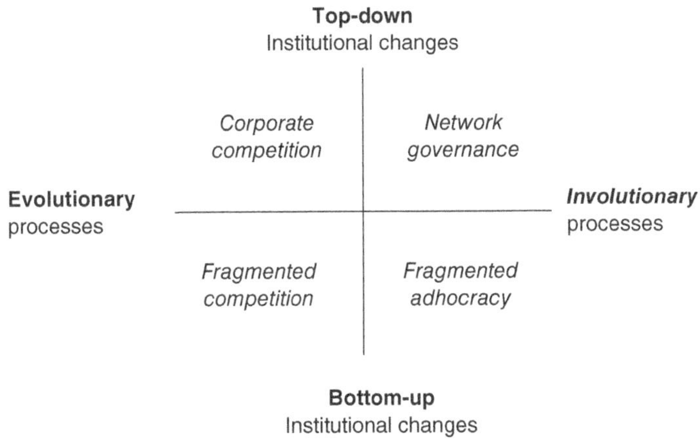


*Figure 10.1* Four different territorial strategies for institutionalising CBRs

We of course know that our theoretical model (see Figure 10.1) does not represent the complexity of the cross-bordering reality either in its context or in its content. However, these four different territorial strategies represent on a general level some significant institutional dynamics in the development of an integrated region:

- *Corporate competition*: This builds on the ambition to integrate a region into a corporate unit that has strong capabilities and a strong coherent identity in the context of other competitive corporate units (cities, regions or states). Corporate competition means that the CBR becomes institutionalised as a core idea of the common future in a competitive market of competing units. Institutional commitment to common capabilities, future and destiny seems strong in this strategy.
- *Fragmented competition*: As a territorial strategy, fragmented competition represents a situation of internal competition among units – i.e., cities and urban areas 'inside' what seems to represent the idea of a coherent CBR The individual units fight for their own progress and success, sometimes using the CBR as a specific content of their own operation and sometimes leaving its context somewhat blurred. Institutional commitment to the cross-border regional idea is low.
- *Fragmented adhocracy*:[1] Fragmented adhocracy represents a territorial strategy that is not supported by a common authority structure but rests on the legitimacy and authority of individual projects and organisations, each having an intention to exploit and explore cross-border potentials. Each project or organisation is relatively de-coupled from the others. Some projects have a more spontaneous approach to the possibilities of cross-bordering, and they could even be disposable border units with a limited lifespan (project-based organisational forms).

- *Network governance:*[2] In network governance the CBR as an idea is managed across institutions and organisations – not as a linear process of development but as an explorative and open process that involves cooperating in an uncertain and complex context of different rules, regulations, capabilities and standards. Network management means to facilitate loosely coupled structures for cooperation that are open to differences and uncertainty among different organisations, projects and institutions.

It is important to bear in mind that there is not necessarily a match between these theoretical arguments and empirical results deriving from previous research on other regions and the territorial strategies adopted in the Øresund region during the period under discussion.

## Two nations separated by natural and political borders but with a common history

In 2000 Denmark and Sweden were connected by a bridge linking Copenhagen, the capital of Denmark, and Malmö in Skåne (in the southern part of Sweden). This fixed link realised the dream of the Øresund region, a dream that had been envisioned by politicians, industrialists and experts for decades. At the opening ceremony the Danish queen and the Swedish king (who are cousins) were prominent symbols of brotherhood and unity.

Øresund takes its name from the sound that separates the two countries and connects the Baltic Sea and the North Sea. With 3.7 million inhabitants, the area is densely populated. Greater Copenhagen is its natural centre and of course the majority are Danes (two-thirds of the population). There are forty-seven municipalities in the Danish part of the region and thirty-three municipalities in Skåne. Øresund is the largest region in Northern Europe, with a strong industrial profile within such areas as food, biotech, medical, IT, energy and maritime. It has nine universities, with 150,000 students and 14,000 researchers, which has been seen to demonstrate the regional potential for growth and prosperity.

The sound is a natural border separating Sweden and Denmark. However, the border is not least a political construction driven by historical conflicts between two power centres in the Nordic arena (Linde-Laursen, 2000). Geopolitically, this passage made it possible to control commerce in and out of the Baltic Sea. There was series of wars between the kings in Copenhagen and Stockholm, and in the middle of the seventeenth century a peace was made between the two kingdoms whereby the Øresund border was internationally recognised and it was decreed that neither country should have sovereignty over it.

Today controlling the border means controlling cross-border activities rather than passage through the sound. Political-administrative borders constituted by two national institutional systems and different jurisdiction in terms of eighty municipalities and three regions (two in Denmark and one in Sweden) create a situation that makes cross-bordering difficult. Besides the natural and political-administrative borders, one should also not underestimate the borders in terms of language and different national cultures. Even though the fixed link has been a success, and more than 25 million people cross the bridge every year, the Øresund region as such is not generally believed to be a success that represents a strong CBR in terms of political and economic collaboration. Rather, there remain many barriers which hinder or perhaps symbolise the unresolved potential of the region.

Cross-border interactions in the Øresund region – commuting; sales, purchases and other business relations; social contacts; media coverage; etc. – have been very limited in modern times. A number of barriers – besides the physical one – have characterised these flows during the last five decades. Besides managing the interests of two nation-states, it is important to recognise the different positions of Copenhagen and Malmö in their national urban hierarchies. Copenhagen is the capital of Denmark and Malmö the third largest city in Sweden with a narrow south Swedish field of influence. This asymmetry has of course had an important influence on the Danish and the Swedish stimulus to engage in the Øresund region project.

Efforts in terms of institutional changes (with the ultimate goal of integrating the two parts of the region) aimed at increasing interactions must be understood with this in mind. These barriers still constitute obstacles to increased cross-border integration. In the last couple of years there has been a slowing down and even a small backlash when it comes to commuting and migration flows, and there has been a decrease in the numbers of commuters (16,000 from southern Sweden to Denmark and 800 from Denmark to Sweden) in the last few years.[3]

### *An old vision of integration was revealed*

Øresund represents an old political vision of regionalisation and cross-bordering. The first idea of a transnational urban space has its origins back in the 1950s, when it was formulated as a vision giving meaning to the idea of connecting Denmark and Sweden. From then on a particular Øresund discourse was developed and institutionalised in both countries, although primarily at the local level. In 1963 the Øresund Council was established to create an arena for cross-border political collaboration. The Nordic Union was an important context for conceptualising cross-border initiatives, in an approach related to the envisioning of possible futures for a region that is explored in chapter 11. For example, at a conference in 1969 organised by the Øresund Council and the Nordic Council it was stated that:

> In the Öresund region in 2000, productivity is three times higher than in 1969. The working week is shortened to 20 hours, but there is no labour shortage and no leisure problems. Universities are at the centre of the region. Universities are the largest workplaces and universities are centres for research.[4]

The Danish and Swedish governments entered into an agreement to build a fixed link, and the Danish government proposed moving Copenhagen Airport to a Danish island in the middle of the sound. (However, the plan was eventually abandoned, and today the island enjoys environmental protection.) In terms of Kingdon's streams model (in Béland, 2005) the policy stream consisted of a flow of ideas, visions, dreams, etc., and the problem stream had an abstract character in terms of future-oriented forecasted problems of modern life, transportation and division of production. Nevertheless, the Danish and Swedish governments agreed to build a fixed link, but new political issues emerged at the beginning of the1970s in terms of financial deficit, the oil crisis, environmental movements and different national strategies towards the European Economic Community, and for the rest of the decade the Øresund region wasn't really on the political agenda. Economic development in Greater Copenhagen and southern Sweden was associated with huge problems of de-industrialisation, a decrease in the number of jobs and people moving away from the Danish capital.

New problems, new policy entrepreneurs and a new context then gave rise to possibilities for policy games wherein the fixed link could return to the agenda. The European Roundtable of Industrialists had success in putting the 'missing links' on the European agenda (Vickerman, 1994; Cowles, 1995; McGowan and Wilks, 1995; Van Apeldoorn, 2000), and one such missing link was the Øresund bridge. The development of what has been labelled 'The New Regionalism' (e.g., Keating, 1998) was an important context for policy development regarding the development of a CBR in the Øresund area. In the 1980s and 1990s there was a regional renaissance in Europe (Dunford and Kafkalas, 1992; Leonardi and Garmise, 1992; Cheshire, 1995; Williams, 1996; Keating, 1998), and new regions were given legitimacy to act as political agents and arenas that could gain European support and influence (Williams, 1996; Smouts, 1998; Keating, 1998). As in the Basque and Welsh cases analysed in chapters 7 and 8, Øresund in this context of 'the Europe of Regions' could now tap into a strong institutionalised discourse of regionalisation. The economic situation in Greater Copenhagen and southern Sweden also had created major challenges for the local and national governments in both countries. The policy window was now open again and the policy entrepreneurs had better success in coupling problems and solutions. In 1991 the Swedish and Danish governments agreed to build the fixed link, and in 1994 the Danish and Swedish parliaments settled on its design and schedule. It was to consist of three parts: a bridge (8 kilometres), an artificial island (Pepper Islet) and a tunnel (4 kilometres). These agreements were the most important events in changing the institutional conditions for organising territorial strategies for a cross-border region in the following two decades.

In the following sections we will describe three different eras in the institutionalisation of the Øresund region. These eras represent the formation of different strategies for creating the right conditions to support the emergence of the region. Each era, rather than being viewed as finite in itself, should be seen as a period in which the institutional rationalities dominated and legitimated the actions aimed at creating and transforming institutions of CBR action and behaviour. Other researchers might argue that more or fewer eras would better validate the formation of specific cross-border strategies. However, our choice of analysis seems to realise some important characteristics of the Øresund region as a CBR in terms of process, content and context.

## Era 1, 1990–96: the emergence of an open-ended network of policy entrepreneurs

The decision to build the fixed link in 1991 had a profound impact on the conditions for institutionalising the Øresund region. One could say that without the bridge there would have been no such concept; however, it is also evident that the decision would not have been made had there been no vision of creating a strong CBR between Sweden and Denmark. The two components were interwoven: the fixed link should realise the vision of a CBR, and the vision should legitimise the decision to build a fixed link.

### *Cities of crisis*

At the beginning of the 1990s the political context of the decision to build or not build a bridge was characterised by the fact that both the Danish capital and southern Sweden were facing economic and industrial challenges and threats. The Initiative Group for recovery of Copenhagen published a report in 1989 with the title *What is the purpose of having a capital?*, which was an existential and provocative political question with the tone of 'crisis' all over it. In southern Sweden another report was published almost at the same time with the title *Why does Malmö exist? The crisis in a historical perspective*. There seemed to be an identity crisis in both places. Since the early 1970s Copenhagen had lost its strong identity as the capital of Denmark through loss of jobs, population and cultural capital, and no longer held an equivalent position to Stockholm (the Swedish capital). Malmö was in a transit from industry-driven economic development to knowledge-driven economic development. The political credo in Denmark seemed to have changed, and the Danish government believed that a strong capital was important. However, the Swedish government was driven less by a vision of regional development in the south of the country than the idea of connecting Sweden to the rest of Europe. Therefore it was regional agents, both public and private, in southern Sweden that developed collective strategies of regional development and identity building.

### *Searching for cross-border potential and the emergence of policy entrepreneurs*

However, the decision to build the bridge introduced a new context for conversations concerning geographical development in terms of 'the Europe of Regions' and CBRs. In this context, Copenhagen and southern Sweden were related in what might be seen as a community of geographical destinies; Copenhagen needed southern Sweden and Malmö and Malmö needed Copenhagen (rather than Gothenburg and Stockholm in the north). The Øresund region became a highly legitimated political project driven by such rationalities as 'regional competition', 'economic synergy', 'the knowledge society', etc. A fixed link could be an important and perhaps the only strategy for recovery, it was argued, because of the new economic and industrial movements seen in Europe in terms of what was labelled 'the Europe of Regions'.

An entrepreneurial mind-set evolved during these years. In the beginning there was an open process of realising the vision of a strong and coherent Øresund region in terms of a free flow of actors, projects, activities and ideas (Tangkjær 2000a, 2000b). Regional agents – especially Danes – could dream up new possibilities of a brighter and better future for Copenhagen, Malmö and southern Sweden. The symbolic analysts (researchers, experts and consultants) held a significant position in this process of creating meaning to and identifying the core components and potentials of the regional idea. The policy entrepreneurs employed the symbolic analysts, or the symbolic analysts were policy entrepreneurs themselves, in trying to position their own ideas and solutions in an emerging CBR market. Mintrom (1997: 739) defines policy entrepreneurs as 'people who seek to initiate dynamic policy change', and who use different strategies to win support for ideas and policy innovation. They do not seek to maintain current power relations and institutional settings but instead attempt to change status quo policy arrangements (Mintrom, 2013: 444). Researchers and consultants produced images and analysis of this emerging CBR in terms of its industrial advantages, its common history, its position in the rankings of European regions, intellectual capital, its potential compared with, e.g., the San Francisco Bay Area, and the development of a strong Baltic region. This work done had huge symbolic significance because of its powerful construction of CBR images and the political construction of the Øresund region.

Mintrom (2013: 443) identifies four different strategies followed by policy entrepreneurs: defining and framing problems; building powerful teams to tap relevant knowledge networks; amassing evidence to show the workability of proposals; and creating strong coalitions of diverse supporters. All four strategies were absolutely present and systematically implemented: the fixed link became a solution to the making of prosperity and regional growth and bureaucratic systems were framed as an obstruction to cross-border aspirations. Networks of (public/private) experts, consultants and researchers evolved and produced visions of a present and future Øresund region in terms of numbers and figures presented at conferences; reports and books were published; and a diverse set of coalitions of private and public stakeholders were created in terms of different policy networks within the labour market, transportation, education, environment, business, etc.

When it comes to organisational and institutional aspects there was a shift from urban government to urban governance, with a multitude of private and public actors collaborating and negotiating development projects in more fragmented processes. Some of these policy networks evolved into more concrete forms and institutionalised the Øresund vision into more specific structures (though the majority no longer exist).

- *Øresund University*: a cross-border collaboration of fourteen universities working on attracting international students to the area and supporting exchanges between the collaborating institutions.
- *Øresund Science Region*: a cross-border initiative that aimed to bring together regional authorities, businesses and universities. This so-called triple-helix model was an approach to cooperation between universities and the wider society.
- *Medicon Valley*: an organisation that connects universities, hospitals and companies within the life sciences. It is perhaps the strongest brand in the Øresund region, even though it is in fact a sub-brand.
- *Scandinavian Academy of Management Studies*: a collaboration between the University of Copenhagen, Copenhagen Business School, Lund University, the Danish Chamber of Commerce, the Confederation of Danish Industry, the Chamber of Commerce and Industry of Southern Sweden, the Øresund Committee and some other interest groups within business and management.
- *The Øresund Business Council*: a policy forum for business organisations to work for growth initiatives in the Øresund region bridging the Scania Business Group and the Copenhagen Business Group. The Scania Business Group represented all business interests in southern Sweden and issued a manifesto for growth (as part of the Øresund region). Shortly afterwards a counterpart to the Scania Group was established in Copenhagen.
- *The Øresund Region Labour Market Council*: a council established by social partners across the region to create a platform for the development of a single and integrated labour market.
- *The Culture Bridge*: a forum for developing cultural events in the Øresund region to attract Swedish inhabitants to Danish events and vice versa.
- *Meeting Place Copenhagen–Malmö*: a collaboration between Wonderful Copenhagen and Magnet Malmö to promote tourism.
- *The Øresund Committee*: one of the first cross-border organisations, it was the platform for politicians from Greater Copenhagen and southern Sweden, a forum for officials and a secretariat. The committee became a strong agent, not least because of its authority as the INTERREG organisation in the Øresund region (INTERREG is a European Commission regional policy programme that supports transnational and cross-border cooperation in Europe). The Øresund Committee still exists, but it is not a strong institutional authority.
- *The Øresund (Identity) Network*: established to own and organise the brand identity of the region.
- *Øresund Entrepreneurship*: an organisation that focused on stimulating entrepreneurship activities within the educational sector.
- *The Øresund Institute*: a non-profit Danish–Swedish association with the purpose of encouraging integration within the region, through analysis, fact finding and boundary-crossing debate regarding different political economic policy issues. It still exists and has institutional legitimacy, but it is not a strong institutional platform.

This network was a mix of governmental and non-governmental organisations working together, yet the agents with the real power to change institutional orders and design were only loosely coupled with them and had no obligation to act on cross-border solutions. Many more small initiatives have been launched over the years and the majority of those still in existence have lost their institutional power. Many projects were also initiated and financially supported by INTERREG, which had approved the Øresund region as a cross-border initiative. The Øresund INTERREG programme was governed by the Øresund Committee, whose strategy was to support many different projects. It had calculated that there was a risk that not many organisations would apply for funding if it was too narrow in scope. However, more than forty applications were received by the very first deadline covering a variety of projects (tourism, research, primary schools, media, culture, the environment, etc.).

Many of these organisations are defunct, having been closed down through lack of support or resources. The Øresund Committee and the Øresund Business Institute still exist, but in general the organisational thickness of the Øresund region seems to have diminished.

## Era 2, 1997–2006: a corporate strategy for a united brand of the region

Every new state form and political power in general introduces its own particular way of partitioning space; it introduces its own administrative classification of discourse about space and about things and people in space (Lefebvre, 1991: 281). The Øresund region was not yet a united political unit and in terms of governance it was definitely very blurred and open ended. New organisations were established, although their primary function was to institutionalise policy networks and none of them really had the power to impact on governance systems in either Denmark or Sweden.

What we have argued in the previous section is that the CBR was an emergent process driven by different policy networks and a mix of governmental and non-governmental organisations collaborating together. It was a process of exploring the transnational potentials in loosely coupled networks of heterogeneous actors and without any corporate strategy or strong governmental control.

In their analysis of place-making in Øresund, Collinge and Gibney (2010) make a distinction between *purposive* and *spontaneous* governance, in which purposive represents an ordered and explicit process that is pursued consciously, and spontaneous represents a self-organising principle without consciousness or process control. They argue that spontaneous self-organising has been the most important approach in the Øresund region. As such this seems to be very much in line with Church and Reid's (1999) findings in their research of the institutionalisation of political space across the English Channel. They use the term 'organic change' as opposed to central governmental control of the process, and according to them it is important that organic changes are based on flexible cooperative networks and associations that can form the basis of a progressive institutional structure allowing for strategic economic governance (ibid.: 653).

However, in terms of political capacity and decision-making power there were as yet no legitimate institutional structures to support the many ideas and images of a strong and competitive CBR across Øresund. The region did not exist in terms of Lefebvre's distinctive concept of spatial competence and performativity (Lefebvre, 1991: 38). However, on the horizon was the bridge, planned to open in 2000. In 1997 a network of policy entrepreneurs representing tourist and marketing agencies created a strategic alliance with the purpose of developing a strategy for the Øresund region. In 1999 the 'Øresund Brandbook' was presented in which a new strategy approach was defined:

> To develop this potential everyone will have to understand what the region holds for them. Inhabitants, neighbours, travellers, local and international business people, all must share an enthusiasm and belief in the future of Øresund. That is why the region needs a brand – to reach people across the Sound, across Europe and across the world. To engage and involve them in the making of Øresund.

The realisation of the Øresund region became a matter of communication, a fight for hearts and minds, not least of those outside the territory (companies, tourists, etc.) but also the logic of auto-communication (communication to oneself about oneself).

Hospers (2006) uses the term 'mindware' to express the kind of branding strategy used in marketing the Øresund region. He argues that a brand stands for the particular things an area is proud of or wants to stand for, and place marketing should close the gap between the regional identity (what the region really is), the image outsiders have about it and how the location wants to be known to the outside world (its brand) (Hospers, 2006: 1016). However, the gap that Hospers talks about was a complex and multidimensional one on account of the fact that the Øresund region wasn't a coherent space and there was no 'organic image' (Hankinson, 2004); rather it was an artificial symbolic construction and a conceptualised space (Hornskov, 2007). However, some of the ideas that were institutionalised in the first era were brought into the marketing of Øresund – for example, the idea of science region. The policy entrepreneurs represented institutional agencies with a strong legitimacy and they introduced a policy innovation in terms of a branding issue that somehow changed the status quo of the regional development.

This new branding strategy was a game changer: (1) there was a change from searching for potentials and industry identity to communicating the essential identity of the Øresund region; (2) this essential identity was marketed to an external audience; and (3) a more formal organisation and purpose was defined, namely that of creating and controlling a brand.

In 1997 a network of public institutions responsible for place marketing from both sides of the region launched the idea that Øresund should be professionally communicated in a global world to attract investors and visitors. Using the distinction made by Collinge and Gibney (2010) there seemed to be a change from spontaneous to purposive governance. Rather than building on heterogeneity and an understanding of the region as having evolved an identity, a governance centre emerged in terms of 'the Øresund Network'. The network published a pamphlet which described its strategy as 'the Birth of a Region'. In this policy text the cross-border potentials of the region were illuminated and the need for developing a strong brand was presented. In an interview one of the founders of the Øresund Network explained that the branding idea was all about timing, since they had up until that point developed the necessary capacity for promoting the Øresund region (Linde-Laursen andTangkjær, 2004: 21). The branding project was funded by the INTERREG II programme and had a budget of approximately 400,000 euros. Competitive tendering was organised and the tender was won by the British consultancy Wolff Olins, which at that time was one of the leading brand consultancies. They made an analysis and concluded from their gathering of empirical data that the Øresund region was something very special because it had:

> a unique attitude to life … People here try to find a balance between social interests and personal ones. Things are measured in human terms. There is a very high investment in people and an inclusive democratic attitude. The best things in life aren't only for the favoured few.[5]

The consultants labelled these findings 'The Human Capital', which was immediately supported by politicians and businesses, and the consultants presented three different suggestions of the region's new brand name – Copenhagen Scania Region, Eko Region and the Sound Region – and even suggested a logo. From opinions gathered in London, New York and Frankfurt the response was absolutely clear that the Øresund region should retain its name and not adopt any of the suggestions made by Wolff Olins. The Danish letter 'Ø', the test groups responded, was unique and something very Scandinavian. So in 1999 Øresund became 'The Øresund region: The Human Capital'. Some journalists were critical of the fact that anyone could pay 400,000 euros to discover something that obvious (Linde-Laursen and-Tangkjær, 2004: 24). A specific Øresund logo was devised that symbolised both the geographical area and the positions of Copenhagen and Malmö. The idea was that this cross-border regional brand should work as a meta-brand for the regional agencies in their communication and marketing. However, besides the new brand name and logo and the professional network of marketing agencies, not many resources were put into the project; the brand name was not widely used, even though it was supposed to epitomise the region's communication and marketing activities. The consultancy company estimated that, for it to become an international brand, an investment of approximately 100 million euros should be made; an effort to reintroduce it was made a couple of years later, but without success.

## Era 3, 2007-onwards: from a corporate regional strategy to city strategies

In our analysis above we have argued that the territorial strategy changed from being open and explorative without any institutional centre to being a more corporate strategy in terms of controlling the image of the region. It could also be argued that the first era was driven by a need for the vision of a future cross-border region to be legimitised and that the second era was driven by the need for some kind of regional identity. The third era, which we believe the Øresund region has entered recently, is that of separate city strategies being followed by governments in both Denmark and Sweden. The Øresund region is not really the core content in these urban strategies but, rather, has become a more blurred context with no strong institutional commitments attached. In the early days an effort was put into the work of identifying the many barriers to cross-bordering (taxes, the price for cross the bridge, legislation, etc.). However, so far only some of these have been eliminated.

### *Cities as centres of and vehicles for economic growth*

In the 1980s and 1990s we witnessed a renaissance of territoriality as an important aspect for understanding economic policy and growth. In these two decades 'the Europe of Regions' was launched to mobilise regions as political and economic actors. Regions had become political and economic actors and competed with each other for resources. This discourse was an important legitimating context for the Øresund region because it brought institutional and financial support to the project – and at a more abstract level it brought a vocabulary that made sense both to the entrepreneurial policy-makers and to their audience.

We argue that the situation has changed in the last decade, namely that the focus on urban life has called for a much more profound position of cities in economic growth and development (e.g., Andersen *et al.*, 2011). Cities seem to be better nodal points in what Castells (1996) called the 'global network of flows' because of their capability to capitalise on the soft capital forms of the global economy (Bayliss, 2007; Nallathiga, 2011). The 'entrepreneurial city' concept that has evolved in urban policies is multifaceted (Harvey, 1989; Jessop, 1998; Swyngedouw *et al.*, 2002; Madureira, 2014). A general view is that the concept covers a shift from city government focusing on welfare and service issues to a mind-set emphasising competition. The city has become a true competitor and the underlying problem is (lack of) competitiveness. Risk-taking, innovation, promotion and economic growth are now central components in such an approach (Madureira, 2014). Two key concepts are 'creativity' and 'attractiveness' – concepts that we see more and more frequently in both national and regional economic growth policies.

As such we have witnessed a renaissance of the city, and perhaps for many reasons:

1. cities are financial centres allocating financial resources in the global economy;
2. the density of cities makes up the necessary context for the logic of adding new work to what already exists;
3. innovation and entrepreneurship have become tremendously important for economic growth and are institutionally supported by institutions often located in cities (universities and educational institutions); and

4 skilled workers are important for innovation and growth as well as internationalisation of business, and skilled workers are to a larger degree located in cities.

These are just some of the characteristics of cities and their special quality in the global economy. However, together they make up what is arguably an extremely important characteristic, namely that of being 'creative'. For many researchers this seems to be of major importance today in developing competitive advantage and to positioning cities among others in the global economy (Healey, 2004; Scott, 2006; Bayliss, 2007; Landry, 2008; Wolfe and Bramwell, 2008; Storper and Scott, 2009; Lysgård, 2012; Freire-Gibb and Nielsen, 2014).

Recent trends in urban and regional policies from a Swedish perspective also focus on the urban or metropolitan core (Swedish Agency for Economic and Regional Growth, 2009, 2011). This can be seen as a logical consequence of the growth discourse that has dominated urban and regional policies for the last two decades. It further represents a belief in the old idea of trickle-down or spreading effects outwards from a concentrated core to the rest of the region.

Looking at the major actors in the Swedish part of the Øresund region – Region Skåne and the cities of Malmö, Lund and Helsingborg – we find strong support for this city-driven approach (MalmöLundregionen, 2012, 2013; Malmö Stad, 2014; Region Skåne 2004, 2014). Although Region Skåne tries to uphold a comprehensive regional perspective, it is doing this from a weak political position. It seems as if the driving force and the power to influence development depends more and more on strategies and actions taken by the cities. When the municipalities in the Malmö–Lund region formulate a programme for joint action, external relations address Copenhagen, not the rest of Skåne or the Øresund region as a whole (MalmöLundregionen, 2012). And the city of Helsingborg is fighting for its own interests in promoting a fixed link to Helsingör on the Danish side (Helsinborg Stad, 2010).

The Øresund region no longer seems to be a high priority for the Danish municipalities. There is some policy-making that supports the development of Øresund, though it seems primarily to be a matter of connecting some policy areas (especially the environment) in Copenhagen with the city of Malmö. Greater Copenhagen has a high growth rate as far as its population is concerned, a strong international brand and a strong identity as a city-region.

The point is that the focus is largely metropolitan. City-regions and city-regionalism are concepts that can be seen as representing a coalescence of two trajectories when it comes to governance of economic growth in a globalising economy – the new regionalism emphasising the central role of the regions (not the nation-state) *and* the big cities as main entities in this process (Allan, 2011; Harrison, 2012; Storper, 2013). Harrison, in describing the failure to create regional governments in England with a strong direct power, argues that city-regions do not replace regions as governance actors; rather, they exist *alongside* the regions. The city-region is a specific meaning of the term region, telling us that the (big) city dominates the region, and that the hinterland is subordinate and very much dependent on policies, institutional frameworks and growth processes embedded in the city.

We can see a similar 'demise' of regional government in Sweden in the central government's resistance to a wide-ranging 'regionalisation' of power. Herrschel (2013), using the examples of Vancouver and Seattle, points at the complexity of the concept 'smart city-regionalism'. On one hand, the big city is seen as the dominant driver of economic growth. On the other, the larger region, with its surrounding suburbs and cities, is taken into account. 'Smart (new) city regionalism is then a fusion of inter-sectoral policy co-ordination with inter-local co-operation at the regional scale' (ibid.: 2338).

When Storper discusses city-regions and economic development he makes a point of talking about different kinds of institutions:

> institutions in the capital *I* sense (states, constitutions, rules, laws, and formal policies). But there is also a small *i sense* of institutions, as the organization of the 'key groups' or 'communities' in the economy – from elite networks to civic associations and neighborhood groups.
>
> (Storper, 2013: 8)

Furthermore, he indicates that metropolitan regions might have the same formal institutions (the big *I*) at the same time having different networks and communities (the small *i*). These arguments fit well the picture previously presented of a multilevel, multi-actor governance and multi-incitement context.

By accepting the notion of the city-region we also acknowledge the fact that the city is embedded in a larger spatial context, the rest of the region, but still dominates this hinterland. In a Danish and Swedish context, cities and municipalities are constitutionally strong actors while regions are rather weak when it comes to political mandate and economic muscle. Hence, the regions are heavily dependent from above on central state politics and allocation of economic resources and from below on the willingness of the cities/municipalities to act in accordance with regional strategies.

The emergence of a city-oriented approach to the cross-border Øresund region during this third era can be seen as a reaction to a less successful regional governance model, reflecting the relatively weak power of the regional policy entrepreneurs. The branding network was a governance network, which gained its legitimacy mostly from normative structures (CBRs, INTERREG funding, branding, the Øresund region) and not from regulative structures and the power of regulation.

## Different eras of cross-bordering and different territorial strategies

From our research on the Øresund region it seems that different territorial strategies have been followed during the last twenty years, and as such it is an excellent example from the point of view of understanding different cross-bordering strategies. In the first era there was an open-ended network wherein no single centre of governance authorised agency and action. Instead the process was driven by a heterogeneous set of policy entrepreneurs mobilising agents and negotiating the framing of cross-bordering in the region. In the second era a corporate institutional framework took over in an endeavor to construct a centre of governance responsible for the meta-branding of the Øresund region. Using the terminology from Murdoch (1998) and his distinction between spaces of prescriptions and spaces of negotiations, this branding strategy was an attempt to institutionalise a new space of prescription that could meta-govern the communication and identity of the region, but it did not have the necessary institutional power to regulate action and behaviour. The last era that we have identified is an period in which we are witnessing a shift from region to cities. Economic and cultural development is driven by cities and their position in the urban hierarchy, meaning that Copenhagen, Malmö and Lund are the key players. While Copenhagen has developed a strong identity and self-understanding as the centre of the Øresund region, Malmö and Lund still need to develop their own strategies. This transformation has made the Øresund region a context for urban development rather than the content of urban strategies, and it is a context without much in the way of institutional structures or authority.

In an analysis of the process of institutionalising a region, Paasi (1986, 1996, 2013) identifies four stages; territorial shaping, symbolic shaping, institutional shaping, and the establishment of the territorial unit in a common social consciousness, a recognised identity. When looking at the Øresund region today we can conclude that, besides territorial shaping – that is, agreeing on the spatial delimitation of the region – there are just fragments of symbolic and institutional shaping but no signs of an Øresund identity.

## Discussion

We can see a development through the three eras, from 1990 to the present, characterised by an accentuated economic growth agenda, on an EU, a nation-state, a cross-border region and a city level. Some would point at sustainability policies and strategies implemented on a regional and an urban level over the last decades as balancing economic growth targets versus social and ecological sustainability. Our argument is that economic growth in its pure sense is actually suppressing the sustainability discourse in the Øresund regional context. A consequence is the promotion of an evolutionary perspective represented in strategies based on existing institutional and organisational structures and on the existing socio-economic paradigm. The major focus today when it comes to promoting extended cross-border interactions is typically investment in transport infrastructure (a necessary measure but far from sufficient).

In fact, the first institutional era in our study of the Øresund region has shown the strongest potential to become involutionary in its approach. Here a multitude of actors, initiatives and visions coexisted. But in the third era, the 'big city' era, our conclusion must be that the involutionary elements have vanished or at least become much more subordinate to a short-term, project-oriented city-economic growth and competition agenda. The practical influence when it comes to such elements as being welcoming, having a willingness to experiment, changing existing regional governance structures, questioning the dominant mind-set, etc., must be seen as having less impact or simply becoming of marginal importance. The creative potential of the Øresund region as the 'extraordinary in-between space' is severely hampered. The dominance of national institutional structures is still very strong, even though cities, city-regions and regions on both sides try to influence development in a number of creative and concrete ways. But cross-border interactions are still hampered by a number of barriers. The circumscribing of the cross-border process in the two nation-states' political agendas is to a large extent defining the room for manoeuvre for regional actors.

Healey (2004: 90) concludes in his discussion on urban governance and creativity that over-management and over-measurement destroy more capacity than they build. National bureaucracies have a tendency to over-manage and over-measure, however, and there is of course a risk that this tendency could be taken over by institutional actors eagerly working for creativity. Healey argues that 'recognition of the need to encourage innovation in a context of dynamic complexity suggests a mode of governance which allows experimentation and understands that experiments fail as well as succeed' (ibid.: 90).

Summarising the institutional changes in the Øresund region in the last twenty-five years, we can see a movement from ad hoc, fragmented, multi-actor exploration towards regional comprehensive strategies in the second era and ending up in fragmented city strategies in era three. There is not any strong element of exploration support that is regionally governed. What we see is a drift towards evolutionary processes that are to a large extent captured in a conventional economic growth and competition mind-set pushing aside involutionary processes. With reference to Healey (2004), it seems that the most popular and legitimated approach to territorial strategy has been management and over-management. Involutionary strategy means to explore and experiment both politically and institutionally. We will not argue, however, that a CBR strategy approach should be involutionary. A CBR is too complex a phenomenon, and a multifaceted approach is needed. Instead we argue that all four territorial strategies are needed to adopt and combine to the making of a CBR. CBRs (as visions and as territories) are laboratories of institutional development. They are in-between spaces of heterogeneity and spaces covering strong institutional structures in terms of regulative institutions and bureaucracies. CBR governance should rest on the capacity to oscillate between the four territorial strategies (see Figure 10.2).

To become more involutionary, and from that more creative and innovative, the Øresund region needs to allow processes that include exploration, experimentation and, not least, a break-up of national institutional frameworks that currently have a lock-in function. There is a need to find a better balance between the evolutionary and the involutionary processes. The latter have to be strengthened. Furthermore, involutionary processes that are coordinated and governed regionally have to coexist with explorative processes characterised by being ad hoc, inclusionary, fragmented and non-governed.

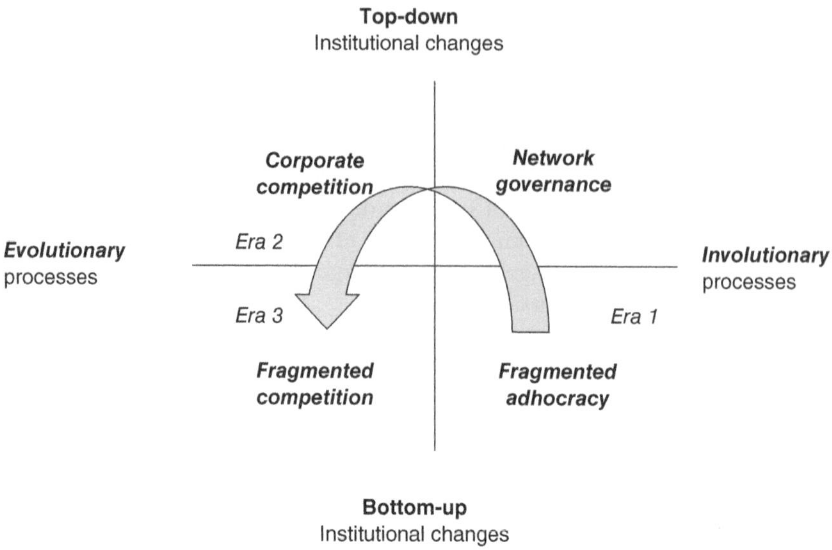


*Figure 10.2* Territorial strategies adopted in the Øresund region

## Notes

1 The term 'fragmented adhocracy' is inspired by Richard Whitley's analysis of the field of management studies (1984).
2 Koppenjan and Klijn (2004), in particular, represent such a perspective, and Agranoff (2007, 2012) represents an interesting network approach.
3 These numbers are presented by the City of Copenhagen: www.kk.dk/da/om-kommunen/fakta-og-statistik/statistik-og-historie/emneopdelt-statistik/oeresundsregionen.
4 The Nordic Council, Øresundsconference, 1964.
5 In 'Øresund: A Name in the World', which was a retrospective narrative of how the brand was developed.

## References

Agranoff, R. (2007) *Managing within Networks: Adding Value to Public Organizations*. Washington, DC: Georgetown University Press.

Agranoff, R. (2012) *Collaborating to Manage: A Primer for the Public Sector*. Washington, DC: Georgetown University Press.

Allan, J. (2011) City-regionalism: a case study of South East-Wales, PhD thesis, Cardiff University.

Alvarez, J. R. R. (1995) The Mexican–US border: the making of an anthropology of borderlands, *Annual Review of Anthropology*, 24(1), pp. 447–70.

Amin, A., and Thrift, N. (1995) Globalisation, 'institutional thickness' and the local economy. In Healey, P., Cameron, S., Davoudi, S., Graham, S., and Madani-Pour, A. (eds), *Managing Cities: The New Urban Context*. Chichester: John Wiley.

Andersen, H. T., Møller-Jensen, L., and Engelstoft, S. (2011) The end of urbanization? Towards a new urban concept or rethinking urbanization, *European Planning Studie*, 19(4), pp. 595–611.
Bayliss, D. (2007) The rise of the creative city: culture and creativity in Copenhagen, *European Planning Studies*, 15(7), pp. 889–903.
Béland, D. (2005) Ideas and social policy: an institutionalist perspective, *Social Policy & Administration*, 39(1), pp. 1–18.
Blatter, J. (2003) Beyond hierarchies and networks: institutional logics and change in transboundary spaces, *Governance*, 16(4), pp. 503–26.
Carmin, J., Hicks, B., and Beckmann, A. (2003) Leveraging local action: grassroots initiatives and transboundary collaboration in the formation of the white Carpathian Euroregion, *International Sociology*, 18(4), pp. 703–25.
Castells, M. (1996) *The Rise of the Network Society*. Oxford: Blackwell.
Cheshire, P. (1995) A new phase of urban development in Western Europe?: the evidence for the 1980s, *Urban Studies*, 32(7), pp. 1045–1063.
Church, A., and Reid, P. (1999) Cross-border co-operation, institutionalization and political space across the English Channel, *Regional Studies*, 33(7), pp. 643–55.
Collinge, C., and Gibney, J. (2010) Place-making and the limitations of spatial leadership: reflections on the Øresund, *Policy studies*, 31(4), pp. 475–89.
Cowles, M. G. (1995) Setting the agenda for a new Europe: the ERT and EC 1992, *Journal of Common Market Studies*, 33(4), pp. 501–26.
Deleuze, G., and Guattari, F. (1988) *A Thousand Plateaus: Capitalism and Schizophrenia*. London: Bloomsbury.
Dunford, M., and Kafkalas, G. (eds) (1992) *Cities and Regions in the New Europe: The Global Interplay and Spatial Development Strategies*. London: Belhaven.
Freire-Gibb, L. C., and Nielsen, K. (2014) Entrepreneurship within urban and rural areas: creative people and social networks, *Regional Studies*, 48(1), pp. 139–53.
Hankinson, G. (2004) The brand images of tourism destinations: a study of the saliency of organic images, *Journal of Product & Brand Management*, 13(1), pp. 6–14.
Harrison, J. (2012) Life after regions? The evolution of city-regionalism in England, *Regional Studies*, 46(9), pp. 1243–59.
Harvey, D. (1989) From managerialism to entrepreneurialism: the transformation in urban governance in late capitalism, *Geografiska Annaler*, 71B(1), pp. 3–17.
Healey, P. (2004) Creativity and urban governance, *Policy Studies*, 25(2), pp. 87–102.
Herrschel, T (2013) Competitiveness and sustainability: can 'smart city regionalism' square the circle? *Urban Studies*, 50, pp. 2332–48.
Hillier, J. (2013) Troubling the place of the border: on territory, community, space and place, *Australian Planner*, 50(2), pp. 103–8.
Hornskov, S. B. (2007) On the management of authenticity: culture in the place branding of Øresund, *Place Branding and Public Diplomacy*, 3(4), pp. 317–31.
Hospers, G.-J. (2006) Borders, bridges and branding: the transformation of the Øresund region into an imagined space, *European Planning Studies*, 14(8), pp. 1015–33.
Jessop, B. (1998) The narrative of enterprise and the enterprise of narrative: place marketing and the entrepreneurial city. In Hall, T., and Hubbards P. (eds), *The Entrepreneurial City: Geographies of Politics, Regime and Representation*. Chichester: John Wiley, pp. 77–99.
Keating, M. (1998) *The New Regionalism in Western Europe: Territorial Restructuring and Political Change*. Cheltenham: Edward Elgar.

Koppenjan, J. F. M., and Klijn, E. H. (2004) *Managing Uncertainties in Networks: A Network Approach to Problem Solving and Decision Making*. Abingdon: Routledge.

Kramsch, O., and Hooper, B. (eds) (2004) *Cross-Border Governance in the European Union*. Abingdon: Routledge

Landry, C. (2008) *The Creative City: A Toolkit for Urban Innovators*. London: Earthscan.

Lefebvre, H. (1991) *The Production of Space*. Oxford: Blackwell.

Leonardi, R., and Garmise, S. (1992) Conclusions: sub-national elites and the European community, *Regional & Federal Studies*, 2(1–2), pp. 247–74.

Linde-Laursen, A. (2000) Bordering improvisations: centuries of identity politics. In Berg, P.-O., Linde-Laursen, A., and Löfgren, O. (eds), *Invoking a Transnational Metropolis: The Making of the Øresund Region*. Copenhagen: Samfundslitteratur.

Linde-Laursen, A., and Tangkjær, C. (2004) *Place-Making in the Global Village. Øresund: a Brand New Future?* Graz: Leykam.

Löfgren, O. (1999) Crossing borders: the nationalization of anxiety, *Ethnologia Scandinavia*, 29, pp. 5–27.

Löfgren, O. (2008) Regionauts: the transformation of cross-border regions in Scandinavia, *European Urban and Regional Studies*, 15(3) pp. 195–209.

Lysgård, H. K. (2012) Creativity, culture and urban strategies: a fallacy in cultural urban strategies, *European Planning Studies*, 20(8), pp. 1281–300.

Madureira, A. M. (2014) (Re)acting the city: physical planning practices and challenges in urban development projects of the entrepreneurial city, dissertation, Blekinge Institute of Technology.

Malmö Stad (2014) *Översiktsplan för Malmö. Planstrategi. Malmö Stad.*

MalmöLundregionen (2012) *Handlingsprogram för MalmöLundregionen.*

MalmöLundregionen (2013) *Strukturbild MalmöLund: En konkretisering av MalmöLund-visionen för 2030*. Samrådsförslag.

McGowan, L., and Wilks, S. (1995) The first supranational policy in the European Union: competition policy, *European Journal of Political Research*, 28(2), pp. 141–69.

Mintrom, M. (1997) Policy entrepreneurs and the diffusion of innovation, *American Journal of Political Science*, 41(3), pp. 738–70.

Mintrom, M. (2013) Policy entrepreneurs and controversial science: governing human embryonic stem cell research, *Journal of European Public Policy*, 20(3), pp. 442–57.

Murdoch, J. (1998) The spaces of actor-network theory, *Geoforum*, 29(4), pp. 357–74.

Nallathiga, R. (2011) Cities under competition: the role of city image(s), *IUP Journal of Brand Management*, 8(4), pp. 25–34.

Nilson, H. R. (1997) Nordic regionalization: on how transborder regions work and why they don't work, *Cooperation and Conflict*, 32(4), pp. 399–426.

Normann, R. (2001) *Reframing Business: When the Map Changes the Landscape*. Chichester: John Wiley.

Paasi, A. (1986) The institutionalization of regions: a theoretical framework for understanding the emergence of regions and the constitution of regional identity, *Fennia*, 164(1), pp. 105–46.

Paasi, A. (1996) *Territories, Boundaries and Consciousness*. Chichester: John Wiley.

Paasi, A. (2013) Regional planning and the mobilization of 'regional identity': from bounded spaces to relational complexity, *Regional Studies*, 47(8), pp. 1206–19.

Region Skåne (2004) *Skånsk livskraft: regionalt utvecklingsprogram (RUP) för Skåne*.

Region Skåne (2014) *Det öppna Skåne 2030: remissförslag Skånes utvecklingsstrategi 2030*.

Rottenburg, R. (2000) Sitting in a bar 1, *Studies in Cultures, Organizations and Societies*, 6(1), pp. 87–100.

Scott, A. J. (2006) Creative cities: conceptual issues and policy questions, *Journal of Urban Affairs*, 28(1), pp. 1–17.

Smouts, M.-C. (1998) The region as the new imagined community. In Le Galès, P., and Lequesne, C. (eds), *Regions in Europe*. London: Routledge.

Storper, M. (2013) *Keys to the City: How Economics, Institutions, Social Interactions, and Politics Shape Development*. Princeton, NJ: Princeton University Press.

Storper, M., and Scott, A. J. (2009) Rethinking human capital, creativity and urban growth, *Journal of Economic Geography*, 9(2), pp. 147–67.

Swedish Agency for Economic and Regional Growth (2009) *Storstadsprogram för nationell tillväxt 2000–2009*. INFO 0070, REV A.

Swedish Agency for Economic and Regional Growth (2011) *Tillväxtens guldägg: Innovation och förnyelse i det regional tillväxtarbetet*. Rapport 0083.

Swyngedouw, E., Moulaert, F., and Rodriguez, A. (2002) Neoliberal urbanization in Europe: large-scale urban development projects and the new urban policy, *Antipode*, 34(3), pp. 542–77.

Tangkjær, C. (2000a) *Åbent hus: organiseringen omkring Øresundsregionen*. Copenhagen: Samfundslitteratur.

Tangkjær, C. (2000b) Öresund as an open house strategy by invitation. In Berg, P.-O., Linde-Laursen, A., and Löfgren, O. (eds), *Invoking a Transnational Metropolis: The Making of the Øresund Region*. Copenhagen: Samfundslitteratur.

Thrift, N. (2001) 'It's the romance, not the finance, that makes the business worth pursuing': disclosing a new market culture, *Economy and Society*, 30(4), pp. 412–32.

Turner, V. (1969) *The Ritual Process: Structure and Anti-Structure*. New York: Cornell University Press.

Turner, V. (1982) *From Ritual to Theatre: The Human Seriousness of Play*. London: Performing Arts Journal.

Van Apeldoorn, B. (2000) Transnational class agency and European governance: the case of the European Round Table of Industrialists, *New Political Economy*, 5(2), pp. 157–81.

Vickerman, R. W. (1994) Transport infrastructure and region building in the European Community, *Journal of Common Market Studies*, 32(1), pp. 1–24.

Whitley, R. (1984) The development of management studies as a fragmented adhocracy, *Social Science Information*, 23(4–5), pp. 775–818.

Williams, R. (1996) *European Union Spatial Policy and Planning*. London: Paul Chapman.

Wolfe, D. A., and Bramwell, A. (2008) Innovation, creativity and governance: social dynamics of economic performance in city-regions, *Innovation: Management, Policy & Practice*, 10(2–3), pp. 170–82.

# 11 Regional social and economic development in the Okanagan, Canada

## Envisioning the future to initiate a strategy

*Keith Culver, Nicky Dhaliwal, Malida Mooken and Roger Sugden*

## Introduction

Our focus in this chapter is regions with little or no experience of a strategy for social and economic development that is conceived, designed and enacted largely from within and across the region itself. We consider the emergence of such a strategy, which we refer to as a "strategy from within," and we do so by reference to the Okanagan in British Columbia, Canada.

Notwithstanding the desires and efforts of different governments to ensure development of the Okanagan, and the fact that from time to time some of its citizens have come to share strategic goals, the region has lacked a strategy substantially conceived and embraced at home undergirded by a shared sense of what the Okanagan is (and could be). In that context we explore the initiation of a strategy based on the aims and desires of local communities (see Sugden and Wilson, 2002) and their collective involvement in envisioning the region's future. We thereby address a common challenge for regions worldwide: the generation of a viable strategy whose imaginative reach is matched by the enthusiasm of its adoption by the citizens who will live with the consequences of its implementation.

In terms of physical geography, the Okanagan comprises numerous communities distributed primarily around various lakes, including Okanagan Lake. For millennia the region has been part of the Okanagan (Syilx) First Nations territory,[1] and over the last century or so it has witnessed an influx of immigrants. Okanagan communities are diverse, in part because of linearity associated with the lake and the development of transportation infrastructure – indeed, it appears that they celebrate and champion aspects of their diversity. Our objective is to consider the prospects for purposely developing a strategy that would benefit Okanagan communities, not only by not sacrificing but also, perhaps, by fostering diversity, which might be positively correlated with advantageous innovation. We argue that the first step in such development could be the engagement of communities in envisioning their futures together, and we explore what this might look like in practice.

The starting point for our analysis is the recent contribution by Navarro *et al.* (2014), many aspects of which have been deepened conceptually in the first six chapters of this book. These authors aim to redress what they consider to be the inadequate conceptualization of regional strategy for the purposes of economic analysis. They see this inadequacy as a consequence of the term having been imported without suitable critique and modification from the field of strategic management. Navarro *et al.* (2014: 534) advocate a holistic perspective requiring consideration of three dimensions – "objectives, content and process" – which they characterize in terms of replies to particular questions: answering "what for?" identifies the objectives, "what?" the content, and "how?" and "who?" the process. Their perspective considers regional strategies in general, and their contention is that all of the questions must be answered for a strategy to be fully identified. They emphasize that their framework is intended for considering past or existing strategies, not for designing and implementing new ones.

Our interest is specifically regions – such as the Okanagan – with little or no experience of a strategy from within. Most especially, we are interested in change – i.e., in such a region introducing a strategy from within. However, taking the analysis of Navarro *et al.* (2014) as given, it follows that, were such change to occur, there would be answers to the "what for, what, how and who" questions (which is not to say that those answers could be readily found).[2] A corollary is that, because such change would in some sense have to start in order for it to be realized, there would also be an answer to a more specific question: In a region with little or no experience of a strategy from within, what is the process for addressing the "what for, what, how and who" of such a strategy?[3] Answering this question is the prime concern of this chapter.

At the outset of our analysis we would also stress a further point of contrast between the approaches of Navarro *et al.* (2014) and ourselves. They find it useful to endorse White's (2004) definition of a strategy as "a coordinated series of actions which involve the deployment of resources to which one has access for the achievement of a given purpose" (Navarro *et al.*, 2014: 533). This is not a definition that explicitly recognizes chosen conduct and habitual behaviors – or, more comprehensively, culture – as an essential element. That could be a drawback, because it risks reducing the inextricable interplay between actions and culture, which not only provides a context but also is a determinant of actions, which in turn influence culture. Our analysis concerns the possibility of introducing a strategy from within that would turn very strongly not only on the actions but also on the culture of people, organizations and communities, as well as on the interplay between culture and actions.

The next section provides an introduction to the Okanagan, particularly its social and economic development. We suggest that, however the region faces its complex context, in the absence of a chosen strategy effectively implemented, its future will be left to luck. The following section takes up the challenge of exploring what would typically be required deliberately to initiate a social and economic strategy from within. We initially step back from details of the Okanagan context to consider issues at a more general level, then draw on the Okanagan example to illustrate various arguments. We highlight envisioning a region's future as an appropriate focal point for initiating a strategy and identify inquiry as a method for addressing that focal point. Our reasoning leads us to hypothesize that a social and economic strategy is typically best initiated by people in the communities of a region undertaking a journey, during which they explore and imagine their futures together, without the constraint of predetermined directions, behaviors and actions. Instead, futures are chosen through interwoven observation, reason and evidence, informed by feeling and sensitivity, as the journey progresses. We then recognize that realizing such a culture of inquiry needs to be developed through deliberate action, and to that end we advocate the desirability in practice of scenario-planning as one integrative approach to imagining possible futures and strategic options. The concluding section provides an integration of our arguments in light of our departure point in Navarro *et al.* (2014) and identifies areas of future work in both independent analysis and comparison among similarly situated regions globally.

## Social and economic development in the Okanagan

The Okanagan is a region located in south-central British Columbia (BC), Canada's westernmost province. Approximately 400 kilometers inland and east of the coastal city of Vancouver, the region features a set of river-connected lakes – the largest of which is Okanagan Lake – in a north–south corridor that stretches 250 kilometers north from Canada's border with the United States. The eastern boundary of the region is formed by the Cascade Mountains, and the Monashee Mountains sit to the west. The effects of the mountains and lakes make for a mild and dry climate; the semi-arid Okanagan is the hottest and driest of any region in BC, albeit average annual preci pitation varies from 300 mm to 750 mm, tending to be higher toward the north and at elevated altitudes (Cohen and Kulkarni, 2001; Belliveau *et al.*, 2006). At about two-thirds the size of Belgium, the total area of the region is approximately 21,000 square kilometers.[4]

Almost two-thirds of the regional population of approximately 350,000 live in and around the city of Kelowna, situated at the center of the Okanagan Valley. Smaller urban concentrations are found in the cities of Vernon to the north (population approximately 40,000) and Penticton to the south (population approximately 30,000), and still smaller settlements are both further north and south.[5]

Notwithstanding the geographic and climatic features marking the Okanagan apart from elsewhere in BC, governance is generally distributed on terms owing more to history than from any intention to regard the region as having a unified geographic and socio-economic identity. Government and governance are complex some writers suppose. European settlers entered what under English law and the international law principle of *terra nullius* was an unclaimed land, open to possession by the first to claim it (Edenhoffer and Hayter, 2013). Yet this is mistaken as a matter of law. As the Supreme Court of Canada makes clear in Tsilhqot'in Nation v. British Columbia, 2014 SCC 44, at paragraph 69, the Royal Proclamation (1763) R.S.C. 1985, App II, No. 1 specifies that the doctrine of terra nullius did not apply to Canada, meaning that land in Canada was not to be regarded as unclaimed and Aboriginal interests in land were to be recognized. European settlers often proceeded nonetheless as though Aboriginal interests were of no great importance and treaty-making unnecessary, notwithstanding this legal fact and the further practical fact that the Okanagan people – aboriginal "First Nations" in Canadian parlance – have for millennia occupied the region and its southern extremity crossing into the United States. Okanagan First Nations continue to maintain that their territory is unceded, leaving governance over contested matters an issue of pragmatic compromise on the back of contingent relations yet to be solidified into a constitutionally clear division of powers and duties (Armstrong *et al.*, 1994).

If some regions are plausibly said to be peripheral to cores, the Okanagan is properly regarded as doubly peripheral, in both geography and time. It is most obviously geographically peripheral to the urban center of Vancouver and the "lower mainland" of BC, home to 70 percent of the province's 4.7 million inhabitants. The Okanagan is also peripheral in a temporal sense, as a latecomer to many of the dimensions of globalization. Each of these aspects of the region's peripheral status has an "echo." Within the region, the north–south orientation around lengthy waterways has been associated historically with distinctive patterns of sub-regional development and senses of identity. Sub-regional core–periphery relations have emerged between rapidly growing Kelowna and slower growth in Vernon and the north and Penticton and the south. An accompanying temporal echo can be seen in the speed at which sub-regions have been affected by globalization: patterns of production for Canadian and export markets have brought sub-regions into contact with global pressures at quite different times. The predominantly southern production of fruit for Canadian markets was shocked, for example, by the conclusion of the North American Free Trade Agreement, bringing producers into competition with generally larger American companies. By contrast, the northern sub-region was much less affected by this particular event, yet it has faced its own particular challenges during a period of consolidation of Canadian mill operations processing timber for export (Edenhoffer and Hayter, 2013).

Much of the story of the Okanagan involves a combination of elements also evident elsewhere. If any special lessons are to be derived, they are likely to be associated with the interaction of two atypical factors: first, the relative youth of this fast-growing region as a part of a young country integrated into the global trade system; second, in the face of rapid changes to the region's social and economic basis, the absence of a strategy for social and economic development that is conceived, designed and enacted largely from within and across the region itself.

In contrast with European regions, for example, with social and economic histories traceable in detail for several centuries, the Okanagan's function as a social and economic region reaches over little more than a single century. Early colonial contact with First Nations resolved into settlement patterns only in the mid-nineteenth century, as ranchers began farming forage crops for cattle, soon accompanied by the trial of grain, potatoes, tobacco and fruit. Opportunities for timber harvest were evident throughout the region (Trenaman and Parminter, 2006), and mining exploration brought minor opportunities in the Okanagan Valley, as well as a major nickel mine in the adjacent Similkameen Valley (Cox, 1995).

The combination of these economic activities drove investment in transport infrastructure, enabling market access, further settlement and population growth

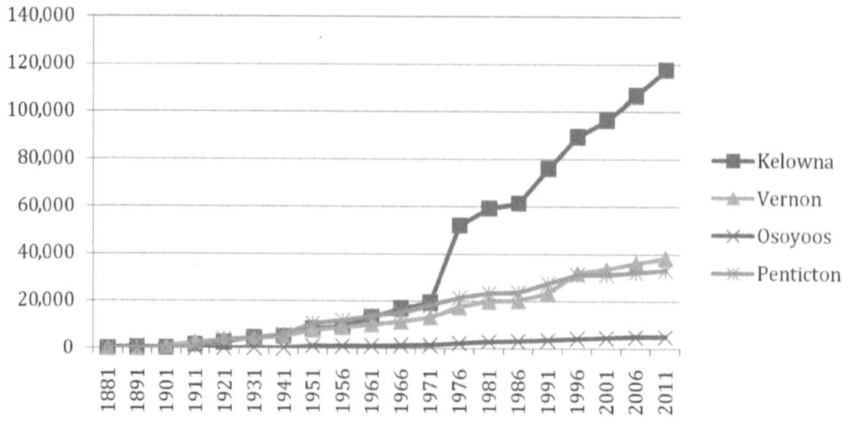


*Figure 11.1* Population data for key settlements in the Okanagan, 1881–2011

Sources: Census of Canada 1881, 1891, 1901 and 1911; Belshaw (2009) for 1911 data for Penticton; BCStats municipal census data for 1921 to 2011.

Notes: As population increased over time, district and sub-district boundaries in the region were expanded; the table reads 'zero' where population data was not available or was not reported.

(see Figure 11.1). By 1891 a steamship service had begun on the Okanagan Lake and the area was reachable by rail from the north. The arrival of rail links to markets, scarcely a century ago, marked the decisive entry of the Okanagan into supra-regional and global commerce. Timber could be sent to ports and eastern markets, and the combination of rapid transport, favorable trade policy and climate gave Okanagan agriculturalists ready markets in Vancouver and the Canadian prairies – particularly for luxury fruits not easily grown in those parts (Pooley, 2012; Wynn, 2013). Settlers and tourists alike were soon attracted to the Okanagan, enticed by means such as English newspaper advertisements boasting of "endless sunshine and bountiful water" and supporting the growth of new settlements, including the carefully named lakeside districts "Summerland" and "Peachland" (Wagner, 2008: 26), and the Okanagan Valley was promoted as a "Garden of Eden" (Koroscil, 2008: 6).

In some ways the first wave of colonization, development and regional connection to distant markets established economic and cultural forms that are yet to be overwritten by endogenous choice or exogenous force. Even once Kelowna and the north were connected to markets via rail, and Penticton followed suit via a separate rail line, the dominant mode of connection between the north and south of the Okanagan was by water until 1937, when the steamer service was made obsolete by improved roads and tug-barge services (Turner, 1995). These improvements were significant yet in a sense incomplete: travel from the southern Okanagan to Kelowna still required a ferry trip across the lake until the construction of a bridge in 1958.[6] Road travel from Kelowna and the central region to Vancouver was accomplished by driving for at least seven hours south through Penticton until the completion in 1986 of the Coquihalla Highway, which reduced the journey time to four hours (Schwindt *et al.*, 2000). The two dimensions of geographic peripherality described above have been measurably attenuated, but they still remain, especially as the region's production is export-oriented and its service industry is focused on tourism and, more recently, the needs of incoming retirees.

As in the early days of the region, the social and economic activities of the intervening to present time have co-evolved with infrastructure development, at length and over a period of extended stability, giving rise to some diversification around historic pillar industries. For example, early orchardists' rapid shipment of fresh fruit to market was soon accompanied by canning operations, adding value to production. A comparatively stable fruit industry thrived for decades before the relatively rapid shift in emphasis from fruit orchards to growing grapes for wine. Globalization-driven challenges to the region's mature initial socio-economic foundations have arrived only quite recently, and at intervals, simultaneously preserving the region from rapid, unchosen change and potentially stultifying preparation for the possibility of such change.

The Okanagan's only age, it might be said, has been a golden age, with carefully curated icons of that age taking disproportionate pride of place in the region's cultural memory and self-presentation. Penticton retains its annual Peach Festival, complete with Peach Queen, Kelowna's city slogan remains "Fruitful in Unity," and curious tourists find BC handily partitioned by Fodor's travel guide into regions including "Okanagan Wine Country."[7] It is understandable, of course, that an attractive image should be presented to potential tourists and retirees, and that marketers seize on slogans enabling that presentation. Yet perhaps trouble may surface when official icons become so distant from the gradually changing factual reality that citizens seeking to choose their future must first overcome a substantial body of well-supported myth.

Evidence drawn from labor-force distribution tends to reinforce the view that there is a troublesome gap between facts and myth in the Okanagan:

> In 2006, 71% of the labour force was employed in the services sector, primarily in retail trade (13%), health care (11%), accommodation & food services (9%) and professional, scientific and technical services (6%). The goods producing sector comprised 28% of the labour force and included construction (11%), manufacturing (9%) and agriculture (4%).[8]

When construction, retail services and health care account for the bulk of labor and iconic agriculture trails in at just 4 percent, re-evaluation of governing myths is clearly warranted. Yet re-evaluation may be unusually difficult because of the rootedness of those myths in a single golden age. There is no regional cultural history and memory of transition from one set of foundations to another – or, less dramatically, culturally perceived and acknowledged transformations of use of foundations.

As foreshadowed above, the most prominent shock and adaptation visible in the Okanagan came with the 1985 negotiation of the North American Free Trade Agreement, exposing the region's orchardists to American competition. An adaptive option was fortunately ready to hand. Wine of poor quality sold for domestic consumption had long been produced in small quantities. Orchardists quickly took advantage of legislation protecting BC wine production and replanted with higher-value grapes, realizing at the same time the land base limitation hampering the scale of fruit production, so beginning efforts to encourage wine tourism (Hira and Bwenge, 2011: 16–19; Aguiar and Marten, 2009). Today some 200 wineries both produce wine largely for the BC market and welcome tourists (see www.winebc.com). Similar stories of shock and adaptation can be told about forestry and tourism, albeit at different dates, leaving the net impression that at least momentary stability and prosperity appear to have been achieved, together with regional population growth, culturally associated with success and prosperity.

We conclude this depiction of the current state of development in the Okanagan by noting two further temporal echoes of the effects of globalization that are still arriving in this peripheral region. The first is a matter of unplanned exogenous support for its current socio-economic status quo. Growth in the exploitation of natural gas and tar-sands energy in the north of BC and Alberta has created a booming market for both skilled and unskilled labor. Comparatively high wages in these industries and the relative isolation of northern communities have combined with regional airlines to create a cadre of commuters from various southern regions, including the Okanagan. In the Kelowna area alone, an estimated 5,000 workers commute to northern employment.[9]

The second echo is a matter of endogenous uncertainty, as First Nations have over time advanced more effectively their assertion that the territory once regarded as *terra nullius* was in fact inhabited and was never ceded. Several Indian bands in the Okanagan have recently taken this fact as inspiration for their own style of entrepreneurial activity. In the south, for example, Chief Clarence Louis and the Osoyoos Indian Band have founded North America's first aboriginal winery (www.nkmipcellars.com), are in the midst of creating a sustainable business park (http://oibdc.ca/businesses/senkulmen-business-park/) and are hosting a provincial prison, among other ventures. This is not an isolated example: in the Central Okanagan, the Westbank First Nation has developed leased land communities and now proposes to use their special legal status as a means to found a private hospital. Where, then, some might see uncertainty facing the region's strategists as First Nations press their land claims, others observe not only social dynamism but also a source of potential regional strength in intercultural competences and experience a kind of Canadian version of the approach to subsidiarity witnessed in parts of Europe, requiring decision-making to occur at the lowest level possible and closest to those most affected.[10] Historic and present conflict between First Nations and settlers may yet become a decisive strategic advantage for the Okanagan region.

### *What next for the Okanagan?*

The complex challenges of globalization bring clear opportunities and threats, expose vulnerabilities, and assist in the identification of impactful uncertainties. So far, despite these challenges, the region has had very little experience with strategies for development that are conceived, designed and enacted from within and across the region itself, and previous attempts at strategy offer more in the way of lessons about the nature of the next possible starting point than they do lessons about successes or failures of strategies per se. As observed above, the early years of the Okanagan's settlement and rapid growth were characterized by actual and perceived distance and difference between internal cores and peripheries. Even as improved transport and communications networks have enabled greater connection, truly regional strategy has not emerged. Explanation of this situation remains elusive as candidate explanations are underdetermined by available evidence.

Some relevant factors and potential explanations may nonetheless be enumerated, all driven by our suggestion that there is an ungrounded perception that no such strategy is needed. Three possible explanations seem especially plausible. The first two are of a piece: they report the Okanagan view that the present approach and regional adaptive capacity are sufficient.

The first arm of this style of explanation might point to both the gradual diversification evident in the Okanagan's forays into manufacturing and software and the region's population growth, and insist that these positive socio-economic features are evidence that sufficient regional development policy coordination, however haphazard and whatever its source, is already occurring. Something like this view appears to have underpinned the gradual failure of the Okanagan Partnership, convened by prominent regional business leaders Brad Bennett and Gordon Fitzpatrick to identify the next bases of sustainable regional development. From its formation in 2004 until its gradual demise, the Okanagan Partnership sought to galvanize regional thinking around what its background studies identified as seven areas of potential comparative advantage: tourism, life sciences, forestry and wood products, wine and beverages, knowledge services, value-added agriculture, and aviation.[11] The leadership and vision advanced by the Okanagan Partnership reached an audience that did not share the group's urgency and, apart from encouraging greater cross-sectorial communication, its legacy is difficult to trace.

A second style of explanation might be still more bold, in effect inverting the suggestion that the Okanagan is peripheral in various ways. It might be argued that the region has a privileged seat at provincial strategic deliberations such that provincial policy is nearly always a reflection of Okanagan interests, ensuring that sufficient resources for socio-economic success flow from government and negating the need for a strategy from within. To see the plausibility of this explanation, consider that the Okanagan was the political base of father and son provincial premiers W. A. C. Bennett (1952–72) and William R. Bennett (1975–86) and that the present premier, Christy Clark, won her seat in the provincial legislature via a by-election in the riding of Westside-Kelowna. Even in the relatively rare interregna when generally conservative BC governments are displaced by others, the Okanagan block of votes may be the decisive granter of comprehensive victory or modest loss in elections effectively decided by the bulk of eligible voters resident in the Lower Mainland.

A third possible explanation suggests that there are Okanagan residents who are aware of the region's need for strategy yet lack both the capacity to gain political priority for the need and, through want of alternative mechanisms for collective deliberation, the preconditions for collective choice of action and strategy. The plausibility of this explanation is supported by the fact of the initiation of the Okanagan Partnership, by the structural facts surveyed regarding the geographic distance between communities with diverse self-conceptions, and by the absence of social institutions enabling alternatives to extant deliberative mechanisms to emerge – there is, for example, no unitary organization uniting private-sector businesses, 94 percent of which have fewer than nineteen employees.[12]

Any available explanation seems to bring to the surface common elements of an analysis showing that the Okanagan's inhabitants should view as unacceptable the present lack of a regional development strategy conceived, designed and enacted from within and across the region itself. The first explanation highlights the danger of complacency regarding present adaptive capacity – this complacency risks failure to take sufficient notice of the magnitude of exogenous forces such as climate change and mobility of labor and capital. The second explanation illuminates the shortcomings of historic strategy-generation institutions and processes: the effects of globalization include increased interdependence, sometimes in unanticipated ways (such as Okanagan workers commuting to jobs in the Alberta tar sands), placing decision-making with potentially profound effects on the region significantly beyond the control of conventional political and legislative processes. In other words, merely relying on the exercise of power in the provincial government is risky. And the third candidate explanation draws attention to whether the region has the cultural and institutional means to understand its past, present context and options, and future challenges in ways leading to effective collective choice.

Taken together, the insights arising from possible explanations of the current status quo set an intriguing challenge for the Okanagan. How might the region initiate a strategy from within so as to benefit its communities without sacrificing and perhaps fostering their diversity, at the same time encouraging advantageous innovation for its long-term social and economic sustainability?

## Community engagement and envisioning a region's future

Strategic planning at the level of a collectivity is notoriously difficult even if universally acknowledged as necessary – and still more difficult if not. Where the need for a strategy is in question, any approach bears an extraordinary burden of justification, obliged to show first that the act of strategizing has any value at all and, further, that the particular chosen strategic process is likely to be effective. Any would-be regional strategist in the Okanagan must face both of these challenges while remembering that the last attempt to develop regional strategy from within, the Okanagan Partnership, ultimately failed to achieve the integrated regional strategic plan and action it sought.

Facing this challenge, any strategist would do well first to inquire into what is different now in the Okanagan and the possibilities created by that difference. In the absence of visible recent shocks to the society and economy of the region, it is unsurprising that some of the most significant differences are amplifications of previously evident factors. Three differences are particularly noteworthy. The first is that, nearly ten years ago, the University of British Columbia (UBC) established a new campus in the region, in Kelowna, and that campus is now maturing. The presence of research-intensive universities has long been associated with innovative capacity, but it must be remembered that this correlation tends to presume the presence of a mature university. As UBC achieves almost a decade of activity in the region, it has nearly completed its initial phase of building from the ground up and is now turning its focus outward, toward the region. UBC is a public university and so a relatively neutral finder of regional fact and curator of regional memory. Its public status also lends it an advantage as a neutral venue for discourse regarding regional strategy, and its institutional capacity includes expertise on diverse approaches to dialogue and multilogue prerequisite to building strategy from within. To this institutional capacity we might add a second development – maturation in information technology platforms and applications – enabling the presentation of facts and arguments in intuitively accessible ways and permitting engagement of a wide range of citizens by diverse means. Third and perhaps most tendentiously, the amalgam of challenges, voices and resources has changed over the past decade as, for example, health-care costs have risen to absorb more than 50 percent of the provincial budget, leading to urgent discussion regarding new ways of achieving better health outcomes in urban and rural areas of the province. The growing Okanagan population is also different, as historic westward migration from the prairies is accompanied by migration from elsewhere, producing more visible ethnic diversity of experience, preference and global connection. Finally, while provincial fiscal resource constraints drive one strand of discussion regarding the future of health care in the region and beyond, the globalization of flows of people, finance and ideas has created a new awareness of international forces and opportunities, freeing the region from exclusive reliance on historic markets and opening the path to thinking of twenty-first-century social and economic pillars in ways that truly overwrite initial dependence on ranching, tourism, lumber and fruit farming.

In this context, acceptance of a need for a strategy from within and the suitability of particular strategy-development techniques depend on the avoidance of critical pitfalls as much as on the choice of viable strategy tools, goals, etc. Assuming *arguendo* that Drucker is correct and that culture does indeed eat strategy for breakfast,[13] preferred approaches to encouraging regional envisioning and realizing of a shared future must be respectful of culture and assist cultural renaissance. These approaches will nonetheless need to achieve goal-setting and the responsibility-allocating functions of strategy-building. This calls for approaches that enable collective sense-making of shared challenges in ways that simultaneously contribute to mutual learning of disparate dimensions of shared history. These approaches must enable collective addressing of culturally resonant problems that are demonstrably beyond the solution capacity of extant institutions and methods while being compatible and continuous with them.

Bearing such arguments in mind – and stepping back from the Okanagan context to consider the issues at a more general level (while returning in due course to a more explicit consideration of the region) – we suggest that deliberately initiating a regional social and economic strategy in a context with little or no experience of a strategy conceived, designed and enacted from within and across the region itself would typically necessitate as part of the process (1) an initial focal point for developing the strategy and (2) a method for addressing the focal point. The need for a focal point stems from the fact that it is not typically feasible for a region to jump immediately to a simultaneous consideration of all of the elements of a holistic strategy. One reason is that, regardless of who is participating in formulating the strategy – whether all in a region or merely a sub-set of those with an interest – each and every person will be constrained by bounded rationality (Williamson, 1975, 1993). A focal point is also necessary as it lessens the risk of going so fast in the introduction of change that much of the population could self-exclude themselves from or resist the process.

Following Navarro and his colleagues (2014: 538), the method for addressing the focal point can vary – for example, be "more top-down/expert based or more bottom-up/participatory," although they also assert that "in the current, advanced and complex systems it is not possible for the leadership to be left to only one agent … It is more and more necessary to move from a governance and leadership based on hierarchy to another based on networks." We would also emphasize the desirability of a method based upon reason and evidence and which accommodates the endogenous verification of critical assumptions. For example, suppose the focal point is searching for solutions – the answers to "what" – on the assumption that the "what for" is known. We would urge that, even assuming the "what for," a method that addresses the solutions by also verifying the assumption would be good practice. Anything less might be thought to leave too much to hope, especially in multicultural situations where diverse modes of expression may lead to a perception of irremediable conflict, while instead there is a need for mutual translation to generate shared understanding of what is in fact common ground.

More generally, whatever the initial focal point for introducing a regional social and economic strategy from within, we would advocate a method that leaves open the possibility of that focal point changing if something more suitable emerges as the strategy is further developed. Flexibility in implementation would increase the likelihood of success. This is to suggest that choice of focal point and method are interconnected. Moreover, we would contend that some focal points are likely to be more suited to certain methods, and vice versa, and that the distinctive culture and history of a region will be a determining factor in all choices, mindful of the observation from Navarro *et al.* that path dependence is a possibly perilous characteristic of regional strategies:

> Regional strategies exhibit a strong path dependence. Institutions and key actors are influenced by historic experience and its consequences: positive evaluations of the past will become a source of inertia in the design

and implementation of strategies and policies, while negative ones will have the opposite effect, generating fractures and changes. The lack of previous experience of limitations or inherited inertia, but also crisis situations (social, economic, political), can act as drivers of change.

(Navarro *et al.*, 2014: 538)

## *Envisioning the future*

With these considerations in mind, we hypothesize: *envisioning a region's future is typically an appropriate focal point for initiating a social and economic strategy from within.*

We offer our hypothesis on more than the familiar grounds that future success is usefully approached via goal-setting and a concentration on manageable segments. Our hypothesis embodies the further insight that envisioning regional futures is a means to taking seriously the diversity of possible futures, both desirable and undesirable, and to strategic thinking which explicitly aims to foster capacity to go beyond reactive adaptation, toward proactive choice of action shaping the way in which emerging forces are experienced and strategic options are chosen and implemented. To be sure, envisioning is compatible with (and for operation requires) goal-setting to support the achievement of desired future states of affairs; but it is more far-ranging in its demands on deliberative methods, as it seeks to answer the "what for" question of regional strategy-building in a way that acknowledges the complexity of regional contexts and the importance of recognition of uncontrolled exogenous forces bearing on strategy development and implementation.

In arguing this we would also recognize that, in many regions currently lacking in terms of strategy for social and economic development, there might be little experience of pan-regional engagement on identity, aims and objectives, therefore little or no basis upon which to imagine the future. This is the case for the Okanagan, where immigrant communities have developed on the lands of the Okanagan Nation over only the last century or so. For much of that period their development has been in relative isolation from one another and impinging upon or in parallel with bands of the Okanagan Nation. As we have previously indicated, there have been few attempts in living memory at forging regional identity and widespread cooperative action – even fewer that have been sustained. In this context, there is no evidence of any consensus on the "what for" of social and economic development. A focus on the future sets the present lack of consensus to one side in favor of exploring alternatives whose future relevance may enable improved reflection on present interests and options.

## *Inquiry*

We also hypothesize: *inquiry is typically a useful method for addressing the focal point for developing a regional social and economic strategy from within.* More accurately, we consider a particular approach to inquiry: an exploratory journey by a group of people where direction, conduct and action are not predetermined but, rather, are chosen through observation, reason and evidence, informed by feeling and sensitivity, as the journey progresses.

Navarro *et al.* (2014) see regional strategy as about the "what for, what, how and who" questions, and Dewey (1938) links questions to inquiry. He argues that "we inquire when we question; and we inquire when we seek for whatever will provide an answer to a question asked" (Dewey, 1938: 105).[14] A situation in which people within a region are contemplating the introduction of a social and economic strategy is what Dewey would call questionable – it is unsettled and indeterminate. There is uncertainty, or at least a lack of clarity, about what action to take or, more judiciously, about what sort of action the situation demands. An inquiry is a means to address such situations. It is "the controlled or directed transformation" of the indeterminate situation into one that is settled, coherent and organized (Dewey 1938: 105; Kaufmann, 1959; Pepper, 1977).

An inquiry involves observation, data collection and inference, guided by ideation and the organization of ideas and materials through reasoning. In arguing this, Dewey points to the importance of inquiry being unfettered by disciplinary boundaries. He suggests that there is a divide between the various aspects of human inquiry that separates economics, politics and morals from a "single and inclusive cultural whole in which their subject matters" are intrinsically connected to each other (Dewey, 1947: 381). According to him, if we break from the divisions (that hinder the cross-fertilization of ideas and methods), adopt intellectual habits and use the resources available fully and freely, we shall release and expand human inquiry (including methods and conclusions) from the shackles of a fixed physical and material framework (inherited from old traditions of physical inquiry) that confines the studies of social subjects.

Dewey also points directly to the significance of feeling and sensitivity:

> It is more or less a commonplace that it is possible to carry on observations that amass facts tirelessly and yet the observed "facts" lead nowhere. On the other hand, it is possible to have the work of observation so controlled by a conceptual framework fixed in advance that the very things which are genuinely decisive in the problem in hand and its solution are completely overlooked. Everything is forced into the predetermined conceptual and theoretical scheme. *The way, and the only way, to escape these two evils, is sensitivity to the quality of a situation as a whole. In ordinary language, a problem must be felt before it can be stated.*
>
> (Dewey, 1938: 70; emphasis added)

Hahn (1977: xi) also identifies a theme in Dewey's work: "knowledge as an affair of the sentient organism interacting with its environment as opposed to a knowing subject seeking to know an alien external world as object." This theme is related to Docherty's (2008) discussion of sense and sensibility. Referring to the study of English, more widely to "the proper place … of literature … within a society," he considers the deficiencies of having "a form of knowledge that was not 'lived', not actually 'felt' at the inner level of sensibility" (2008: 4). The result of such a form might be seen as "a triumph of the industrialisation of the human spirit," a failure to balance appropriately "sense or reason and sensibility or feeling" (ibid.: 4–5).

Consistent with these arguments, we suggest that inquiry as a method for developing a regional strategy should not be constrained by a predetermined conceptual framework that might control or pre-empt the direction and outcomes, hence the actual strategy, and in so doing overlook key elements in the situation. Similarly, the means used should not precede or impede the development of the inquiry itself. An inquiry involves the transformation of a situation and so it is important, first, to assess the situation, then to develop accordingly the means required for the inquiry to be successful (see also Kaufmann, 1959). This method explicitly invalidates an approach that assumes complete understanding of the problematic situation being faced or of what needs to be done. Such an assumption would be based on predetermined conceptual frameworks and means, and not necessarily on the observation, reason and evidence, informed by feeling and sensitivity, required in an inquiry. Along those lines, a regional strategy that addresses the "what," "how" and "who," without identifying the "what for," would be based on predetermined notions that are not necessarily based on observation, reason and evidence, feeling and sensitivity. Moreover, the objectives, content and process of the strategy would be influenced by "who" is involved in the inquiry.

An inquiry is a continuous process of change: "rational operations grow out of organic activities, without being identical with that from which they emerge" (Dewey, 1938: 19). The implication is not merely that inquiry takes time but also "that the objective subject-matter of inquiry undergoes temporal modification" (ibid.: 118). Inquiry is a journey in which people in a region strive to understand and refine their development possibilities in a situation that evolves as their behaviors and actions also evolve. Hence, we envisage that a journey of inquiry might enable people in the Okanagan to go beyond simply devising adaptive tactics/strategies in response to globalization-induced change, as was seemingly the case after the 1985 negotiation of the North American Free Trade Agreement which put the region's orchardists in competition with larger American producers. In a journey of inquiry, the objectives, content and process of development are centered on the capacities, chosen conduct and unconscious habits of people, which are in part shaped through their shared interactions and actions. Through inquiry, development possibilities are not necessarily reactionary. Rather, they emerge out of organic operations that take into consideration the region's context (including its opportunities, threats, vulnerabilities and uncertainties) and explore new avenues in order to build social and economic resilience over time.

Moreover, an inquiry is a revisable process:

> The "settlement" of a particular situation by a particular inquiry is no guarantee that *that* settled conclusion will always remain settled ... the criterion of what is taken to be settled, or to be knowledge, is being *so* settled that it is available as a resource in further inquiry; not being settled in such a way as not to be subject to revision in further inquiry.
>
> (Dewey, 1938: 8–9)

This is to suggest that conclusions obtained in one inquiry might in turn trigger or be used in subsequent inquiries but that those conclusions are not finalities. Operations in one inquiry might yield significantly different conclusions in subsequent inquiries – not least because the situation might have evolved or might be different – and thus conclusions reached in a previous inquiry are tested and revised in subsequent inquiries.

An implication for the development of a regional strategy is that previous inquiries on strategies are relevant but can by no means provide final proof of what should be done. Consider the possibility of inquiries within inquiries – for example, embedding into a wide-ranging inquiry on a region's future distinct inquiries on aspects of that future. Once those embedded inquiries are settled and fed into the broader inquiry it might emerge that, the previous settlement notwithstanding, the embedded inquiries warrant reopening. For example, from the late nineteenth century, gravity-fed irrigation systems that used wooden flumes and open ditches to transport water to the land in the Okanagan Valley allowed the growth of tree fruits such as cherries and apricots (Wagner, 2008). The consequent alteration in natural habitat that occurred was viewed positively by the settlers – orchardists – but not by the indigenous Syilx people, who placed high value on the grassland and wetland environments. A journey of inquiry, which would ideally incorporate all of those concerned – including orchardists and Syilx people – would further explore the possibilities (and suitability) of irrigation systems for the land and the impact on the natural habitat. Any previous settlement regarding the use of irrigation systems would not be so settled that it could not be reopened to inquiry.

### *Community engagement*

Combining the arguments for envisioning a region's future with those for inquiry as a method, we further hypothesize: *a social and economic strategy is typically best initiated by people in the communities of a region undertaking a journey, during which they explore and imagine their futures together without the constraint of predetermined directions, conduct and actions, which are instead chosen through observation, reason and evidence, informed, as their journey progresses, by feeling and sensitivity.*

How such a journey might be undertaken in practice would depend on the particular circumstances – the histories, experiences and cultures – of people and communities living in a region. It would also depend on the relation of those people and communities to people, communities, regions and metropolitan centers in other parts of the world. Drawing on Amin and Thrift (2002), Amin refers to regions "as places of overlapping – *but not necessarily locally connected* – relational networks, as perforated entities with connections that stretch far in time and space, and, resulting from all of this, as spatial formations of continuously changing composition, character, and reach" (Amin, 2004: 34; emphasis added). Thus he refers to the potential for regions to be "immersed in global networks of organization and routinely implicated in distant connections and influences" (ibid.: 33), unleashing forces that we would expect to impact the development of a regional social and economic strategy, not least through influencing people's aims and desires for their futures.

Typically, the creation of public fora (Sacchetti *et al.*, 2009) and spaces (Sacchetti, 2013) that enable inquiry would be important for people on a journey that initiates a social and economic strategy. The idea of public fora is that they would offer purposely created arenas for people and communities to learn to inquire about their social and economic futures together (Sacchetti *et al.*, 2009). In a particular region we might envisage a plethora of overlapping fora, developed over time to ensure accessibility and interaction. For example, in the Okanagan there are people and organizations sharing concerns about healthy lifestyles (such as the Okanagan Similkameen Healthy Living Coalition, a case to which we return later). That shared concern might provide a basis for them to meet together so as to discuss and deliberate, to imagine their futures, and thus think about and explore the possibilities for shared aims and objectives in a regional social and economic strategy. Others in the Okanagan share an interest in the development of particular sectors, such as wine, defense, digital technologies and advanced construction materials. Each of these provides a reason and foundation for interaction, thus inquiry.

The possibility of fora is also linked to the significance of public spaces. These can include ice rinks, parks, town squares and streets, as well as cafes and canteens and office corridors, not to mention galleries, theatres and exhibition sites. They are spaces in which people interact in their everyday lives. They also afford opportunities for individuals to communicate and deliberate, to reflect critically on their beliefs and choices, and thus to envision new possibilities and indeed new futures (Sacchetti, 2013). In line with our earlier comments about regions and relational networks, we would also stress that these public spaces are not necessarily merely locally bounded: it would be

> an error to imagine the local public sphere in purely localist terms. The public sphere, that is the discursive arena in which any individual here or there can participate with aid of many "traveling" technologies such as books, newspapers, billboards, the media, the internet, is trans-territorial by very definition.
> (Amin, 2004: 11)

The creation of public fora and spaces would involve inputs from many actors, including municipalities with their town planning (Sacchetti, 2013) and enterprises and community organizations with their choices that affect working cultures and lives. Universities, perhaps especially public universities, would also be significant.

Of their essence, public universities are concerned with observation, data collection and inference, guided by ideation and the organization of ideas and materials through reason, evidence and sensibility. That is, universities are concerned with inquiry. Moreover, they have always been purposeful in impacting the societies and economies of which they are a part. From their origins, their focus on medicine, law and theology was explicitly concerned with influence in practice (Graham, 2005), and in recent years there has been much focus on universities interacting with, and impacting, social and economic development (Nowotny,

2000). For example, the potential opportunities, challenges and tensions for universities to contribute to regional innovation and growth are widely acknowledged in academic and policy literature (see Goddard *et al.*, 2013, and references therein). These characteristics provide a basis from which universities might enable people and communities to undertake a journey of inquiry, an exploration together of their social and economic futures. In doing so, universities might not only facilitate public forums, for example, but also synthesize their proceedings and cross-fertilize their deliberations, so as to move toward an inclusive strategy.

In the case of the Okanagan, what is especially interesting in this regard is the presence of UBC in the region. Through the Okanagan campus, UBC is committed to impacting the region's social and economic development. Supporting the people and communities of the Okanagan to imagine their futures, thus to undertake a journey of regional strategy formulation and implementation so as to realize their vision, could be an important role for the university.

### *Scenario-planning*

All of these points accepted, however, even if a regional strategy is indeed best initiated through a journey of inquiry, there needs to be a starting point to that journey – or, perhaps more accurately, a catalyst for its initiation. To that end, and recalling our previously stated concern that preferred approaches to encouraging regional envisioning of a shared future must be respectful of culture and assist cultural renaissance, we hypothesize: *in practice, scenario-planning is likely a suitable catalyst for a journey of inquiry during which people in the communities of a region will explore and imagine their futures together.*

Scenario-planning in the Oxford intuitive analytics tradition is an approach to sense-making and identification of strategic options in situations dominated by complexity and uncertainty, where what is subjectively experienced as "turbulence" overwhelms extant planning processes and institutions (Ramirez *et al.*, 2010; Emery and Trist, 1965). These scenario-planning methods were first developed in military and private-sector contexts from the 1960s onward (Bradfield *et al.*, 2005). They enjoyed perhaps their most celebrated deployment by Shell during the first oil shock of the 1970s, when the company sought new strategic options as its supply of oil suddenly became uncertain, and planning for the future of oil companies seemed overwhelmed by complex, fast-moving and unpredictable facts (Bradfield *et al.*, 2005; Schoemaker, 1995). In the hands of Shell and others, scenario-planning has been used to enable typically unitary, hierarchically organized organizations to "re-perceive" their current strategic position. This is achieved by facilitated deployment of a set of knowledge-gathering and knowledge-recombination techniques within the organization, harnessing facts to specified areas of uncertainty to construct possible future worlds imagined to be between thirty-five and a hundred years from the present. These future worlds, which an organization might inhabit, are expressed in fact-driven, story-like narratives, which concretize and express what might occur when present uncertainties become certainties (Wilkinson *et al.*, 2013).

In contrast to the probabilistic pictures of future states of affairs familiar from forecasting, the "possibilistic" pictures of multiple futures delivered by scenario-building make no claims to truth or likelihood, nor are they normatively directed toward identification of preferred futures. Rather, their value lies in their plausible exploration of the possible consequences of various chains of facts arising even in situations where shortages of information preclude probabilistic reasoning. These stories "making sense" of presently overwhelming strategic contexts can then be used to challenge the current conceptions or rosters of action possibilities within an organization, potentially illuminating new options or foreshadowing the frailty of specific options in all possible futures (Wilkinson and Ramirez, 2010).

The term "scenario-planning" is evidently something of a misnomer to the extent that it is not in itself intended to generate any particular kind of plan – or indeed any specific plan (Schoemaker, 1995). Scenario-planning is, however, a precursor to strategy and its resolution into planning, insofar as it enables a given organization to reassess what it knows about itself and its context. As typically facilitated, it has an important social flattening effect within an organization. Participants' daily roles and titles matter less than their contribution to surfacing and integration of explicit and tacit knowledge, which may be supplied in quantitative or qualitative terms, and expressly includes acknowledgement and specification of uncertainty. Further, critical distance from present interests is driven by the projection of possible futures sufficiently far into those futures that all participants can be safely presumed at least to have unpredictably different interests. Even those inclined to be sceptical regarding the use-value of the resulting narratives regarding possible futures may find value in the organizational learning effects fostered by scenario-planning (Wilkinson, 2009; Goodwin and Wright, 2001). Those more sympathetic to the claimed effect of "re-perception" of present and future contexts may see in the attempt to reason rigorously about uncertainty a valuable further heightening of participants' sensitivity to the diversity of action options available in a context which is far less predictable and more malleable than previously believed.

Bringing these methods to the Okanagan would be difficult yet possible, beginning with the challenge found in translating methods originating in unitary, hierarchical organizations to a much more heterogeneous situation. The key in doing so, we suggest, lies in recognizing that, while the region does not resemble actors such as Shell, its citizens can, with respect to certain problems, conduct themselves as members of a soft-bordered unitary organization – even if bound by ties little more than those found in single-issue political advocacy groups. A second challenge arrives with the question of whether the Okanagan is experiencing the metaphorical turbulence to which scenario-planning has been judged an effective response. We have early and incomplete yet indicative evidence that there are issues experienced as turbulence sufficient to motivate participation in scenario-planning as a gateway to a broader collective journey of inquiry and onward to construction of new social institutions for deliberative engagement around a regional strategy.

In October of 2013 two of the present authors, Culver and Dhaliwal, conducted a scenario-planning exercise with a sub-regional coalition of community actors self-organized to respond to the growing challenge of chronic disease prevention. Actors in the Okanagan Similkameen Healthy Living Coalition include the relevant regional district, school district, City of Penticton and Interior Health Authority, as well as others seeking culture change in the community response to a preventable disease burden whose treatment cost is soaring. When the coalition was frustrated in its efforts to secure fresh funding to support new collective efforts as a corrective to the perceived limitations of existing government-sponsored actions, it sought new sources of strategic insight and opted to engage in the previously unfamiliar process of scenario-planning. The scenario-planning exercise enabled consideration of future contexts arising from present high-impact certainties becoming certain.

One usefully illustrative example arose from consideration of the relation thirty-five years hence between, on the one hand, the health of the population, public-sector planners and private-sector developers and, on the other, the quantity and distribution of health-care resources. Participants explored possible interactions between these "driving forces" intentionally amplified and brought into intersection, projecting, for example, a world in which public-sector planners and private-sector developers are increasingly at odds and so distracted from public-health concerns by other disagreements, all while diminishing public investment is controlled from a center little inclined to adapt approaches to local areas. In exploring this future possible world, credibly imagined as an amplification of "weak signals" presented by facts today, participants identified new opportunities for the magnification of the roles of existing community organizations and saw the need for the creation of others – for example, regional data collection and archiving. Participants further realized the need for enhanced and additional collaboration with similarly situated others beyond their sub-region, supporting as a consequence the subsequent development and hosting at UBC of a BC Interior Healthy Living Hub, providing an interchange point for communities, private, public and NGO sectors, and university-based researchers.

For the purposes of this chapter, the details of this scenario narrative are of only passing interest: what is important is the demonstration via this exercise that a shared major challenge – a regional shock in the making – can become an impetus for the reconception of a collective's place in the world and options for living together.

With this encouraging early result in hand, we are prompted toward the establishment of a broader collective agenda for a regional culture and practice of inquiry, open to novel deliberative techniques, to the use of novel visualization techniques enabling better access to complex data, and to the renewal of efforts to record the region's cultural history in a way likely to enable self-understanding and chosen self-transformation.

## Concluding remarks

Our concluding remarks are as much an indication of future work as a recapitulation of a completed argument, as might be expected in the context of a discussion substantially focused on the preconditions and conditions of regional strategy. Revisiting our departure point in the "what for," "what," "how" and "who" dimensions of regional strategy that are the focus of the first part of this book, in addition to an economic macro-picture, our discussion of the Okanagan has brought attention to an additional "when" element. The significance of this element has been explored in the context of the Okanagan as a region relatively new to globalization. The sense in which the Okanagan is "new" provides an instructive contrast to the elements of regional strategy in similarly industrialized European regions. Its newness is within the region a barrier to envisioning a different future, to the extent that there is little experience and cultural memory of significant transformations. At the same time, its relatively brief history in its colonized form gives rise to the possibility that it might be easier in the Okanagan to build a journey of inquiry leading to new deliberative institutions, insofar as the bonds of history and cultural memory are fewer and more diverse in a region yet to establish its own identity. Where it is a commonplace in Europe to hear frustration at regions' feeling bound by a kind of historical or cultural or geographic determinism, the same forces are less thickly intertwined in the Okanagan, though no less present in type in the interaction between indigenous peoples and newer arrivals, the presence of an international border, and regionally internal core–periphery relations. The experience and the potential of the Okanagan, we suggest, open rich opportunities for comparative analysis with European regions in particular and with other peripheral regions worldwide. Let us close with an invitation to collaborative work in two illustrative problem contexts which may be usefully explored in comparative contrast between new and old worlds.

From a European perspective, the Okanagan as a nationally and globally peripheral region may be viewed as *de facto* concerned to enact a Canadian version of a familiar Treaty on the European Union commitment to strive to ensure that "decisions are taken as closely as possible to the citizen in accordance with the principle of subsidiarity."[15] As European regions work in various ways to determine what this open-textured principle means in practice, Canadian experimentation in exploring a similar political impulse may be of comparative interest to the extent of the similarity and significant historical difference of the Canadian setting. Might it be possible to explore more rapidly and more thoroughly in Canada the merits of particular deliberative approaches likely to be bogged down in Europe in debate over, for example, the factual basis for starting points? Might the differently oriented and differently constitutionally rooted Canadian experience of engagement of national minorities offer a contrast illuminating fresh strategic possibilities for European regions? We suggest that the answers to these questions may offer intriguing new perspectives on familiar challenges, not least because the intersection of the Okanagan's stakeholders, while complex, is certain to be somewhat less complex, in at least some respects, than the intersection of twenty-eight member states and their interests.

Returning from regions in national and supranational contexts to the place and options of regions under globalization, observations offered regarding the use of air travel for labor mobility in Canada remind us of the fragility of historic presumptions regarding the stability of core–periphery relations. In our networked world demanding less hierarchy and more collaborative governance, flows of labor and capital have also been liberalized, allowing reconsideration of the extent to which regions might by their strategies take core–periphery relations to be to some extent chosen and not just imposed. Regions exploring official and *de facto* subsidiarity have yet to develop truly twenty-first-century models for inquiry, and, for social institutions enabling collective choice expressed in strategies as opposed to mere self-regulation, we might observe the Scottish Parliament and similar quasi-national assemblies of limited jurisdiction. Where such self-regulation might even be considered retrograde, to the extent that it recapitulates historic choice-making institutions with less than due consideration for the demands of globalization, the Okanagan's *de facto* rather than *de jure* enjoyment of subsidiarity in a currently strategy-free status quo may make it an ideal partner to European and other regions struggling to find new ways of imagining strategic choice in uncertain futures. What similarities or differences might we find in Scotland's deliberations aimed at the development of a "Silicon Glen" while the Okanagan chooses to pursue high-technology interests in software? Might the situation of Bordeaux and the Okanagan bring comparison-based insights into regional choice to remain core to agricultural expertise, even while climate change pushes actual production to what is now peripheral to historic core production regions?

We conclude with a final observation regarding academic inquiry into regional strategy. In many regions academics hold a kind of stylized observer status relative to regional strategy. Academics are only occasionally invited to give direct policy advice, which is still more occasionally given direct implementation. Yet under globalization there may be a special role for academics in regional strategy, insofar as regions need the kind of international knowledge network that academics pride themselves on building and using. When there is a United Nations but not a "Globally United Regions" organization, the task and role of academics in regional strategy may yet require both better theory and better translation to practice than ever before: this volume may, in addition to carrying scholarly insights, function as a welcome call to arms to academics to engage with one another in scholarly ways, and with regions in practical ways, to create a needed and otherwise absent circulation between theory and practice to enable all to make best use of the forces of globalization. Academics once thought to sit at the periphery of relevance may yet find a seat near the core.

## Notes

1 See the self-description of the Syilx people and their conception of land-holding at www.syilx.org/who-we-are/the-syilx-people/.

2 We would suggest there would also be answers to "where" and "when" questions, by analogy to the manner in which language learning analysis refers to who, where, why, when, how and what as a coherent set of queries (Hutchinson and Waters, 1987). This approach is further consistent with our proposed use of scenario-planning methods to enable collective construction of shared possible futures, expressed in narratives bearing the virtues of memorable and in that way potentially action-galvanizing stories containing who, where, when, why and how elements.

3 The answers to all of the questions would tend to evolve over time and, as they are interrelated, a change in one would affect another.
4 Our Okanagan, "Okanagan Valley Profile", p. 1 (www.ourokanagan.ca).
5 See ibid., and www.bcstats.gov.bc.ca/StatisticsBySubject/Demography/PopulationEstimates.aspx.
6 The Okanagan Lake Bridge was the first and largest floating bridge in Canada, stretching seven-eighths of a mile. Until 1963 it was a toll bridge. In 2008 it was rebuilt to reduce traffic and improve access into Kelowna (www.kelownabc.com/kelowna/kelowna10.php).
7 See www.fodors.com/world/north-america/canada/british-columbia/okanagan-wine-country/.
8 Our Okanagan, "Okanagan Valley Profile", p. 12.
9 Personal communication. Janelle Hynes (Airport Marketing and Media Relations), states that almost 5,000 of the passengers travelling to Northern Alberta in 2013 commuted for employment purposes.
10 See http://europa.eu/legislation_summaries/glossary/subsidiarity_en.htm.
11 See http://okanaganpartnership.blogspot.ca/ and the Okanagan Partnership Progress Report at www.paulbaran.com/okpartner2.pdf.
12 Our Okanagan, "Okanagan Valley Profile", p. 11.
13 Attributed to Peter Drucker by Mark Fields, present CEO of the Ford Motor Company, as reported by Jeffrey McCracken, "'Way forward' requires culture shift at Ford," *Wall Street Journal*, January 23, 2006; http://online.wsj.com/news/articles/SB113797951796853248.
14 According to Nagel (1986: x), Dewey (1938) is clear that his work is "a hypothesis, the detailed confirmation of which would have to be supplied by others in the future." Similarly, when we hypothesize here that inquiry is a useful method, and that envisioning a region's future might be appropriate, we recognize that detailed confirmation awaits future work.
15 Preamble, Consolidated Version of the Treaty on European Union, 2010/C 83/01.

## References


Aguiar, L., and Marten, T. (2009) Scripting taste, marking distinction: wine tourism and post-Fordist restructuring in the Okanagan Valley, British Columbia. In Pupo, N., and Thomas, M. P. (eds), *Interrogating the New Economy: Restructuring Work in the 21st Century*. Toronto: University of Toronto Press.

Amin, A. (2004) Regions unbound: towards a new politics of place, *Geografiska Annaler*, 86B(1), pp. 33–44.

Amin, A., and Thrift, N. (2002) *Cities: Rethinking Urban Theory*. Cambridge: Polity.

Armstrong, J., Maracle, L., and Derickson, D. (1994) *We Get our Living Like Milk from the Land*. Penticton: Theytus Books.

Belliveau, S., Smit, B., and Bradshaw, B. (2006) Multiple exposures and dynamic vulnerability: evidence from the grape industry in the Okanagan Valley, Canada, *Global Environmental Change*, 16(4), pp. 364–78.

Belshaw, I. (2009) *Becoming British Columbia: A Population History*. Vancouver: UBC Press.

Bradfield, R., Wright, G., Burt, G., Cairns, G., and Van Der Heijden, K. (2005) The origins and evolution of scenario techniques in long range business planning, *Futures*, 37(8), pp. 795–812.

Cohen, S., and Kulkarni, T. (eds) (2001) *Water Management and Climate Change in the Okanagan Basin*. Vancouver: Environment Canada and University of British Columbia.

Cox, D. (1995) *S.S. Sicamous: Queen of Okanagan Lake*. Penticton: Skookum.

Dewey, J. (1938) *Logic: The Theory of Inquiry*. New York: Henry Holt.

Dewey, J. (1947) Liberating the social scientist, *Commentary*, 4, pp. 378–85.

Docherty, T. (2008) *The English Question, or Academic Freedoms*. Brighton: Sussex Academic Press.

Edenhoffer, K., and Hayter, R. (2013) Restructuring on a vertiginous plateau: the evolutionary trajectories of British Columbia's forest industries 1980–2010, *Geoforum*, 44, pp. 139–51; doi: http://dx.doi.org/10.1016/j.geoforum.2012.10.002.

Emery, F. E., and Trist, E. (1965) The causal texture of organizational environments, *Human Relations*, 18, pp. 12–32.

Goddard, J., Kempton, L., and Vallance, P. (2013) Universities and smart specialisation: challenges, tensions, and opportunities for the innovation strategies of European regions, *Ekonomiaz*, 83(2), pp. 82–101.

Goodwin, P., and Wright, G. (2001) Enhancing strategy evaluation in scenario planning: a role for decision analysis, *Journal of Management Studies*, 38(1), pp. 1–16.

Graham, G. (2005) *The Institution of Intellectual Values: Realism and Idealism in Higher Education*. Exeter: Imprint Academic.

Hahn, L. E. (1977) Introduction. In Boydston, J. A. (ed.), *The Middle Works of John Dewey 1899–1924*, Vol. 4: *Essays on Pragmatism and Truth 1907–1909*. Carbondale: Southern Illinois University Press.

Hira, A., and Bwenge, A. (2011) *Wine Industry in British Columbia: Issues and Potential*, American Association of Wine Economists working paper no. 89; www.wine-economics.org/workingpapers/AAWE_WP89.pdf.

Hutchinson, T., and Waters, A. (1987) *English for Specific Purposes: A Learning Centered Approach*. Cambridge: Cambridge University Press.

Kaufmann, F. (1959) John Dewey's theory of inquiry, *Journal of Philosophy*, 56(21), pp. 826–36.

Koroscil, P. M. (2008) *The British Garden of Eden: Settlement History of the Okanagan Valley, British Columbia*. Vancouver: Simon Fraser University.

Nagel, E. (1986) Introduction. In Boydston, J. A. (ed.), *The Later Works, 1925–1953: John Dewey*, Vol. 12: *Logic: The Theory of Inquiry*. Carbondale: Southern Illinois University Press.

Navarro, M., Valdaliso, J. M., Aranguren, M. J., and Magro, E. (2014) A holistic approach to regional strategies: the case of the Basque Country, *Science and Public Policy*, 41(4), pp. 532–47.

Nowotny, H. (2000) The production of knowledge beyond the academy and the market: a reply to Dominique Pestre, *Science, Technology and Society*, 5(2), pp. 183–94.

Pepper, D. M. (1977) John Dewey: inquiry: knowledge and truth, PhD dissertation, Pepper.

Pooley, I. (2012) When the titans met: railway rivalry in the Okanagan and Kelowna's rise as a fruit-shipping centre, *BC Studies*, 176, p. 57.

Ramirez, R., van der Heijden, K. and Selsky, J. W. (2010) Introduction: why write this book and for whom? In Ramirez, R., Selsky, J. W., and van der Heijden, K., *Business Planning for Turbulent Times: New Methods for Applying Scenarios*. London: Earthscan.

Sacchetti, F., Sacchetti, S., and Sugden, R. (2009) Creativity and socio-economic development: space for the interests of publics, *International Review of Applied Economics*, 23(6), pp. 653–72.

Sacchetti, S. (2013) The creation of public spaces in a small Italian town, mimeo, Stirling Management School, University of Stirling, December.Schwindt, R., Vining, A., and Globerman, S. (2000) Net loss: a cost–benefit analysis of the Canadian Pacific salmon fishery, *Journal of Policy Analysis and Management*, 19(1), pp. 23–45.

Sugden, R., and Wilson, J. R. (2002) Economic development in the shadow of the consensus: a strategic decision-making approach, *Contributions to Political Economy*, 21(1), pp. 111–34.

Trenaman, R., and Parminter, J. (2006) History of the British Columbia Forest Service, http://members.shaw.ca/wolfpatch/Forestry/History/.

Turner, R. (1995) *The Sicamous and the Naramata: Steamboat Days in the Okanagan*. Winlaw, BC: Sono Nis Press.

Wagner, J. (2008) Landscape aesthetics, water, and settler colonialism in the Okanagan Valley of British Columbia, *Journal of Ecological Anthropology*, 12(1), pp. 22–38.

White, C. (2004) *Strategic Management.* Basingstoke: Palgrave Macmillan.

Wilkinson, A. (2009) Scenarios practices: in search of theory, *Journal of Futures Studies*, 13(3), pp. 107–14.

Wilkinson, A., and Ramirez, R. (2010) Canaries in the mind: exploring how the financial crisis impacts 21st century future-mindfulness, *Journal of Futures Studies*, 14(3), pp. 45–60.

Wilkinson, A., Kupers, R., and Mangalagiu, D. (2013) How plausibility-based scenario practices are grappling with complexity to appreciate and address 21st century challenges, *Technological Forecasting and Social Change*, 80(4), pp. 699–710.

Williamson, O. E. (1975) *Markets and Hierarchies: Analysis and Antitrust Implications.* New York: Free Press.

Williamson, O. E. (1993) Calculativeness, trust, and economic organization, *Journal of Law and Economics*, 36, p. 453.

Wynn, G. (2013) Timber trade history. In: *The Canadian Encyclopaedia*, www.thecanadianencyclopedia.ca/en/article/timber-trade-history/

# 12 Constructing research and innovation strategies for smart specialisation (RIS3)

## Lessons from practice in three European regions

*Mari José Aranguren, Mikel Navarro and James R. Wilson*[1]

### Introduction

The cases analysed in most other chapters of this book have taken an essentially historical perspective in reflecting on the past trajectories of competitiveness strategy in specific territories. Like the previous chapter by Culver *et al.*, here we deal with the present and the future. Moreover, while analysis in other cases has been structured around the necessary components that a territorial strategy should deal with, here the focus is on the steps to be accomplished in order to construct a territorial strategy. In the European context, this process has been and continues to be heavily influenced by the European Commission, which has encouraged the development of regional innovation strategies for some time (European Commission, 2007). More concretely, for the 2014–2020 period of European Regional Development Funding it has introduced an *ex ante* condition that requires all EU member states and regions to have a research and innovation strategy for smart specialisation (an RIS3) in place before their operational programmes are approved (European Commission, 2014). This has resulted in a scrambling around by regional governments to demonstrate the existence of a smart specialisation strategy amid considerable confusion as to how this should be done – something that is reflected in the diversity of approaches and experiences that are currently emerging. It is an interesting and important moment therefore to analyse specific cases with the aim of increasing both our understanding of how RIS3 are being developed in practice and what shape regional strategies for competitiveness are likely to take in the future.

The RIS3 concept as seen now in Europe emerged initially from the observation that many regional governments have adopted a mimetic approach to investing in certain areas of STI without truly taking the plurality and diversity of their specific contexts into consideration. What are required, it is argued, are regional STI strategies that are smart, in the sense of specialising in areas where there are clear synergies with the existing and potential productive capacities and capabilities of the region. Building such a strategy is a *living process* which is ongoing in time. In particular, RIS3 advocates identifying a region's priorities by means of an *entrepreneurial discovery process* (Foray *et al.*, 2012). In other words, territorial strategy is defined not only by *what* it prioritises (on which see chapters 2 and 3 of this book) but also by *how* this is done (on which see chapters 4, 5 and 6). The strategy must be the result of a participatory process which involves all of the various stakeholders that form the *quadruple helix* of the innovation process: public authorities; the business community; the academic world and knowledge-based institutions; and civil society. It requires not only scientific and technological know-how but also market knowledge and entrepreneurial capacities. It also needs suitable multilevel governance to articulate interconnections between the regional level and the sub-regional, national and supranational levels. In this sense, an RIS3 is envisaged not as a government strategy but, rather, as a truly territorial strategy in which government participates in the identification of (and pursuit of investment in) STI priorities together with all elements of the quadruple helix.

Yet the entrepreneurial discovery process underlying RIS3 remains very much a black box. Analysis in the earlier chapters of this book, and particularly by Aranguren and Larrea in chapter 4, suggests that the shift from more formal planning approaches to the more flexible process-based approaches inherent in the notion of an entrepreneurial discovery process is not automatic. It requires the generation of new capabilities in the territory, in a context in which there is typically a strong element of path dependence, such that the approach with which institutions and policy-makers in a territory address the issue of strategy is highly influenced by the way in which territorial strategy was constructed in the past (Valdaliso *et al.*, 2014; chapter 7 in this volume). This implies that the specific regional context in which RIS3 are constructed will strongly condition their development, which in turn suggests the need to study and learn from a range of currently ongoing experiences.

While much of the mystery of territorial strategy lies in the entrepreneurial discovery process, it is also true to say that policy-making and strategy-making in general is a black box that needs opening up. Indeed, there is a widespread perception that the human element of how policies are designed has been neglected in regional studies (Collinge and Gibney, 2010; Gibney, 2011; Sotarauta, 2005; Stimson *et al.*, 2009). This chapter contributes to the challenge of looking inside this black box with a comparative analysis of three regional cases of RIS3 strategy-making: the Basque Country, Navarre and Murcia.

All three of these are located in Spain, where regions have among the highest levels of policy autonomy in Europe and where the processes of preparing RIS3 for the European Commission have been led at the regional level (rather than at the national level, as is the case in some countries). The Basque Country and Navarre are neighbouring regions in the north of Spain that at first glance look very similar. They are both industrial areas, with relatively strong economic performance, relatively well-developed innovation systems and their own unique (in Spain) tax-raising powers.They are both currently governed by regionalist/nationalist political parties in minority in the regional assembly. Yet the RIS3 process of each is taking shape quite differently. Murcia, in the south of Spain, has quite different fundamental characteristics in terms of its economy (a low presence of industry, a less-developed innovation system and a weaker economic performance), administration (no tax-raising powers, which fall under the general Spanish regime) and politics (the ruling political party is a national one, in a majority at the regional assembly). A comparative analysis of the process in these three cases opens up learning with regard to the specific issues that European regions are addressing in practice in seeking to develop RIS3 in line with the European Commission's requirements.

In the second section of the chapter we present some methodological considerations regarding the structure that is followed in the three case studies. In the third section the construction of RIS3 in the three regions is analysed, which serves to highlight some of the barriers that currently exist in the development of regional RIS3 in Europe. Reflections on the issues highlighted are then brought together and summarised in a series of concluding comments.

## A structure for the case analysis: six steps to RIS3

To organise analysis of the three cases we follow the explicit structure that was proposed by the European Commission for the development of RIS3 in their *Guide to Research and Innovation Strategies for Smart Specialisation* (Foray *et al.*, 2012). This guide proposes six steps for the development of an RIS3:

1 analysis of the regional context and potential for innovation;
2 governance and ensuring participation and ownership;
3 elaboration of an overall vision for the future of the region;
4 identification of priorities;
5 definition of coherent policy mix, roadmap and action plan; and
6 integration of monitoring and evaluation mechanisms.

As the guide highlights, the six steps 'should not be thought of as separate and autonomous stages in the process, but as interacting components of a comprehensive design scheme whose implementation pattern depends on the specificity of the regional context' (Ibid.: 18).

With regard to the *first step* of analysing regional context and innovation potential, the guide refers to economic differentiation as 'one of the central principles behind smart specialization'. It is argued that 'the key to successful differentiation is to exploit *related variety*, which suggests that a regional economy can build its competitive advantage by diversifying its unique, localized know-how into new combinations and innovations which are close or adjacent to it.' Several methods can be used to support the identification of potential niches for smart specialisation, and Foray *et al.* (2012: 29) recognise that 'an integrated method that delivers a unique solution to this question does not exist: it is the combination of an array of evidence that is most likely to provide a suitable basis for this identification process.' They suggest that the most relevant methods include analysis of scientific and technological specialisation, analysis of regional economic specialisation, in-depth cluster case studies, peer reviews and foresight. This analysis should cover three main dimensions: regional assets; linkages with the rest of the world and the position of the region in the global economy; and the dynamics of the entrepreneurial environment.

The *second step* refers to governance and highlights the relevance of ensuring participation and ownership of different actors from the quadruple helix in the development of RIS3. In order to ensure that all stakeholders own and share the strategy, governance schemes should allow for 'collaborative leadership', meaning that decision-making hierarchies should be flexible enough to let each actor have a role and eventually take the lead in specific phases of RIS3 design, according to their characteristics, background and capacities. The *third step* is strongly related and emphasises the importance of having a clear and shared vision of the future development of the region around which stakeholders can be engaged in the process, a task that is particularly challenging given that an RIS3 is a long-term process. In particular it highlights the importance of communication for an RIS3 that is alive and constantly evolving.

*Step four* refers to the identification of priorities, and here the guide underlines that

> RIS3 entails an effective match between a top-down process of identification of broad objectives aligned with EU policies and a bottom-up process of emergence of candidate niches for smart specialization, areas of experimentation and the future development stemming from the discovery activity of entrepreneurial actors.
>
> (Foray *et al.*, 2012: 22)

It is of crucial importance to focus on a limited number of innovation and research priorities in line with the potential for smart specialisation detected in the analysis phase. These priorities will be the areas in which a region can realistically hope to excel. In addition to vertical, activity-based priorities, it is important to pay attention to defining horizontal-type priorities in terms of broad regional competences (see chapters 2 and 3 of this book).

The final two steps are connected with the policies to support the development of RIS3 and the integration of evaluation mechanisms (see chapters 5 and 6 of this book). *Step five* is to define a coherent policy mix, and Foray *et al.* (2012: 23) emphasise that the RIS strategy 'should be implemented through a road map with an effective action plan allowing for a degree of experimentation through pilot projects', adding that 'pilot projects constitute the main tools for policy experimentation and allow testing unprecedented mixes of policy measures at a small scale, before deciding or implementing at a larger or more expensive scale.' *Step six* follows from this logically, with the suggestion that mechanisms for monitoring and evaluating policies should be integrated in the strategy from the very beginning. In this sense the design effort in an RIS3 does not come to an end when the strategy moves on to the implementation phase. A strategy for smart specialisation should evolve and adjust to changes in economic and framework conditions, as well as to the emergence of new evidence during implementation through evaluation and monitoring activities.

In order to conduct a comparative analysis of how regions are pursuing each of these steps in practice, we suggest that it is important to conduct a prior analysis of two other more general elements that will condition the practice of RIS3 in regions. Firstly, while step one of the guide refers to 'analysis of the regional context and potential for innovation', this is linked to specific diagnostics that the region should carry out to provide strategic intelligence about its position and potential as regards innovation. Yet, in making a comparative analysis of regions, there is a broader context to be considered in terms of characteristics that will facilitate or hinder the development of RIS3. Here we refer, for example, to things such as the region's size, concentration of the economic activity in space, multilevel governance (including regional competences and decentralisation within the region), general quality of government, political stability, sectoral specialisation and type of firms. Secondly, we suggest that it is important to ask a general question regarding the type of strategy that the region envisages – what it understands by RIS3. This will have roots in the legacy of each region in planning and strategy-making (where there is likely to be some path dependency) and will revolve around questions such as whether the region conceives of RIS3 as an R&D strategy or as a broader strategy, whether the RIS3 fits with other regional plans and/or strategies, and whether it is understood in terms of writing a plan or of developing processes. Along with the general context of the region, these questions will mark how the six steps are pursued.

In terms of the data used for the case analysis, the involvement and knowledge of the authors has not been the same in all three instances. The authors have particularly strong knowledge of the Basque case, having studied the competitiveness of the region for many years (see, for example, Orkestra, 2007, 2009, 2011, 2013) and having played an active role over the last two years in discussions with government and other agents around the development of its RIS3. While they might therefore be seen as 'insiders' in the Basque case, they are acting as 'outsiders' in the cases of Navarre and Murcia, where they are conducting ongoing analysis of these 'living labs' for understanding RIS3 in a European research project on 'smart specialisation for regional innovation' (SmartSpec).[2] Specifically, the data for this chapter concerning these two regions come from an analysis of secondary sources surrounding their RIS3 alongside around a dozen in-depth interviews with key players in the process of each that were conducted during June–July 2014.

## Learning from practice: constructing RIS3 in the Basque Country, Navarre and Murcia

### *Regional context*

In practice RIS3 strategy development throughout Europe is taking place in very different regional contexts, and there are several characteristics that might be seen to facilitate or hinder its construction – above all of the entrepreneurial discovery processes that are central to it. Even across the three Spanish regions that we have analysed we can identify significant differences in elements related to space and demography (the size of the region, geographic concentration of the economic activity, immigration, etc.), governance and politics (regional competences, decentralisation within the region, legacy and quality of government, political stability, etc.), productive structure (sectoral specialisation, kind of firms, internationalisation, etc.) and innovation system (prevalent actors, innovative performance, etc.) (see Table 12.1), for example. These result in different degrees and combinations of complexity for the construction and development of RIS3. Regional complexity in this sense largely reflects the governance reality that characterises the region as a result of certain fundamental features of its geography, history, industrial structure, etc. Greater complexity should not therefore be judged as either positive or negative *per se*: there are cases when complex structures are necessary to govern complex realities and also cases where unnecessary complexity is created – for example, in the proliferation of intermediate institutions without clear functions.

While all three regions are quite small in terms of population, the Basque Country is the largest and has the least concentration of economic activity in space, features which tend to add elements of complexity for RIS3 development, although the lower growth of population and immigration may work in the opposite direction. It is also the case that the decentralisation of competences within the region towards sub-regional administrative bodies is much higher in the Basque Country, where there are three provinces with their own governments, provincial capitals with their own economic development strategies, and even local strategies in some counties and municipalities. In comparison with Navarre and Murcia, which are single provincial regions with insignificant economic development structures at the local level, such features again point to greater challenges for articulating governance relationships and developing RIS3 processes.

On the other hand, the better quality of the government in the Basque Country and higher political stability in Murcia, and to a lesser extent in the Basque Country too, compared with Navarre can also be seen as a more conducive context for RIS3 development. Meanwhile, the Basque Country and Navarre have a more advantageous context than Murcia in terms of their overall economic performance and the development and level of sophistication of their innovation systems. However, the higher degree of sector specialisation in Navarre and Murcia suggests that decisions around the prioritisation of activities are potentially easier than they are in the Basque Country. Finally, the characteristics of firms across the three regions can also signal differences in the RIS3 decision-making processes in the sense that it may be easier to involve endogenous firms in processes with a regional frame of reference than multinational corporations (MNCs) or large national firms. Our message here is that all of these (and potentially other) contextual characteristics will in different ways condition the development of RIS3 processes; while they are asked to follow a similar 'six-step' process (Foray *et al.*, 2012), regions do not begin the strategy process on a level playing field.

*Table 12.1* Regional context in the Basque Country, Navarre and Murcia

| | *Basque Country* | *Navarre* | *Murcia* |
|---|---|---|---|
| Population (size) | Medium (2.2 million) | Small (0.6 million) | Small-medium (1.6 million) |
| Density and urbanisation | Medium-high (average EU) | Very low density, but urban concentration | Low density, but urban concentration |
| Population growth | Stability and little immigration | Dynamic, linked to immigration | Very dynamic, linked to immigration |
| Decentralisation | Highest (including S&T and taxes); regional government with elected assembly | Highest (including taxes); regional government with elected assembly | Very high; regional government with elected assembly |
| General quality of government* | Medium-high (above Spanish average) | Medium-low (below Spanish average) | Medium-low (Spanish average) |
| Regional organisation | Three provinces, each with own government; provincial capitals with own economic development strategies; local strategies in some counties | Provincial and regional governments coincide; no noticeable economic strategies in the capital city and counties | Provincial and regional governments coincide; no noticeable economic strategies in the main cities and counties |
| Political stability | Rotation in ruling party since 2008 after long period of PNV control (regionalist, centre-right); currently PNV has no majority in the assembly, but there is broad consensus of almost all parties on industrial R&D and innovation policy (political clashes take place in other areas) | UPN (regionalist, right-wing) in power since 1996, but currently has a minority in the assembly; until 2011, consensus among the two main parties; afterwards severe institutional and political crisis that affects even the management of the RIS3 | PP (national, right-wing) has a large majority in the assembly |

| | | | |
|---|---|---|---|
| Sectoral specialisation | Specialisation in industry (around metals and metal manufacture) and to a lesser extent in KIBS & ICT | Very high specialisation in industry (automobile and agri-business) and health | Very high specialisation in agriculture and water-related business and to a lesser extent in petro-chemical and tourism |
| Export orientation | Medium-low (1.5 times Spanish average) due to industrial specialisation | Medium-high (double Spanish average) due to industrial specialisation | Low (1.1 times Spanish average) but high in specialised sectors (agri-business …) |
| Firms | Medium size (above Spanish average due to industrial specialisation); largely endogenous firms | Medium-high (double Spanish average due to industrial specialisation); high presence of MNCs | Low (similar to Spanish average); endogenous firms, in consumer-end production, are smaller; external (national) firms, in basic and heavy equipment, are bigger |
| Innovation system | Innovation follower (RIS2014); strong business R&D, technological infrastructures and VET centres; weak university and public research centres; very high educational level of population | Innovation follower (RIS2014); strong business R&D and universities; high educational level of population | Moderate innovator (RIS2014); reasonable universities and public research centres but weak business R&D and innovation; low educational level of population |
| Economic performance | High productivity, medium labour participation, high unemployment (but lowest in Spain) and very high per capita GDP (highest in Spain) | High productivity, medium labour participation, high unemployment (but second lowest in Spain) and very high per capita GDP (second highest in Spain) | High productivity, low labour participation, very high unemployment and low per capita GDP (84% of EU average; 'transition region') |

Source: Based on secondary sources and interviews.

Note: *Classification of general quality of government from Charron *et al.* (2012); KIBS: Knowledge Intensive Business Services; PNV: Basque National Party; PP: Popular Party; UPN: Union of the Navarran People; VET: Vocational Education and Training.

### *Type of strategy*

Alongside the general context in which the region develops its RIS3, we have argued that it is important to understand something about the type of strategy being envisaged when embarking on the RIS3 process. To gain insight on this question we can analyse the legacy of each region in planning and strategy-making (which could generate some path dependency and facilitate or hinder the change to RIS3) and the frames of reference for the current process (questions around the focus of the RIS3, its integration with other regional plans/strategies, and whether it is understood as a plan, a process, or both).

Regarding the legacy of plans and strategy-making, it could be argued that those regions with a longer experience in STI plans, in fostering public–private collaboration, and in bottom-up or participatory strategic approaches are likely to possess more of the capabilities needed to develop the types of process and prioritisation required by an RIS3. In this aspect the Basque Country and to a lesser extent Navarre stand out from Table 12.2 as having longer experience in government-led planning and strategy-making, and Navarre in particular has developed this experience with a strong presence of bottom-up processes. It could also be argued, however, that a strong government lead in planning processes doesn't necessarily develop the capabilities across a broader set of agents that are required for an RIS3 and could result in government strategy rather than a territorial strategy.

More generally, what each region understands about RIS3 will be reflected to some extent in the scope and approach to its development. For instance, in the case of Navarre, the Moderna plan, which is considered to be their RIS3 strategy, has wider scope as a socio-economic development strategy than that in Murcia, where the focus of RIS3Mur is on R&D and innovation, and in the Basque Country, where the focus of the PCTI-2020 is narrower still (largely on R&D). This is also reflected in the relationship between the RIS3 and other plans and strategies. In the Basque Country the PCTI-2020 sits under a Plan for Reactivation and Employment and parallel to many other economic, social, environmental and educational plans, a situation that is similar in Murcia. In Navarre, however, the Moderna plan ranks highest in the region and is being developed, in determined areas, by more specific plans (e.g., a plan for S&T).

### *Analysis of the regional context and potential for innovation*

Bearing in mind that the three regions being analysed have quite different contexts and prior understandings of what an RIS3 should look like, we now turn to analyse the development of their RIS3 in terms of the six steps proposed in the RIS3 guide (Foray *et al.*, 2012). The first step is to make a diagnosis of the region's unique and distinctive capabilities around which the strategy should be constructed. Statistical availability is critical for this step, and in our three cases this availability is very high. In contrast with some other European countries, there is abundance of regional data available in Spain and regional agents

*Table 12.2* Type of strategy in the Basque Country, Navarre and Murcia

| | *Basque Country* | *Navarre* | *Murcia* |
|---|---|---|---|
| Short name | PCTI-2015 → PCTI-2020 | Moderna | RIS3Mur |
| Scope | R&D and innovation strategy (but mostly R&D strategy) | Socio-economic development strategy | R&D & innovation strategy |
| Legacy of plans | Long history of plans and strategies; active role of government in the emergence and development of new activities (bios, nanos …) | Long history of plans and strategies, without thematic priorities until 2010; less direct role of government and greater presence of bottom-up processes | Moderate history of plans and strategies, including vertical choices; less direct role of government in emergence of economic activities |
| Integration with other regional strategies/plans | The PCTI sits under the Plan for Reactivation and Employment and ranks parallel to many other economic, social, environmental and educational plans | Moderna ranks highest in the region and is being developed, in determined areas, by more specific plans (e.g., plan for S&T) under Moderna's framework | RIS3Mur is under the IRIS-2020 general strategy; there were other plans (on S&T, industry, vocational training …), some of which have expired, and their integration with RIS3Mur is not clear |
| RIS3 document | The existing PCTI-2015 (passed in 2012) has been presented as the Basque RIS3, but a new PCTI-2020 is now in process | The existing Moderna (passed in 2010) has been presented as the Navarre RIS3 | The RIS3Mur is an entirely new plan, passed in 2014 |

Source: Based on secondary sources and interviews.

respond positively to information requirements from regional governments. In the Basque Country the regional statistical institute (Eustat) also has its own statistical operations and the regional and local administrations have a large number of administrative records, while IEN in Navarre and CREM in Murcia mainly collaborate with and diffuse data collected by the national office and, again, there are a large number of administrative records in the hands of the regional government (including tax records in the case of Navarre).

It is also important to have access to good analysis conducted by regional and/or international agents. In this aspect, the Basque Country has a wealth of diagnostic analysis and, though to a lesser extent, there is also plenty in Navarre and Murcia. In the cases of the Basque Country and Navarre these diagnostics are published by the government, by quasi-governmental agencies such as regional development agencies and innovation agencies, and by independent or academic organisations such as Orkestra in the Basque Country and Institución Futuro in Navarre.[3] While Navarre has a good consultant in innovation policy, an active think-tank on competitiveness and departments of economics and business at the universities, these lack the academic profile, orientation, resources or structures to assist the process properly. Indeed, the well-designed process of the Moderna plan was partly conducted with non-local consultants. Murcia has no research organisations or relevant consultants who specialise in competitiveness and territorial strategy analysis, and, despite being reasonably good, the universities do not meet that need either. As can be seen in Table 12.3, the presence of international analysis mirrors that of regional analysis, with the Basque Country leading the way, followed by Navarre and then Murcia.

In terms of analysis that benchmarks against other regions, all three cases are lacking. Diagnostics of the Basque system have included the identification of other EU regions with similar structural conditions, but until now those regions have not been analysed to draw lessons for the Basque Country. In Navarre some regions and countries with successful development models were studied and visited, even though they did not share the same structural conditions. And the diagnostics included in the RIS3Mur have been carried out without comparing Murcia with regions sharing similar structural conditions, although the analysis did identify potential reference regions for the future. What is perhaps most revealing is that in none of our three cases have neighbouring regions been included in the diagnostic analysis so as to identify synergies and complementarities. This would appear short-sighted given that economic activity does not generally respect administrative boundaries, and indeed lack of consideration of the cross-border dimension is a general shortcoming of RIS3 processes across Europe.

Finally, regarding the content of the diagnostics, there are strong similarities between the three cases that we suggest are probably symptomatic of how the first step has been applied in most regions. The analysis has been based on a very complete SWOT analysis, with detailed specialisation analyses, analysis of the science, technology and industry/cluster fields, and studies of the impact of international trends and societal challenges. Yet analysis on the dynamics of the regional entrepreneurial environment is lacking.

### *Governance: ensuring participation and ownership*

This second step highlights the relevance of ensuring participation and ownership among different actors of the quadruple helix in the development of RIS3. As suggested above, the emergence of this governance is likely to be more complex if there are more departments in the government, many agencies and different levels of government operating in the territory. Navarre and Murcia present a less complex system for coordination and governance development than the Basque Country (with nine departments in the regional government, several of them with R&D competences, and a vast set of agencies and intermediary organisations). The smaller size and concentration of R&D competences in Navarre (eight departments and R&D competences quite concentrated, a small number of agencies and intermediary organisations, and stability and continuity of public staff) and Murcia (seven departments and R&D competences very concentrated, an average number of agencies and intermediary organisations, with plans to merge some of

*Table 12.3* Comparing step 1: analysis of regional context and potential for innovation

| | *Basque Country* | *Navarre* | *Murcia* |
|---|---|---|---|
| Statistical availability | Exceedingly high | Very high | Very high |
| Analysis conducted by regional agents | Plenty of diagnostics, published by the government or quasi-governmental organisations, as well as by more independent and academic organisations (e.g., Orkestra) | Sufficient number of studies published by the government or quasi-governmental organisations, as well as some by more independent organisations (e.g., Institución Futuro) | Sufficient number of studies published by the government or quasi-governmental organisations, and fewer and less in-depth studies carried out by independent organisations |
| International analyses of the region | The region has been the subject of numerous academic analyses published in international journals or forums; additionally, the OECD (2011, 2013) reviewed the Basque innovation system and its tertiary education system, the European expert K. Morgan (2013) assessed its RIS3, and an RIM report (Magro, 2014) has been written on the Basque innovation policy system | Although the Navarre case is mentioned as a case of good practice in several EC and OECD documents, the only complete documents available are the RIM report on Navarre (Bergera and Arive, 2011) and the assessment of the RIS3 by the European expert V. Harmaakorpi (2013); Navarre is taking part as a living-lab in the EU SmartSpec project, and Orkestra (2014) has elaborated a report on it | Although a European expert assessed the elaboration process of RIS3Mur, there is no publicly available report; Murcia is taking part as a living-lab in the SmartSpec project, and Orkestra (2014) has elaborated a report on it |
| Regional benchmarking | Some regional benchmarking without in depth analysis; studies and visits to some regions and countries | Studies and visits to some regions and countries | Planned in-depth analysis of some reference regions |
| Type of analysis | Very complete SWOT, specialisation (in industry/cluster, science and technology) and trends analysis, but lack of analysis on the entrepreneurial environment | Very complete SWOT, specialisation (in industry/cluster, science and technology) and trends analysis relying on opinions of local experts, but lack of analysis on the entrepreneurial environment | Very complete SWOT, specialisation (in industry/cluster, science and technology) and trends analysis relying on opinions of local researchers and business people, but lack of analysis on the entrepreneurial environment |

Source: Based on secondary sources and interviews.

them) favour coordination. In the Basque Country there is also a greater diversity of territorial actors at different levels who are developing economic development strategies (provinces, capital-city municipalities, and even local development agencies) (see Table 12.4). While there have been some attempts to initiate and foster coordination of these initiatives at the regional level, this has proved difficult to put into practice. In the cases of Navarre and Murcia, in contrast, almost all of the competences linked to economic promotion are in the hands of regional government.

Coordination with neighbouring regions, the national government, EU institutions and other non-governmental agents is another critical aspect of RIS3 governance. As already anticipated when discussing the first, diagnostic step, in all three cases coordination with neighbouring regions is scarce to non-existent. All Spanish regions are members of the national IDI (Research, Development and Innovation) network, which was established in 2010 to generate synergies between regions in their R&D and innovation policies and has organised a series of meetings for exchanging experiences in the building of RIS3.[4] Apart from potential interactions with neighbouring Spanish regions that are included in these groups, in none of the three cases have we detected explicit attempts to coordinate RIS3 with a neighbouring region. In Murcia, however, there are some signs that this is seen as a challenge for the future (at least in terms of generating funding), as there are plans to collaborate with neighbours (Valencia, Balearic Islands) to apply to the European Regional Development Fund (ERDF).

When it comes to coordination with the national government, in all three regions there is communication as opposed to strict coordination as such, although there is also an element of control in that the national government has the final decision whether or not to accept the resulting regional strategies; the regional RIS3 must be integrated with the national one and channelled by the central government to the European Commission. In this regard representatives of the three regions have taken part in the RIS3 meetings of the IDI network, which have been based largely on exchanging experiences so as to facilitate the preparation of regional RIS3 and can be seen to have played a loose coordinating role. The decisions made in the elaboration of their RIS3 have been taken very much at the regional level, however, which is reflective of the approach to R&D and innovation policy more generally. The Basque Country tends to be particularly protective of its autonomy and singularity in this area, and yet it is very successful in capturing funds from national R&D programmes. Collaboration in the R&D field is more explicit in the cases of Navarre and Murcia, with a number of national research centres in fields of great importance for their regions being located there, and it could be argued that the connection with and recognition of the role of national government is stronger in Murcia on account of a national party being in power in the regional assembly (as opposed to regionalist parties in the other two regions).

Each of the three regions has an office in Brussels, which is significant for coordination with EU institutions. The Basque Country was the first Spanish region to have a presence in Brussels, efforts through which have helped to capture 0.9 per cent of funding in the seventh framework programme (2007–13), superior to the

*Table 12.4* Comparing step 2: governance

| | *Basque Country* | *Navarre* | *Murcia* |
|---|---|---|---|
| Regional government | Nine departments and a vast set of agencies and intermediary organizations; little coordination | Eight departments with R&D competences quite concentrated and a small number of agencies and intermediary organisations; easier informal coordination | Seven departments with R&D competences very concentrated and an average number of agencies and intermediary organisations; easier coordination |
| Sub-regional levels | Many territorial actors launching economic development strategies | Almost all the competences linked to economic promotion are in the hands of regional government | Almost all the competences linked to economic promotion are in the hands of regional government, but clear local productive systems and some agents are organised locally |
| Coordination with neighbouring regions | Scarce coordination with neighbouring regions | Scarce coordination with neighbouring regions | Scarce coordination with neighbouring regions |
| Coordination with national government | Decisions in the regional government but minimal communication with the national one; participation in IDI network | Decisions in the regional government but communication with the national one; participation in IDI network | Decisions in the regional government but fluid communication with the national one; participation in IDI network |
| Coordination with the EU institutions | An office in Brussels, participation in several EU initiatives and many funds from EU programmes | An office in Brussels, participation as living lab in Smartspec and not many funds from EU programmes | An office in Brussels with much less noticeable presence, participation as living lab in Smartspec and scarce funds from EU programmes |

*(continued)*

*Table 12.4* (continued)

| | *Basque Country* | *Navarre* | *Murcia* |
|---|---|---|---|
| Coordination with non-governmental agents for general strategy | Basque Council of STI (the regional government presides over it and provincial governments, universities, technological centres and firms participate), but it is mainly an advisory body | The board and permanent committee of the Moderna plan (members of regional government and political parties, business associations, firms, universities, technological centres and trade unions); broad participation for the elaboration, implementation and monitoring of the Moderna plan, including the civil population | The steering committee of RIS3Mur (representatives of the government, the public universities and the business association); monitoring and evaluation committees (members of regional government, the business association and the technological centres) |
| Leadership of strategy | Change in leadership, but 'collaborative leadership' not generated | Change in leadership, but 'collaborative leadership' not generated | Change in leadership, but 'collaborative leadership' not generated |
| Entrepreneurial discovery processes | Design/characteristics of entrepreneurial discovery processes not yet explicit | Entrepreneurial discovery processes designed and in development, mainly through clusters | Design/characteristics of entrepreneurial discovery processes not yet explicit |
| Innovation agencies for participation | Innobasque has acted as secretariat for the PCTI-2015 and for the working group of the PCTI-2020 | Moderna lacks the support from the regional government to have this role | Not an agency with this role |

Source: Based on secondary sources and interviews.

0.5 per cent weight of Basque GDP in the EU. Relationships have been developed with high-level officers in the European Commission's DG Regional and Urban Policy and the RIS3 platform, and the Basque government participated in the first peer review of RIS3. It later agreed that an EU expert should assess their RIS3 (Morgan, 2013), an input that is proving to be influential to ongoing processes. The regional government is also participating in EU initiatives such as the Vanguard Initiative for new growth through smart specialisation, the Enterprise Europe Network, ERA-NET and the ERRIN network,[5] and a researcher from Orkestra participated in the EU's mirror group for the RIS3 and was thus able to communicate developments to the Basque government. The proportion of funds received from EU programmes in Navarre and Murcia is significantly lower than that in the Basque Country, and in Murcia is well below what might be expected according to their regional R&D and innovation expenditure. This indicates a lower level of connection in general with EU institutions, but both regions have demonstrated proactiveness when it comes to engaging around their RIS3. Navarre's Brussels office supports the diffusion and debate of its Moderna plan among EU institutions, and as a result it has become well known and is frequently showcased at EU events. The Navarre RIS3 was also assessed by a European expert, but until now that document has not received such wide diffusion in the region and has been less influential than that in the Basque case. Being members of ERRIN, both Navarre and Murcia applied to be and were selected as 'living-labs' for the SmartSpec project and are currently engaging in reflection processes and a series of 'learning journey' workshops along with the other fourteen living lab regions.

Finally, regarding coordination with non-governmental agents, the mechanisms are different in each region. In the Basque Country there is a Science, Technology and Innovation Council with representation from regional government, provincial governments, universities, technological centres and a few large firms. This is mainly an advisory body. In past plans participation of non-governmental actors was present in the elaboration phase but not in the subsequent implementation and evaluation, and although their participation in the current PCTI-2020 is acknowledged, it remains to be seen precisely how it will be configured. In Navarre the board and the permanent committee of the Moderna plan are composed of members of the regional government and political parties, of business associations and firms, of universities and technological centres, and of trade unions. The broad participatory process for the elaboration of the plan included civil society, and for its implementation and monitoring there are several 'Moderna teams' composed of the type of agents mentioned above. In Murcia the steering committee of RIS3Mur and the evaluation and monitoring committees consist of representatives of the government, the public universities, the business association and the technological centres. There is no direct representation of firms, entrepreneurs or agents of civil society.

In order to ensure that all stakeholders own and share what should be a territorial strategy, the RIS3 guide emphasises that governance schemes should allow for 'collaborative leadership'. This means that hierarchies in decision-making should be flexible enough to let different actors play roles and eventually take the lead in specific phases of RIS3 design, according to their characteristics, backgrounds and capacities. In the Basque Country and Murcia leadership is dominated by government. In Navarre other quadruple helix agents played key initial roles and continue to sustain their activity, with the government role affected by the current political crisis. Indeed, despite some changes of leadership within the groups involved in all three cases, in none of the regions have we seen the emergence of what might be called collaborative leadership.

In the Basque Country the notion of an RIS3 was initially pursued by the Department of Economic Development and Competitiveness (DEDC) within the regional government, at the request of the president. It was then decided to bind together the RIS3 process with the elaboration of the new PCTI-2020, which was already timetabled within this legislature under the responsibility of the presidency. That the president should lead the process from this moment was also supported by the emergence of certain tensions between different departments around the selection of vertical priorities. While the thinking behind a new economic model for Navarre was started by non-governmental actors (firms, business and labour associations, universities, savings bank), the project was later taken over by the vice-president of the region and head of the Department of Economy and Treasury and led publicly by the president. At present the Department of Economy and Treasury includes competences related to industry and employment, and alongside the presidency this is the main department supporting the process. In Murcia the RIS3Mur was launched in parallel with the more general regional development strategy (IRIS-2020) led by the president and a steering committee. While this steering committee includes the Department of Economy and Finance, the universities and the main business association, it appears that the actual leadership of the project corresponds in practice with the Department of Industry, Tourism, Enterprise and Innovation, where policy competences on research (including university research) are concentrated.

The last two rows of Table 12.4 comment on the *entrepreneurial discovery processes* from which prioritisation decisions should theoretically emerge in RIS3. In both the Basque Country and Murcia there is not yet an explicit formulation of these entrepreneurial discovery processes that is linked to the current strategy document (the PCTI-2020 and RIS3Mur plans).The RIS3Mur made a great effort to identify new activities, related to the existing or potential strengths of Murcia and to appealing technologies/markets as yet unexploited. This was more of a theoretical exercise, however, and it is explicitly acknowledged as a starting point of entrepreneurial discovery processes oriented to action among the region's firms and other agents that is currently lacking. In the Basque Country there is a long trajectory of informal entrepreneurial discovery processes where different agents share knowledge so as to foster new activities and products. These have taken place in clusters and sector associations, in networks and projects backed by strategic agencies (Biobasque and Nanobasque), in Innobasque (the Basque Innovation agency) and in local development agencies. While much of this participation was fed into the previous PCTI-2015, it is currently not clear how the new PCTI-2020 will explicitly integrate these processes in arriving at prioritisation decisions. The Moderna plan of Navarre, on the other hand, has explicitly set out entrepreneurial discovery processes from the beginning, to be developed mainly by clusters. For each cluster or transversal priority working roundtables were set up, which operate with a similar method and develop action plans that feed into the overall strategy.

Finally, for the development of entrepreneurial discovery processes, the existence and role of innovation agencies that make possible other stakeholder participation is critical. In the Basque Country at present, Innobasque acts as secretariat for the process in the PCTI-2020 and fulfils the tasks that the government defines, but it is neither the initiator of the processes nor the permanent forum that makes the effective participation of other actors in the RIS3 possible. As such the processes of entrepreneurial discovery that it can support on its own are quite limited. In Navarre, the attempt to create a new public–private organisation, the Moderna Foundation, to develop the RIS3 was quite successful, but since 2012 the functioning of Moderna has been hindered by a severe economic, institutional and political crisis in the region. As a consequence, Moderna currently lacks the necessary support and resources from the regional government, and the governmental policies are not aligned with the reflections developed by quadruple helix agents. In Murcia, although it is planned in the IRIS-2020 strategy, at present there is no agency that offers a permanent space for interaction between the government and the main components of the quadruple helix. Some intermediary organisations supported by the regional government keep connections with those agents, but those relations are of a more informal nature, and the behaviour of firms, universities, research centres, etc., is quite reactive.

### *Shared vision*

The third step – generating shared vision – forms the basis from which a truly territorial strategy can emerge. Building a shared vision requires interaction between different agents, and in that sense it goes hand in hand with much of the discussion around governance in the previous sub-section. Like the entrepreneurial discovery processes, the notion of shared vision can be made more or less explicit. For example, the RIS3Mur has tried explicitly to set a shared vision, linked to the one included in the more general IRIS-2020 plan for Murcia's development. Among objections to this vision, however, are that it is too general, it is applicable to any Mediterranean region, and it is too optimistic and detached from reality – comments that would suggest that the vision is not so much 'shared' as it was 'established'.

Navarre has also worked explicitly towards a shared vision, but in this case through the engagement of a wide range of agents in the process of developing the Moderna plan. The thrust of the vision is around the necessity to change Navarre's existing economic model and, in a participatory way, to identify the 'roots and the branches' of the new model. As a consequence of such a broad participatory process, it could be argued that the vision has lacked focus, but it has been a good starting point that could be fine-tuned in subsequent steps. Unfortunately, since

2011 a deep institutional, political and economic crisis has shaken Navarre and the shared vision has been negatively affected, with the process now very much at a standstill.

The Basque Country, in contrast to the other two regions and in line with analysis of the governance step, is a case of a shared vision existing in the background but not being explicitly linked to and expressed as part of the RIS3. Since the early 2000s there has been a widely shared vision among agents of the quadruple helix that competitiveness should no longer be efficiency driven, which served the region well during the 1990s, but innovation driven, which is necessary because of the rise in wages. The PCTI-2015 did not properly address the main activities and agents on which that shift should be hinged; in order to keep all participants content, there was no real selection or prioritisation. The new PCTI-2020 is trying to correct this by establishing more focused priorities, but it has taken longer than initially thought to get some kind of agreement even among the main departments of the regional government as to what these should be. In the next steps, that agreement over priorities and actions will have to be discussed and debated with the other agents of the quadruple helix to work towards a properly shared vision of how the Basque economy should be upgraded towards innovation-led competiveness.

### *Vertical and horizontal priorities*

The thematic or vertical priorities in the three cases are all based on an assessment of scientific, technological and economic strengths, as carried out in the diagnostic step, as well as on the market opportunities opened up by societal challenges. In the Basque Country, they are based on both existing (energy and advanced manufacturing) and potential (bio-sciences) economic strengths. In the PCTI-2020 there is an attempt to narrow the focus of thematic priorities (until then, it was much too broad) and rebalance them (upgrading and diversification tends to rely more on the former than on the latter). In Navarre, thematic priorities refer to capabilities both existing (mainly in the so-called green and health economies) and emerging (the talent economies), but the general perception is that there are too many thematic priorities included in the plan. The degree of thematic prioritisation in Murcia is low in practice because, instead of focusing on those areas in which the region actually has unique advantages, priorities include many activities in which it doesn't stand out or cannot be expected to be a leader in the future.

Horizontal priorities have been understood in a different way in each case. In the Basque Country they are seen in the PCTI-2020 as key cross-cutting issues that require determined interventions. Although apparently well designed and arranged, in fact they are concentrated too much on R&D (neglecting non-R&D-based innovation and social innovation) and tackled without enough coordination (e.g., separating the restructuring of the technological innovation sub-system from the restructuring of the scientific sub-system). Key elements for the success of the Basque RIS3 are also developed by other plans, without, to date, sufficient coordination among them. In Navarre, horizontal priorities have been understood as key areas of production and innovation that the plan should take into account; thus they have not been chosen because the diagnostic analysis detected them as important current system failures. Finally, in Murcia there is a list of strategic priorities that could be understood as horizontal priorities, but there is no sign of the relevance or actual priority of each of them, and it could also be argued that certain key issues for the innovation system are somehow overlooked by the RIS3Mur (e.g., the need for changing the governance of the university system).

### *Policy mix and action plan*

The fifth step in the RIS3 guide refers to configuring a policy mix and action plan to support the strategy, in line with the analysis in chapter 5 of this book. In the case of the Basque Country, the initial RIS3 document (the PCTI-2015) did not include a real financial scenario and did not provide the basis for an action plan for the current government (which was not in power when it was written). The new PCTI-2020 has not yet developed the part of the plan related to the policy mix, except for the total budgetary forecast. Under this, the amount of funding from the public administration is supposed to be reduced (from 39 per cent in 2014 to 32 per cent in 2020) and that from business and international sources should rise (from 55 per cent and 6 per cent respectively, to 60 per cent and 8 per cent in 2020). The regional government is the main source of public finance, followed by the national government and then the provincial governments. So far, there is no estimate for distribution by priorities or fields.

The Moderna plan gave Navarre a very well-designed process by which to arrive at concrete actions from the chosen priorities. But since there were neither budgetary projections for the deployment of actions nor mechanisms that would ensure the alignment of the regional government's policies and measures with those stemming from the plan, when the region was shaken by a severe institutional, political and economic crisis, the action plan was strongly affected. Thus, because of budgetary constraints, in the last two to three years many regional R&D and innovation programmes (which constituted the main source of public finance) have been on hold.

In Murcia, the unfolding process from strategic lines and objectives to actions has been developed in an orderly fashion in the RIS3Mur. As a result, there is a list of actions, and for each of them a card with basic points (challenges, targeted groups …). The only budgetary data contained in the RIS3Mur, however, refers to estimated funds coming from each source (public, private and abroad) but not to their allocation among thematic priorities and strategic objectives. Besides, as resources 'are all subject to the budgetary availability', there is no guarantee that they are going to be spent. Unlike the situation in the Basque Country and Navarre, most of the resources for the RIS3Mur will come from the ERDF. Private and foreign funds (excluding ERDF funds) are supposed to double and triple, respectively, from 2014 to 2020. But, despite this, they will reach only 43 per cent and 3 per cent, respectively. The concentration of R&D and innovation policy competences in one department favours the coordination of the actions, although there is a perception that it could be improved with the planned creation of an innovation agency.

All three regions are in the early stages of articulating the policy mixes that will support their strategies, therefore, and it is instructive to look at the current general picture of R&D and innovation policies to get an idea of existing inertias. In the Basque Country and Navarre there is a prevalence of supply-side tools, which give preference to R&D activities over demand-side and non-R&D activities. Tax incentives are supposed to form a large part of the incentives for R&D but are not managed with strategic goals in mind, and public procurement has not been effectively developed until now. In Murcia, even if the plan appears in favour of non-R&D activities, due to inertia the amount of resources allocated to demand-side and non-R&D-based innovation are still far from being comparable with those devoted to R&D and supply-side policies; likewise, there are no specific plans to develop the stated objective of promoting innovative public procurement.

### *Monitoring and evaluation*

The final step refers to monitoring and evaluation, which it is argued should be integrated into the RIS3 process from the beginning (see chapter 6 in this volume). In the Basque Country, although in all previous PCTIs there was a scorecard with indicators related to goals or planned activities, beneficiaries were not normally consulted and, at best, only monitoring was carried out. The new PCTI-2020 announces that an integrated monitoring and evaluating system is going to be set out. The new system differentiates four levels of monitoring and evaluation: the innovation system; the strategy and plan; the instruments and programmes; and the agents of the STI network. For each of them, objectives and goals will be previously established. Each of these levels will be the responsibility of a different assessment agent: the innovation system by Innobasque; the PCTI-2020 by the president; and both the instruments and programmes and the agents of the STI network by the corresponding departments. This new system should bring important improvements with respect to past practices, but there are also grounds for questions as regards the extent to which the systemic nature of the policy mix will be accounted for, the extent to which practices will evaluate as opposed to monitor, and the internal nature of the processes (as opposed to assuring input from external agents).

In the case of Navarre, the Moderna plan incorporates a defined set of indicators to measure its degree of advancement and periodically request the opinion of the beneficiaries. However, at present there is a sincere recognition that through these mechanisms it is impossible to measure or know the actual contribution of the plan to the established goals. Moreover, the organisation responsible for the evaluation of the contribution of the plan to the established goals is also responsible for its management, which goes against of the RIS3 guide's recommendation. Finally, the set of indicators established to measure the degree of advancement of the plan are very general and not easy to change by means of policies in the short run. Alongside those general targets it can be argued that there should be more manageable short- to medium-term objectives and indicators.

In Murcia, following the RIS3 Guide, the RIS3Mur tries to differentiate monitoring and evaluating. For the first, it distinguishes among three kinds of indicators: execution, result and context indicators. Execution indicators measure progress in implementation. Result indicators (which could also be named as 'output indicators') measure changes produced as a consequence of the implemented actions. Context indicators are related to the objectives and vision of the strategy. However, RIS3Mur doesn't pinpoint how evaluation will be done, and it is doubtful that in fact it is going to measure the real contribution of each of the levels (agents, instruments or programmes, priorities and the whole RIS3Mur) to the objectives established for them. On the other hand, evaluation is, again, expected to be conducted by the same organisation responsible for the management of the RIS3Mur (the technical secretariat), and it seems that the RIS3Mur overlooks enquiries to beneficiaries as a complementary source of quantitative indicators and analyses.

## Concluding comments

The comparative step-by-step analysis of three ongoing cases in RIS3 development has highlighted a number of general features of the current 'state of practice' in territorial strategy, in Europe at least. These general features indeed mirror many of the concerns pointed to by analysis in other chapters in this book – both the conceptual analysis in Part I and other cases in Part II – and give us some hints as to where the practice of territorial strategy-making needs to look in the future.

First of all, it is clear that regional context is a critical factor influencing the development of the processes that underlie territorial strategies, in particular entrepreneurial discovery processes. Territories are characterised by different types of complexity, made up of a multitude of geographical, structural and institutional factors that interact with one another in different ways and by strong degrees of path dependence that mark the very vision of what territorial strategy means. This implies that there are no single recipes for developing the right processes that will set in motion entrepreneurial discovery and lead to the appropriate identification of priorities that are then supported by ideal policy mixes and bolstered by effective evaluations. Each region has to find its own way, based upon its own complexity in existing governance relationships and its own history of where it has come from.

The six steps of territorial strategy set out in the European Commission's RIS3 guide (Foray *et al.*, 2012), therefore, must be adapted to the context of each region. The steps in themselves embody the basic elements that should form all territorial strategies (diagnosis, governance across the quadruple helix, shared vision, clear prioritisation, policy alignment and ongoing evaluation), but the context of each region implies that the route towards these basic elements will contain differences. Indeed, our three case studies illustrate these differences in practice. Yet there are nevertheless some general patterns and arguments that emerge in our analysis of the pursuit of the six steps.

Reflecting a more general perception of how European regions have approached meeting the European Commission's RIS3 requirements, there is a sense in which the first diagnostic step is the easy part and that for many regions the serious thought stops there. An analysis of the region's strengths, weaknesses and capabilities, combined with strategic intelligence on technological and market trends (step 1) can lead to a convincing justification of areas for prioritisation (step 4), and there may be a temptation for regional governments to avoid becoming too deeply embroiled in the messy, uncertain processes of governance and development of shared vision that are critical for igniting entrepreneurial discovery processes (steps 2 and 3). Thus RIS3 might easily revert to a technocratic, intelligence-based plan rather than being the emergent and living process of experimentation and discovery that is in fact necessary to make effective prioritisation decisions. Indeed, the cases illustrate different difficulties in linking (explicitly defined and implicit) entrepreneurial discovery processes and shared vision to the government's plan-based perception of what a strategy should look like, and even where this link does appear to have been made with some success (in Navarre) it was temporary and has not been continued.

The analysis also highlights the severe practical difficulties in setting actual priorities where there are always conflicting interests (step 4), in aligning policy mixes with those priorities in the face of existing policy inertias (step 5) and in establishing effective evaluation mechanisms (step 6). The challenges of steps 5 and 6 in particular have been accentuated here by timing issues, in the sense that European regions have been under great pressure to present RIS3 in a short space of time. In such a context it is logical to move from diagnostic (step 1) to prioritisation (step 4), as these are the most tangible parts of what is typically understood by a strategic plan. While policy alignment and evaluation should be integral parts of an RIS3 from the very beginning, especially if existing inertias are to be overcome, in this context of time pressure it is tempting to leave them as afterthoughts to the more visible parts of the strategy. Such reflections echo much of the analysis in the earlier conceptual chapters of this book (particularly chapters 4 to 6) concerning 'how' territorial strategy takes place, and they emphasise the inherent challenges in translating concepts developed in academia and among EU policy-makers into real-life scenarios.

## Notes

1 This work was supported by the European Commission (FP7 SSH.2012.1.1-3) under Grant number 320131. Any errors are the responsibility of the authors.
2 The project is led by the University of Cardiff (UK) and is financed by the European Commission (FP7). See www.cardiff.ac.uk/cplan/research/smartspec.
3 See www.orkestra.deusto.es and www.ifuturo.org. See also Aranguren *et al.* (2014) for detail on the case of Orkestra as an academic institution with an explicit mission to support regional competitiveness, and Goddard *et al.* (2013) on the general role that universities can play in RIS3 processes in this regard.
4 See www.rededi.es for more information.
5 See www.s3vanguardinitiative.eu, http://een.ec.europa.eu/, and www.errin.eu for more information.

## References


Aranguren, M. J., Guibert, J. M., Valdaliso, J. M., and Wilson, J. R. (2014) Academic institutions as change agents for territorial development, mimeo, Orkestra-Basque Institute of Competitiveness.

Bergera, M., and Arive, M. (2011) *Regional Innovation Monitor: Regional Innovation Report (Region of Navarre): To the European Commission Enterprise and Industry Directorate-General*, https://webgate.ec.europa.eu/ENTR/rim_cp/report/innovation/regional-innovation-report-navarre.

Charron, N., Lapuente, V., and Dijkstra, L. (2012) *Regional Governance Matters: A Study on Regional Variation in Quality of Government within the EU*, Regional Policy Working Papers WP01/2012. Brussels: European Commission.

Collinge, C., and Gibney, J. (2010) Connecting place, policy and leadership, *Policy Studies*, 31(4), pp. 379–91.

European Commission (2007) *Innovative Strategies and Actions: Results from 15 Years of Regional Experimentation*. Brussels: European Commission.

European Commission (2014) *National/Regional Innovation Strategies for Smart Specialisation (RIS3)*, Cohesion Policy 2014–2020 Factsheet. Brussels: European Commission.

Foray, D., Goddard, J., Goenaga, X., Landabaso, M., McCann, P., Morgan, K., Nauwelaers, C., and Ortega-Argilés, R. (2012) *Guide to Research and Innovation Strategies for Smart Specialisations (RIS 3)*. Brussels: European Commission.

Gibney, J. (2011) Knowledge in a 'shared and interdependent world': implications for a progressive leadership of cities and regions, *European Planning Studies*, 19(4), pp. 613–27.

Goddard, J., Kempton, L, and Vallance, P. (2013) Universities and smart specialisation: challenges, tensions and opportunities for the innovation strategies of European regions, *Ekonomiaz*, 83, pp. 83 102.

Harmaakorpi, V. (2013) Expert assessment smart specialisation Navarre. Unpublished document, Susinno Ltd.

Magro, E. (2014) *Regional Innovation Monitor: Regional Innovation Report (Basque Region): To the European Commission Enterprise and Industry Directorate-General*, http://ec.europa.eu/enterprise/policies/innovation/policy/regional-innovation/monitor/sites/default/files/report/2014%20RIM%20Plus_Regional%20Innovation%20Report_Basque%20Country.pdf.

Morgan, K. (2013) *Basque Country RIS3: An Expert Assessment on behalf of DG Regional and Urban Policy*. Brussels: European Commission.

OECD (2011) *OECD Reviews of Regional Innovation: Basque Country, Spain*. Paris: OECD.

OECD (2013) *Basque Country, Spain: Higher Education in Regional and City Development*. OECD Report, 26 February.

Orkestra (2007) *Competitiveness Report of the Basque Country: Towards a Unique Value Proposition*. Bilbao: Deusto.

Orkestra (2009) *Second Report on the Competitiveness of the Basque Country: Towards an Innovation-Based Competitive Stage*. Bilbao: Deusto.

Orkestra (2011) *The Basque Country Competitiveness Report 2011: Leading the New Complexity*. Bilbao: Deusto.

Orkestra (2013) *The Basque Country Competitiveness Report 2013: Productive Transformation for Tomorrow*. Bilbao: Deusto.

Orkestra (2014) Region of Murcia: regional profile and analysis of smart specialization practices. Unpublished document, October.

Sotarauta, M. (2005) Shared leadership and dynamic capabilities in regional development. In Sagan, I., and Haikier, H. (eds), *Regionalism Contested: Institutions, Society and Governance*. Aldershot: Ashgate.

Stimson, R., Stough, R. R., and Salazar, M. (2009) *Leadership and Institutions in Regional Endogenous Development*. Cheltenham: Edward Elgar.

Valdaliso, J. M., Magro, E., Navarro, M., Aranguren, M. J., and Wilson, J. R. (2014) Path dependence in policies supporting smart specialisation strategies: insights from the Basque case, *European Journal of Innovation* Management, 17(4), pp. 390–408.

# 13 Where next for territorial strategy?

## Concluding remarks and a call to arms

*Jesús M. Valdaliso and James R. Wilson*[1]

This book began from the premise that territories need to develop strategies for their economic development – a premise around which there is widespread agreement, rapidly evolving practice, but a lack of rigorous academic reflection. Its main contribution twofold: first, it provides a conceptual framework for the analysis (of past strategies) and for the design, implementation and evaluation of (present and future) strategies (and their corresponding policy measures); and, second, it offers case studies of seven territories in Europe and the Americas that demonstrate different experiences with territorial strategy, each of which contributes to deepening our real-world understanding of one or several dimensions of that conceptual framework.

The case analysis is particularly important because there can be no *one size fits all* strategy. In their very nature territorial strategies are context-, place- and path- dependent, which demands holistic approaches with long-term perspectives (Aranguren *et al.*, 2012; Navarro *et al.*, 2014). Nevertheless, it is possible to go beyond the isolated analysis of individual cases to make some broader generalisations, and even to infer some general propositions related to the different stages and questions of a territorial strategy. That is indeed what this book has attempted to do by setting these seven cases alongside a detailed exploration of a conceptual framework – a framework which was previously discussed with the authors of each of the cases as a (very) broad guide for their analysis. In this concluding chapter our challenge is, briefly, to bring together these general propositions and reflect on what is now required to take our understanding of the critical process of territorial strategy-making to the next stage.

Our concluding remarks are organised around the three main questions that we argued in the introduction that every territorial strategy should address – 'what for', 'what' and 'how/who' – alongside the two further practical challenges of translating strategy into the policy arena and of strategy evaluation – that is, the conceptual structure developed in Part I of the book. However, although this differentiation makes sense for the sake of a better analytical insight, one of the messages of the analysis of the previous twelve chapters is that in real life it is in fact very difficult to separate them out into discrete elements. They all overlap with one another, and indeed a key finding of the empirical cases in the book has been that the 'how/who' question in particular is always strongly related to and conditions the 'what for' and the 'what' questions. Thus we begin our concluding reflections with the 'how/who' question, because this dimension plays a key role in all of the other questions and practical challenges.

## Territorial strategies: when (visioning), who (leadership) and how (process)

Historical analysis of the growth in popularity of the territorial strategy concept in chapter 1 highlighted the importance of an external stimulus as an impetus behind the development of territorial strategies. This is indeed reflected in most of the cases analysed in Part II of the book, where territorial strategies have appeared mainly as government-led responses to external shocks or to economic crisis – in the early 1980s in the Basque Country, although in a very informal and non-deliberate form, and in the early 1990s in Wales, the Basque Country, the Øresund and Rafaela. In all of these cases crisis was seen as an opportunity for change and, specifically, to formulate a vision for the territory and to develop a strategy. When these external shocks are absent or the need for a strategy is not widely perceived, as the Okanagan case shows, it takes much more time and effort to initiate the process.

In 'old' territories it was the established institutional structures (governments) that took the initiative, and over time other actors became involved and engaged in the process of strategy design and implementation. However, a lack of supporting institutional structures, because of the cross-border nature of the region (Øresund) or the relative youth and/or peripheral character of the region (Okanagan), is found to pose an additional challenge to launching territorial strategy processes. The 'who' and 'how', then, become preliminary key questions to be addressed and solved before reflections around the 'what for' and the 'what' are able to take place in earnest. The Øresund case makes very clear, for example, that the original vision of several policy entrepreneurs concerning a cross-border region eventually failed as a result of the difficulties of having two different governments in two separate countries. On the contrary, the Okanagan case shows that the absence of a strong regional government potentially makes it easier to initiate from the very beginning a participatory process to envision the region's future because it is necessary to bring together different parties.

The trend towards decentralisation and 'devolution' of powers to regions and cities, quite visible in the world since the 1980s (Rodríguez-Pose and Tjimstra, 2009; Walendowski *et al.*, 2011), has been a driving factor in the expansion of territorial strategy-making; there are more territories, with greater policy competences, and at a smaller geographical scale that facilitates the proximity relationships required for strategic reflection. Indeed, Walendowski *et al.* (2011) find a strong relationship between the degree of regional autonomy and the extent of regional strategy development. Yet to have a regional or a local government with significant policy competences is not enough, as the juxtaposition of the Welsh and Basque cases clearly shows. Whereas successive Basque governments since the mid-1980s have been able to implement a long-term strategy supported by several policy actions sustained over a long period of time, the Welsh experience is one of rent-seeking and interdepartmental differences that have generated short-termism and produced a multitude of plans and programmes that have changed continually with successive regional governments.

Related to decentralisation, and associated with its vision of a 'Europe of the Regions', the European Union has also played an important role in the rise of territorial strategy. The regional policy that began to be implemented in the mid-1970s has indeed been significant not only in Europe (such as in the Basque Country, Wales, Navarre and Murcia, and even in the cross-border Øresund region) but also in regions in the Americas that have looked to Europe as a point of reference in certain respects – something that comes across in the cases of Rafaela and Okanagan. This influence is perhaps even greater now than in the past, in the context of the strong impulse in Europe behind research and innovation strategies for smart specialisation (RIS3). As highlighted in chapter 12, the funding conditionality attached to RIS3 has ensured the spread of territorial strategy-making guided by certain principles (or steps) throughout Europe's regions (Foray *et al.*, 2012; European Commission, 2014). And this influence has also spread to other parts of the world, in part as a result of the promotion of the smart specialisation concept by the OECD and the World Bank (Foray, 2014).

There is a sense, however, in which a particular, structured approach to territorial strategy-making has been pushed on European regions too quickly; governments have scrambled around to demonstrate the existence of an RIS3 so as to meet EU funding requirements, amid considerable confusion around the concept itself. The analysis of this book suggests that such confusion shouldn't surprise us. The question of 'how' territorial strategy should be formed in different contexts is a very difficult one; it takes time to come to terms with and to develop the required 'dynamic territorial capabilities' (in the language of chapter 4). Under time pressure, the temptation for regions must be to jump to the most visible parts of what is typically understood by a strategic plan: diagnosis and prioritisation. The entrepreneurial discovery processes among quadruple helix agents that should build from diagnosis and uncover prioritisations, feeding a territorial strategy that is 'alive' and constantly adapting itself, do not appear overnight. Indeed, time and again in the case analyses we see the importance of building up over time the type of dynamic territorial capabilities emphasised in chapter 4 through a long-term process of policy and strategy learning.

In the cases of Rafaela and the Basque Country it was visionary politicians with a long-term perspective and sufficient political power who played the initial role of catalyst, whereas in other spaces with weaker or fragmented institutional structures, such as the Okanagan or the Øresund, other actors assumed or are assuming that role (universities, policy entrepreneurs from business and civil society). Engagement and alignment of different territorial agents around common goals and the associated capacities for shared leadership are revealed as critical in all these cases. Yet they take time, requiring significant learning and trust-building. Indeed, the cases of Rafaela and the Basque Country show that processes that started around the early 1990s did not begin to bear fruit until ten years or so later. This divergence between the long-term horizon of strategies and the short-term horizon of politicians adds a further challenge to the process of strategy formation and implementation. Politics and political power, for better or for worse, make the difference in these processes, something that other studies with a long-term perspective have also stressed (Breznitz, 2007; Martinelli *et al.*, 2013; Morgan, 2013).

Acknowledging this need for time, perhaps the key message of the book concerns the centrality of the question of 'how' territorial strategy takes place. Chapters 2 and 3 highlighted the challenges in making choices around priorities, which is the 'what' at the visible core of any strategy, but these challenges can only ever be met through the better articulation of decision-making processes. What is more, to get the decisions right there must be a vision of what the strategy wants to achieve, a vision that again requires processes of dialogue and construction among agents. Chapters 4, 5 and 6 all emphasised the importance of learning about decision-making processes in different ways, and each of the case studies has highlighted the implications of the presence or lack of such learning. Indeed, we can take some important lessons from this analysis regarding key elements that might guide how places look to learn in their pursuit of territorial strategies: the ability to make the time horizon of strategy independent – or partly independent – of the political cycle; the need for establishing 'spaces' for dialogue and the exchange of views and ideas; the importance of developing social capital among implicated agents; the evolution from individual leadership to shared leadership; the significance of the ownership of the strategy being truly territorial, as opposed to pertaining to government or to any other unique agent; and the roles that different forms of training and research can play in all of the above.

## Territorial strategies: what for (vision and ambition)

Alongside recognition of the need for a strategy, whether through a specific external stimulus or an internal process of reflection, there is the need to build a consensus around the direction that the territory should take so as to guide that strategy (Porter and Rivkin, 2012). In the jargon of chapter 11, territories need to 'envision' their future if the strategy is to reflect where they really want to be; in the jargon of chapter 3, this involves formulating an 'ambition' that articulates the unique value proposition differentiating the territory. This ambition is ultimately about creating a supportive environment for the prosperity of both citizens and firms, bearing in mind that prosperity can be defined in different ways and that the type of prosperity sought is in fact a key dimension of the 'what for' of a territorial strategy.

The envisioning process thus involves at least three challenges. First, territories should identify and align social, economic and environmental goals so that they are not in conflict with one another. Second, territories should be aware that their ambition and their corresponding goals co-evolve over time and with the stages of their economic development. The combination of these first two challenges makes necessary a process of strategy and policy learning and evaluation, as emphasised in chapter 6, which allows for introducing changes if necessary. A third challenge is to formulate an ambition that is highly specific to the territory's legacy, assets and resources and that is closely aligned to the activities, sectors, markets and actors that constitute the 'what' of the strategy.

Several of the cases highlight the argument that a strong identity (based on history, culture, etc.) may facilitate this process of envisioning a common future (the Basque Country, for example). Others illustrate that this can also work the other way around; strategies, if they succeed, may contribute to strengthen territorial identities (Rafaela, for example; see also Walendowski *et al.*, 2011). Whatever the case, those who take the lead in envisioning processes need to design broad and inclusive goals aligned with the needs of the territory (Sugden and Wilson, 2002) – hence the necessity of participatory approaches that create dialogue and learning and, even better, the emergence of leadership that is itself shared across agents. Generating shared vision is a continuous process that cannot be controlled by one agent (which often attempts to do so), that takes time (to overcome mistrust among different agents and build common understanding and social capital) and that is easier said than done (as chapters 11 and 12 in particular have highlighted). We see here clear overlap, therefore, with the considerations made in the previous section regarding 'how' territorial strategy is made.

## Territorial strategies: what (positioning and prioritisation)

The interrelationship between how a territorial strategy is constructed and what it aims to achieve must ultimately become concrete in defining the actual content of the strategy: 'what' will the strategy focus on to shape the future competitiveness of the territory? Building from an understanding of business strategy, chapter 3 frames this in terms of deciding what markets to compete in, how to win in those markets, and therefore what capabilities to create in the territory – that is, the strategy must 'position' the territory in terms of its future competitiveness and set up priorities for action accordingly. These priorities, as chapter 2 has stressed, should be set up not only in terms of the economic activities and scientific and technological areas to promote and support but also with regard to the assets and resources of the territory, its actors (SMEs, MNEs, clusters, knowledge centres, etc.), its external relationships and its internal articulation. In their need to be tangible and to result in concrete actions, positioning and prioritisation form the most visible parts of a territorial strategy that ultimately shape the trajectory of its economic development.

While defining the content of strategy may appear a relatively easy exercise, we have seen in both the conceptual and the case analyses and have argued above that the process of making decisions towards defining this content (the 'how') is anything but straightforward at the territorial level. Indeed, there is an important distinction to be made here between the strategy concept applied to the firm and that applied to the territory. When it comes to the process of strategy formation leading to real choices between activities, and therefore agents, territories face far more formidable challenges than firms. The power school of business strategy

(Mintzberg *et al.*, 1998) recognises that firms themselves are made up of different interest groups, but this set of different interests is far more complex and diverse at the territorial level. Defining the content of a strategy for a territory involves choosing some things (sectors, areas, activities, technologies, actors) over others, which is likely to result in conflicts between different stakeholders and implies that strategy is ultimately a political process. As we have seen, governments may be tempted to escape from these decisions either by working only with horizontal priorities or by having too many vertical priorities, but both of these defeat the very object of constructing a strategy. Working towards consensus in the context of a shared vision, achieved as we have argued above through processes of dialogue, can make choices easier, or at least help mitigate the potential conflicts of interests that may appear. Once again, therefore, we see how the 'how' strongly conditions the achievement of the 'what'.

As highlighted in chapter 3, we should also remember that, while territories compete with one another – as firms do – they also trade among themselves; they are always producers and consumers. As consumers, territories always win from interregional competition; but, as producers, the attraction of particular 'traded' economic activities is very much a zero-sum game. This, essentially, is what lies behind the need for territories to position themselves strategically, which they can do through offering an attractive business environment and a supportive institutional architecture for competitiveness, both in general (horizontally) and in specific areas (vertically). However, while a territory can choose to focus on business environment conditions in areas in which it aims to differentiate itself from competing locations (the 'necessary'), it will always, in the last resort, have to address both the full range of market failures and public-sector roles that it is constitutionally required to cover and the full set of economic sectors, whether 'traded' or 'local' (the 'urgent'). Sometimes, particularly in time of crisis, the 'urgent' becomes more pressing than the 'necessary'.

We tend to see this competition as a game between different regions around the world, but it also happens between different regions that belong to the same country (or the same supranational space, such as the European Union) and increasingly between different territorial levels – for example, between a region and its most important cities or between regions and cities worldwide. The Øresund case indicates, precisely, that the growing power of two key cities has left the concept of a cross-border regional strategy at a dead end. Indeed, more generally it highlights the challenges of interregional strategy interaction, something that is also revealed in chapter 12 as a key and unresolved issue in the implementation of RIS3. Indeed, there seems to be a broad margin for improvement with regard to the coordination of different strategies across regions and cities within the EU (and surely also elsewhere). Economic activity does not tend to respect administrative boundaries, and if synergies are not to be lost then it is critical when defining the content of territorial strategies to bear in mind the cross-over with neighbouring (and potentially indeed non-neighbouring) territories, and also to exploit synergies across different territorial levels that may each be developing their own strategies (a city and a region, for example).

Taking the above arguments further still, territories themselves are dynamic constructs whose configuration is constantly open to change. In the old Europe, processes of 'devolution' and of territorial reconfiguration that began in the 1980s became a source of 'breaking with the past' or, in other words, allowed for a new institutional architecture from which a change process emerged – as the Basque and Welsh cases in this book show. But outside Europe, and in 'younger' countries with a rather short history, new regions or territorial units can be built up, as is highlighted by the Okanagan case. Indeed, long-term perspectives of urban and regional development help to understand the changeable and artificial nature of concepts such as regions or cities (Martinelli *et al.*, 2013).

## From strategy to the policy arena

When it comes to operationalising territorial strategies, there is a critical link with public policies, an aspect that was explored in detail in chapter 5 and is reflected in different ways in all of the case studies. Literature and analysis of territorial strategy tends to focus on the design of strategy, with an assumption that good design will lead to straightforward implementation. In reality, however, territories experience an implementation gap which has its roots in several interrelated factors: policy complexity; policy path dependency; the requirements of institutional learning; and, related to the arguments in the last section, the issue of how well territories and policies correspond in geography.

The competitiveness policies that should be aligned with territorial strategies in order to support their development in fact have a wide range of origins. Competences for relevant policies are located in different departments of government (industry, education, health, environment, etc.) and at different administrative levels (national, regional, city, local), and are often operationalised by different sets of intermediate agents (development agencies, innovation agencies, etc.). They also employ different combinations of policy instruments, more or less effectively, which interact and overlap in various ways. This scenario of complexity raises important coordination issues in the leap from strategy to policy, and these coordination issues are complicated further by the fact that existing policies in each of these domains and levels have their own history, trajectory, and established stakeholders/beneficiaries. When looking to align policy with strategy there are therefore significant challenges in overcoming policy inertias. While it is easier to navigate these power relationships with respect to the more general policies supporting horizontal priorities, the policies that support vertical priorities are particularly sensitive because they involve choices with direct financial impact on distinct groups of firms and other agents. As we have seen, in particular in the European cases, these challenges can slow down the translation of strategy into concrete policy mixes that move the strategy forward.

Some solutions to these issues are also emerging. For example, while the speed with which the European Commission has pushed forward the smart specialisation agenda has been criticised above, there is no doubt that its action in this field (and its clear articulation of the need to align policy with strategy within RIS3) is serving an important purpose in raising consciousness of these challenges and facilitating peer learning across regions. In regions with weak governments and little trajectory in territorial strategy, the influence of the European Commission on policies and programmes has arguably been stronger, and many of the regions with stronger governments and a history of developing territorial strategies have been held up as examples. This is a positive process that supports the long-term learning that the cases analysed here have highlighted as critical if territorial strategies are to be implemented well and ultimately to bear fruit.

The analysis of several of the chapters has also highlighted an interesting link between the operationalisation and the formalisation of strategy. The cases of the Basque Country and Rafaela both illustrate that more formal planning processes (and associated public policies) emerge only over time, requiring first the establishment of processes of social change and learning. In this sense the Welsh case also highlights the 'start-up costs' of new government, and the Øresund case suggests that too quick a move towards formalisation of strategy and away from the less hierarchical, 'involutionary processes' from which strategy starts to emerge, rather than advancing operationalisation, can lead to setbacks. The 'journey' emphasised in the Okanagan case, aiming to establish a culture of inquiry among different agents in the territory, is also in line with such a conclusion.

## Learning from the past: strategy and policy evaluation

Few would disagree that it is important to learn lessons from the past when designing and implementing new strategies (Martinelli *et al.*, 2013: xxiv; Morgan, 2013). Going even further, an outstanding scholar from the field of evolutionary economic geography has advocated that history's role 'should be an integral part of regional policy analysis' (Martin, 2011: 207). Indeed, another issue common to most of the empirical chapters is their implicit or explicit historical perspective, with that general aim of learning from the past. But, beyond the broad acknowledgement that history matters in regional development, there is another assumption – subtle in the Welsh and Øresund cases, strong in the Basque, Rafaela and Okanagan cases – that strategy-making itself is a path-dependent process.

The process of designing, implementing and developing territorial strategies is iterative and cumulative. It takes time and builds on existing territorial capabilities, policy mixes, and experiences of previous policies. The process and learning approaches to strategy suggested in chapter 4 and emphasised in the Rafaela and Okanagan cases (and somehow visible in the Basque case too) appear to be critical. On the contrary, the case of Wales seems to indicate that policy learning did not happen effectively, for various reasons, and that of Øresund that it didn't have time to happen properly. Indeed, in general the empirical chapters appear to pinpoint a positive relationship between the diffusion of process and learning approaches to strategy and the degree of path dependency in strategy-making. Learning from the past allowed for sustaining strategies that were perceived as successful but also for making changes and adjustments to cope with errors or to avoid risks of lock-in, as chapter 7 highlights.

A key conclusion, therefore, is that strategy learning is important. Given the link between strategy and policy established in chapter 5, and illustrated in most of the empirical chapters, an implication is that policy learning is also important for territorial strategy. Furthermore, the importance of both highlights the role that evaluation should play as a key element of learning. Chapter 6 dealt in detail with this issue and set out a framework for linking policy evaluation and strategy evaluation so as to unlock new learning potential. While there is likely to be little disagreement that evaluation should play an integral role in territorial strategy – it is one of the six steps in the RIS3 process, for example (Foray *et al.*, 2012) – it tends to remain something that is talked about a lot and done very little. Chapter 12 suggests that it has been tempting for regions to leave the evaluation and monitoring step as an afterthought in the RIS3 process rather than integrating it into the strategy process from the beginning, and other cases are also illustrative of a lack of evaluation practice. In the case of Wales, for example, lack of policy evaluation processes is cited as one of the causes for lack of policy learning; and in the Basque case, which has been associated with relatively successful policies over a long period of time, the lack of evaluation practice has meant that we struggle to know which policies have been the most influential and effective in supporting the strategy and why. It is clear that, in order to provide strategic intelligence to the strategy-making process in ways that support the evolution of the 'what for', the 'what' and indeed the 'how', we need to get better at evaluation.

## The role of academic research: a call to arms

We are mindful that it is much easier to formulate recommendations than to get them implemented. Still, we firmly believe that territories, and in particular the governments of these territories, need sound and non-partisan academic advice based on careful knowledge and assessment in order to design and implement strategies for economic development and competitiveness. We hope that the analysis in this book provides a small part of this input and, more importantly, an encouragement for the research community to engage further in these critical issues that ultimately shape the future of our territories and the welfare of the people living in them. Echoing previous works about economic strategy that made a call for action not to despair (Dertouzos *et al.*, 1989: 167; Porter and Rivkin, 2012: 9), we finished chapter 1 with a call to arms to all those interested in processes of territorial change. We now finish the book with a call to arms to academics and academic institutions to be more engaged and involved in territorial development processes, particularly in evolving coherent territorial strategies, from the diagnosis to the design, implementation, monitoring and evaluation.

One of the salient features of the conceptual and empirical chapters of this book has indeed been the recurring role of academic research, academic institutions and academic researchers in territorial strategy processes, which is reflective of wider debates around the roles that academia plays and should play in territorial development processes (Aranguren *et al.*, 2014; Drabenstott, 2008; Etzkowitz *et al.*, 2000; Goddard and Puukka, 2008; Karlsen *et al.*, 2012). The cases of Rafaela and Okanagan in particular make strong arguments as to the role that 'academic inquiry' has played and could play in influencing territorial strategies. As argued in chapter 11, taking forward this role requires both better theory and better translation to practice than ever before – a sentiment that echoes the call in chapter 4 for more praxis, linking thought and action, if we are to deepen our understanding and practice of the core question of 'how' territorial strategy is constructed. Indeed, the sheer experience of some of the authors in this book with some of the processes of change analysed in its pages demonstrates clearly that scholars themselves may learn a lot from engaging in such praxis, although this is another story. More generally, the book has shown that successful territorial strategies require shared vision, leadership and governance, and, to play a role in this, academics 'have to be there'.

## Note

This work was supported by the Spanish Ministry of Economy and Competitiveness under Grant number HAR2012-30948 (Valdaliso); by the Basque Government Department of Education, Language and Culture under Grant number IT807-13 (Valdaliso) and IT629-13 (Wilson); and by the European Commission (FP7 SSH.2012.1.1-3) under Grant number 320131 (Wilson). Any errors are the responsibility of the authors.

## References

Aranguren, M. J., Guibert, J. M., Valdaliso, J. M., and Wilson, J. R. (2014) Academic institutions as change agents for territorial development, mimeo, Orkestra-Basque Institute of Competitiveness.

Aranguren, M. J., Magro, E., Navarro, M., and Valdaliso, J. M. (2012) *Estrategias para la construcción de ventajas competitivas regionales: el caso del País Vasco.* Madrid: Marcial Pons.

Breznitz, D. (2007) *Innovation and the State: Political Choice and Strategies for Growth in Israel, Taiwan and Ireland.* New Haven, CT: Yale University Press.

Dertouzos, M., Lester, R., and Solow, R. (1989) *Made in America: Regaining the Productive Edge.* Cambridge, MA: MIT Press.

Drabenstott, M. (2008) Universities, innovation and regional development: a view from the United States, *Higher Education Management and Policy*, 20(2), pp. 43–55.

Etzkowitz, H., Webster, A., Gebhardt, C., and Cantisano, B. R. (2000) The future of the university and the university of the future: evolution of ivory tower to entrepreneurial paradigm, *Research Policy*, 29, pp. 313–30.

European Commission (2014) *National/Regional Innovation Strategies for Smart Specialisation (RIS3)*, Cohesion Policy 2014–2020 Factsheet. Brussels: European Commission.

Foray, D. (2014) *Smart Specialisation: Opportunities and Challenges for Regional Innovation Policy.* Abingdon: Routledge.

Foray, D., Goddard, J., Goenaga, I., Landabaso, M., McCann, P., Morgan, K., Nauwelaers, C., and Ortega-Argilés, R. (2012) *Guide to Research and Innovation Strategies for Smart Specialisation.* Brussels: European Commission.

Goddard, J., and Puukka, J. (2008) The engagement of higher education institutions in regional development: an overview of the opportunities and challenges, *Higher Education Management and Policy*, 20(2), pp. 11–41.

Karlsen, J., Larrea, M., Wilson, J. R., and Aranguren, M. J. (2012) Bridging the gap between academic research and regional development in the Basque Country, *European Journal of Education*, 47(1), pp. 122–38.

Martin, R. (2011) Regional economies as path-dependent systems: some issues and implications. In Cooke, P. (ed.), *Handbook of Regional Innovation and Growth*. Cheltenham: Edward Elgar.

Martinelli, S., Moulaert, F., and Novy, A. (eds) (2013) *Urban and Regional Development Trajectories in Contemporary Capitalism*. London: Routledge.

Mintzberg, H., Ahlstrand, B., and Lampel, J. (1998) *Strategy Safari*. New York: Free Press.

Morgan, K. (2013) Path dependence and the state: the politics of novelty in old industrial regions. In Cooke, P. (ed.), *Re-framing Regional Development: Evolution, Innovation and Transition*. London: Routledge.

Navarro, M., Valdaliso, J. M., Aranguren, M. J., and Magro, E. (2014) A holistic approach to regional strategies: the case of the Basque Country, *Science and Public Policy*, 41(4), pp. 532–47.

Porter, M. E., and Rivkin, J. W. (2012) The looming challenge to U.S. competitiveness, *Harvard Business Review*, March, pp. 1–9.

Rodríguez-Pose, A., and Tijmstra, S. (2009) *On the Emergence and Significance of Local Economic Development Strategies*. Caracas: CAF Working Paper 2009/07.

Sugden, R., and Wilson, J. R. (2002) Economic development in the shadow of the consensus: a strategic decision-making approach, *Contributions to Political Economy*, 21(1), pp. 111–34.

Walendowski, J., Kroll, H., Wintjes, R., and Hollanders, H. (2011) *Innovation Patterns and Innovation Policy in European Regions: Trends, Challenges and Perspectives: 2010 Annual Report*. Project no. 0932 for the European Commission. Brussels: Technopolis.

# Index

Note: References to figures and tables are in **bold** type.

For Product Safety Concerns and Information please contact our EU representative GPSR@taylorandfrancis.com Taylor & Francis Verlag GmbH, Kaufingerstraße 24, 80331 München, Germany